SATURDAY AM

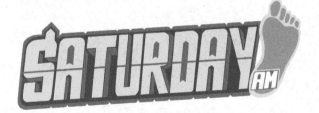

PRESENTS...

VOLUME 1

THE PAYBACK

STORY AND ART BY **Morganne Walker**

ROCKPORT

Contents

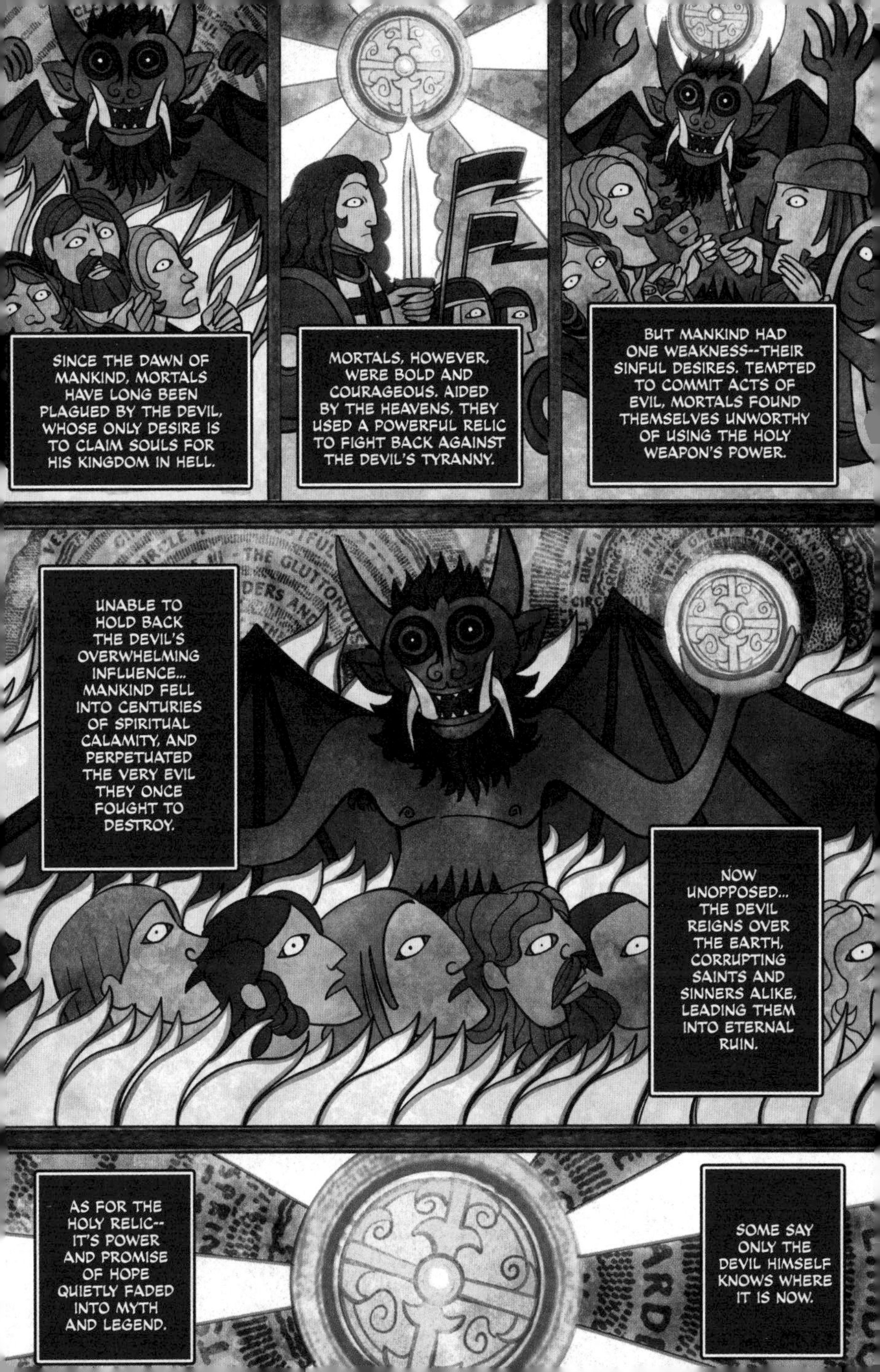
SINCE THE DAWN OF MANKIND, MORTALS HAVE LONG BEEN PLAGUED BY THE DEVIL, WHOSE ONLY DESIRE IS TO CLAIM SOULS FOR HIS KINGDOM IN HELL.
MORTALS, HOWEVER, WERE BOLD AND COURAGEOUS. AIDED BY THE HEAVENS, THEY USED A POWERFUL RELIC TO FIGHT BACK AGAINST THE DEVIL'S TYRANNY.
BUT MANKIND HAD ONE WEAKNESS--THEIR SINFUL DESIRES. TEMPTED TO COMMIT ACTS OF EVIL, MORTALS FOUND THEMSELVES UNWORTHY OF USING THE HOLY WEAPON'S POWER.
UNABLE TO HOLD BACK THE DEVIL'S OVERWHELMING INFLUENCE... MANKIND FELL INTO CENTURIES OF SPIRITUAL CALAMITY, AND PERPETUATED THE VERY EVIL THEY ONCE FOUGHT TO DESTROY.
NOW UNOPPOSED... THE DEVIL REIGNS OVER THE EARTH, CORRUPTING SAINTS AND SINNERS ALIKE, LEADING THEM INTO ETERNAL RUIN.
AS FOR THE HOLY RELIC-- IT'S POWER AND PROMISE OF HOPE QUIETLY FADED INTO MYTH AND LEGEND.
SOME SAY ONLY THE DEVIL HIMSELF KNOWS WHERE IT IS NOW.

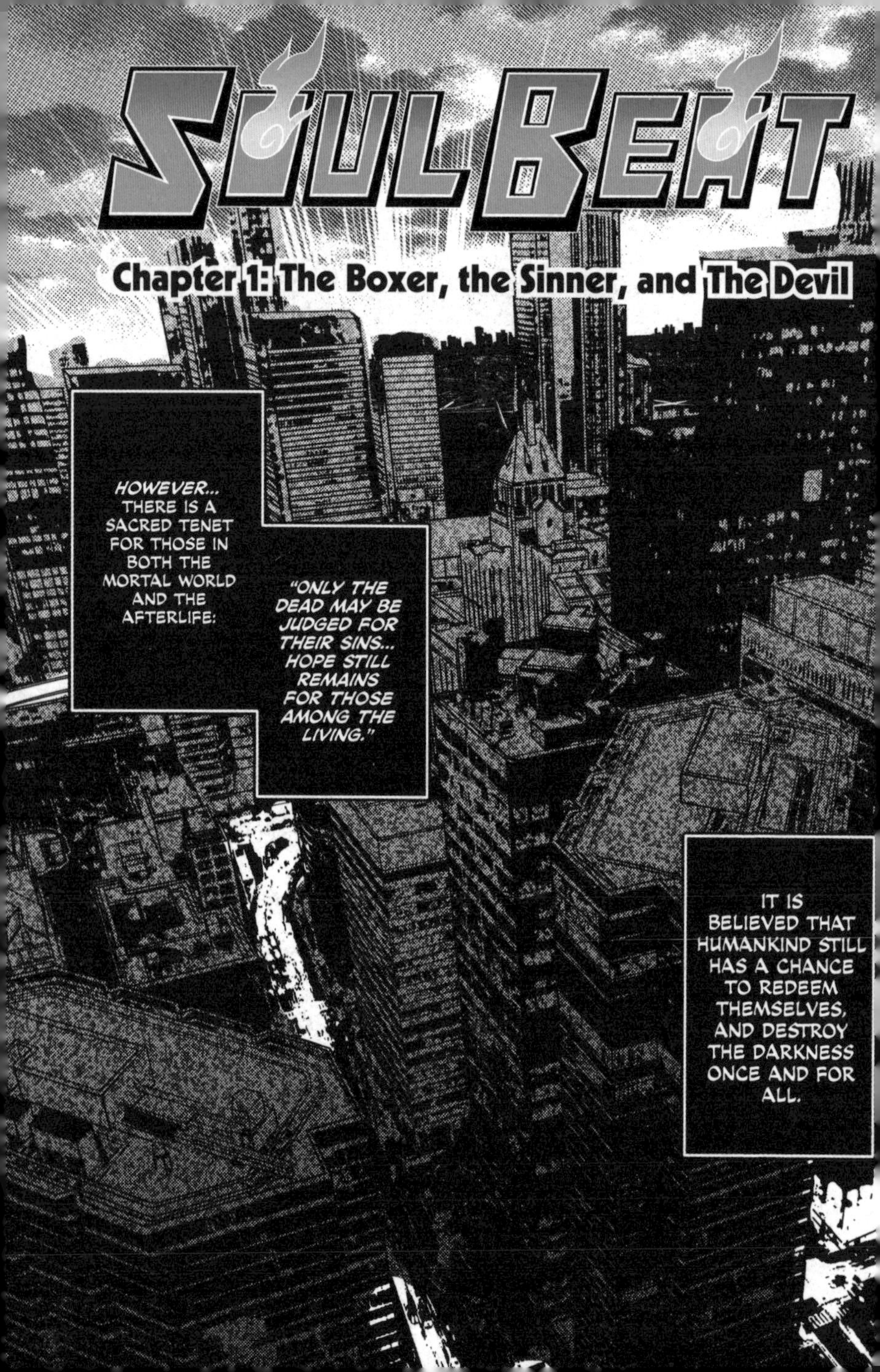
SOUL BEAT
Chapter 1: The Boxer, the Sinner, and The Devil
HOWEVER... THERE IS A SACRED TENET FOR THOSE IN BOTH THE MORTAL WORLD AND THE AFTERLIFE:
"ONLY THE DEAD MAY BE JUDGED FOR THEIR SINS... HOPE STILL REMAINS FOR THOSE AMONG THE LIVING."
IT IS BELIEVED THAT HUMANKIND STILL HAS A CHANCE TO REDEEM THEMSELVES, AND DESTROY THE DARKNESS ONCE AND FOR ALL.

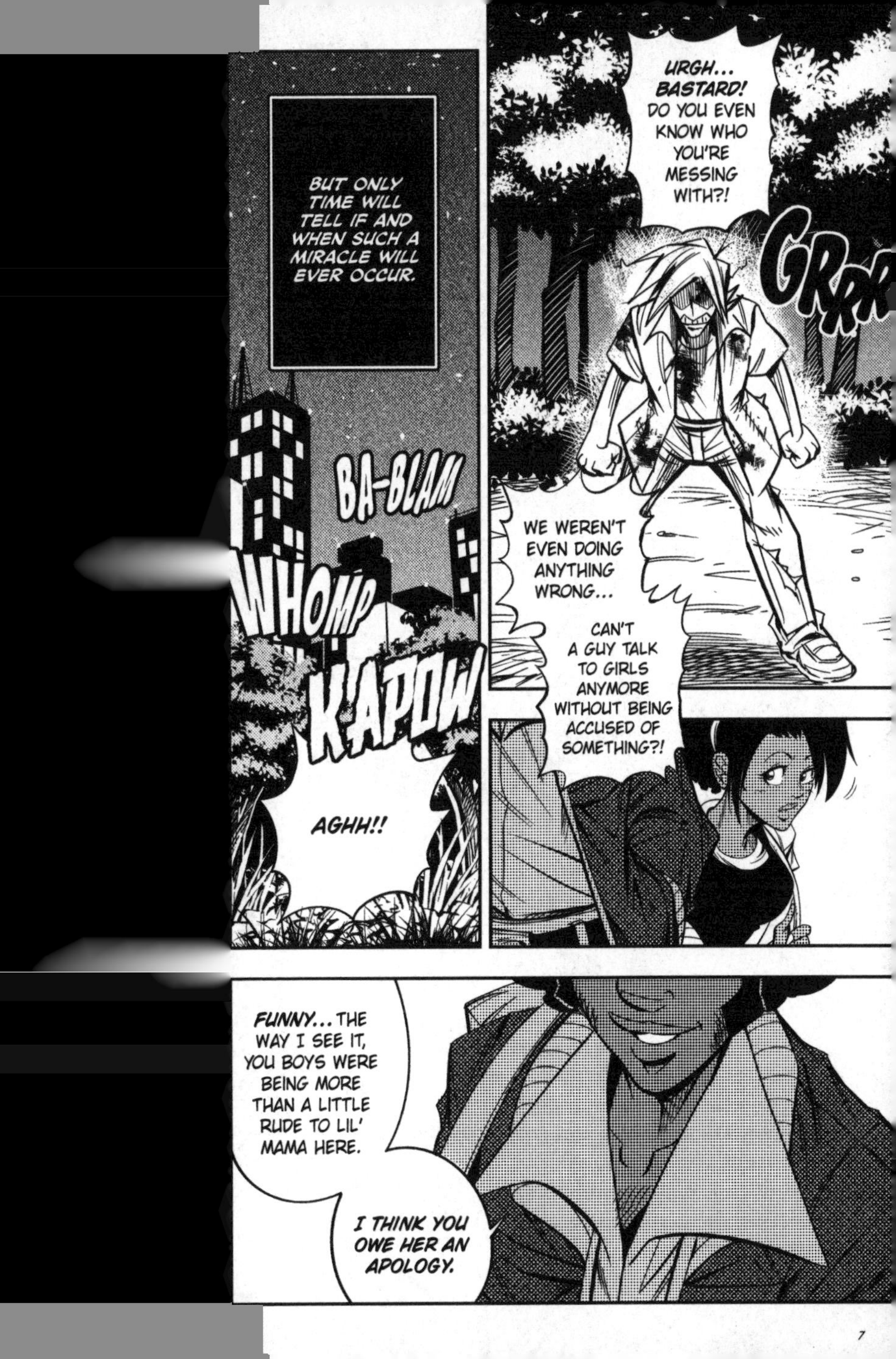

BUT ONLY TIME WILL TELL IF AND WHEN SUCH A MIRACLE WILL EVER OCCUR.
BA-BLAM
WHOMP
KAPOW
AGHH!!
URGH... BASTARD! DO YOU EVEN KNOW WHO YOU'RE MESSING WITH?!
GRRR
WE WEREN'T EVEN DOING ANYTHING WRONG...
CAN'T A GUY TALK TO GIRLS ANYMORE WITHOUT BEING ACCUSED OF SOMETHING?!
FUNNY... THE WAY I SEE IT, YOU BOYS WERE BEING MORE THAN A LITTLE RUDE TO LIL' MAMA HERE.
I THINK YOU OWE HER AN APOLOGY.

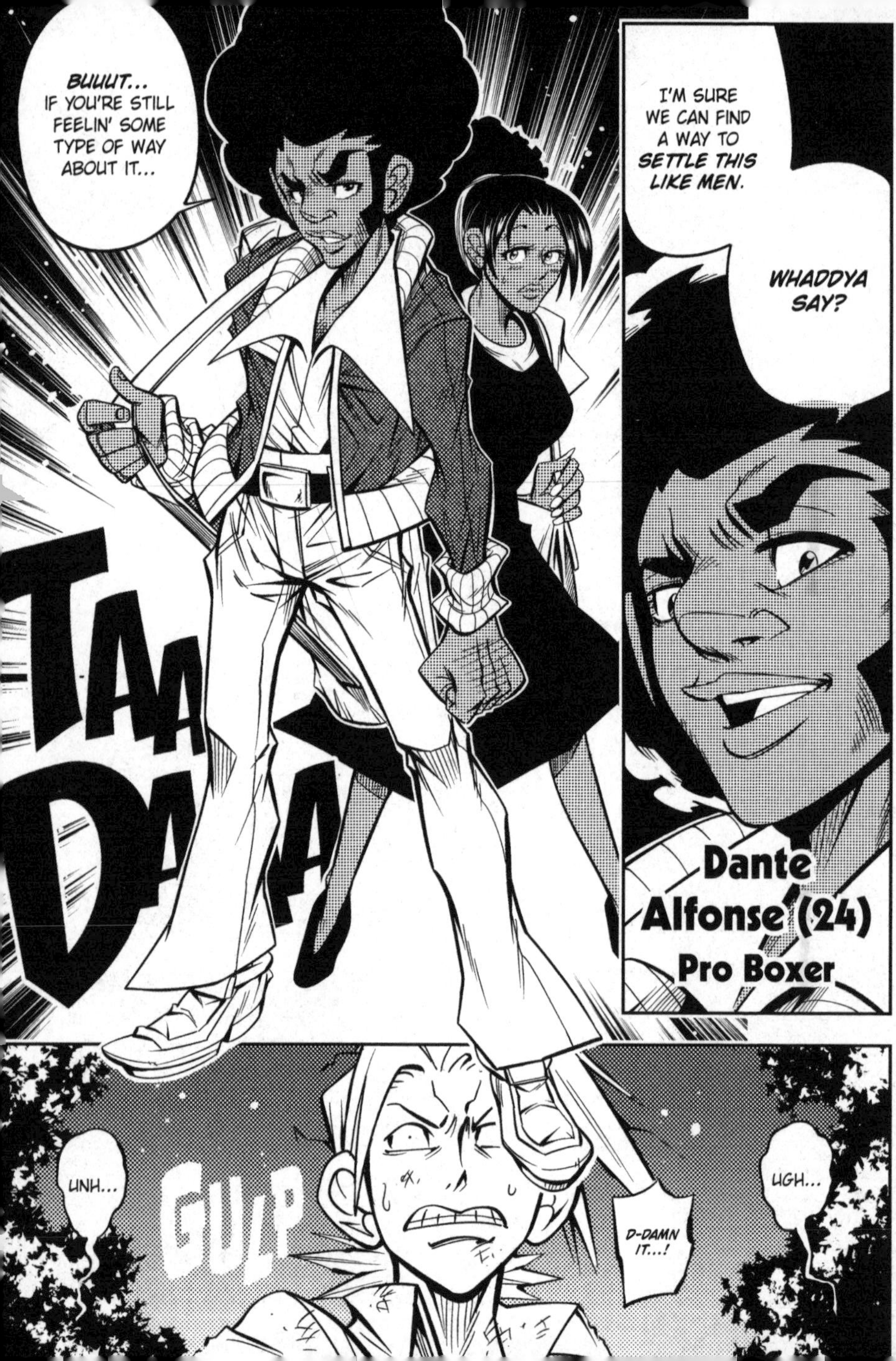
BUUUT... IF YOU'RE STILL FEELIN' SOME TYPE OF WAY ABOUT IT...
TAA DAAA
I'M SURE WE CAN FIND A WAY TO SETTLE THIS LIKE MEN.
WHADDYA SAY?
Dante Alfonse (24)
Pro Boxer
UNH...
GULP
D-DAMN IT...!
UGH...

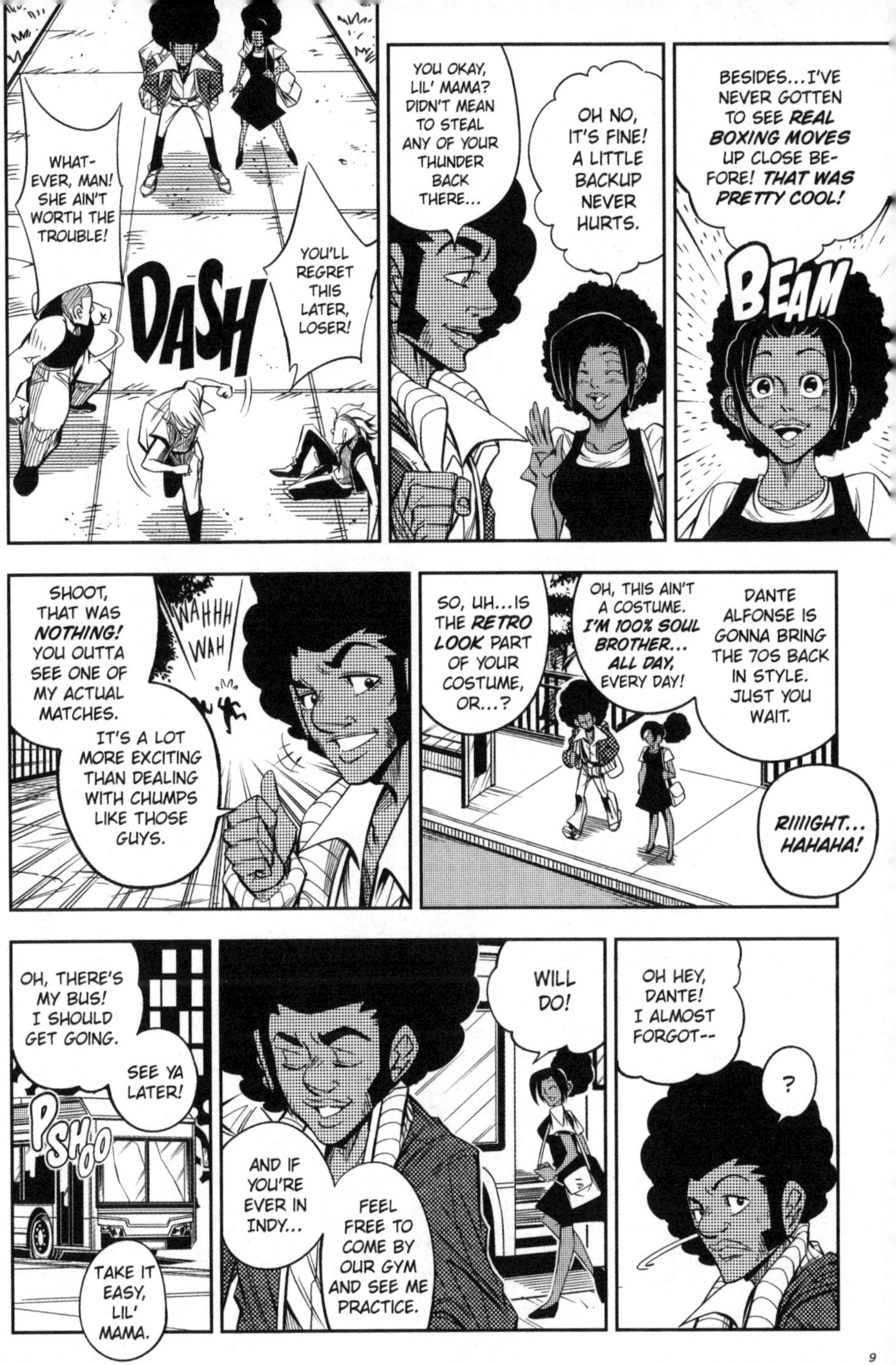
WHAT-EVER, MAN! SHE AIN'T WORTH THE TROUBLE!
DASH
YOU'LL REGRET THIS LATER, LOSER!
YOU OKAY, LIL' MAMA? DIDN'T MEAN TO STEAL ANY OF YOUR THUNDER BACK THERE...
OH NO, IT'S FINE! A LITTLE BACKUP NEVER HURTS.
BESIDES...I'VE NEVER GOTTEN TO SEE REAL BOXING MOVES UP CLOSE BE-FORE! THAT WAS PRETTY COOL!
BEAM
SHOOT, THAT WAS NOTHING! YOU OUTTA SEE ONE OF MY ACTUAL MATCHES.
WAHHH WAH
IT'S A LOT MORE EXCITING THAN DEALING WITH CHUMPS LIKE THOSE GUYS.
SO, UH...IS THE RETRO LOOK PART OF YOUR COSTUME, OR...?
OH, THIS AIN'T A COSTUME. I'M 100% SOUL BROTHER... ALL DAY, EVERY DAY!
DANTE ALFONSE IS GONNA BRING THE 70S BACK IN STYLE. JUST YOU WAIT.
RIIIIGHT... HAHAHA!
OH, THERE'S MY BUS! I SHOULD GET GOING.
SEE YA LATER!
PSHOO
TAKE IT EASY, LIL' MAMA.
WILL DO!
AND IF YOU'RE EVER IN INDY...
FEEL FREE TO COME BY OUR GYM AND SEE ME PRACTICE.
OH HEY, DANTE! I ALMOST FORGOT--
?

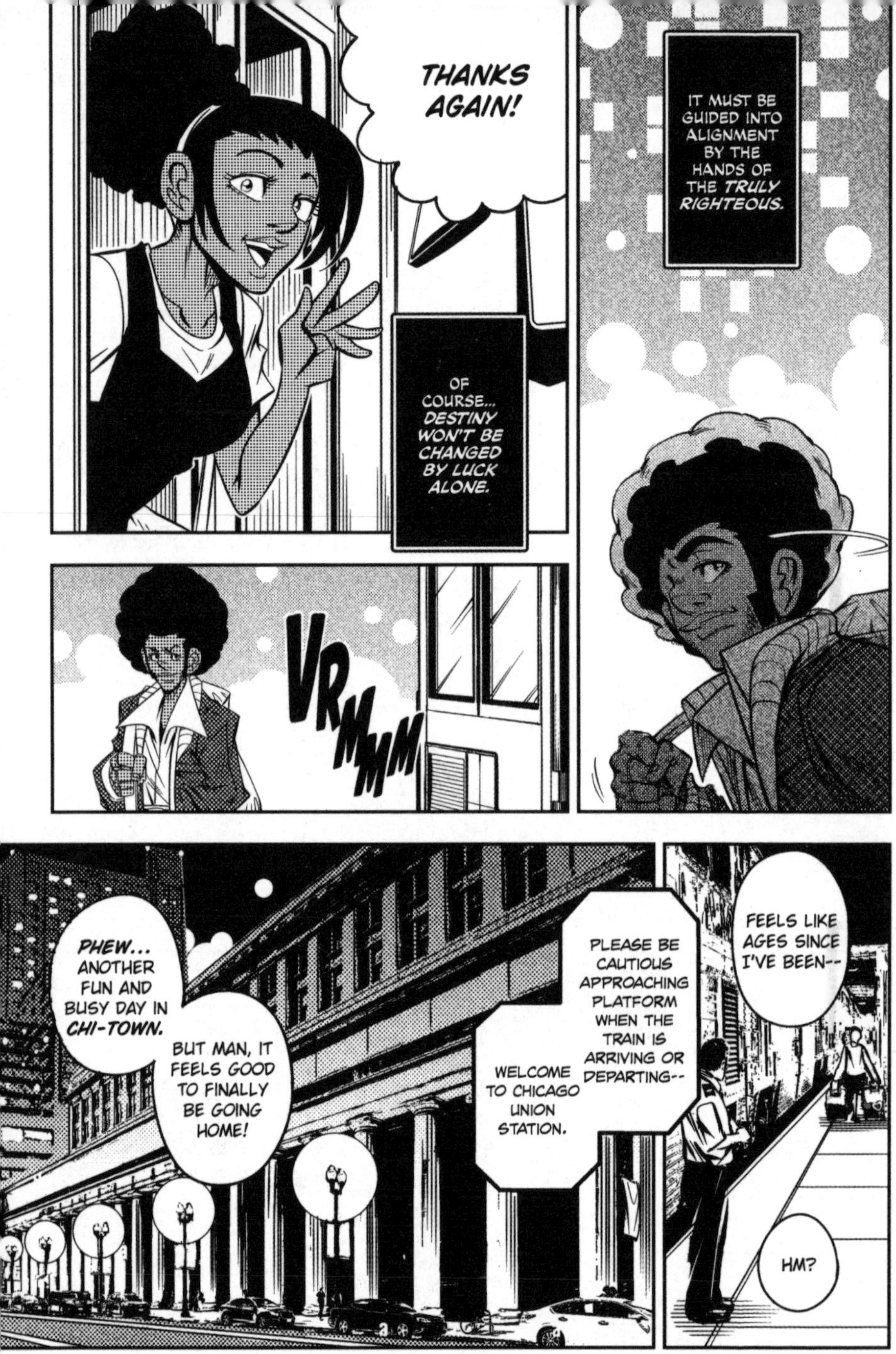
THANKS AGAIN!
OF COURSE... DESTINY WON'T BE CHANGED BY LUCK ALONE.
VRMMMM
IT MUST BE GUIDED INTO ALIGNMENT BY THE HANDS OF THE TRULY RIGHTEOUS.
PHEW... ANOTHER FUN AND BUSY DAY IN CHI-TOWN.
BUT MAN, IT FEELS GOOD TO FINALLY BE GOING HOME!
WELCOME TO CHICAGO UNION STATION.
PLEASE BE CAUTIOUS APPROACHING PLATFORM WHEN THE TRAIN IS ARRIVING OR DEPARTING--
FEELS LIKE AGES SINCE I'VE BEEN--
HM?

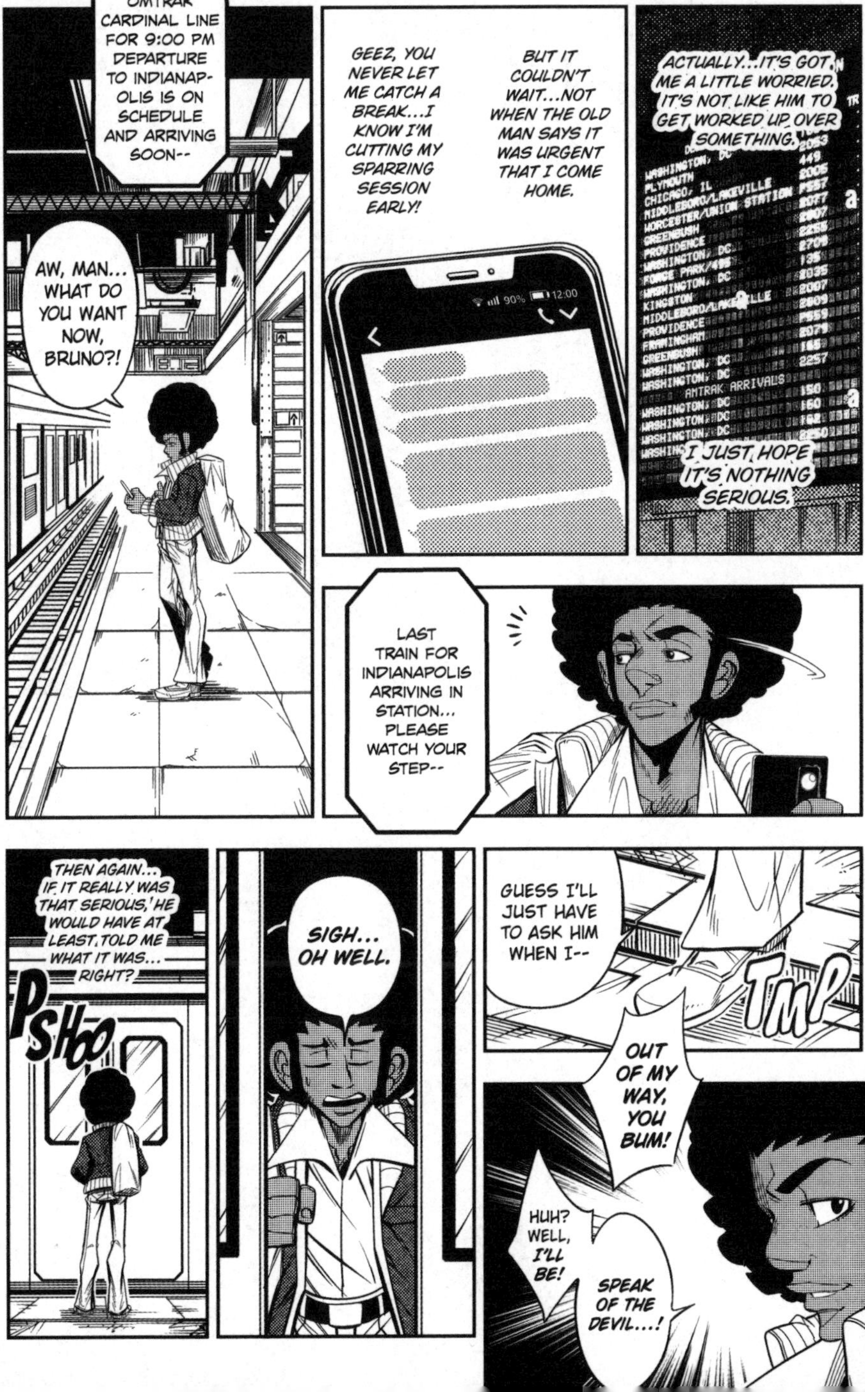
OMTRAK CARDINAL LINE FOR 9:00 PM DEPARTURE TO INDIANAPOLIS IS ON SCHEDULE AND ARRIVING SOON--
AW, MAN... WHAT DO YOU WANT NOW, BRUNO?!
GEEZ, YOU NEVER LET ME CATCH A BREAK...I KNOW I'M CUTTING MY SPARRING SESSION EARLY!
BUT IT COULDN'T WAIT...NOT WHEN THE OLD MAN SAYS IT WAS URGENT THAT I COME HOME.
90% 12:00
ACTUALLY...IT'S GOT ME A LITTLE WORRIED. IT'S NOT LIKE HIM TO GET WORKED UP OVER SOMETHING.
AMTRAK ARRIVALS
I JUST HOPE IT'S NOTHING SERIOUS.
LAST TRAIN FOR INDIANAPOLIS ARRIVING IN STATION... PLEASE WATCH YOUR STEP--
THEN AGAIN... IF IT REALLY WAS THAT SERIOUS, HE WOULD HAVE AT LEAST TOLD ME WHAT IT WAS... RIGHT?
PSHOO
SIGH... OH WELL.
GUESS I'LL JUST HAVE TO ASK HIM WHEN I--
TMP
OUT OF MY WAY, YOU BUM!
HUH? WELL, I'LL BE!
SPEAK OF THE DEVIL...!

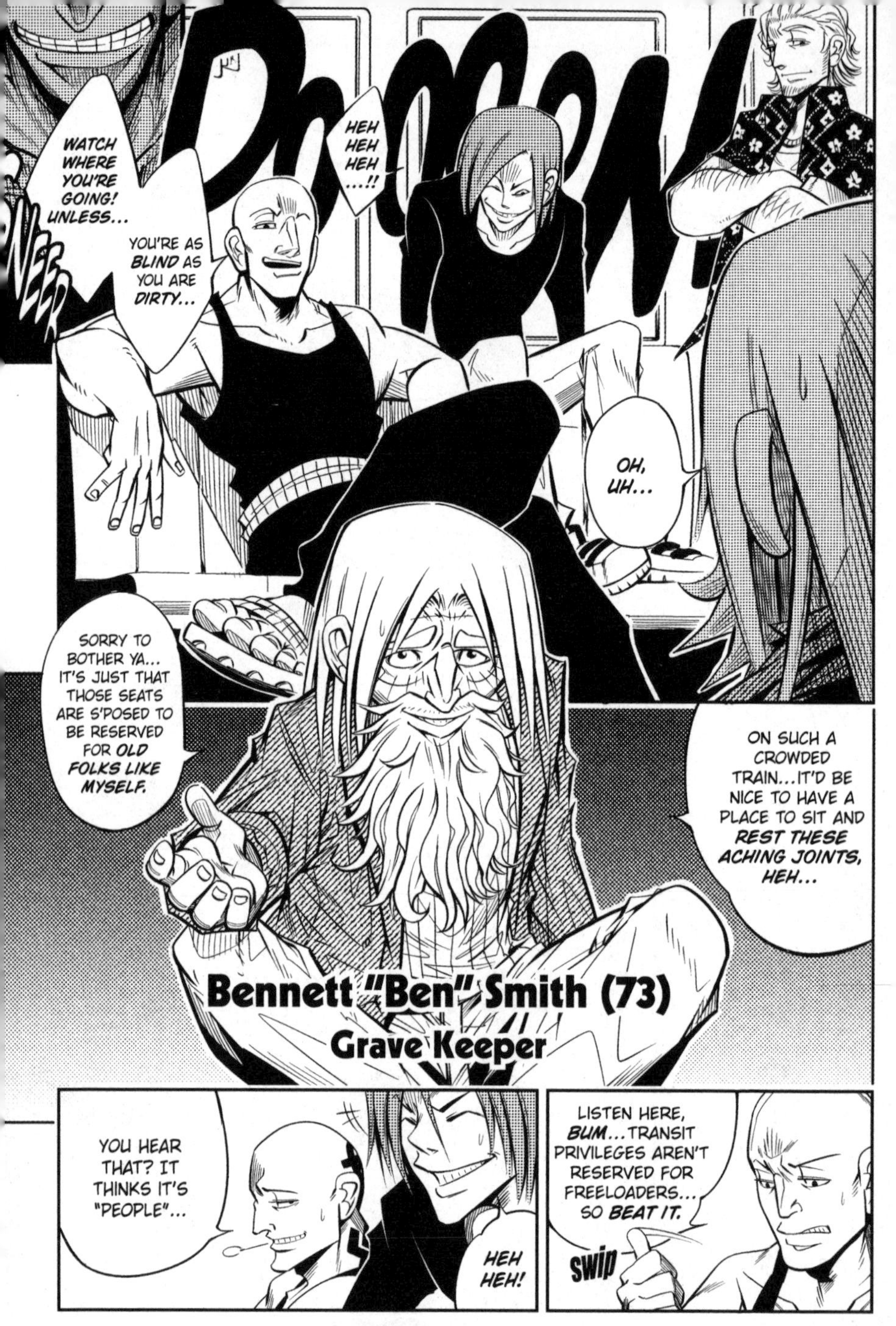
WATCH WHERE YOU'RE GOING! UNLESS...
YOU'RE AS BLIND AS YOU ARE DIRTY...
HEH HEH HEH ...!!
OH, UH...
SORRY TO BOTHER YA... IT'S JUST THAT THOSE SEATS ARE S'POSED TO BE RESERVED FOR OLD FOLKS LIKE MYSELF.
ON SUCH A CROWDED TRAIN...IT'D BE NICE TO HAVE A PLACE TO SIT AND REST THESE ACHING JOINTS, HEH...
Bennett "Ben" Smith (73)
Grave Keeper
YOU HEAR THAT? IT THINKS IT'S "PEOPLE"...
HEH HEH!
LISTEN HERE, BUM...TRANSIT PRIVILEGES AREN'T RESERVED FOR FREELOADERS... SO BEAT IT.
swip

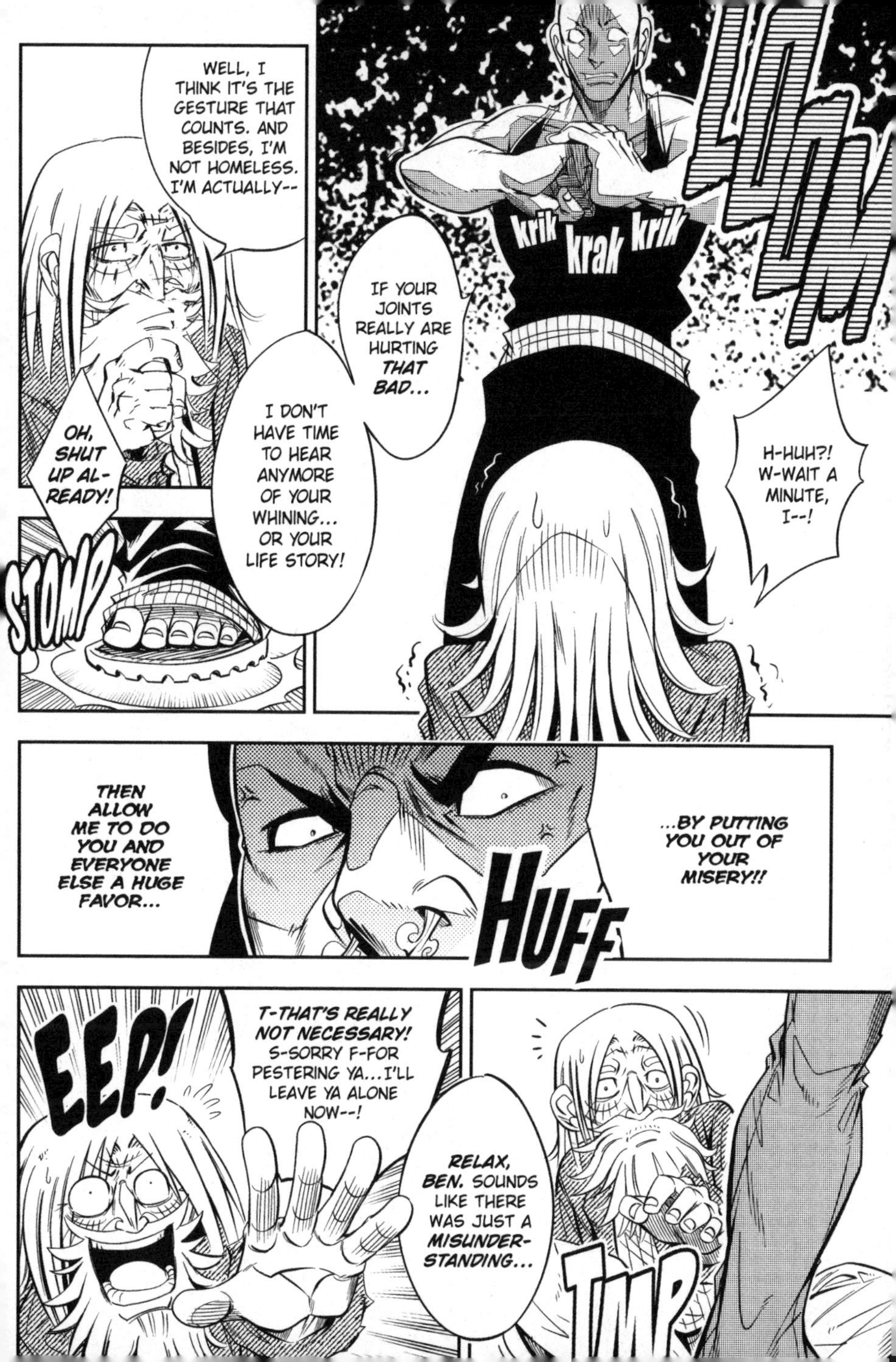

WELL, I THINK IT'S THE GESTURE THAT COUNTS. AND BESIDES, I'M NOT HOMELESS. I'M ACTUALLY--
OH, SHUT UP AL-READY!
STOMP
krik krak krik
IF YOUR JOINTS REALLY ARE HURTING *THAT BAD...*
I DON'T HAVE TIME TO HEAR ANYMORE OF YOUR WHINING... OR YOUR LIFE STORY!
H-HUH?! W-WAIT A MINUTE, I--!
THEN ALLOW ME TO DO YOU AND EVERYONE ELSE A HUGE FAVOR...
HUFF
...BY PUTTING YOU OUT OF YOUR MISERY!!
EEP!
T-THAT'S REALLY NOT NECESSARY! S-SORRY F-FOR PESTERING YA...I'LL LEAVE YA ALONE NOW--!
RELAX, BEN. SOUNDS LIKE THERE WAS JUST A *MISUNDER-STANDING...*
TMP

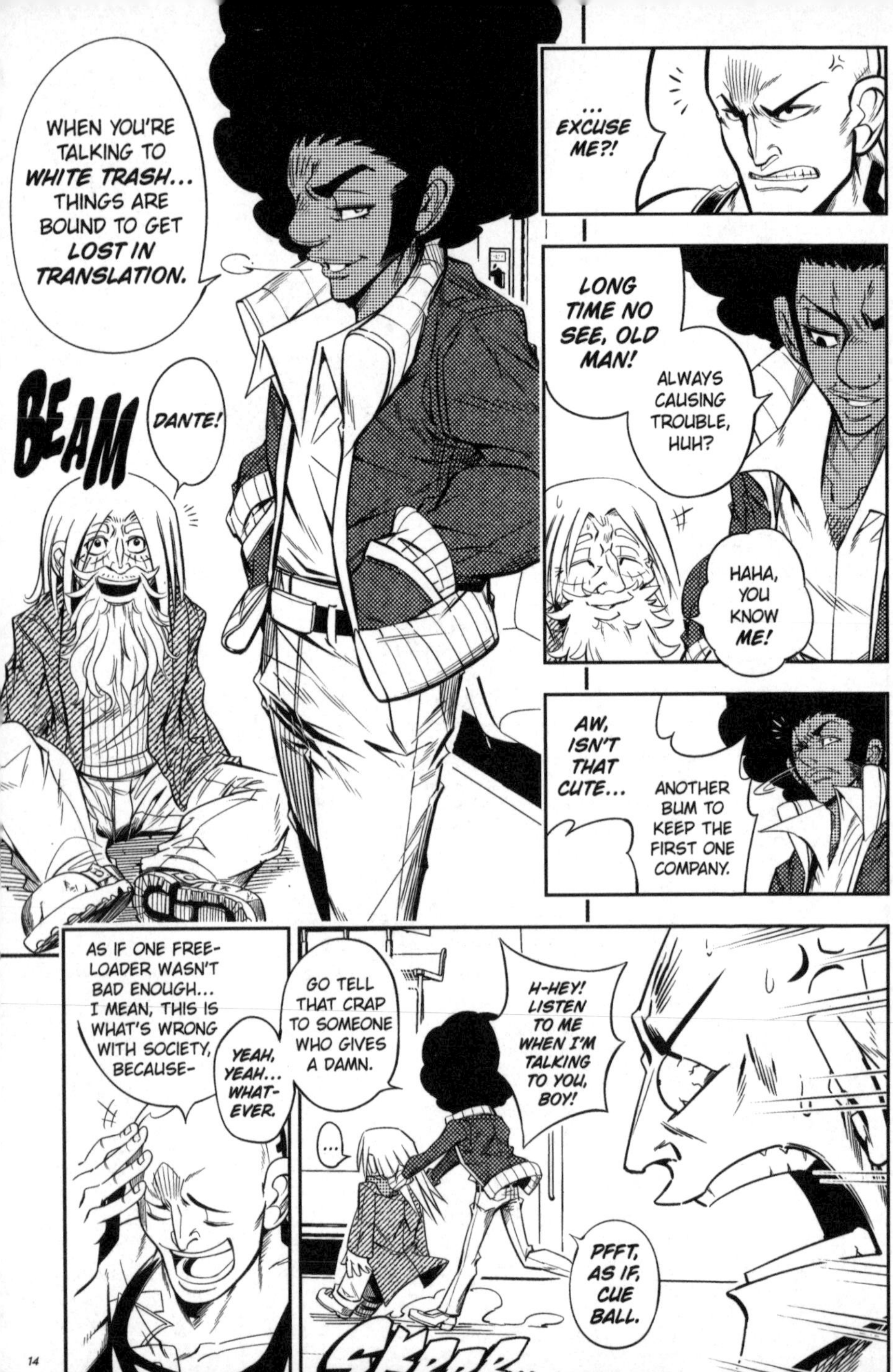
WHEN YOU'RE TALKING TO WHITE TRASH... THINGS ARE BOUND TO GET LOST IN TRANSLATION.
BEAM
DANTE!
... EXCUSE ME?!
LONG TIME NO SEE, OLD MAN!
ALWAYS CAUSING TROUBLE, HUH?
HAHA, YOU KNOW ME!
AW, ISN'T THAT CUTE...
ANOTHER BUM TO KEEP THE FIRST ONE COMPANY.
AS IF ONE FREE-LOADER WASN'T BAD ENOUGH... I MEAN, THIS IS WHAT'S WRONG WITH SOCIETY, BECAUSE-
YEAH, YEAH... WHAT-EVER.
GO TELL THAT CRAP TO SOMEONE WHO GIVES A DAMN.
...
H-HEY! LISTEN TO ME WHEN I'M TALKING TO YOU, BOY!
PFFT, AS IF, CUE BALL.

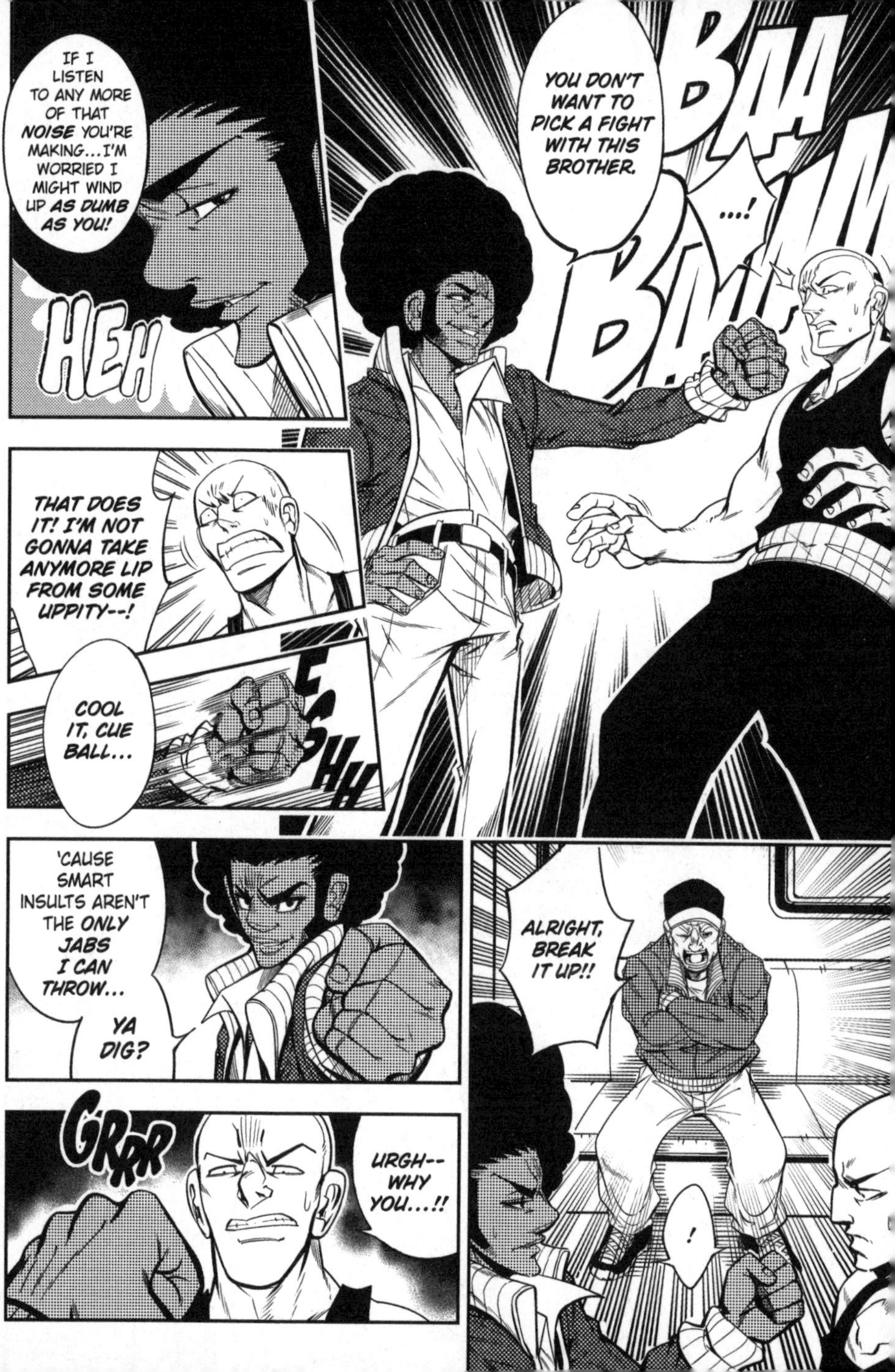
IF I LISTEN TO ANY MORE OF THAT *NOISE* YOU'RE MAKING... I'M WORRIED I MIGHT WIND UP *AS DUMB AS YOU!*
HEH
THAT DOES IT! I'M NOT GONNA TAKE ANYMORE LIP FROM SOME UPPITY--!
COOL IT, CUE BALL...
FSHH
YOU DON'T WANT TO PICK A FIGHT WITH THIS BROTHER.
BAAM
BAM
...!
'CAUSE SMART INSULTS AREN'T THE *ONLY JABS* I CAN THROW...
YA DIG?
GRRR
URGH-- WHY YOU...!!
ALRIGHT, BREAK IT UP!!
!

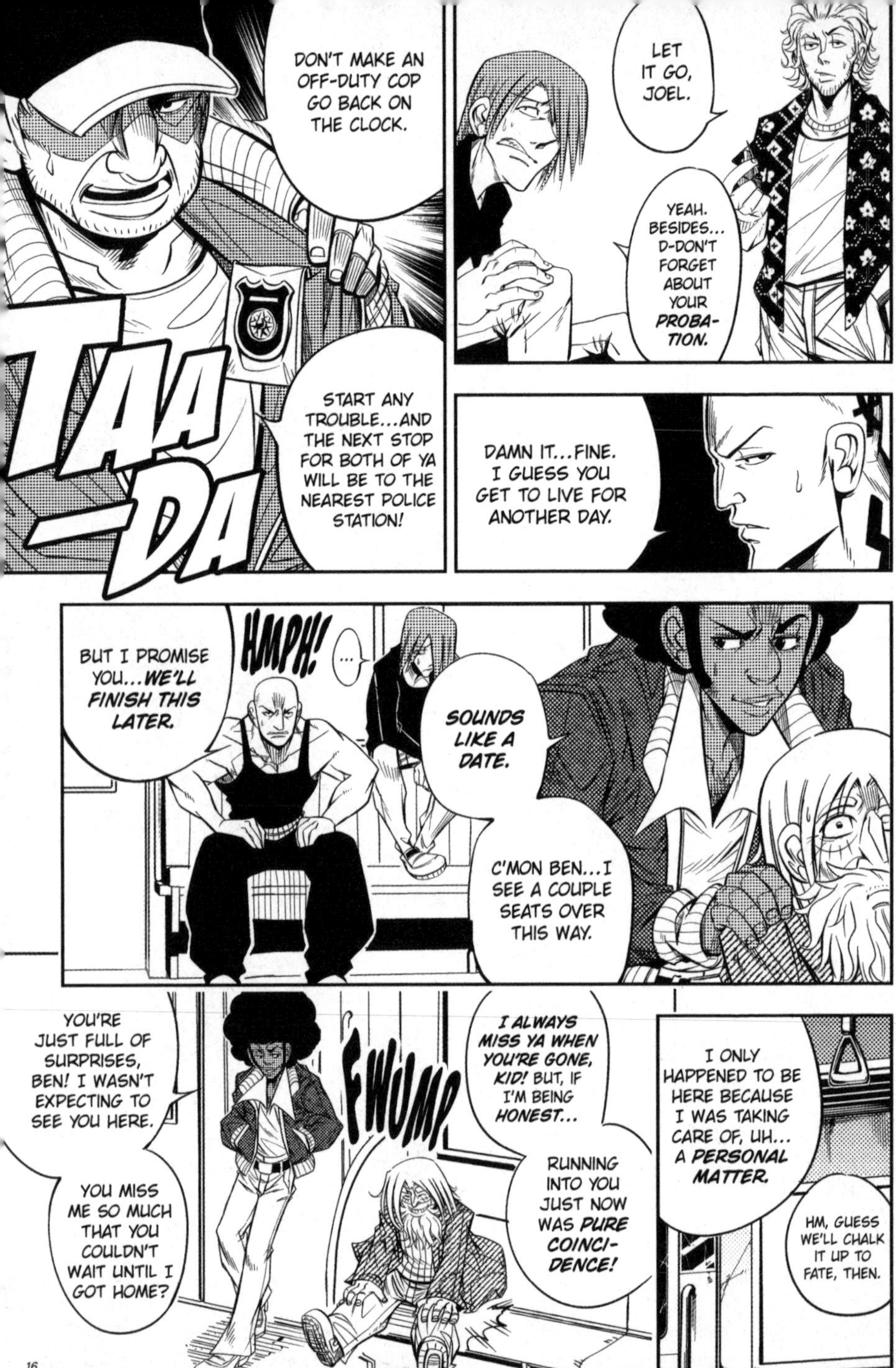
DON'T MAKE AN OFF-DUTY COP GO BACK ON THE CLOCK.
TAA-DA
START ANY TROUBLE...AND THE NEXT STOP FOR BOTH OF YA WILL BE TO THE NEAREST POLICE STATION!
LET IT GO, JOEL.
YEAH. BESIDES... D-DON'T FORGET ABOUT YOUR PROBATION.
DAMN IT...FINE. I GUESS YOU GET TO LIVE FOR ANOTHER DAY.
BUT I PROMISE YOU...WE'LL FINISH THIS LATER.
HMPH!
...
SOUNDS LIKE A DATE.
C'MON BEN...I SEE A COUPLE SEATS OVER THIS WAY.
YOU'RE JUST FULL OF SURPRISES, BEN! I WASN'T EXPECTING TO SEE YOU HERE.
YOU MISS ME SO MUCH THAT YOU COULDN'T WAIT UNTIL I GOT HOME?
FWUMP
I ALWAYS MISS YA WHEN YOU'RE GONE, KID! BUT, IF I'M BEING HONEST...
RUNNING INTO YOU JUST NOW WAS PURE COINCI-DENCE!
I ONLY HAPPENED TO BE HERE BECAUSE I WAS TAKING CARE OF, UH... A PERSONAL MATTER.
HM, GUESS WE'LL CHALK IT UP TO FATE, THEN.

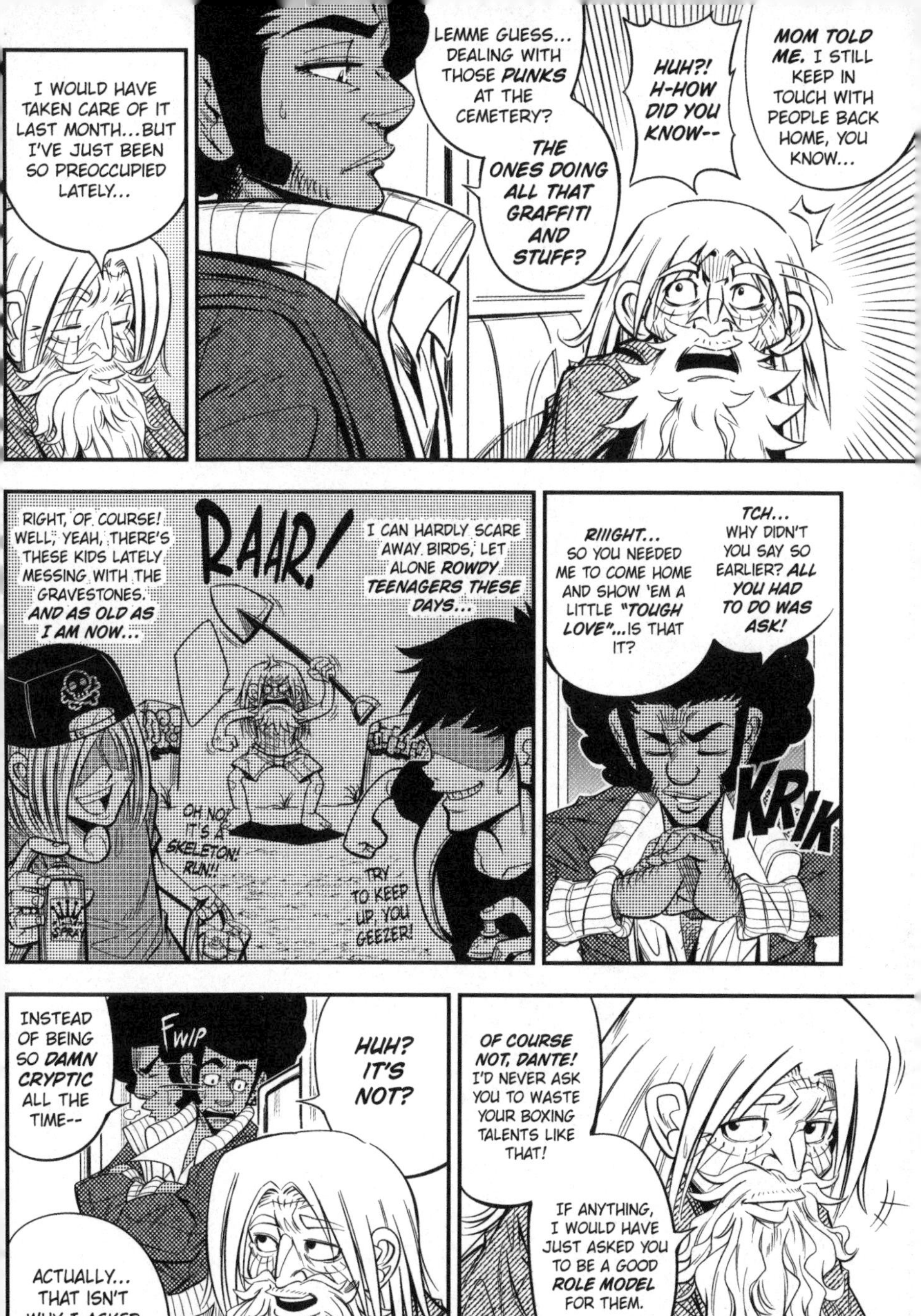

I WOULD HAVE TAKEN CARE OF IT LAST MONTH...BUT I'VE JUST BEEN SO PREOCCUPIED LATELY...
LEMME GUESS... DEALING WITH THOSE PUNKS AT THE CEMETERY?
THE ONES DOING ALL THAT GRAFFITI AND STUFF?
HUH?! H-HOW DID YOU KNOW--
MOM TOLD ME. I STILL KEEP IN TOUCH WITH PEOPLE BACK HOME, YOU KNOW...
RIGHT, OF COURSE! WELL, YEAH, THERE'S THESE KIDS LATELY MESSING WITH THE GRAVESTONES. AND AS OLD AS I AM NOW...
RAAR!
I CAN HARDLY SCARE AWAY BIRDS, LET ALONE ROWDY TEENAGERS THESE DAYS...
OH NO! IT'S A SKELETON! RUN!!
SPRAY
TRY TO KEEP UP, YOU GEEZER!
RIIIGHT... SO YOU NEEDED ME TO COME HOME AND SHOW 'EM A LITTLE "TOUGH LOVE"...IS THAT IT?
TCH... WHY DIDN'T YOU SAY SO EARLIER? ALL YOU HAD TO DO WAS ASK!
KRIK
INSTEAD OF BEING SO DAMN CRYPTIC ALL THE TIME--
FWIP
HUH? IT'S NOT?
ACTUALLY... THAT ISN'T WHY I ASKED YOU TO COME HOME, KID.
OF COURSE NOT, DANTE! I'D NEVER ASK YOU TO WASTE YOUR BOXING TALENTS LIKE THAT!
IF ANYTHING, I WOULD HAVE JUST ASKED YOU TO BE A GOOD ROLE MODEL FOR THEM.

THEY'RE JUST A BUNCH OF KIDS DOING PRANKS... THEY'RE NOT SO BAD TO HURT ANYONE.

IN TIME, THEY'LL GROW UP AND COME TO THEIR SENSES EVENTUALLY.

YOU, UH... SURE ABOUT THAT?

YOU BET! I KNOW BECAUSE I USED TO BE QUITE THE *HELLION* MYSELF AT THAT AGE!

BUT TIME AND PATIENCE HELPED ME SEE THE LIGHT... *SO TO SPEAK.*

HMPH... HAVE IT YOUR WAY, THEN.

BUT, PROMISE ME SOMETHING, OLD MAN...

STOP MAKING UP CRAZY STORIES ABOUT YOU BEING A TOUGH GUY OR SOMETHING!

BA-BAM

HUH?! WHAT ARE YOU TALKING ABOUT? I'M NOT MAKING ANYTHING UP!

YEAH RIGHT! I DOUBT A BORING GOODY-TWO-SHOES LIKE YOU HAS DONE A BAD THING YOUR WHOLE LIFE!

IN FACT, YOU'RE SUCH A *GODDAMN SAINT--*

I BET THE DEVIL HIMSELF COULDN'T LAY A FINGER ON YOU, OLD MAN.

...!

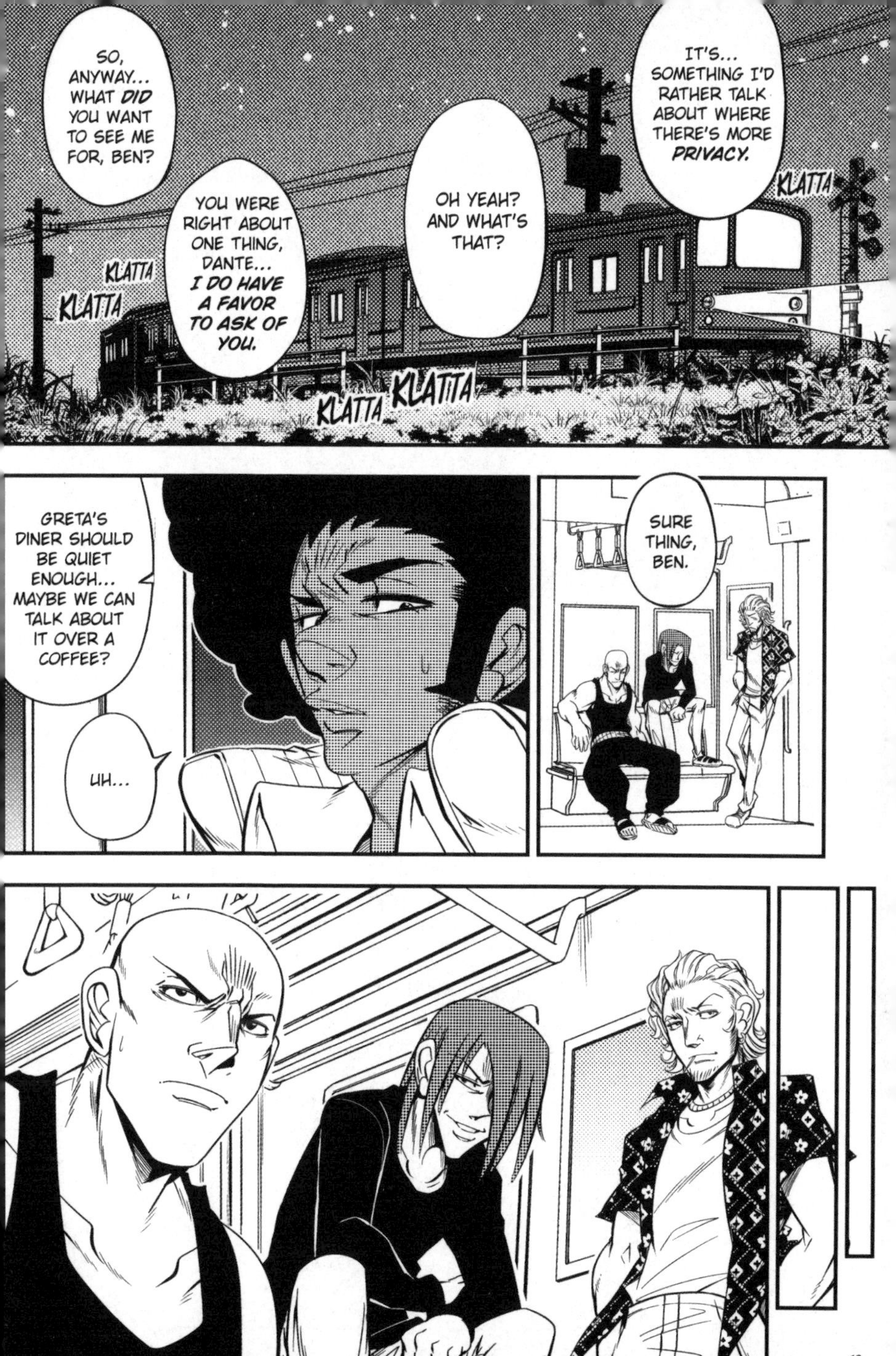
SO, ANYWAY... WHAT *DID* YOU WANT TO SEE ME FOR, BEN?
KLATTA
KLATTA
YOU WERE RIGHT ABOUT ONE THING, DANTE... *I DO HAVE A FAVOR TO ASK OF YOU.*
KLATTA
KLATTA
OH YEAH? AND WHAT'S THAT?
IT'S... SOMETHING I'D RATHER TALK ABOUT WHERE THERE'S MORE *PRIVACY.*
KLATTA
GRETA'S DINER SHOULD BE QUIET ENOUGH... MAYBE WE CAN TALK ABOUT IT OVER A COFFEE?
UH...
SURE THING, BEN.

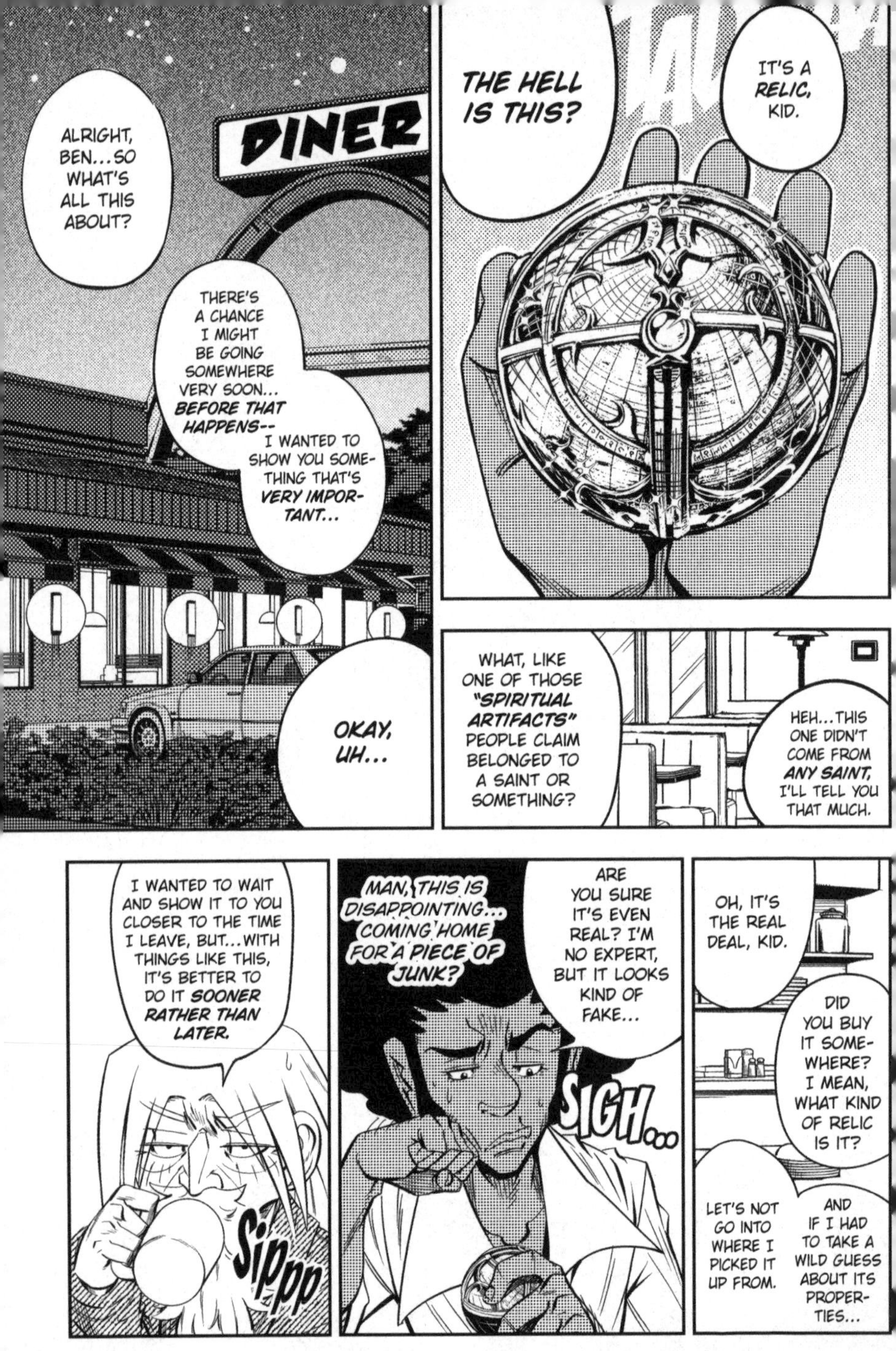
ALRIGHT, BEN...SO WHAT'S ALL THIS ABOUT?
DINER
THERE'S A CHANCE I MIGHT BE GOING SOMEWHERE VERY SOON... **BEFORE THAT HAPPENS--** I WANTED TO SHOW YOU SOMETHING THAT'S **VERY IMPORTANT...**
OKAY, UH...
THE HELL IS THIS?
IT'S A **RELIC,** KID.
WHAT, LIKE ONE OF THOSE **"SPIRITUAL ARTIFACTS"** PEOPLE CLAIM BELONGED TO A SAINT OR SOMETHING?
HEH...THIS ONE DIDN'T COME FROM **ANY SAINT,** I'LL TELL YOU THAT MUCH.
I WANTED TO WAIT AND SHOW IT TO YOU CLOSER TO THE TIME I LEAVE, BUT...WITH THINGS LIKE THIS, IT'S BETTER TO DO IT **SOONER RATHER THAN LATER.**
SIPPP
MAN, THIS IS DISAPPOINTING... COMING HOME FOR A PIECE OF JUNK?
ARE YOU SURE IT'S EVEN REAL? I'M NO EXPERT, BUT IT LOOKS KIND OF FAKE...
SIGH...
OH, IT'S THE REAL DEAL, KID.
DID YOU BUY IT SOMEWHERE? I MEAN, WHAT KIND OF RELIC IS IT?
LET'S NOT GO INTO WHERE I PICKED IT UP FROM.
AND IF I HAD TO TAKE A WILD GUESS ABOUT ITS PROPERTIES...

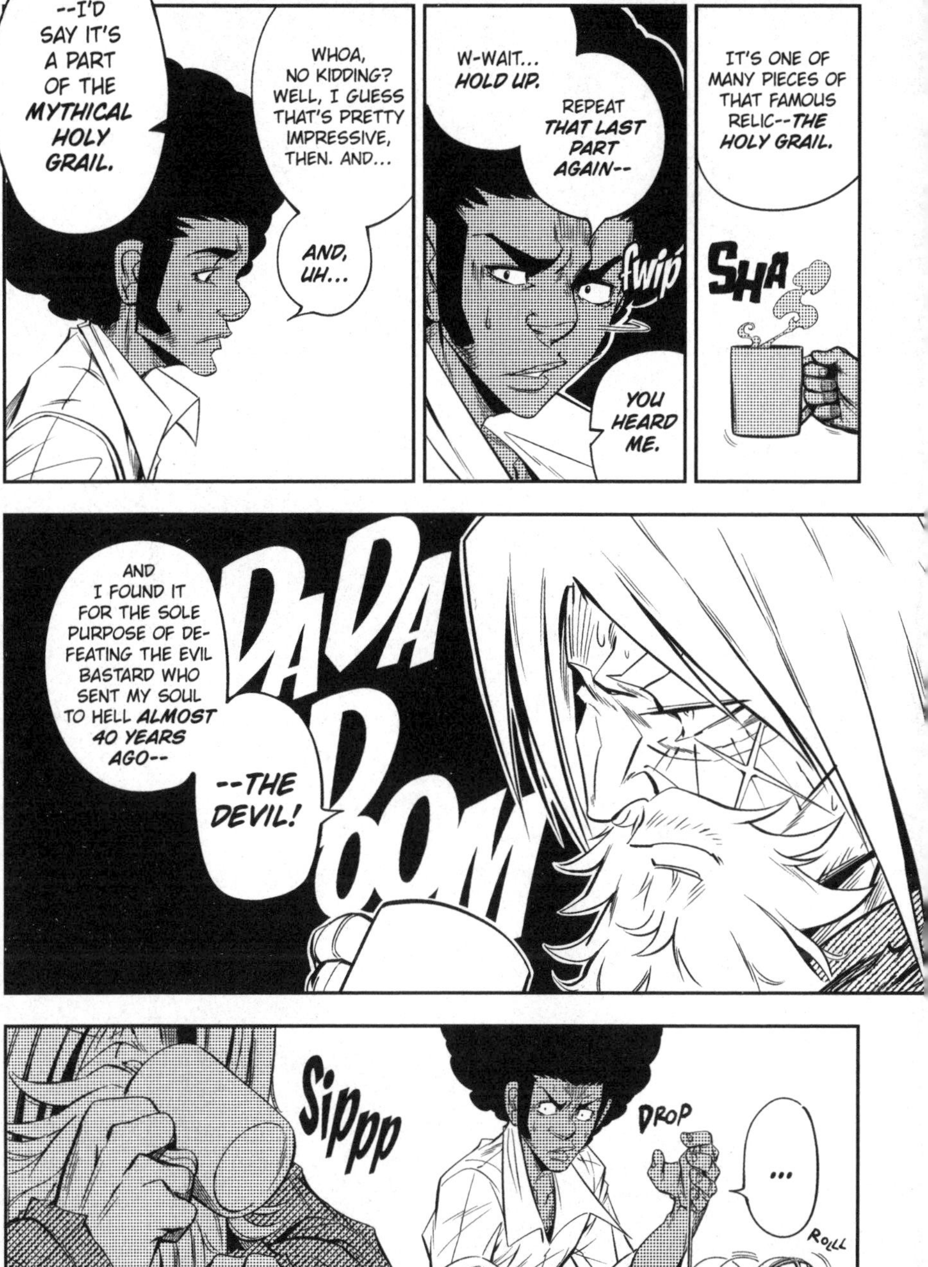
--I'D SAY IT'S A PART OF THE MYTHICAL HOLY GRAIL.
WHOA, NO KIDDING? WELL, I GUESS THAT'S PRETTY IMPRESSIVE, THEN. AND...
AND, UH...
W-WAIT... HOLD UP.
REPEAT THAT LAST PART AGAIN--
fwip
YOU HEARD ME.
IT'S ONE OF MANY PIECES OF THAT FAMOUS RELIC--THE HOLY GRAIL.
SHA
AND I FOUND IT FOR THE SOLE PURPOSE OF DE-FEATING THE EVIL BASTARD WHO SENT MY SOUL TO HELL ALMOST 40 YEARS AGO--
DADADA DOOM
--THE DEVIL!
Sippp
DROP
...
ROLL

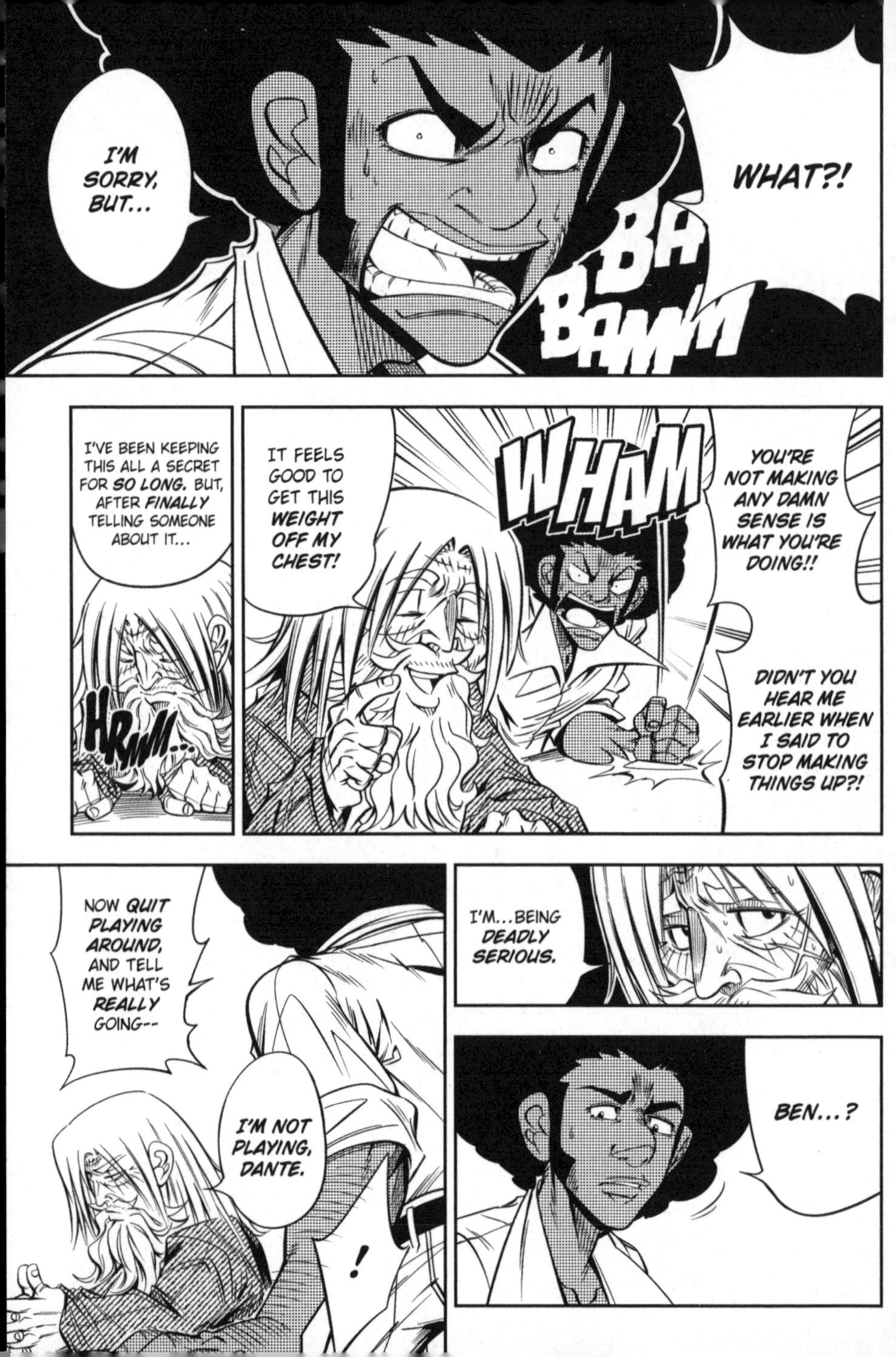
I'M SORRY, BUT...
WHAT?!
BA BAMM
I'VE BEEN KEEPING THIS ALL A SECRET FOR SO LONG. BUT, AFTER FINALLY TELLING SOMEONE ABOUT IT...
HRMM...
IT FEELS GOOD TO GET THIS WEIGHT OFF MY CHEST!
WHAM
YOU'RE NOT MAKING ANY DAMN SENSE IS WHAT YOU'RE DOING!!
DIDN'T YOU HEAR ME EARLIER WHEN I SAID TO STOP MAKING THINGS UP?!
NOW QUIT PLAYING AROUND, AND TELL ME WHAT'S REALLY GOING--
I'M NOT PLAYING, DANTE.
!
I'M...BEING DEADLY SERIOUS.
BEN...?

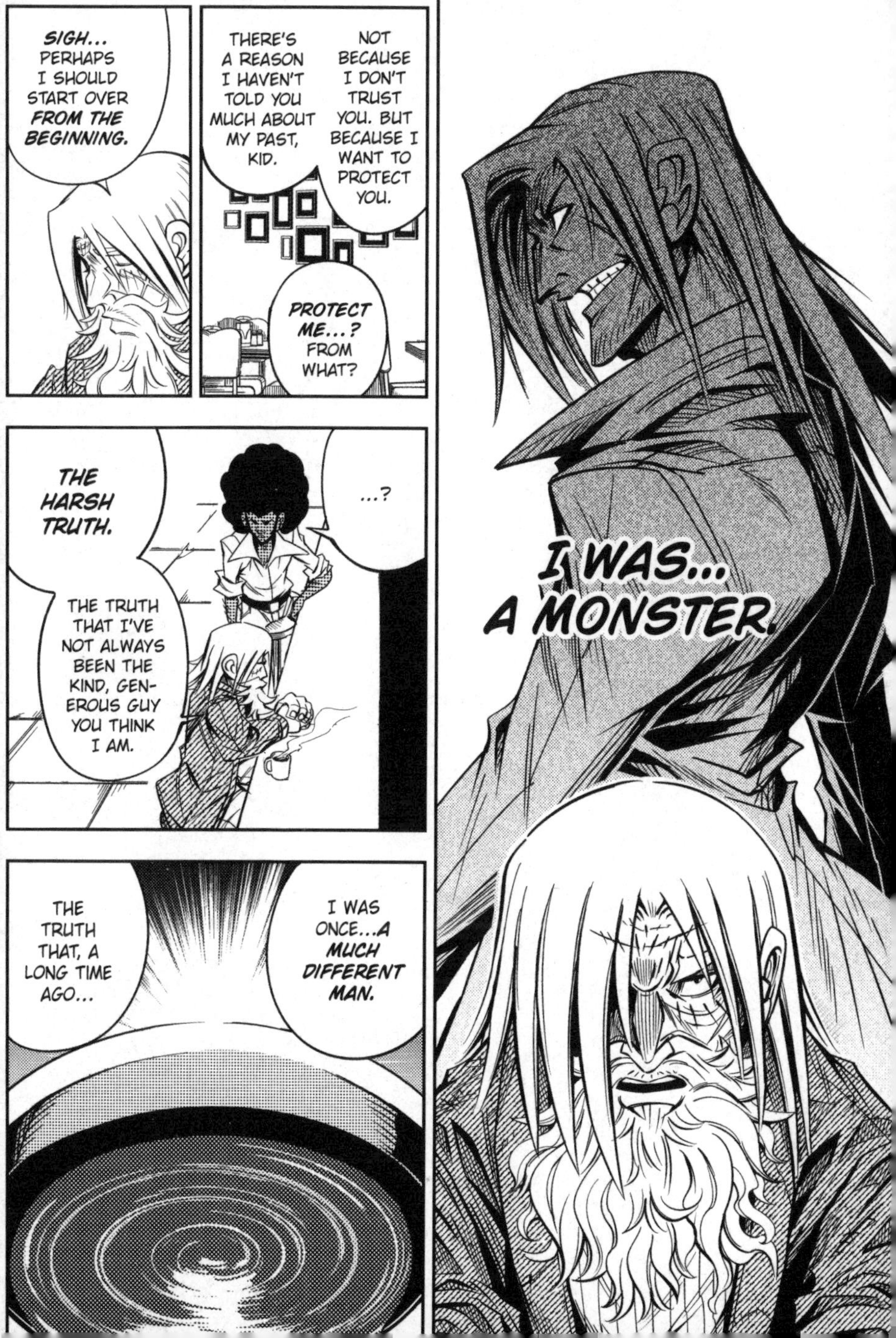
SIGH... PERHAPS I SHOULD START OVER FROM THE BEGINNING.
THERE'S A REASON I HAVEN'T TOLD YOU MUCH ABOUT MY PAST, KID.
NOT BECAUSE I DON'T TRUST YOU. BUT BECAUSE I WANT TO PROTECT YOU.
PROTECT ME...? FROM WHAT?
THE HARSH TRUTH.
...?
THE TRUTH THAT I'VE NOT ALWAYS BEEN THE KIND, GEN-EROUS GUY YOU THINK I AM.
THE TRUTH THAT, A LONG TIME AGO...
I WAS ONCE...A MUCH DIFFERENT MAN.
I WAS... A MONSTER.

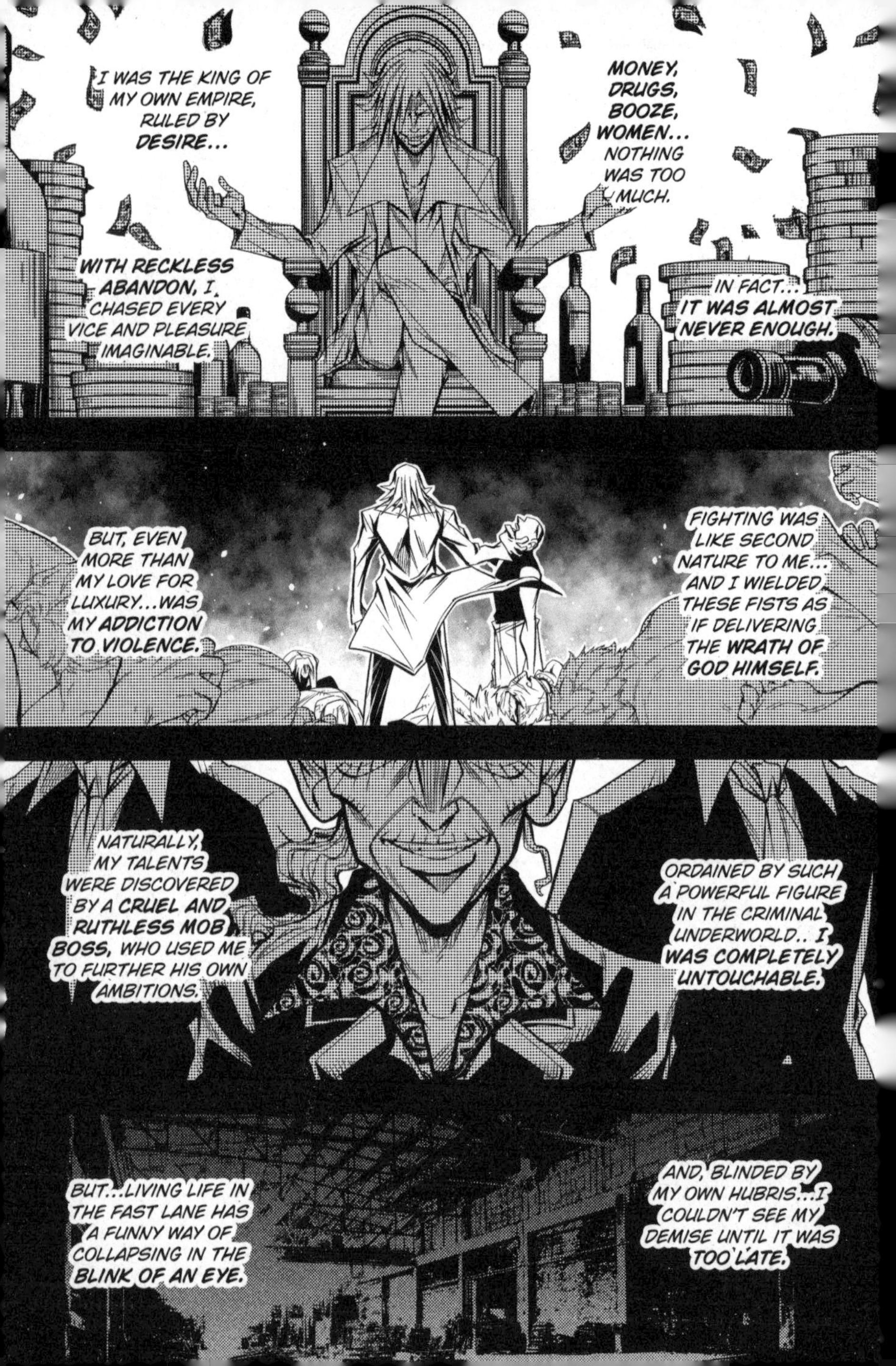
I WAS THE KING OF MY OWN EMPIRE, RULED BY DESIRE...
MONEY, DRUGS, BOOZE, WOMEN... NOTHING WAS TOO MUCH.
WITH RECKLESS ABANDON, I CHASED EVERY VICE AND PLEASURE IMAGINABLE.
IN FACT... IT WAS ALMOST NEVER ENOUGH.
BUT, EVEN MORE THAN MY LOVE FOR LUXURY...WAS MY ADDICTION TO VIOLENCE.
FIGHTING WAS LIKE SECOND NATURE TO ME... AND I WIELDED THESE FISTS AS IF DELIVERING THE WRATH OF GOD HIMSELF.
NATURALLY, MY TALENTS WERE DISCOVERED BY A CRUEL AND RUTHLESS MOB BOSS, WHO USED ME TO FURTHER HIS OWN AMBITIONS.
ORDAINED BY SUCH A POWERFUL FIGURE IN THE CRIMINAL UNDERWORLD.. I WAS COMPLETELY UNTOUCHABLE.
BUT...LIVING LIFE IN THE FAST LANE HAS A FUNNY WAY OF COLLAPSING IN THE BLINK OF AN EYE.
AND, BLINDED BY MY OWN HUBRIS...I COULDN'T SEE MY DEMISE UNTIL IT WAS TOO LATE.

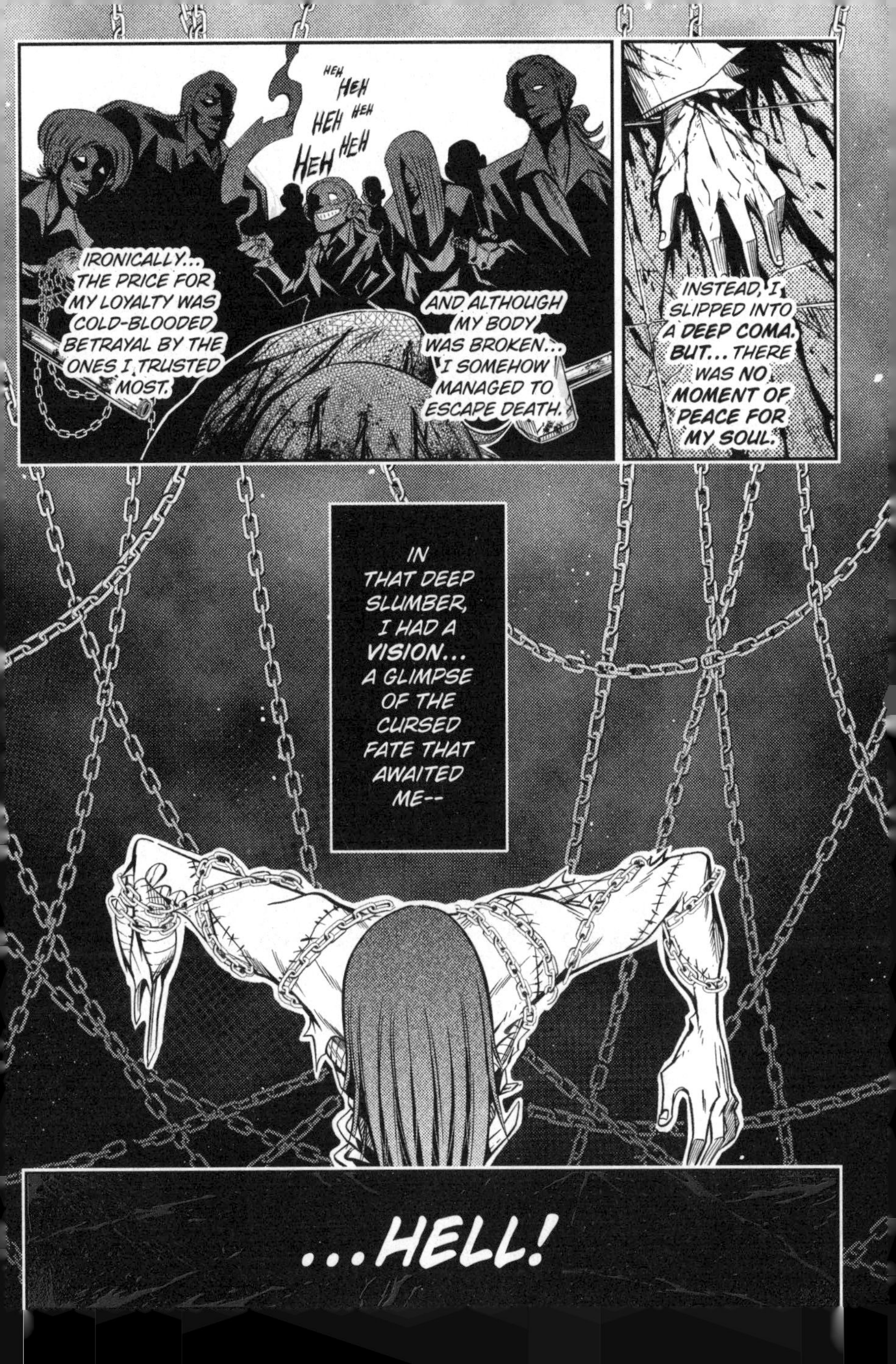
HEH HEH HEH HEH HEH HEH
IRONICALLY... THE PRICE FOR MY LOYALTY WAS COLD-BLOODED BETRAYAL BY THE ONES I TRUSTED MOST.
AND ALTHOUGH MY BODY WAS BROKEN... I SOMEHOW MANAGED TO ESCAPE DEATH.
INSTEAD, I SLIPPED INTO A DEEP COMA. BUT... THERE WAS NO MOMENT OF PEACE FOR MY SOUL.
IN THAT DEEP SLUMBER, I HAD A VISION... A GLIMPSE OF THE CURSED FATE THAT AWAITED ME--
...HELL!

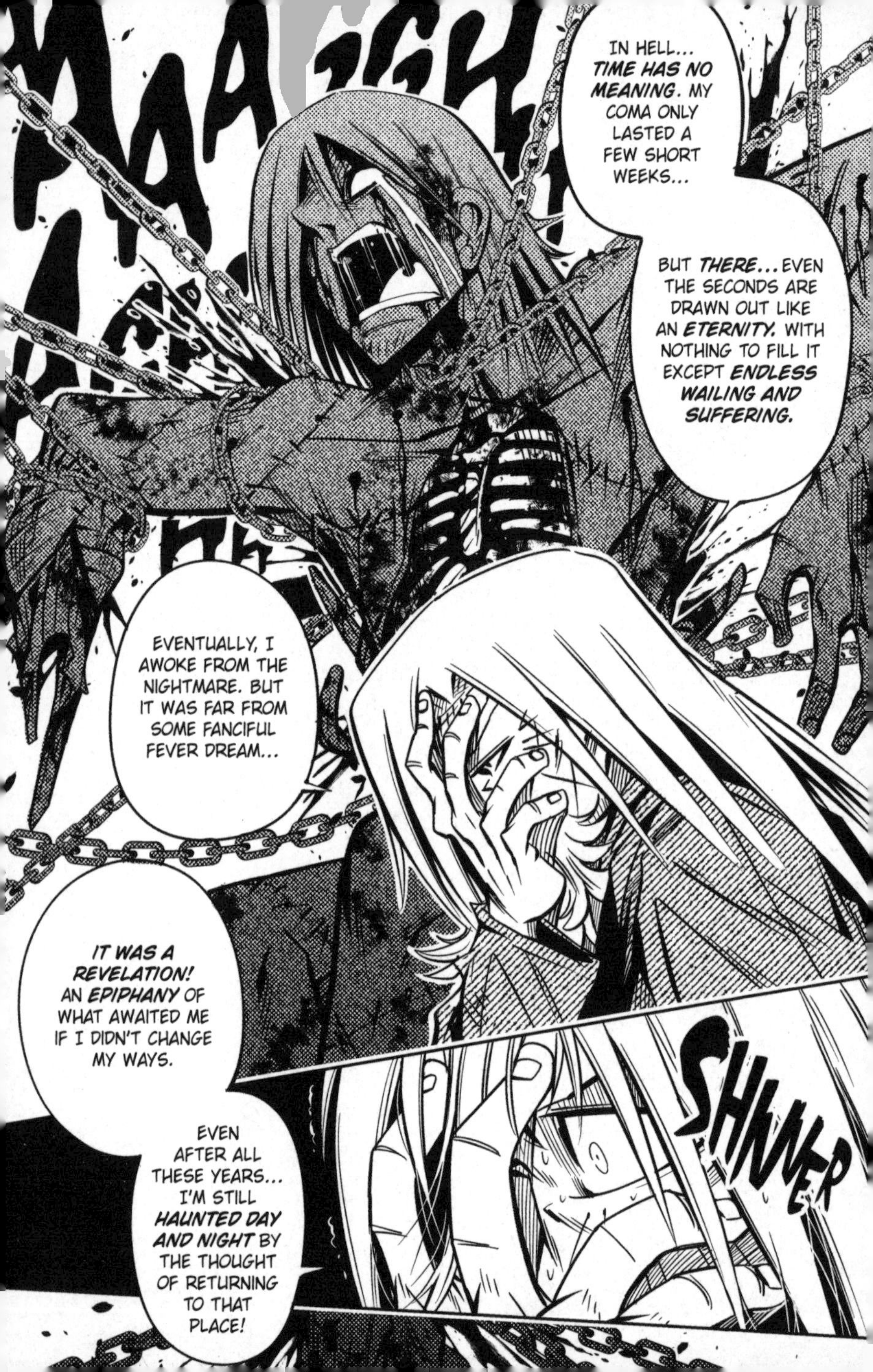
IN HELL... TIME HAS NO MEANING. MY COMA ONLY LASTED A FEW SHORT WEEKS...
BUT THERE... EVEN THE SECONDS ARE DRAWN OUT LIKE AN ETERNITY. WITH NOTHING TO FILL IT EXCEPT ENDLESS WAILING AND SUFFERING.
EVENTUALLY, I AWOKE FROM THE NIGHTMARE. BUT IT WAS FAR FROM SOME FANCIFUL FEVER DREAM...
IT WAS A REVELATION! AN EPIPHANY OF WHAT AWAITED ME IF I DIDN'T CHANGE MY WAYS.
EVEN AFTER ALL THESE YEARS... I'M STILL HAUNTED DAY AND NIGHT BY THE THOUGHT OF RETURNING TO THAT PLACE!
SHIVER

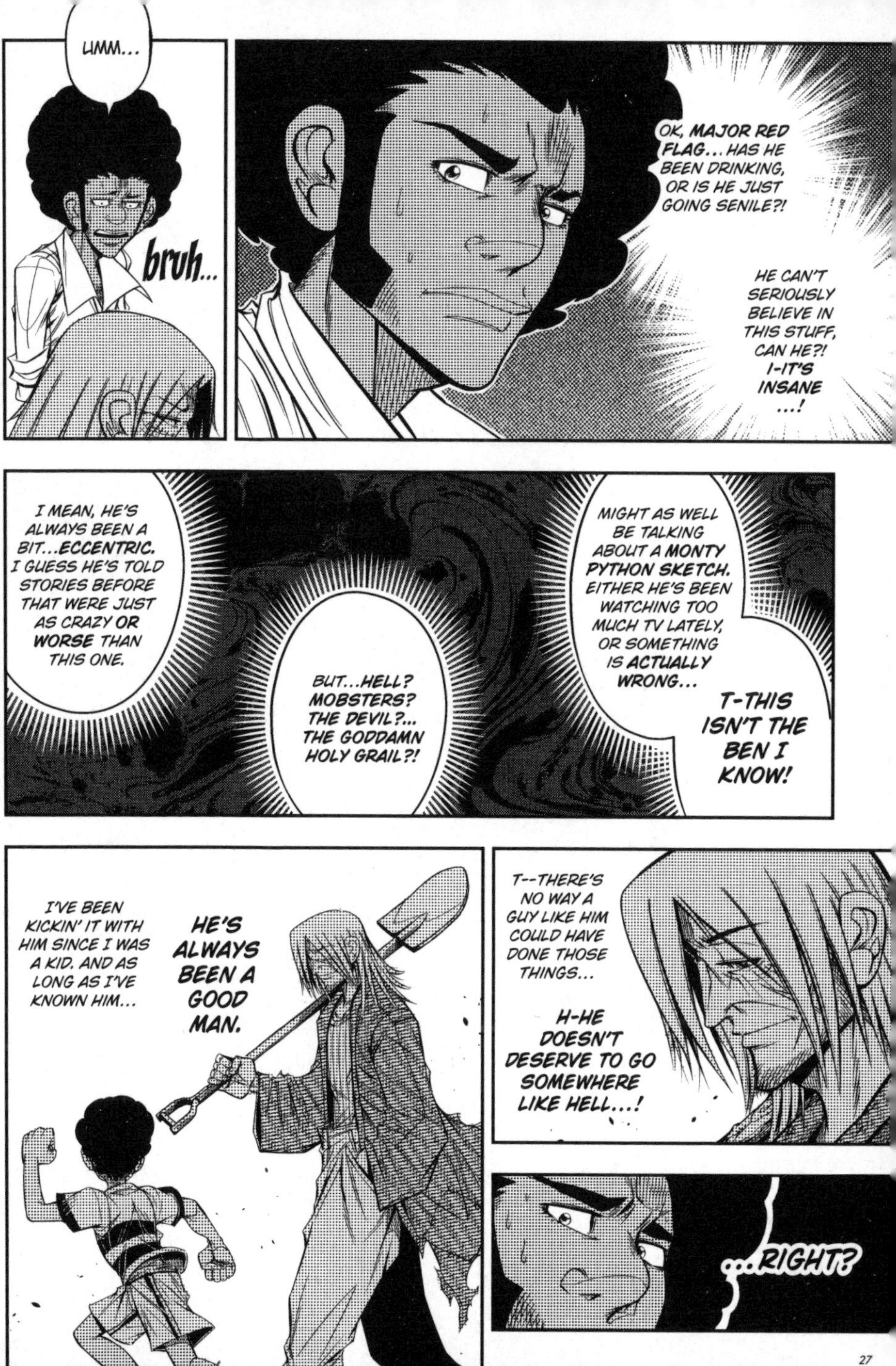
UMM…
bruh…
OK, **MAJOR RED FLAG…** HAS HE BEEN DRINKING, OR IS HE JUST GOING SENILE?!
HE CAN'T SERIOUSLY BELIEVE IN THIS STUFF, CAN HE?! **I-IT'S INSANE …!**
I MEAN, HE'S ALWAYS BEEN A BIT… **ECCENTRIC.** I GUESS HE'S TOLD STORIES BEFORE THAT WERE JUST AS CRAZY **OR WORSE** THAN THIS ONE.
BUT… HELL? MOBSTERS? THE DEVIL?… THE GODDAMN HOLY GRAIL?!
MIGHT AS WELL BE TALKING ABOUT A **MONTY PYTHON SKETCH.** EITHER HE'S BEEN WATCHING TOO MUCH TV LATELY, OR SOMETHING IS **ACTUALLY WRONG…**
T-THIS ISN'T THE BEN I KNOW!
I'VE BEEN KICKIN' IT WITH HIM SINCE I WAS A KID. AND AS LONG AS I'VE KNOWN HIM…
HE'S ALWAYS BEEN A GOOD MAN.
T--THERE'S NO WAY A GUY LIKE HIM COULD HAVE DONE THOSE THINGS…
H-HE DOESN'T DESERVE TO GO SOMEWHERE LIKE HELL…!
…RIGHT?

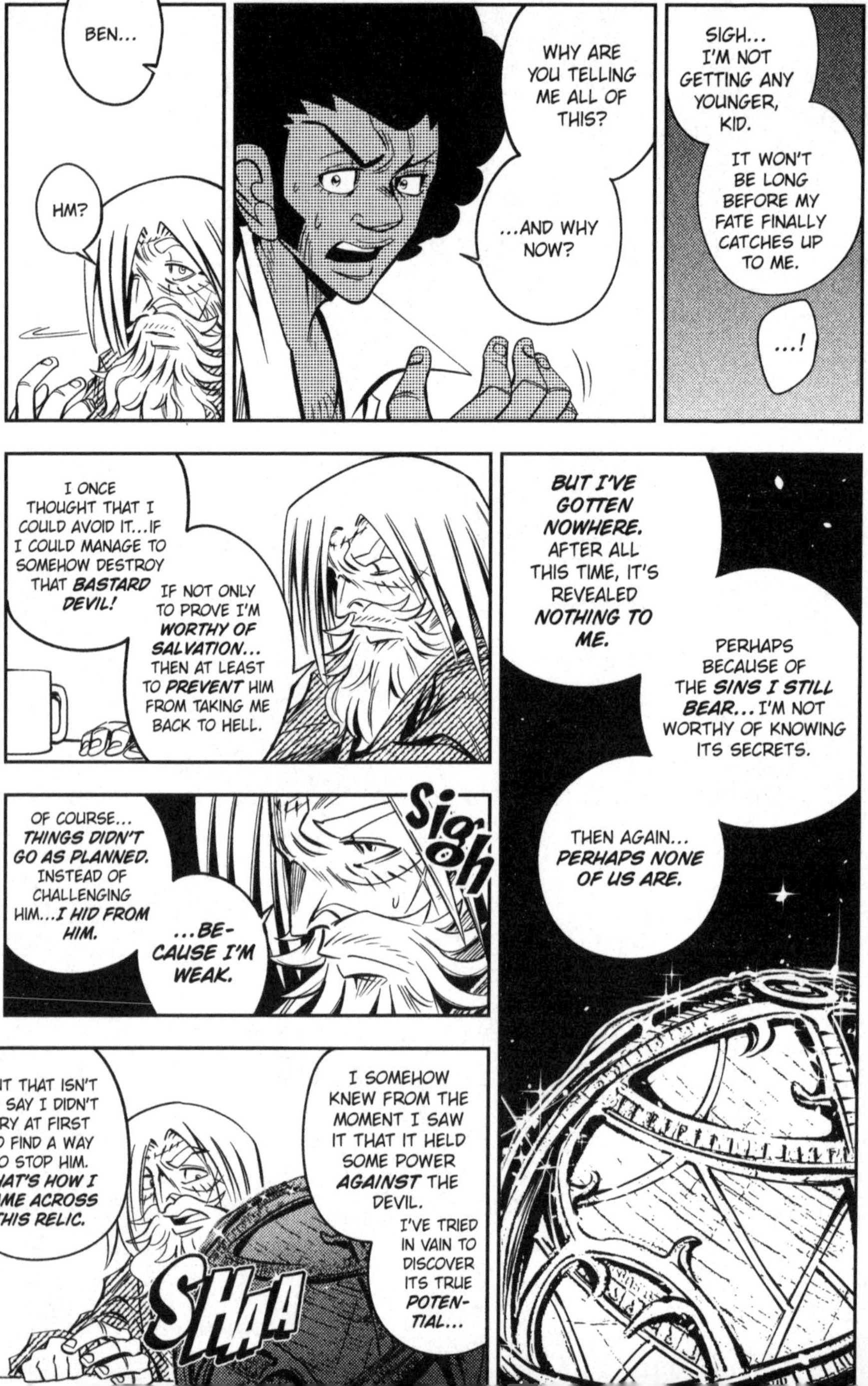
BEN...
HM?
WHY ARE YOU TELLING ME ALL OF THIS?
...AND WHY NOW?
SIGH... I'M NOT GETTING ANY YOUNGER, KID.
IT WON'T BE LONG BEFORE MY FATE FINALLY CATCHES UP TO ME.
...!
I ONCE THOUGHT THAT I COULD AVOID IT...IF I COULD MANAGE TO SOMEHOW DESTROY THAT BASTARD DEVIL!
IF NOT ONLY TO PROVE I'M WORTHY OF SALVATION... THEN AT LEAST TO PREVENT HIM FROM TAKING ME BACK TO HELL.
OF COURSE... THINGS DIDN'T GO AS PLANNED. INSTEAD OF CHALLENGING HIM...I HID FROM HIM.
SIGH
...BE-CAUSE I'M WEAK.
BUT THAT ISN'T TO SAY I DIDN'T TRY AT FIRST TO FIND A WAY TO STOP HIM. THAT'S HOW I CAME ACROSS THIS RELIC.
I SOMEHOW KNEW FROM THE MOMENT I SAW IT THAT IT HELD SOME POWER AGAINST THE DEVIL.
I'VE TRIED IN VAIN TO DISCOVER ITS TRUE POTEN-TIAL...
SHAA
BUT I'VE GOTTEN NOWHERE. AFTER ALL THIS TIME, IT'S REVEALED NOTHING TO ME.
PERHAPS BECAUSE OF THE SINS I STILL BEAR... I'M NOT WORTHY OF KNOWING ITS SECRETS.
THEN AGAIN... PERHAPS NONE OF US ARE.

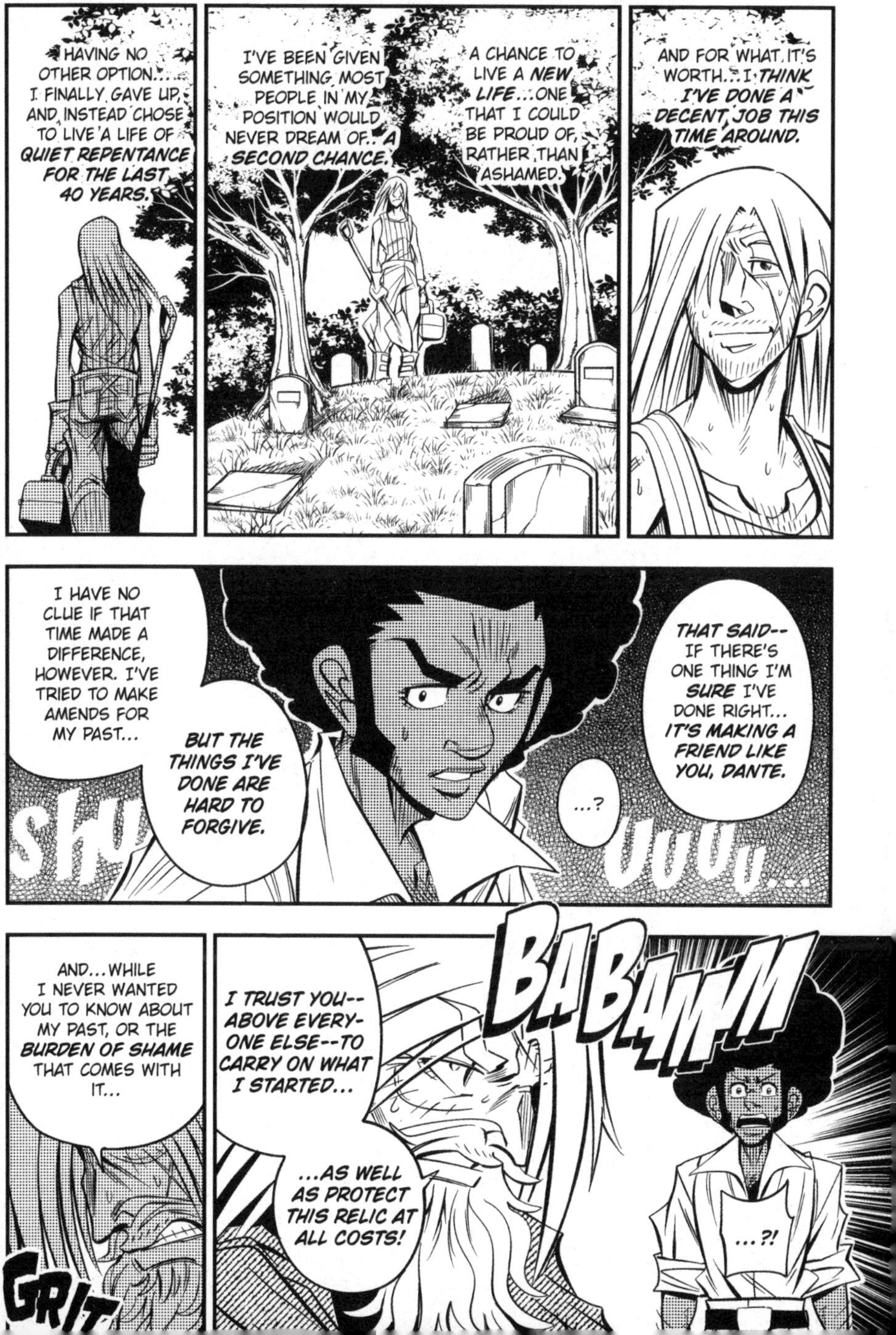
HAVING NO OTHER OPTION... I FINALLY GAVE UP, AND INSTEAD CHOSE TO LIVE A LIFE OF QUIET REPENTANCE FOR THE LAST 40 YEARS.
I'VE BEEN GIVEN SOMETHING MOST PEOPLE IN MY POSITION WOULD NEVER DREAM OF... A SECOND CHANCE.
A CHANCE TO LIVE A NEW LIFE... ONE THAT I COULD BE PROUD OF, RATHER THAN ASHAMED.
AND FOR WHAT IT'S WORTH... I THINK I'VE DONE A DECENT JOB THIS TIME AROUND.
I HAVE NO CLUE IF THAT TIME MADE A DIFFERENCE, HOWEVER. I'VE TRIED TO MAKE AMENDS FOR MY PAST...
BUT THE THINGS I'VE DONE ARE HARD TO FORGIVE.
SHU
...?
THAT SAID-- IF THERE'S ONE THING I'M SURE I'VE DONE RIGHT... IT'S MAKING A FRIEND LIKE YOU, DANTE.
UUUU...
AND... WHILE I NEVER WANTED YOU TO KNOW ABOUT MY PAST, OR THE BURDEN OF SHAME THAT COMES WITH IT...
GRIT
I TRUST YOU-- ABOVE EVERY-ONE ELSE--TO CARRY ON WHAT I STARTED...
...AS WELL AS PROTECT THIS RELIC AT ALL COSTS!
BABAMM
...?!

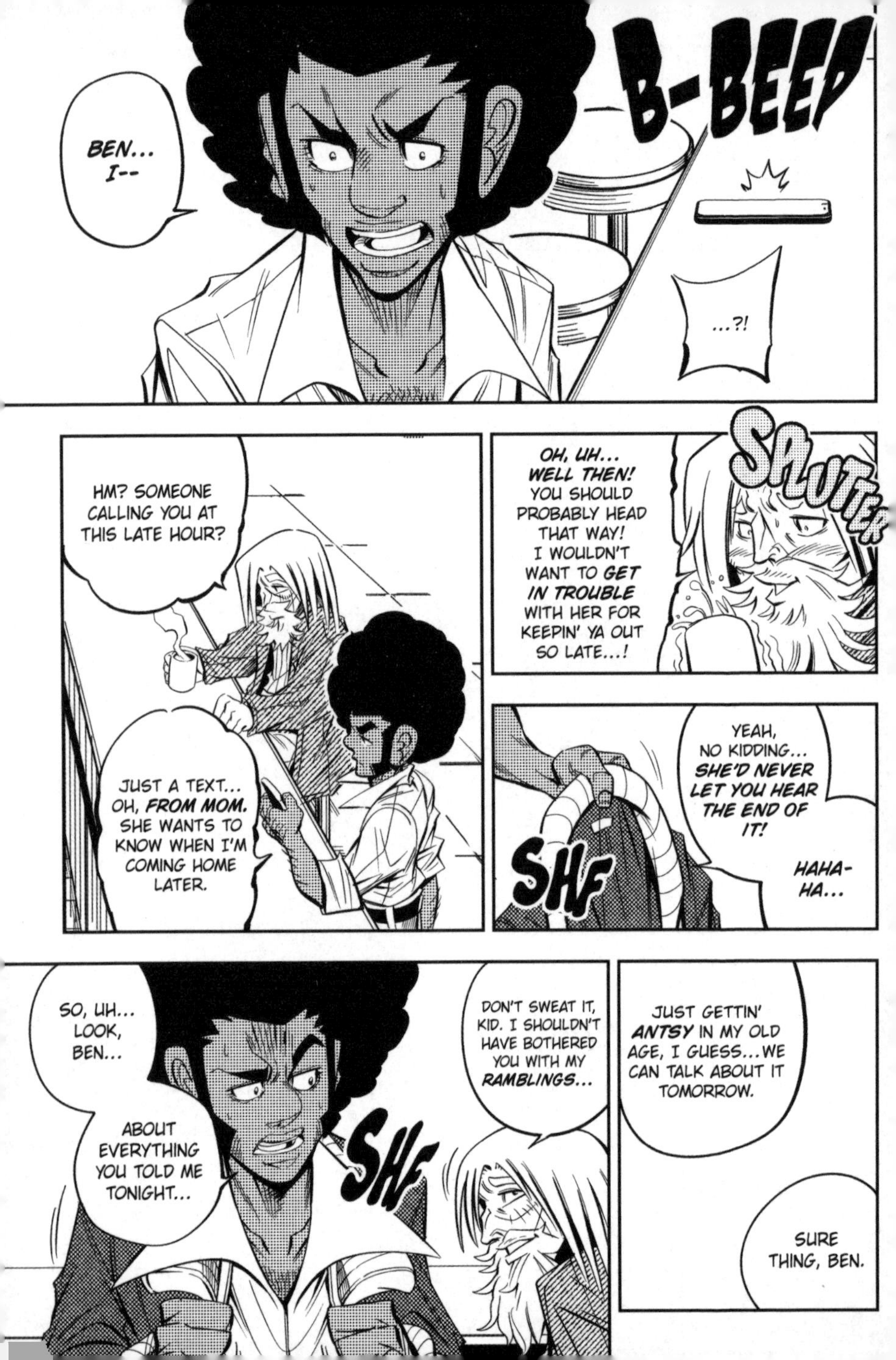
BEN... I--
B-BEEP
...?!
HM? SOMEONE CALLING YOU AT THIS LATE HOUR?
JUST A TEXT... OH, **FROM MOM.** SHE WANTS TO KNOW WHEN I'M COMING HOME LATER.
SPUTTER
OH, UH... **WELL THEN!** YOU SHOULD PROBABLY HEAD THAT WAY! I WOULDN'T WANT TO **GET IN TROUBLE** WITH HER FOR KEEPIN' YA OUT SO LATE...!
SHF
YEAH, NO KIDDING... **SHE'D NEVER LET YOU HEAR THE END OF IT!**
HAHA-HA...
SO, UH... LOOK, BEN...
ABOUT EVERYTHING YOU TOLD ME TONIGHT...
SHF
DON'T SWEAT IT, KID. I SHOULDN'T HAVE BOTHERED YOU WITH MY **RAMBLINGS...**
JUST GETTIN' **ANTSY** IN MY OLD AGE, I GUESS...WE CAN TALK ABOUT IT TOMORROW.
SURE THING, BEN.

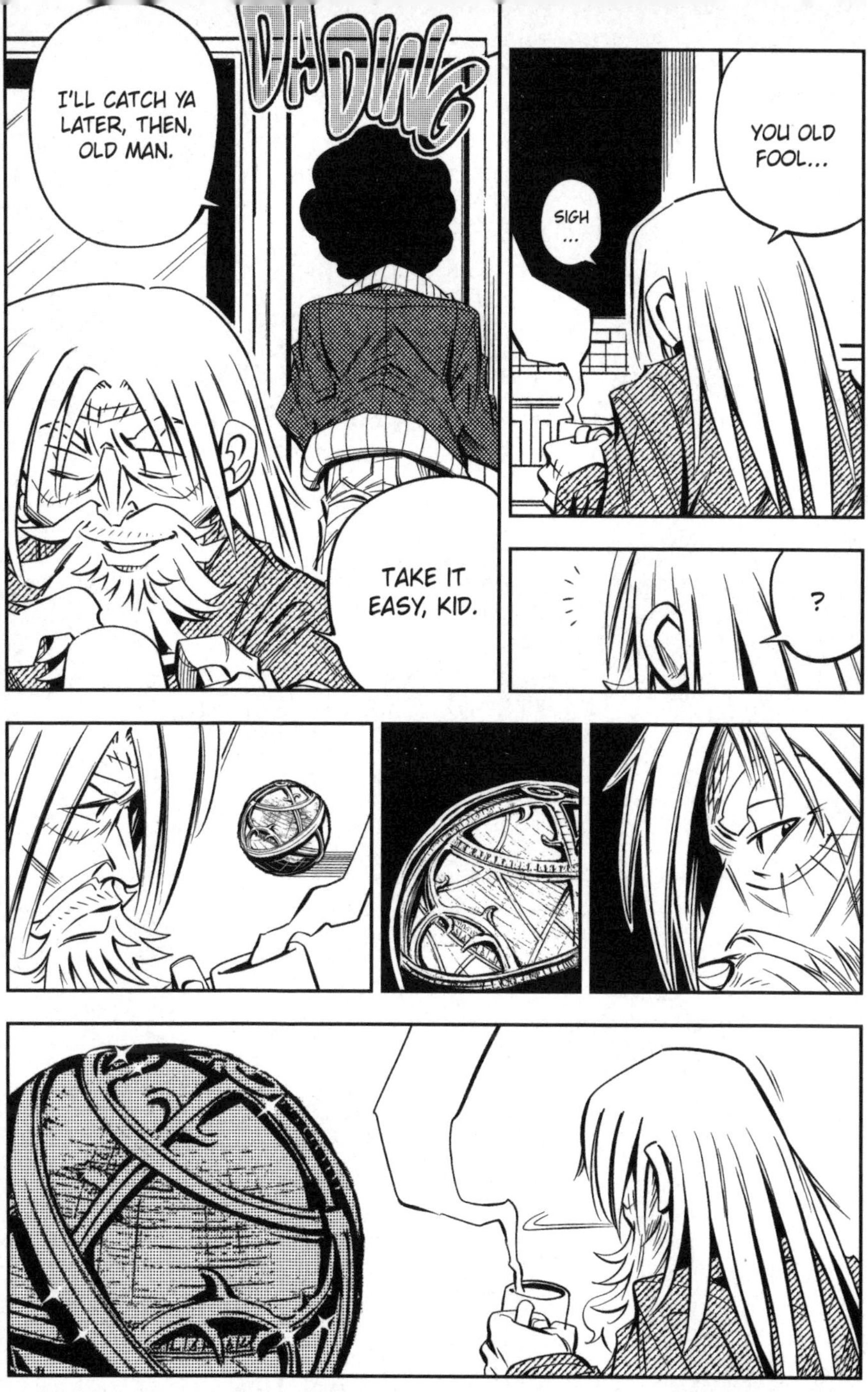
I'LL CATCH YA LATER, THEN, OLD MAN.
DA DING
TAKE IT EASY, KID.
SIGH ...
YOU OLD FOOL...
?

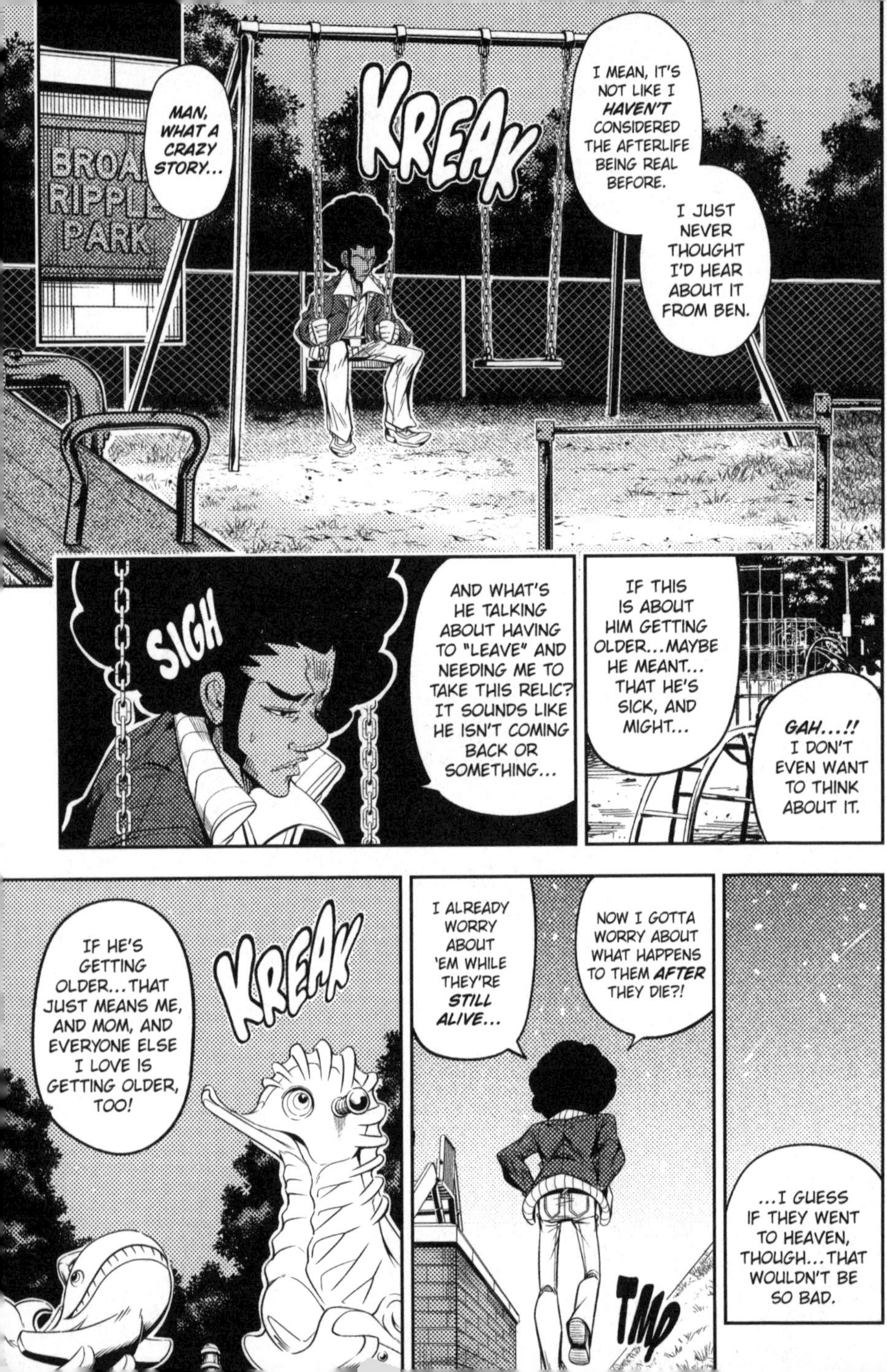
MAN, WHAT A CRAZY STORY...
KREAK
I MEAN, IT'S NOT LIKE I *HAVEN'T* CONSIDERED THE AFTERLIFE BEING REAL BEFORE.
I JUST NEVER THOUGHT I'D HEAR ABOUT IT FROM BEN.
SIGH
AND WHAT'S HE TALKING ABOUT HAVING TO "LEAVE" AND NEEDING ME TO TAKE THIS RELIC? IT SOUNDS LIKE HE ISN'T COMING BACK OR SOMETHING...
IF THIS IS ABOUT HIM GETTING OLDER...MAYBE HE MEANT... THAT HE'S SICK, AND MIGHT...
GAH...!! I DON'T EVEN WANT TO THINK ABOUT IT.
IF HE'S GETTING OLDER...THAT JUST MEANS ME, AND MOM, AND EVERYONE ELSE I LOVE IS GETTING OLDER, TOO!
KREAK
I ALREADY WORRY ABOUT 'EM WHILE THEY'RE *STILL ALIVE*...
NOW I GOTTA WORRY ABOUT WHAT HAPPENS TO THEM *AFTER* THEY DIE?!
TMP
...I GUESS IF THEY WENT TO HEAVEN, THOUGH...THAT WOULDN'T BE SO BAD.

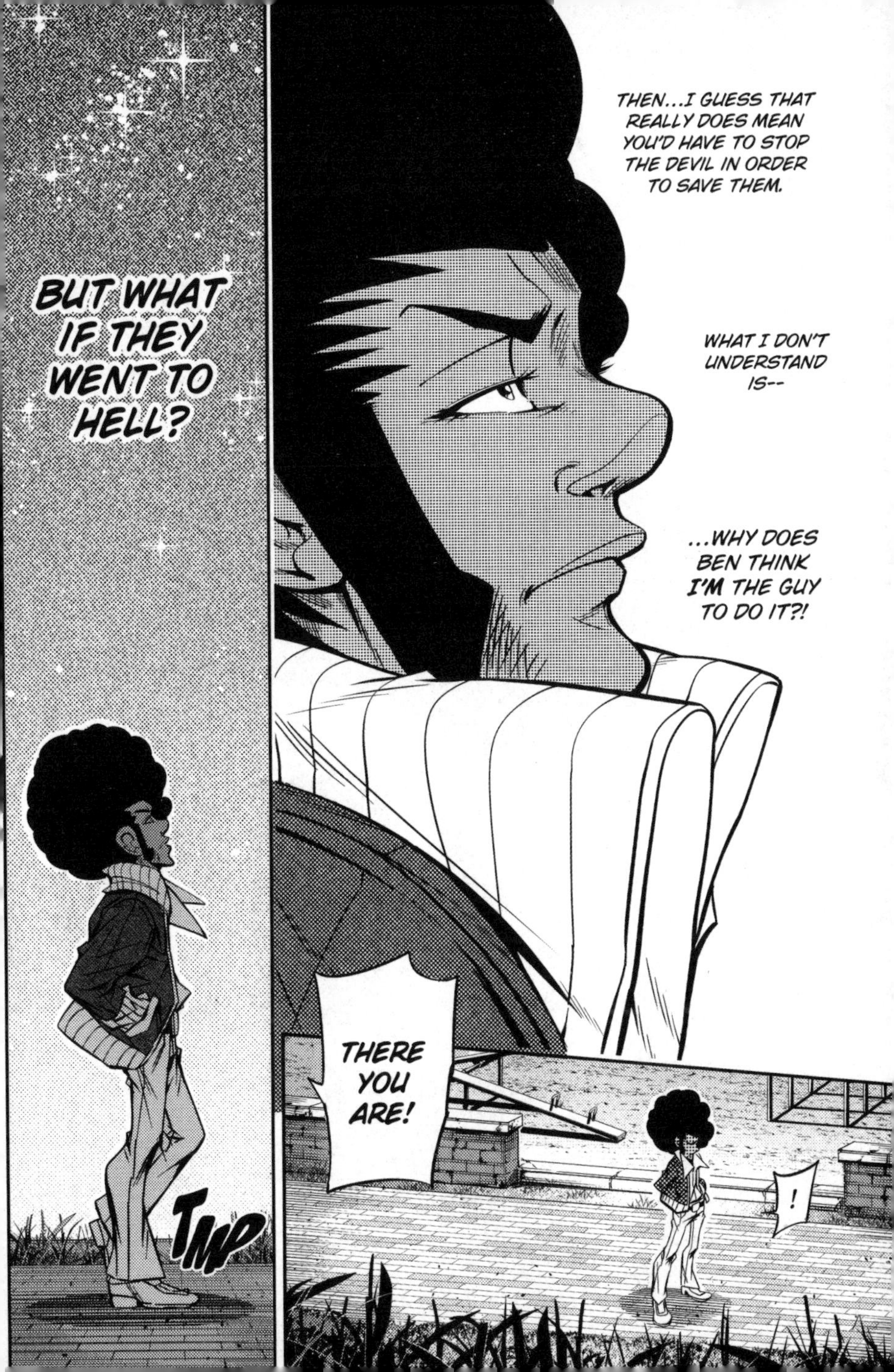
BUT WHAT IF THEY WENT TO HELL?
TMP
THEN...I GUESS THAT REALLY DOES MEAN YOU'D HAVE TO STOP THE DEVIL IN ORDER TO SAVE THEM.
WHAT I DON'T UNDERSTAND IS--
...WHY DOES BEN THINK *I'M* THE GUY TO DO IT?!
THERE YOU ARE!
!

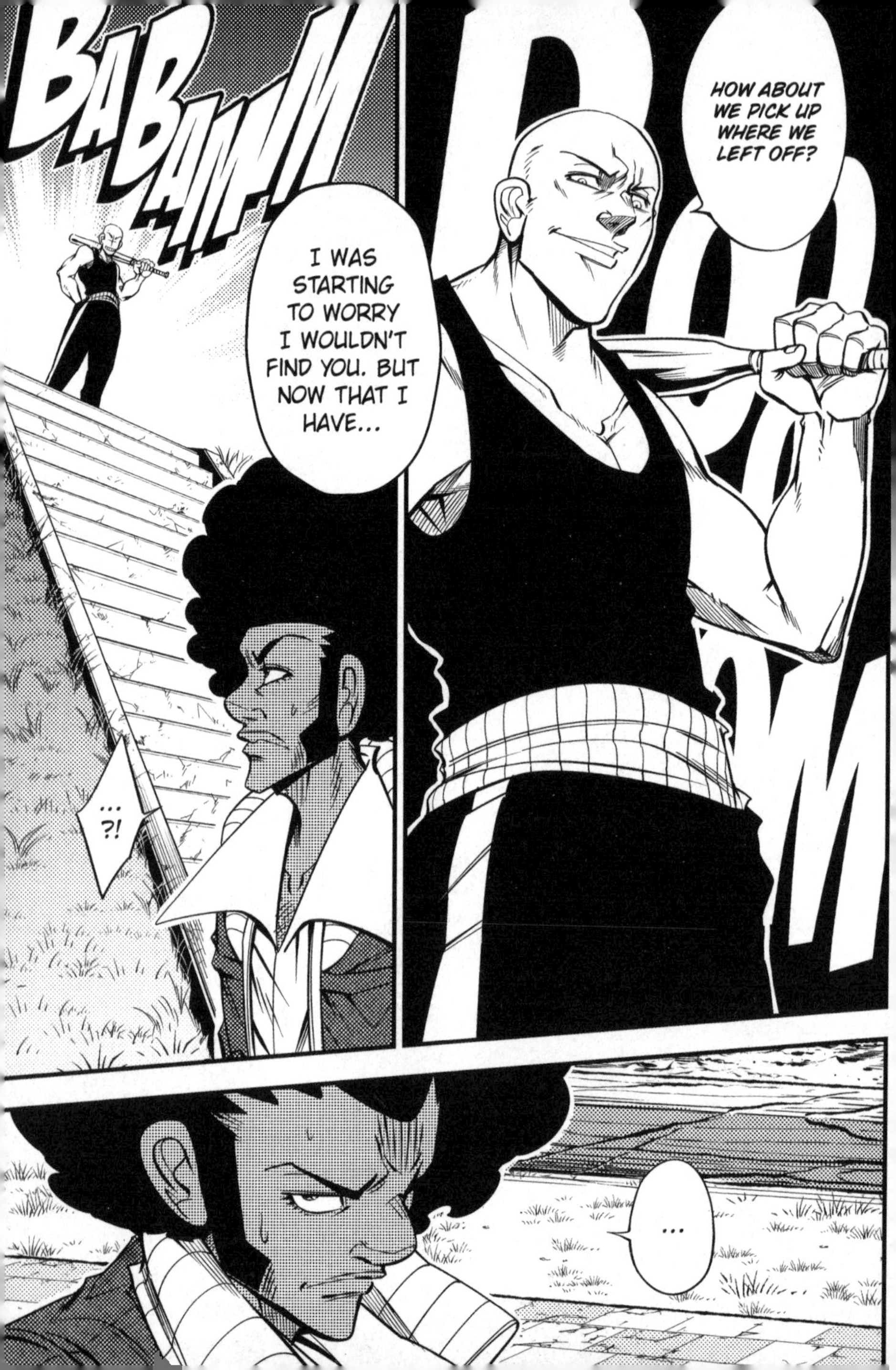
BABAMM
I WAS STARTING TO WORRY I WOULDN'T FIND YOU. BUT NOW THAT I HAVE...
...?!
DOOOM
HOW ABOUT WE PICK UP WHERE WE LEFT OFF?
...

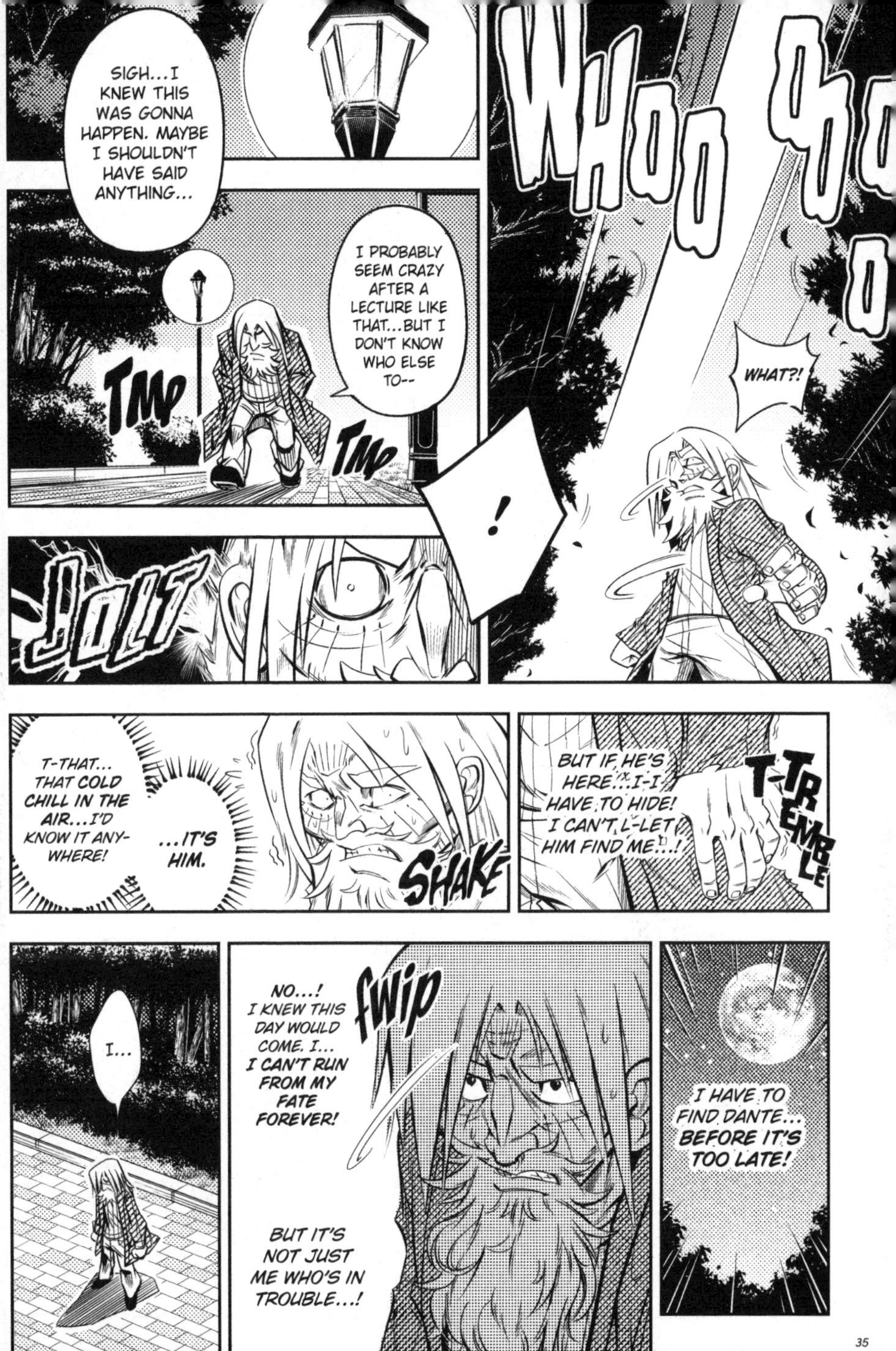
SIGH...I KNEW THIS WAS GONNA HAPPEN. MAYBE I SHOULDN'T HAVE SAID ANYTHING...
TMP
I PROBABLY SEEM CRAZY AFTER A LECTURE LIKE THAT...BUT I DON'T KNOW WHO ELSE TO--
TMP
!
JOLT
WHOOOOOO
WHAT?!
T-THAT... THAT COLD CHILL IN THE AIR...I'D KNOW IT ANY-WHERE!
...IT'S HIM.
SHAKE
BUT IF HE'S HERE...I-I HAVE TO HIDE! I CAN'T L-LET HIM FIND ME...!
T-TREMBLE
I...
NO...! I KNEW THIS DAY WOULD COME. I... I CAN'T RUN FROM MY FATE FOREVER!
fwip
BUT IT'S NOT JUST ME WHO'S IN TROUBLE...!
I HAVE TO FIND DANTE... BEFORE IT'S TOO LATE!

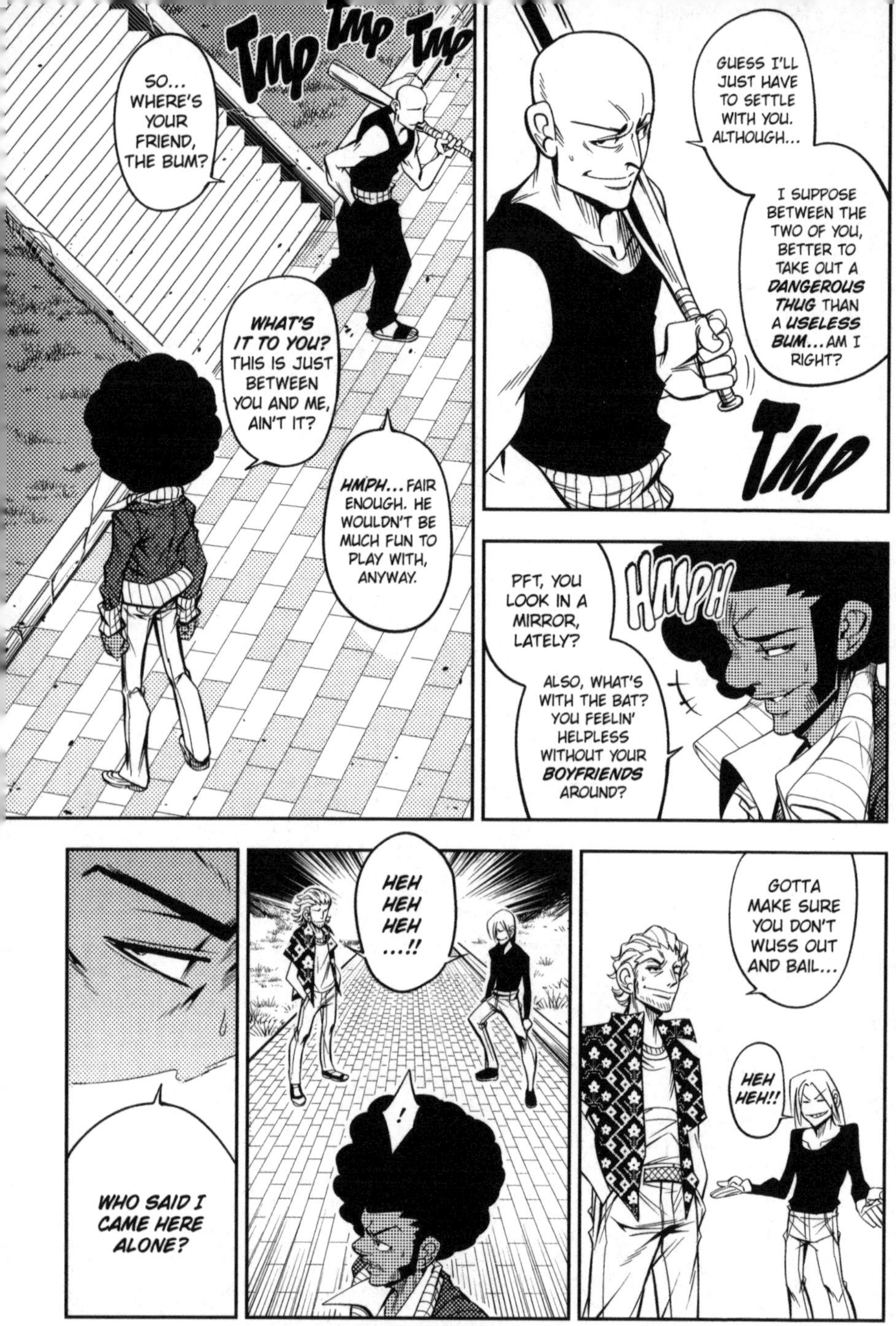

TMP TMP TMP
SO... WHERE'S YOUR FRIEND, THE BUM?
WHAT'S IT TO YOU? THIS IS JUST BETWEEN YOU AND ME, AIN'T IT?
HMPH... FAIR ENOUGH. HE WOULDN'T BE MUCH FUN TO PLAY WITH, ANYWAY.
GUESS I'LL JUST HAVE TO SETTLE WITH YOU. ALTHOUGH...
I SUPPOSE BETWEEN THE TWO OF YOU, BETTER TO TAKE OUT A DANGEROUS THUG THAN A USELESS BUM... AM I RIGHT?
TMP
PFT, YOU LOOK IN A MIRROR, LATELY?
HMPH
ALSO, WHAT'S WITH THE BAT? YOU FEELIN' HELPLESS WITHOUT YOUR BOYFRIENDS AROUND?
WHO SAID I CAME HERE ALONE?
HEH HEH HEH ...!!
!
GOTTA MAKE SURE YOU DON'T WUSS OUT AND BAIL...
HEH HEH!!

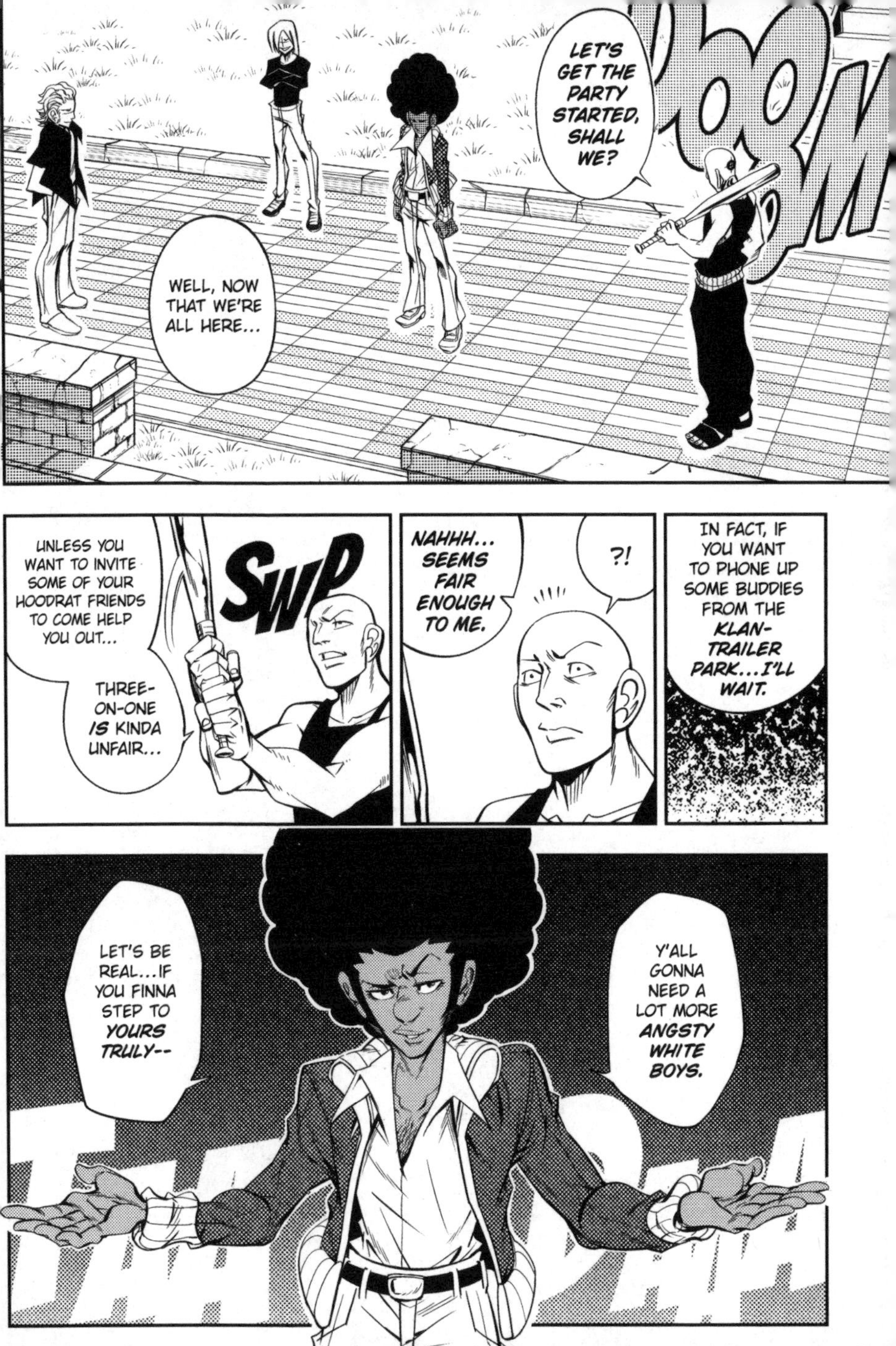
WELL, NOW THAT WE'RE ALL HERE...
LET'S GET THE PARTY STARTED, SHALL WE?
UNLESS YOU WANT TO INVITE SOME OF YOUR HOODRAT FRIENDS TO COME HELP YOU OUT...
SWP
THREE-ON-ONE *IS* KINDA UNFAIR...
NAHHH... SEEMS FAIR ENOUGH TO ME.
?!
IN FACT, IF YOU WANT TO PHONE UP SOME BUDDIES FROM THE ***KLAN-TRAILER PARK...I'LL WAIT.***
LET'S BE REAL...IF YOU FINNA STEP TO ***YOURS TRULY--***
Y'ALL GONNA NEED A LOT MORE ***ANGSTY WHITE BOYS.***

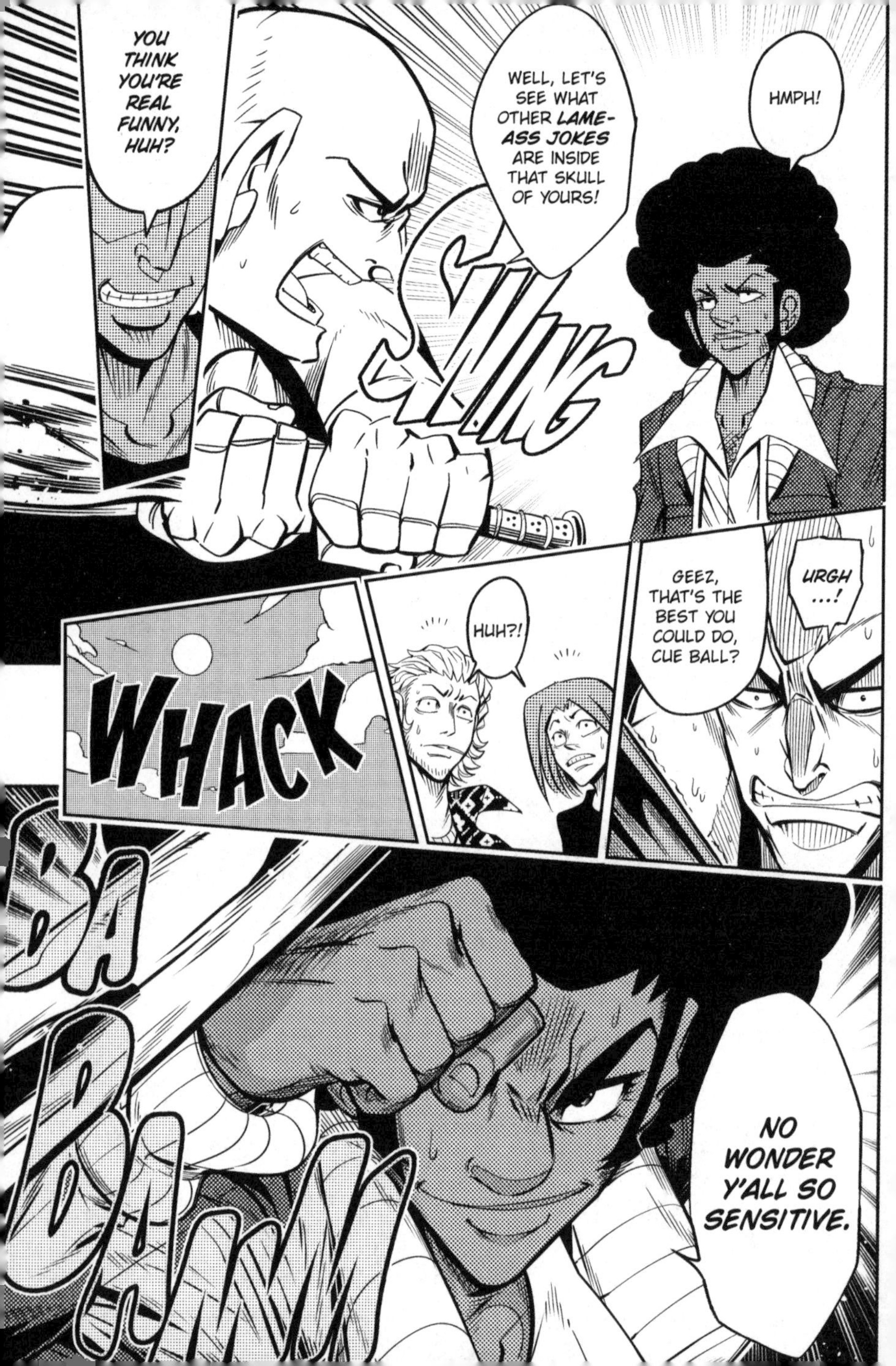
YOU THINK YOU'RE REAL FUNNY, HUH?
SHING
WELL, LET'S SEE WHAT OTHER **LAME-ASS JOKES** ARE INSIDE THAT SKULL OF YOURS!
HMPH!
WHACK
HUH?!
GEEZ, THAT'S THE BEST YOU COULD DO, CUE BALL?
URGH ...!
NO WONDER Y'ALL SO SENSITIVE.

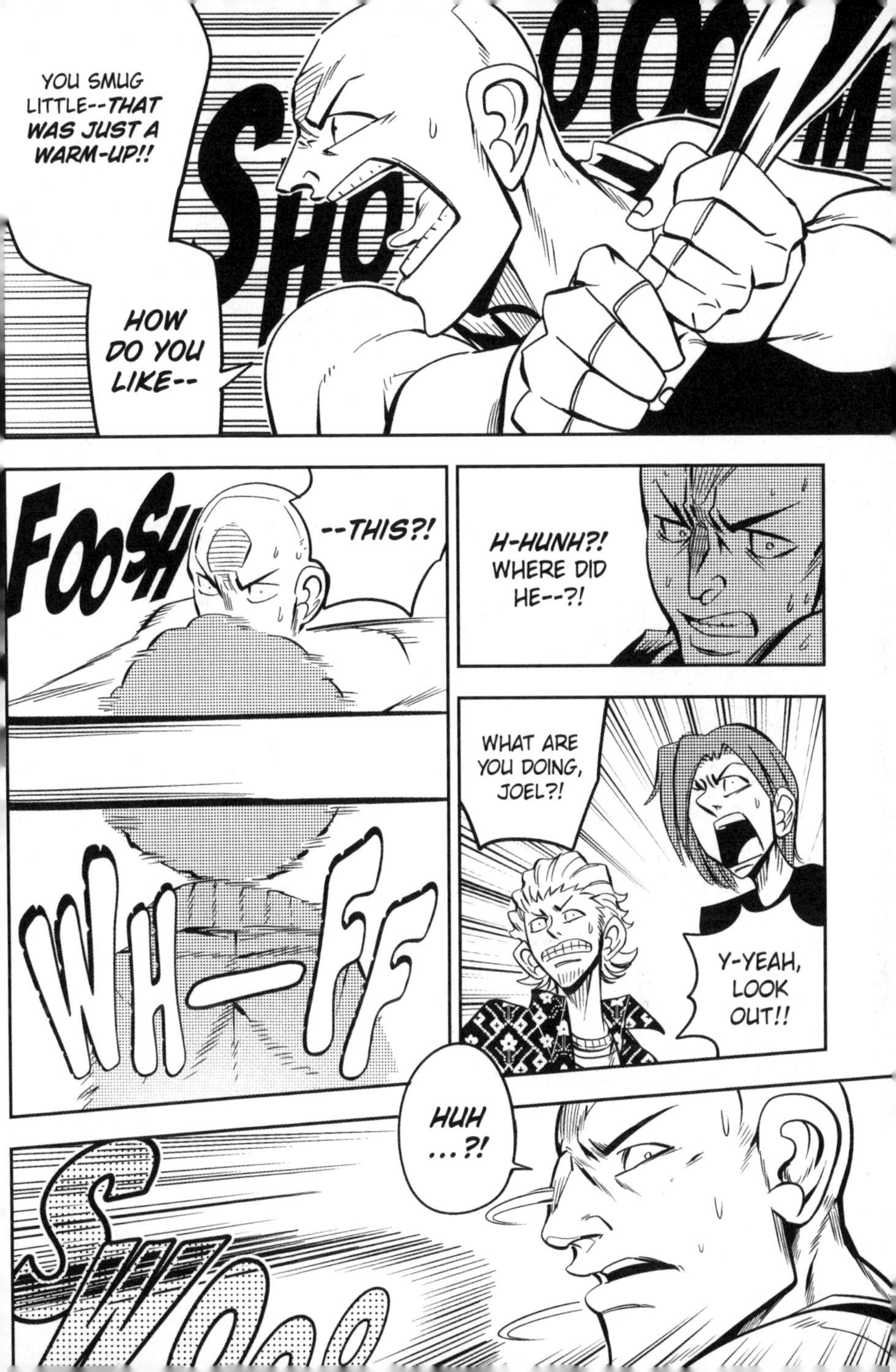

YOU SMUG LITTLE--THAT WAS JUST A WARM-UP!!
SHO
OOOM
HOW DO YOU LIKE--
FOOSH
--THIS?!
H-HUNH?! WHERE DID HE--?!
WH-FF
WHAT ARE YOU DOING, JOEL?!
Y-YEAH, LOOK OUT!!
SWOOO
HUH ...?!

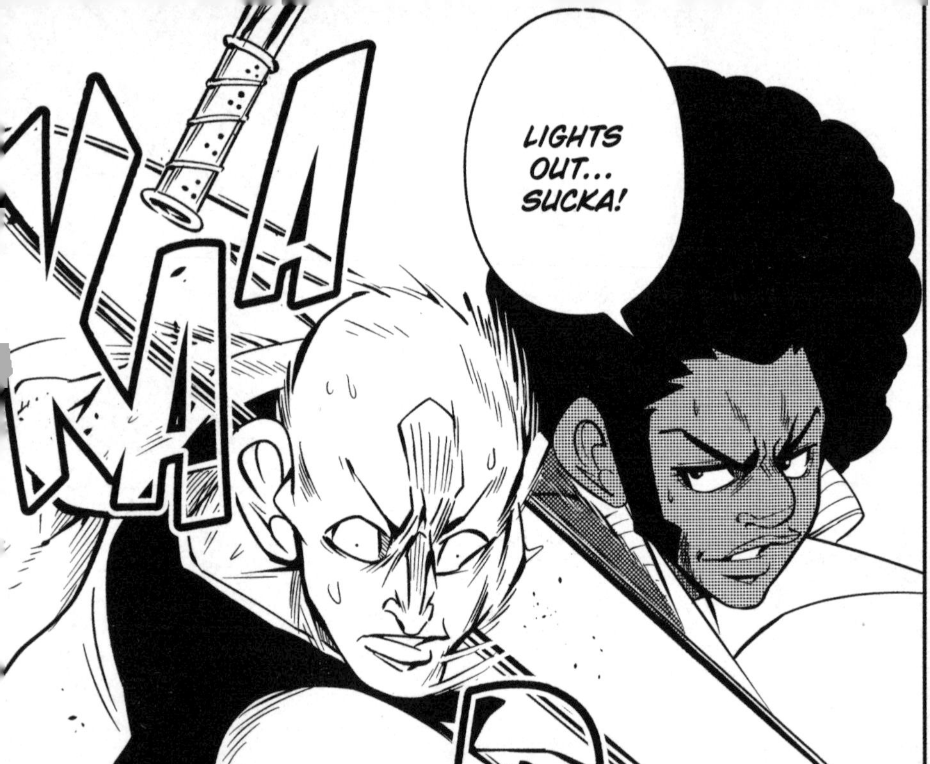
LIGHTS OUT... SUCKA!
POW

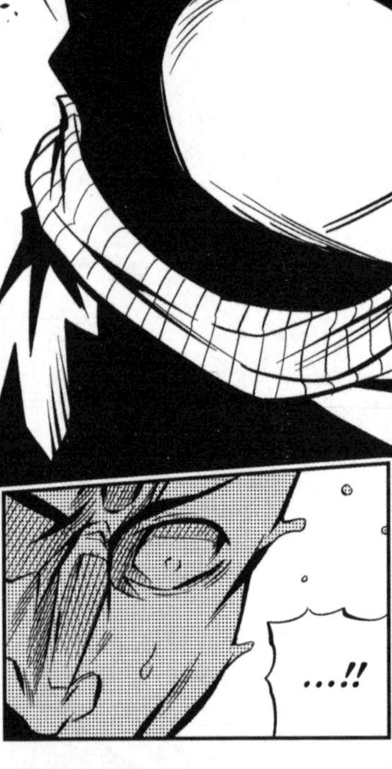
...!!

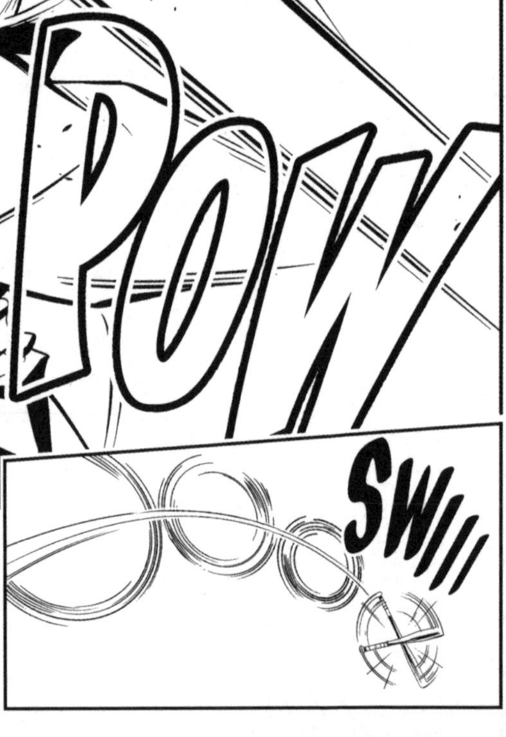
SWIII

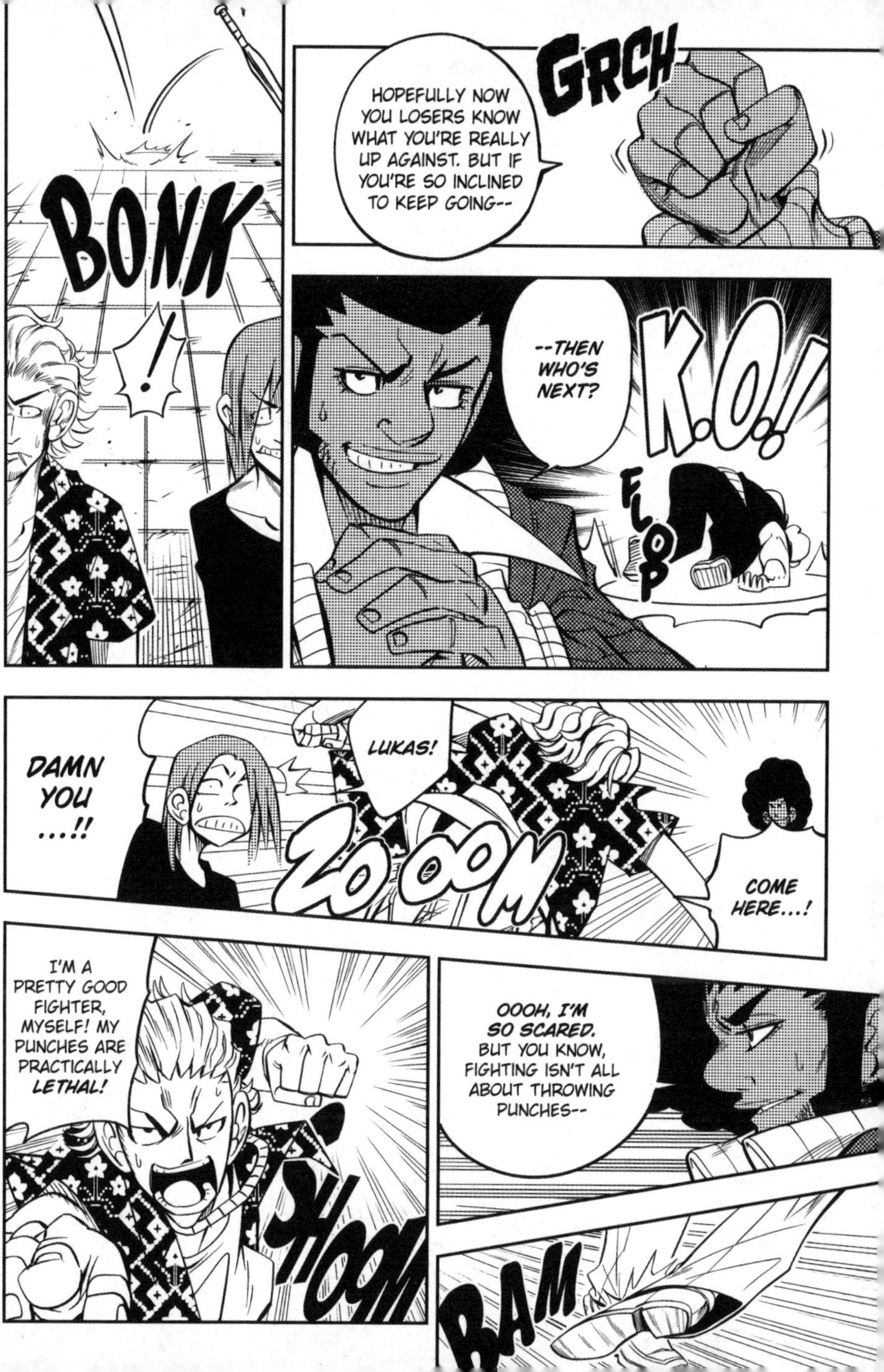
BONK
!
HOPEFULLY NOW YOU LOSERS KNOW WHAT YOU'RE REALLY UP AGAINST. BUT IF YOU'RE SO INCLINED TO KEEP GOING--
GRCH
--THEN WHO'S NEXT?
K.O.!!
FLOP
DAMN YOU ...!!
LUKAS!
ZOOOM
COME HERE...!
I'M A PRETTY GOOD FIGHTER, MYSELF! MY PUNCHES ARE PRACTICALLY LETHAL!
SHOOM
OOOH, I'M SO SCARED. BUT YOU KNOW, FIGHTING ISN'T ALL ABOUT THROWING PUNCHES--
BAM

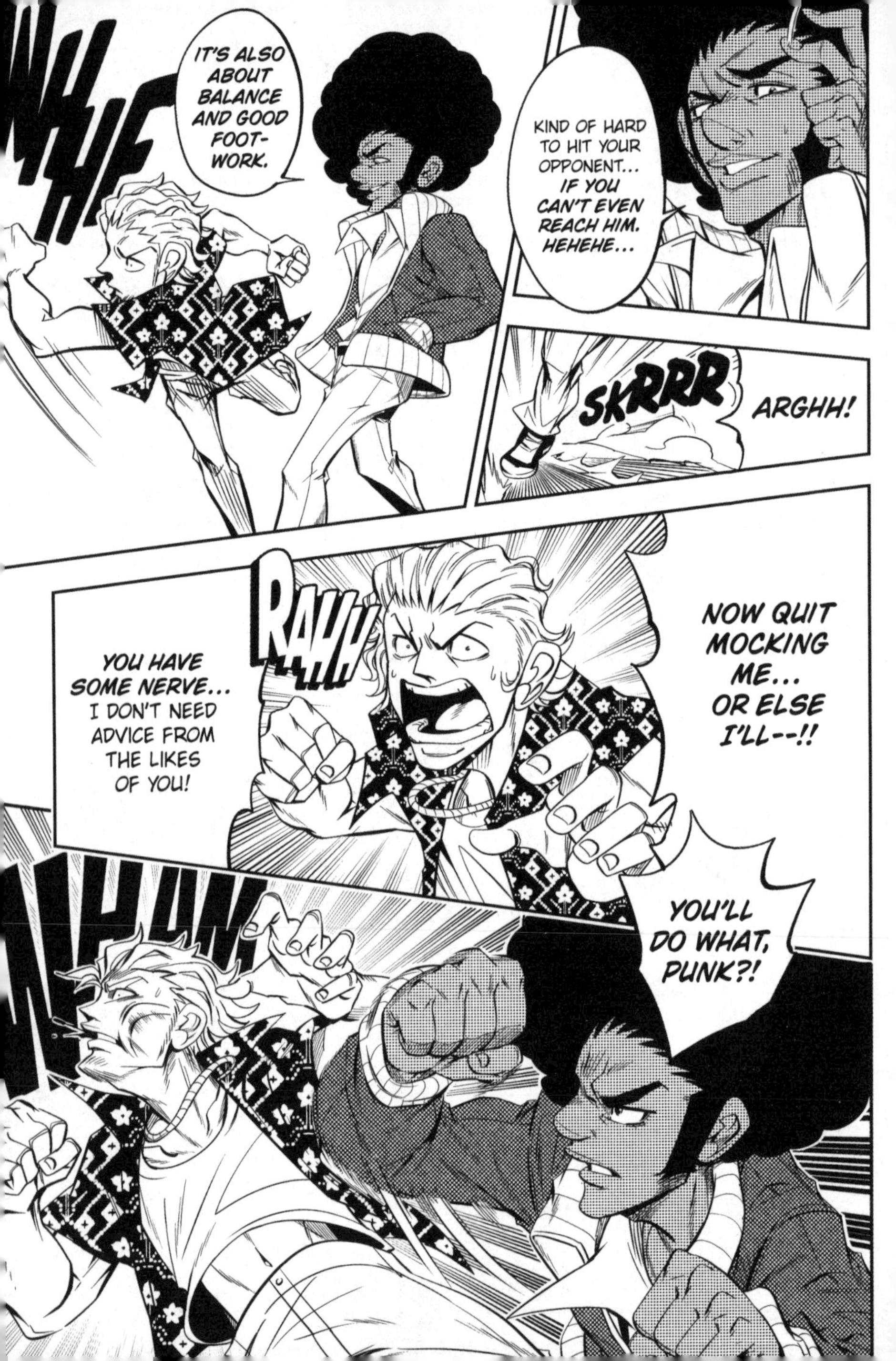
IT'S ALSO ABOUT BALANCE AND GOOD FOOT-WORK.
KIND OF HARD TO HIT YOUR OPPONENT... IF YOU CAN'T EVEN REACH HIM. HEHEHE...
SKRRR
ARGHH!
RAHH
YOU HAVE SOME NERVE... I DON'T NEED ADVICE FROM THE LIKES OF YOU!
NOW QUIT MOCKING ME... OR ELSE I'LL--!!
YOU'LL DO WHAT, PUNK?!

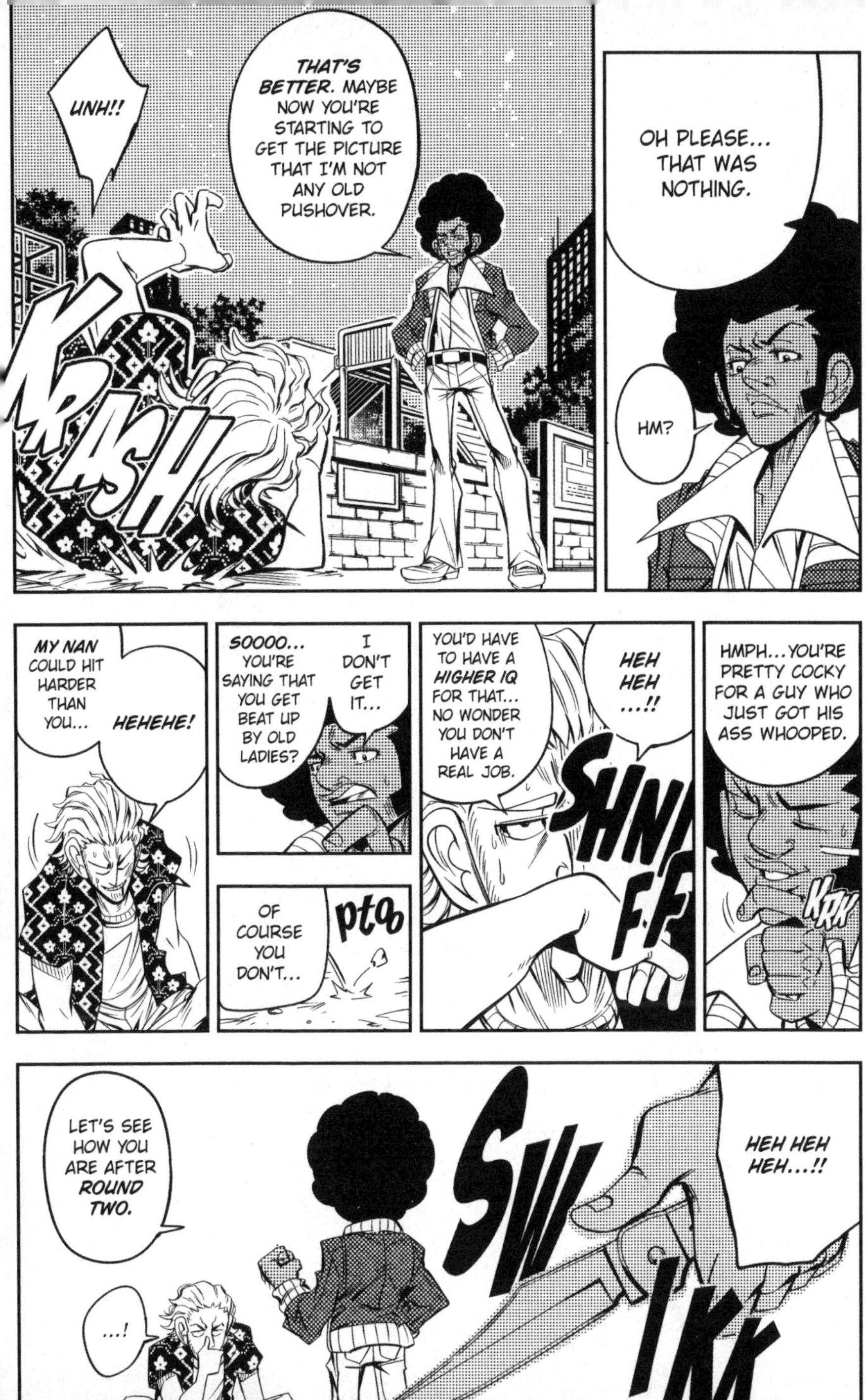
UNH!!
KRASH
THAT'S BETTER. MAYBE NOW YOU'RE STARTING TO GET THE PICTURE THAT I'M NOT ANY OLD PUSHOVER.
OH PLEASE... THAT WAS NOTHING.
HM?
MY NAN COULD HIT HARDER THAN YOU...
HEHEHE!
SOOOO... YOU'RE SAYING THAT YOU GET BEAT UP BY OLD LADIES?
I DON'T GET IT...
OF COURSE YOU DON'T...
ptoo
YOU'D HAVE TO HAVE A ***HIGHER IQ*** FOR THAT... NO WONDER YOU DON'T HAVE A REAL JOB.
HEH HEH ...!!
SHNIFF
HMPH...YOU'RE PRETTY COCKY FOR A GUY WHO JUST GOT HIS ASS WHOOPED.
KRK
LET'S SEE HOW YOU ARE AFTER ***ROUND TWO.***
...!
SWIKK
HEH HEH HEH...!!

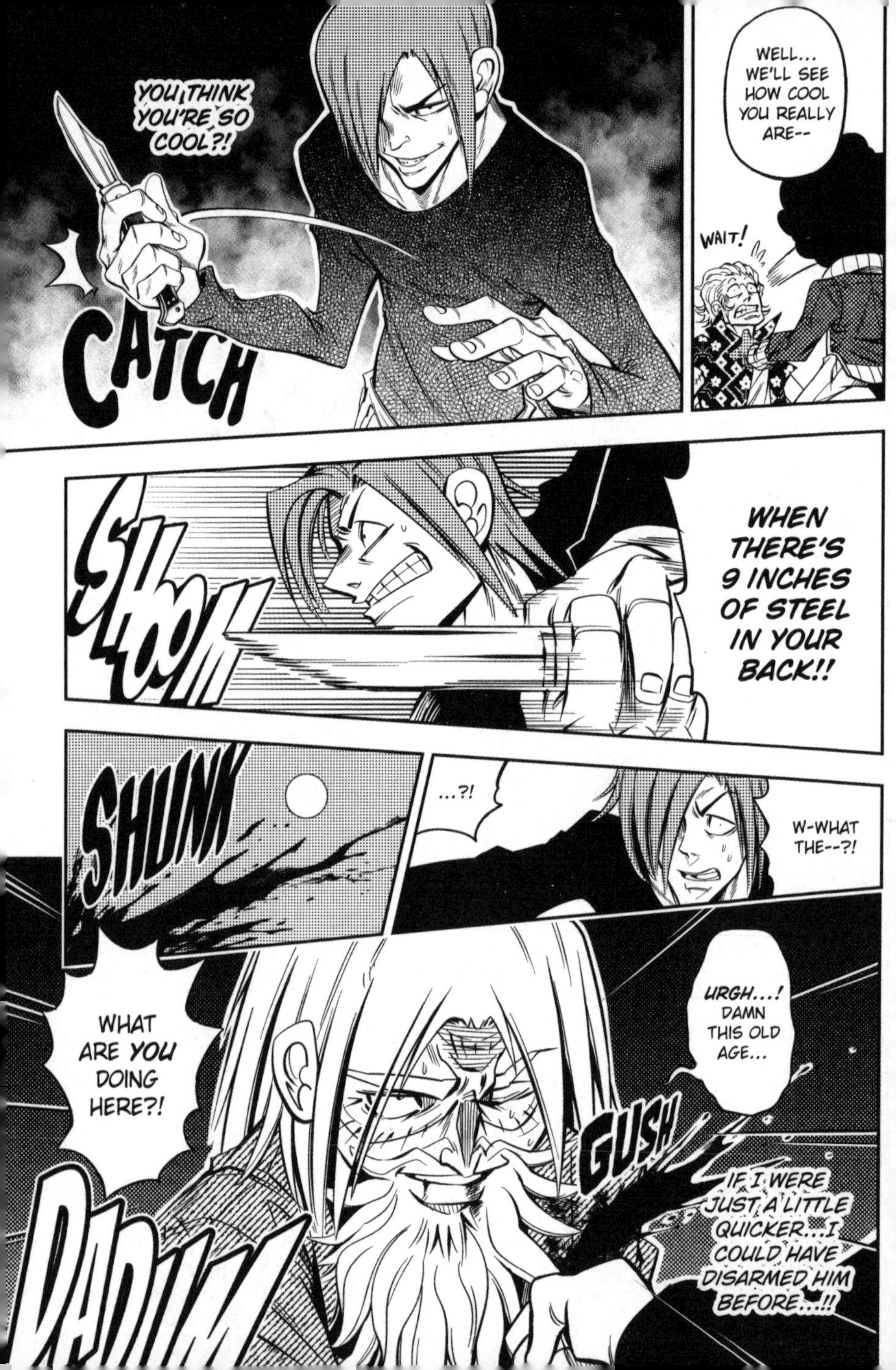
YOU THINK YOU'RE SO COOL?!
CATCH
WELL... WE'LL SEE HOW COOL YOU REALLY ARE--
WAIT!
SHOOM
WHEN THERE'S 9 INCHES OF STEEL IN YOUR BACK!!
SHUNK
...?!
W-WHAT THE--?!
WHAT ARE YOU DOING HERE?!
DADUM
GUSH
URGH...! DAMN THIS OLD AGE...
IF I WERE JUST A LITTLE QUICKER...I COULD HAVE DISARMED HIM BEFORE...!!

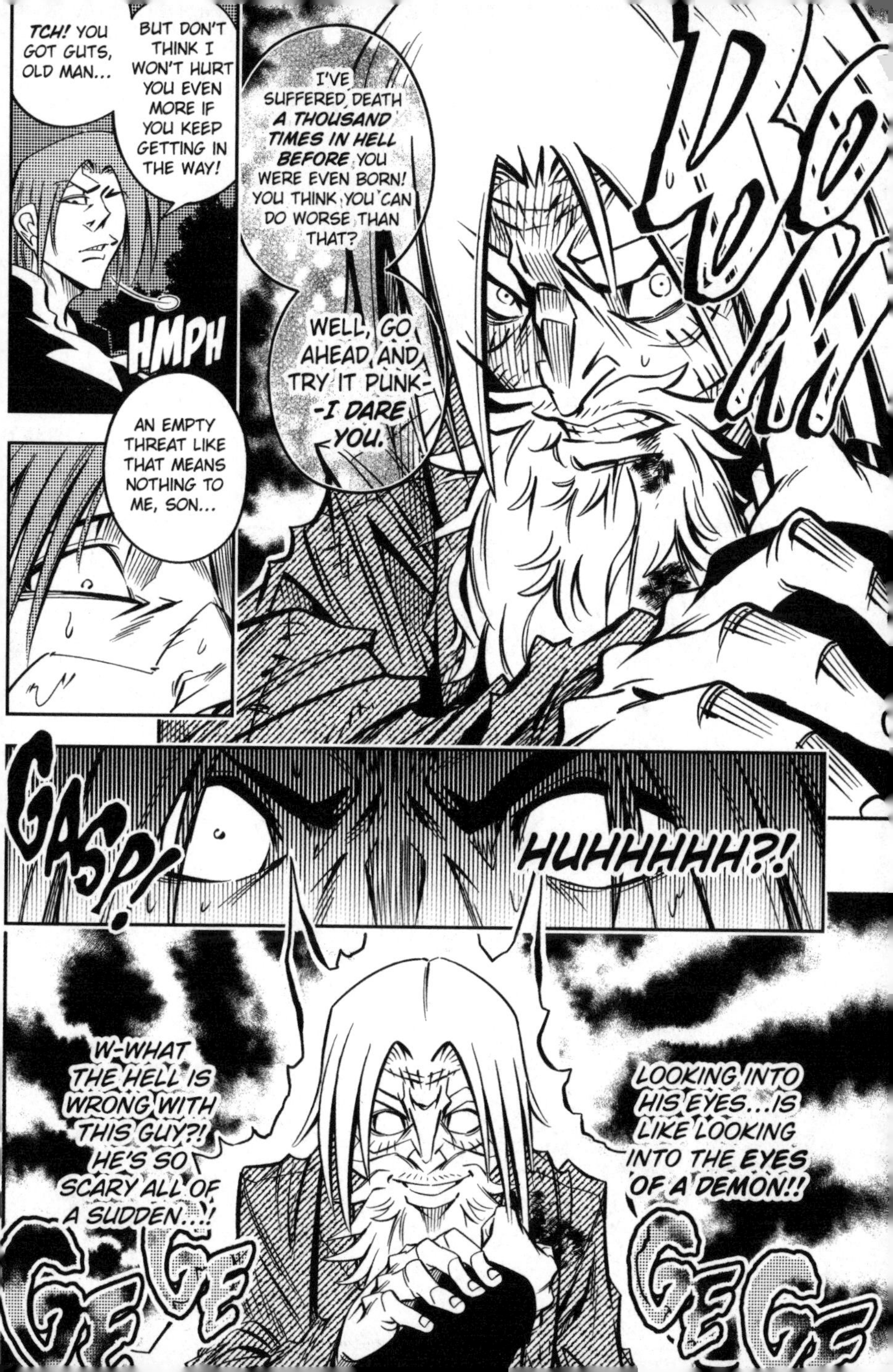
TCH! YOU GOT GUTS, OLD MAN...
BUT DON'T THINK I WON'T HURT YOU EVEN MORE IF YOU KEEP GETTING IN THE WAY!
HMPH
AN EMPTY THREAT LIKE THAT MEANS NOTHING TO ME, SON...
I'VE SUFFERED DEATH A THOUSAND TIMES IN HELL BEFORE YOU WERE EVEN BORN! YOU THINK YOU CAN DO WORSE THAN THAT?
WELL, GO AHEAD AND TRY IT PUNK--I DARE YOU.
GASP!
HUHHHHHH?!
W-WHAT THE HELL IS WRONG WITH THIS GUY?! HE'S SO SCARY ALL OF A SUDDEN...!
LOOKING INTO HIS EYES...IS LIKE LOOKING INTO THE EYES OF A DEMON!!
GE GE
GE GE

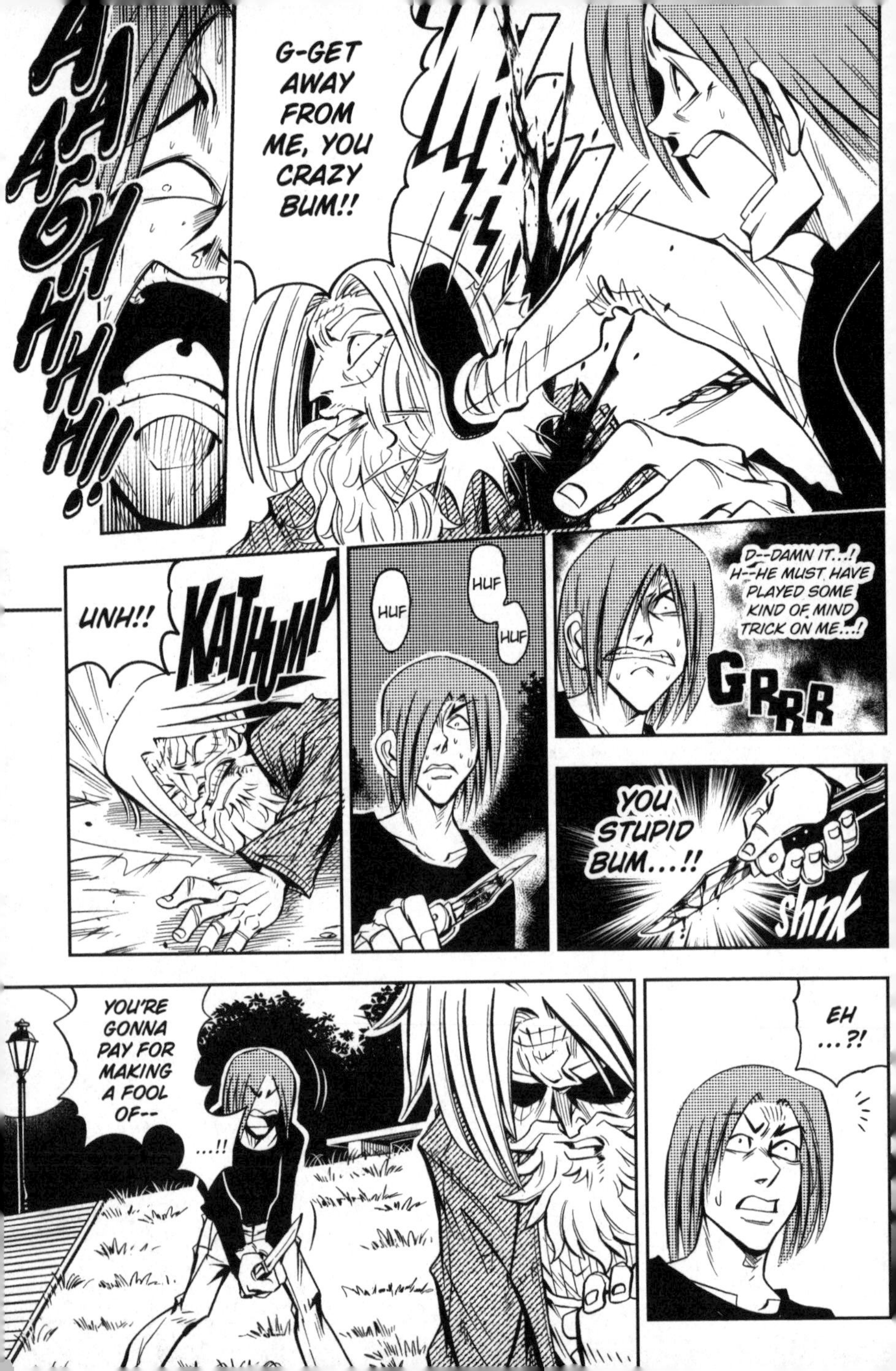
AAAGHHHH!!
G-GET AWAY FROM ME, YOU CRAZY BUM!!
UNH!!
KATHUMP
HUF
HUF
HUF
D--DAMN IT...! H--HE MUST HAVE PLAYED SOME KIND OF MIND TRICK ON ME...!
GRRR
YOU STUPID BUM...!!
shnk
YOU'RE GONNA PAY FOR MAKING A FOOL OF--
...!!
EH ...?!

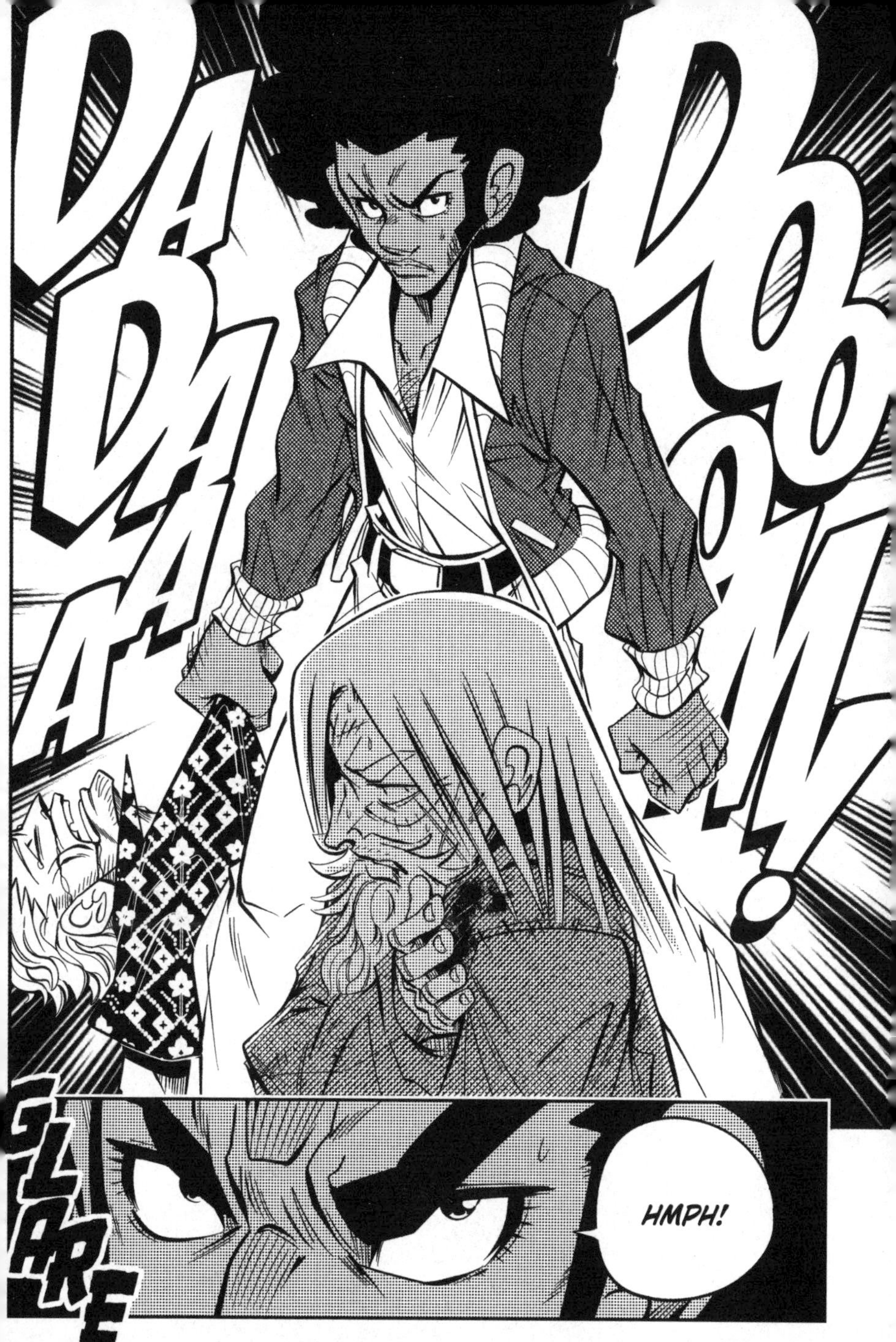
DADADA
DOOOOM!
GLARE
HMPH!

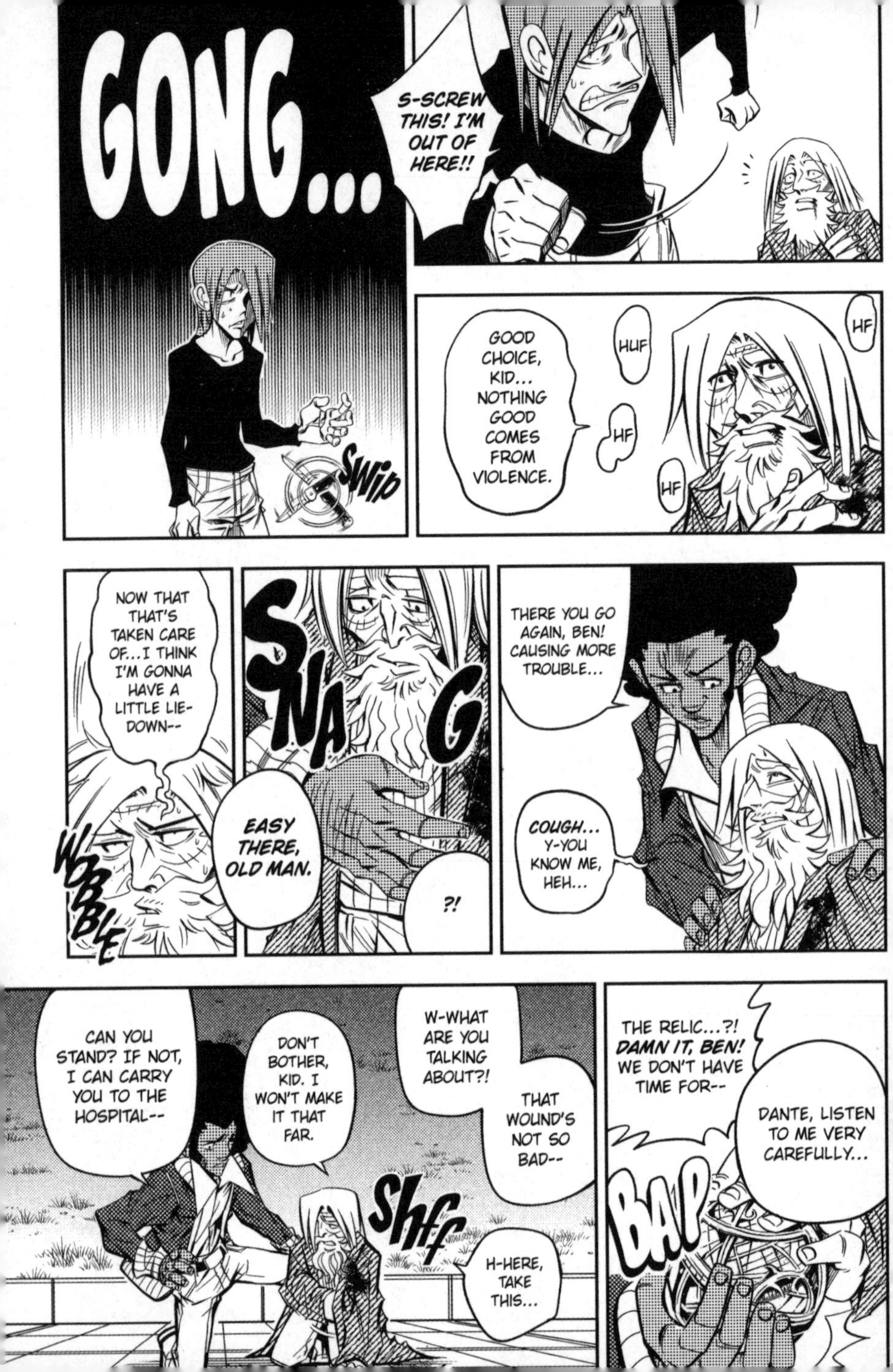
GONG...
SWIP
S-SCREW THIS! I'M OUT OF HERE!!
GOOD CHOICE, KID... NOTHING GOOD COMES FROM VIOLENCE.
HUF
HF
HF
HF
NOW THAT THAT'S TAKEN CARE OF...I THINK I'M GONNA HAVE A LITTLE LIE-DOWN--
WOBBLE
SNAG
EASY THERE, OLD MAN.
?!
THERE YOU GO AGAIN, BEN! CAUSING MORE TROUBLE...
COUGH... Y-YOU KNOW ME, HEH...
CAN YOU STAND? IF NOT, I CAN CARRY YOU TO THE HOSPITAL--
DON'T BOTHER, KID. I WON'T MAKE IT THAT FAR.
W-WHAT ARE YOU TALKING ABOUT?!
THAT WOUND'S NOT SO BAD--
SHFF
H-HERE, TAKE THIS...
THE RELIC...?! DAMN IT, BEN! WE DON'T HAVE TIME FOR--
DANTE, LISTEN TO ME VERY CAREFULLY...
BAP

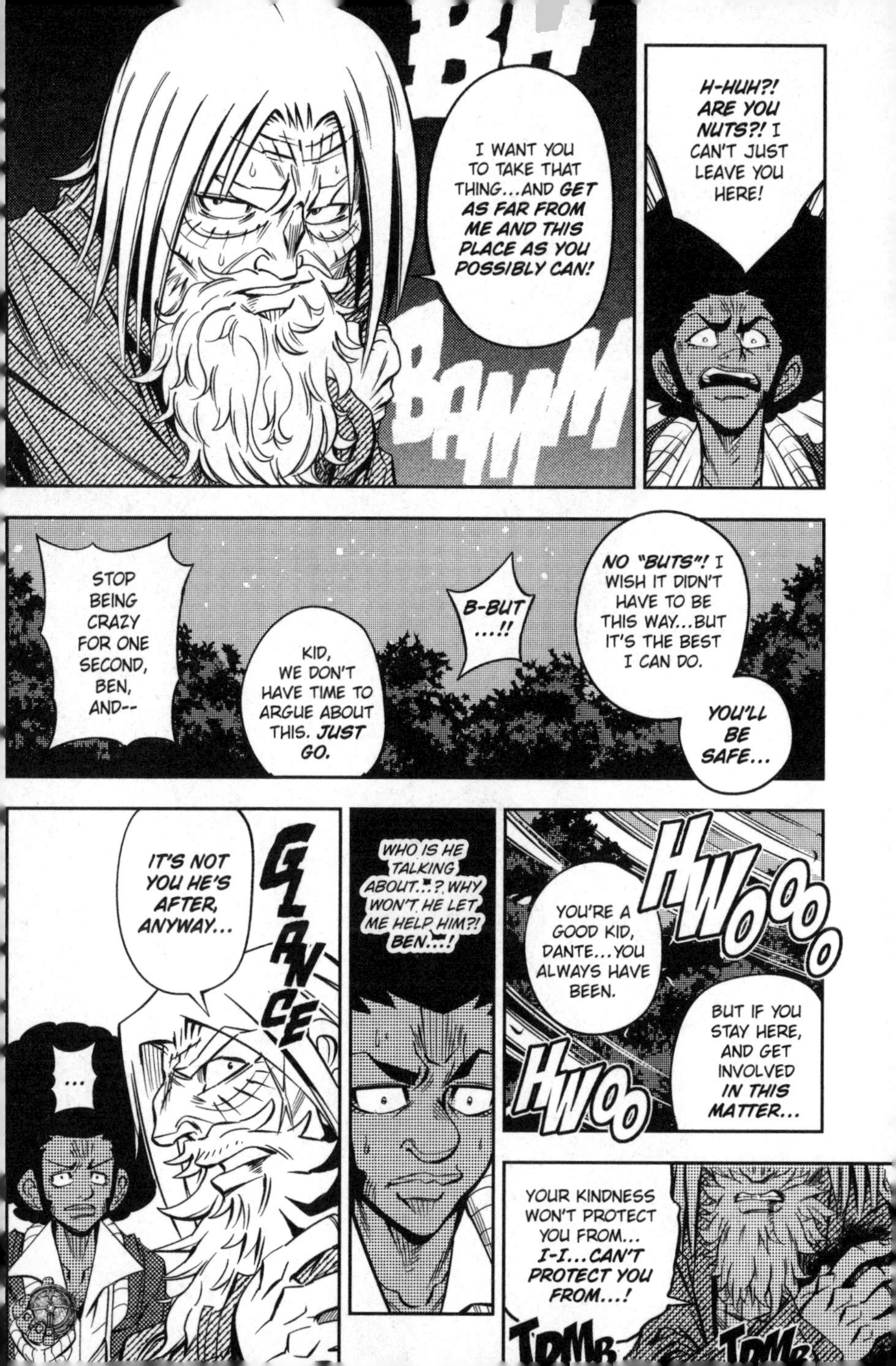
I WANT YOU TO TAKE THAT THING...AND GET AS FAR FROM ME AND THIS PLACE AS YOU POSSIBLY CAN!
BAMM
H-HUH?! ARE YOU NUTS?! I CAN'T JUST LEAVE YOU HERE!
STOP BEING CRAZY FOR ONE SECOND, BEN, AND--
KID, WE DON'T HAVE TIME TO ARGUE ABOUT THIS. JUST GO.
B-BUT...!!
NO "BUTS"! I WISH IT DIDN'T HAVE TO BE THIS WAY...BUT IT'S THE BEST I CAN DO.
YOU'LL BE SAFE...
IT'S NOT YOU HE'S AFTER, ANYWAY...
GLANCE
...
WHO IS HE TALKING ABOUT...? WHY WON'T HE LET ME HELP HIM?! BEN...!
HWOOOO
YOU'RE A GOOD KID, DANTE...YOU ALWAYS HAVE BEEN.
BUT IF YOU STAY HERE, AND GET INVOLVED IN THIS MATTER...
HWOO
YOUR KINDNESS WON'T PROTECT YOU FROM... I-I...CAN'T PROTECT YOU FROM...!
TDMB
TDMB

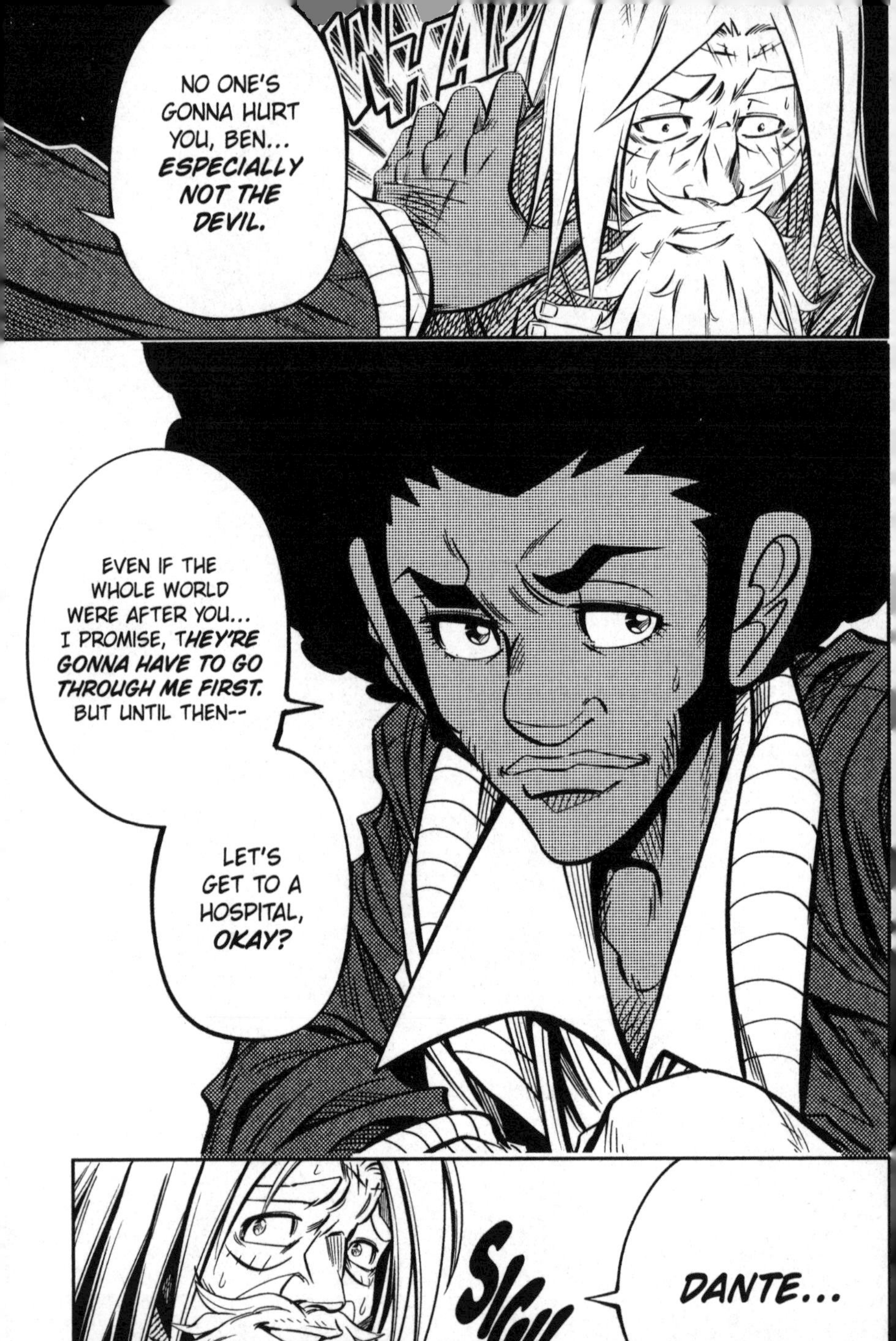
NO ONE'S GONNA HURT YOU, BEN... ESPECIALLY NOT THE DEVIL.
EVEN IF THE WHOLE WORLD WERE AFTER YOU... I PROMISE, THEY'RE GONNA HAVE TO GO THROUGH ME FIRST. BUT UNTIL THEN--
LET'S GET TO A HOSPITAL, OKAY?
SIGH
DANTE...

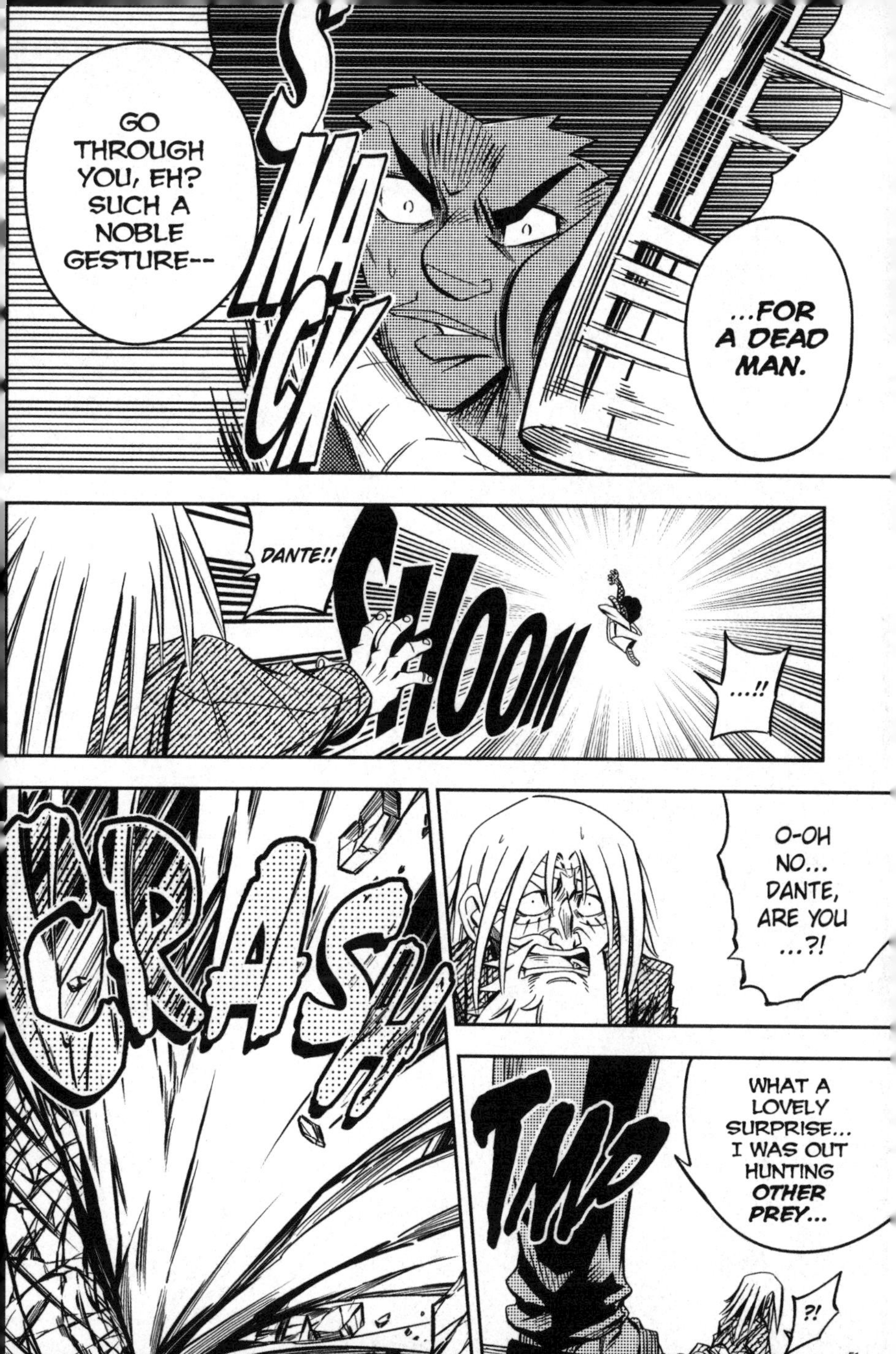
GO THROUGH YOU, EH? SUCH A NOBLE GESTURE--
SMACK
...FOR A DEAD MAN.
DANTE!!
SHOOM
...!!
CRASH
O-OH NO... DANTE, ARE YOU ...?!
TMP
WHAT A LOVELY SURPRISE... I WAS OUT HUNTING OTHER PREY...
?!

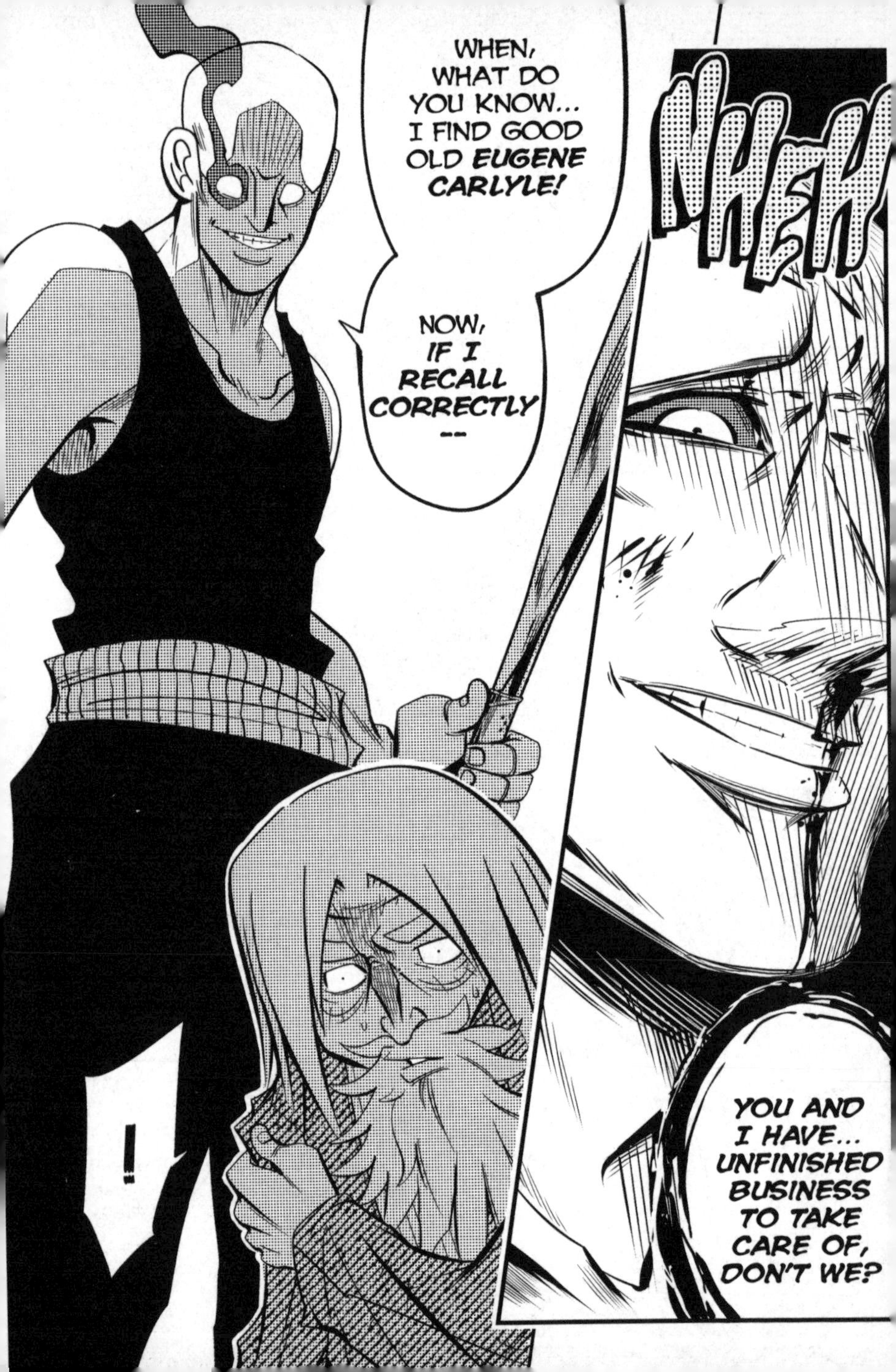
WHEN, WHAT DO YOU KNOW... I FIND GOOD OLD EUGENE CARLYLE!
NOW, IF I RECALL CORRECTLY --
!
NHEH
YOU AND I HAVE... UNFINISHED BUSINESS TO TAKE CARE OF, DON'T WE?

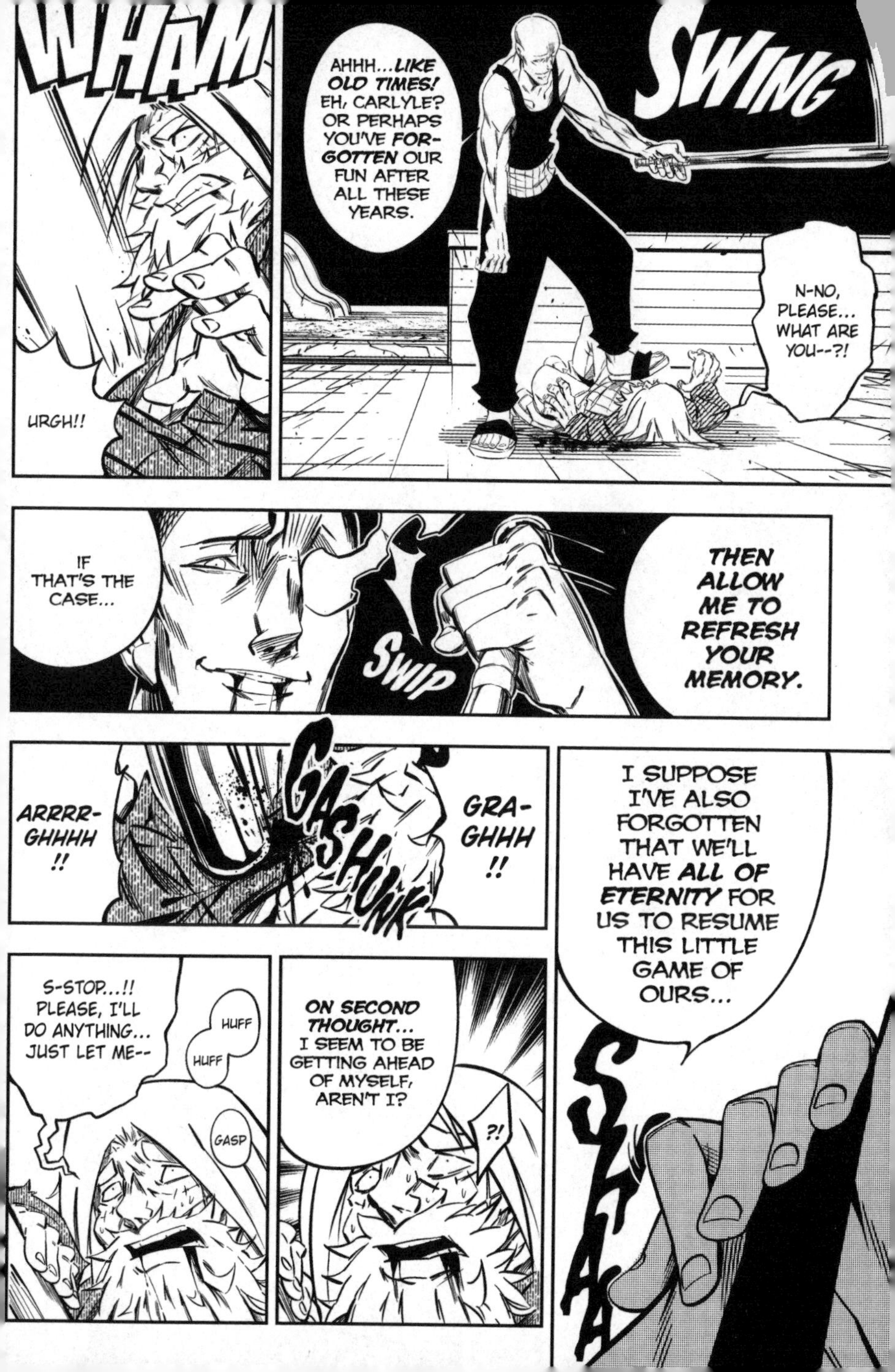
WHAM
URGH!!
AHHH...LIKE OLD TIMES! EH, CARLYLE? OR PERHAPS YOU'VE FORGOTTEN OUR FUN AFTER ALL THESE YEARS.
SWING
N-NO, PLEASE... WHAT ARE YOU--?!
IF THAT'S THE CASE...
SWIP
THEN ALLOW ME TO REFRESH YOUR MEMORY.
ARRRR-GHHHH!!
GASHUNK
GRA-GHHH!!
I SUPPOSE I'VE ALSO FORGOTTEN THAT WE'LL HAVE ALL OF ETERNITY FOR US TO RESUME THIS LITTLE GAME OF OURS...
S-STOP...!! PLEASE, I'LL DO ANYTHING... JUST LET ME--
HUFF
HUFF
GASP
ON SECOND THOUGHT... I SEEM TO BE GETTING AHEAD OF MYSELF, AREN'T I?
?!
SHAAA

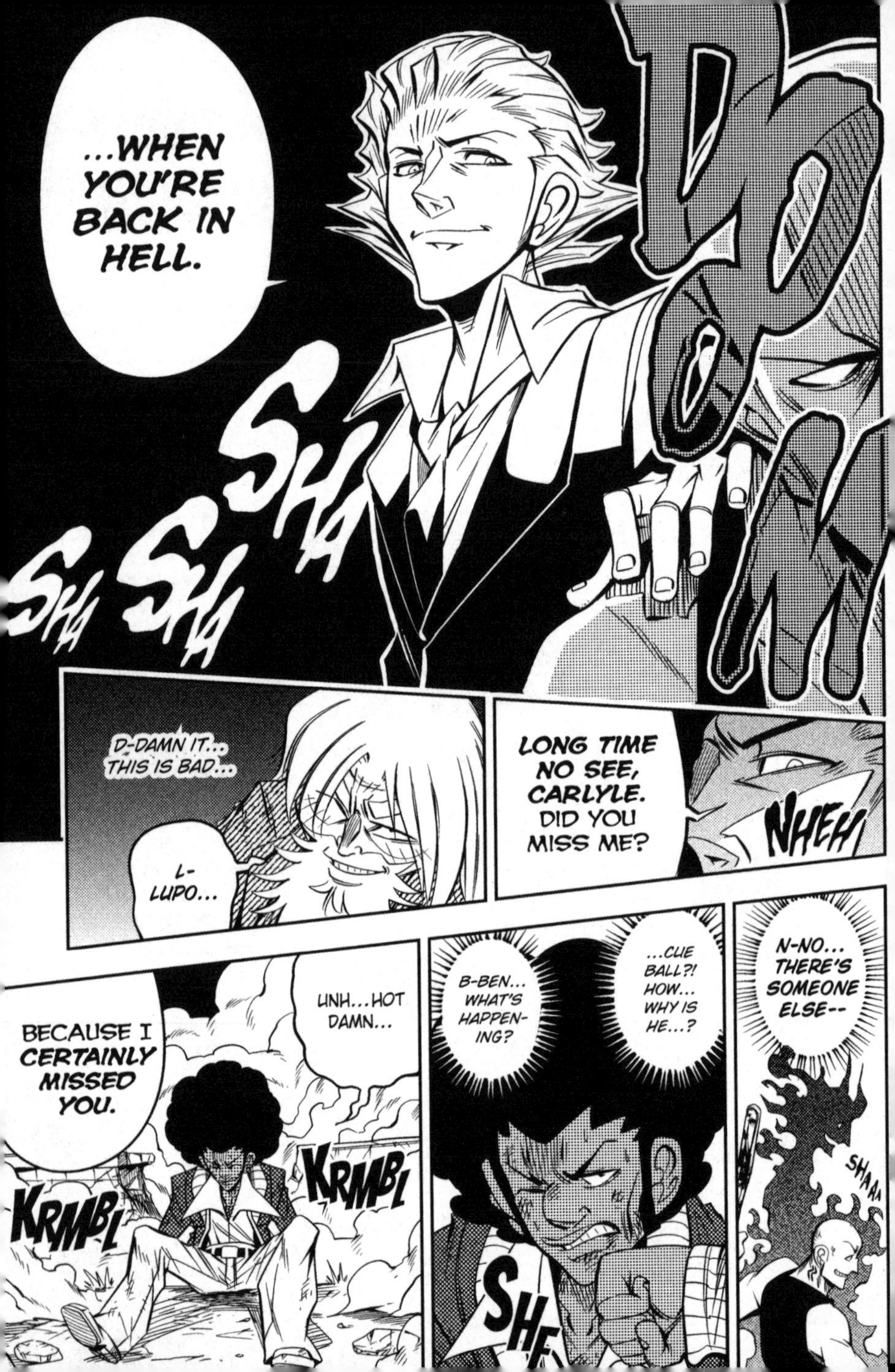
...WHEN YOU'RE BACK IN HELL.
SHA SHA SHA SHA
D-DAMN IT... THIS IS BAD...
L-LUPO...
LONG TIME NO SEE, CARLYLE. DID YOU MISS ME?
NHEH
BECAUSE I CERTAINLY MISSED YOU.
UNH...HOT DAMN...
KRMBL
KRMBL
B-BEN... WHAT'S HAPPEN-ING?
...CUE BALL?! HOW... WHY IS HE...?
N-NO... THERE'S SOMEONE ELSE--
SHAAA

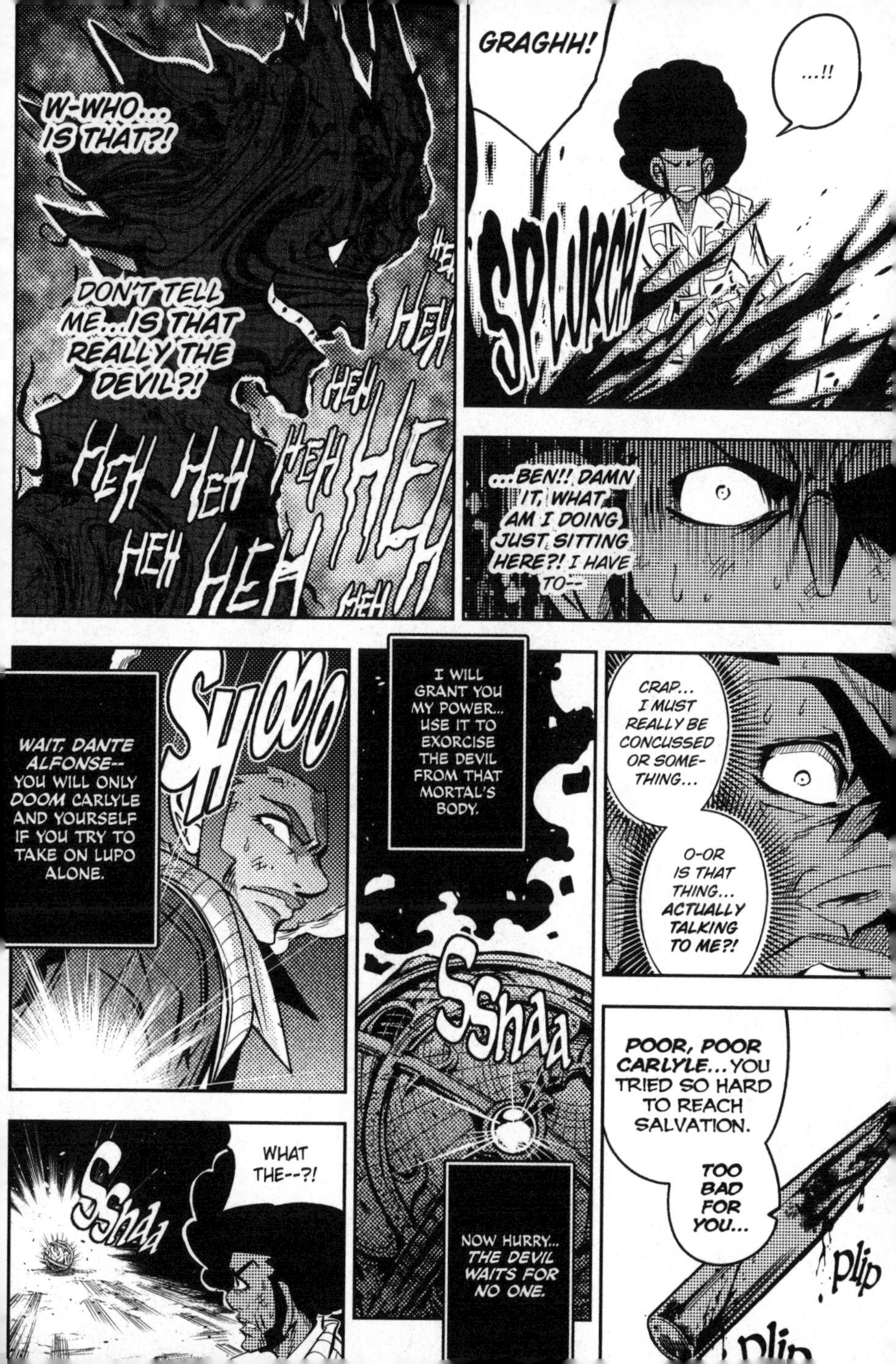
W-WHO... IS THAT?!
DON'T TELL ME...IS THAT REALLY THE DEVIL?!
HEH HEH HEH HEH HEH HEH HEH HEH HEH
GRAGHH!
...!!
SPLURCH
...BEN!! DAMN IT, WHAT AM I DOING JUST SITTING HERE?! I HAVE TO--
WAIT, DANTE ALFONSE-- YOU WILL ONLY DOOM CARLYLE AND YOURSELF IF YOU TRY TO TAKE ON LUPO ALONE.
SHOOOO
Sshaa
WHAT THE--?!
I WILL GRANT YOU MY POWER... USE IT TO EXORCISE THE DEVIL FROM THAT MORTAL'S BODY.
Sshaa
NOW HURRY... THE DEVIL WAITS FOR NO ONE.
CRAP... I MUST REALLY BE CONCUSSED OR SOME-THING...
O-OR IS THAT THING... ACTUALLY TALKING TO ME?!
POOR, POOR CARLYLE... YOU TRIED SO HARD TO REACH SALVATION.
TOO BAD FOR YOU...
plip
plip

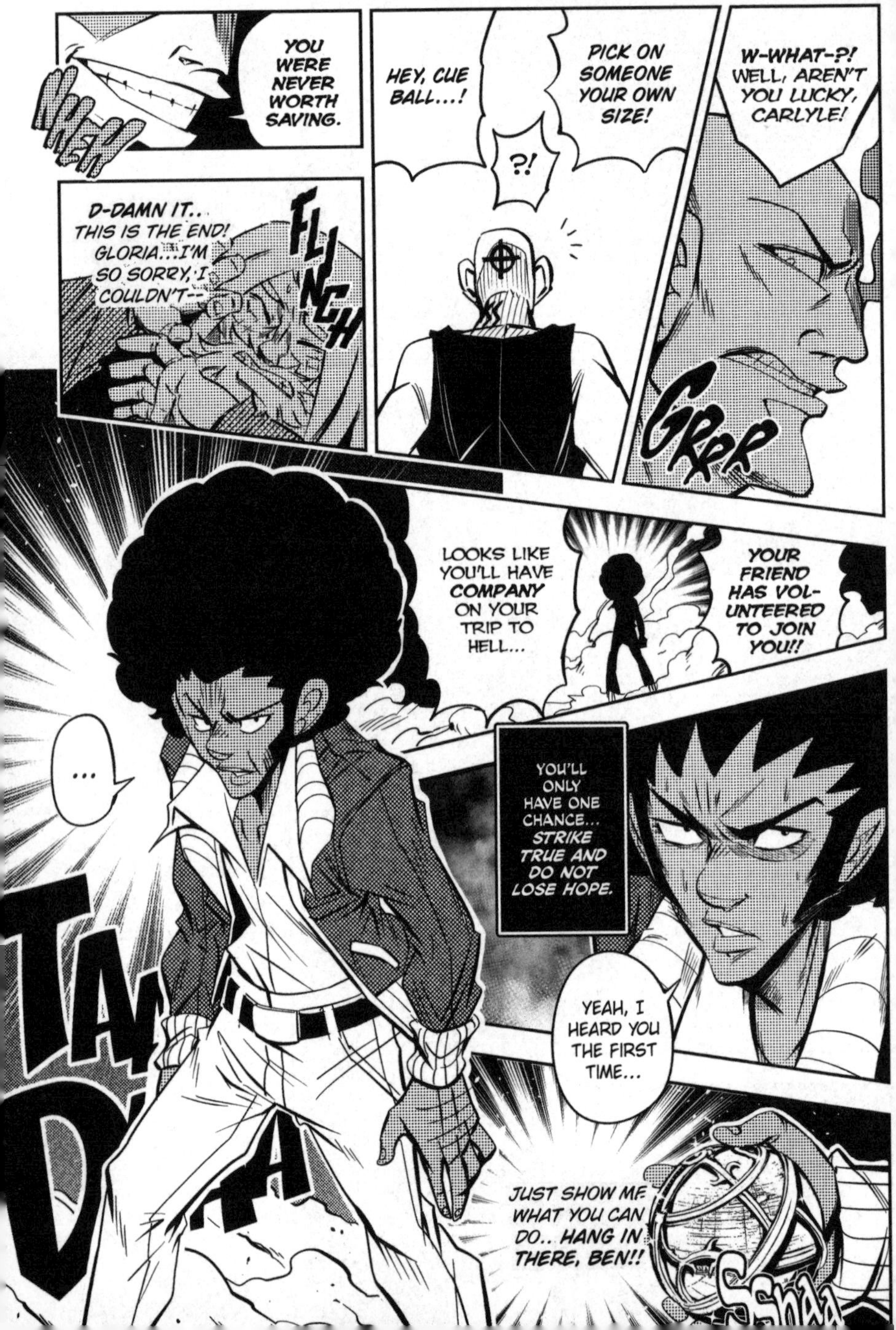
YOU WERE NEVER WORTH SAVING.
D-DAMN IT.. THIS IS THE END! GLORIA...I'M SO SORRY, I COULDN'T--
FLINCH
HEY, CUE BALL...!
PICK ON SOMEONE YOUR OWN SIZE!
?!
W-WHAT-?! WELL, AREN'T YOU LUCKY, CARLYLE!
GRRR
...
LOOKS LIKE YOU'LL HAVE **COMPANY** ON YOUR TRIP TO HELL...
YOUR FRIEND HAS VOL-UNTEERED TO JOIN YOU!!
YOU'LL ONLY HAVE ONE CHANCE... *STRIKE TRUE AND DO NOT LOSE HOPE.*
YEAH, I HEARD YOU THE FIRST TIME...
JUST SHOW ME WHAT YOU CAN DO.. HANG IN THERE, BEN!!

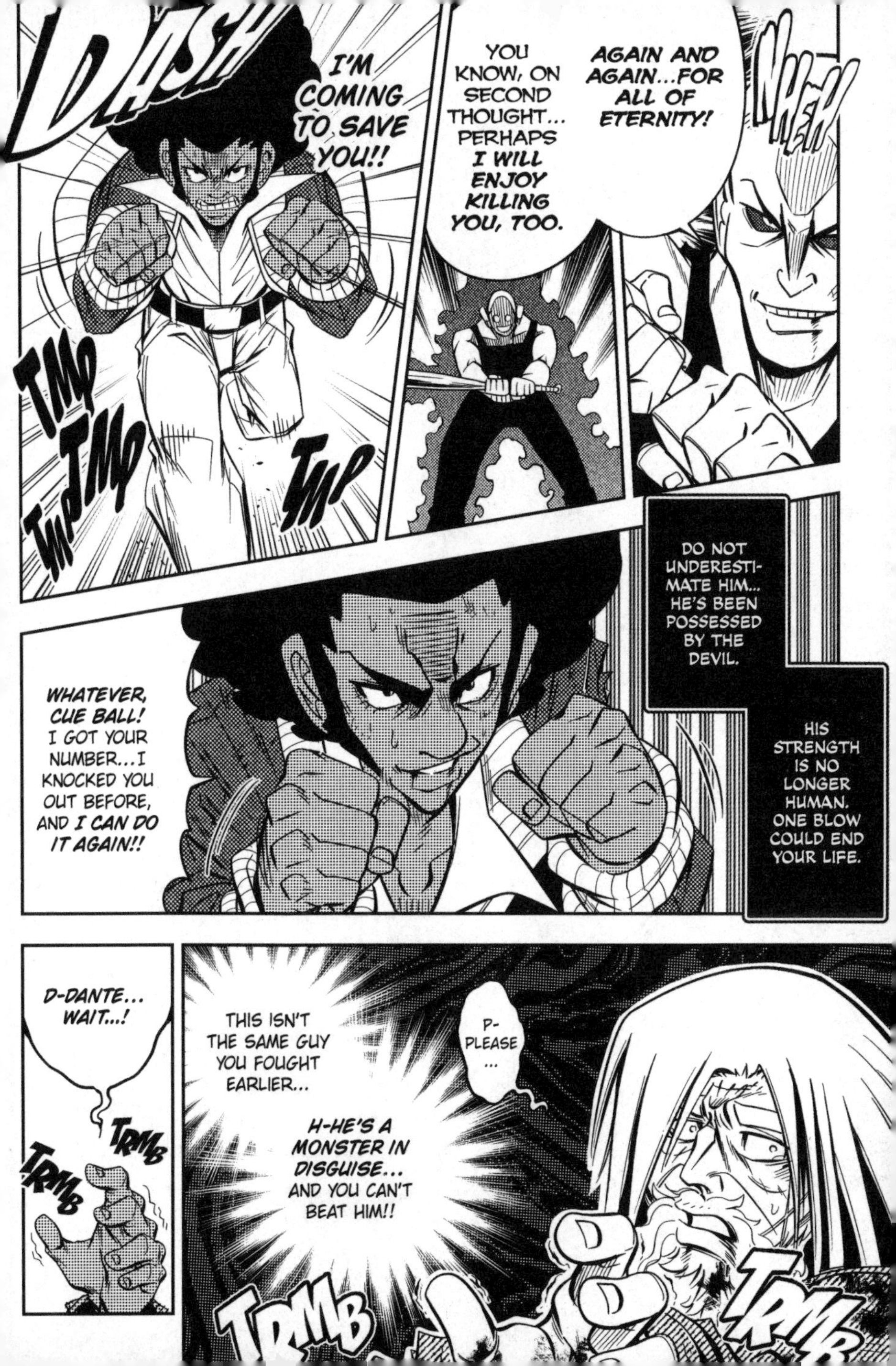
DASH
I'M COMING TO SAVE YOU!!
TMP TMP TMP
TMP
YOU KNOW, ON SECOND THOUGHT... PERHAPS I WILL ENJOY KILLING YOU, TOO.
AGAIN AND AGAIN...FOR ALL OF ETERNITY!
NHEH
WHATEVER, CUE BALL! I GOT YOUR NUMBER...I KNOCKED YOU OUT BEFORE, AND I CAN DO IT AGAIN!!
DO NOT UNDERESTI-MATE HIM... HE'S BEEN POSSESSED BY THE DEVIL.
HIS STRENGTH IS NO LONGER HUMAN. ONE BLOW COULD END YOUR LIFE.
D-DANTE... WAIT...!
TRMB TRMB
THIS ISN'T THE SAME GUY YOU FOUGHT EARLIER...
H-HE'S A MONSTER IN DISGUISE... AND YOU CAN'T BEAT HIM!!
P-PLEASE...
TRMB
TRMB

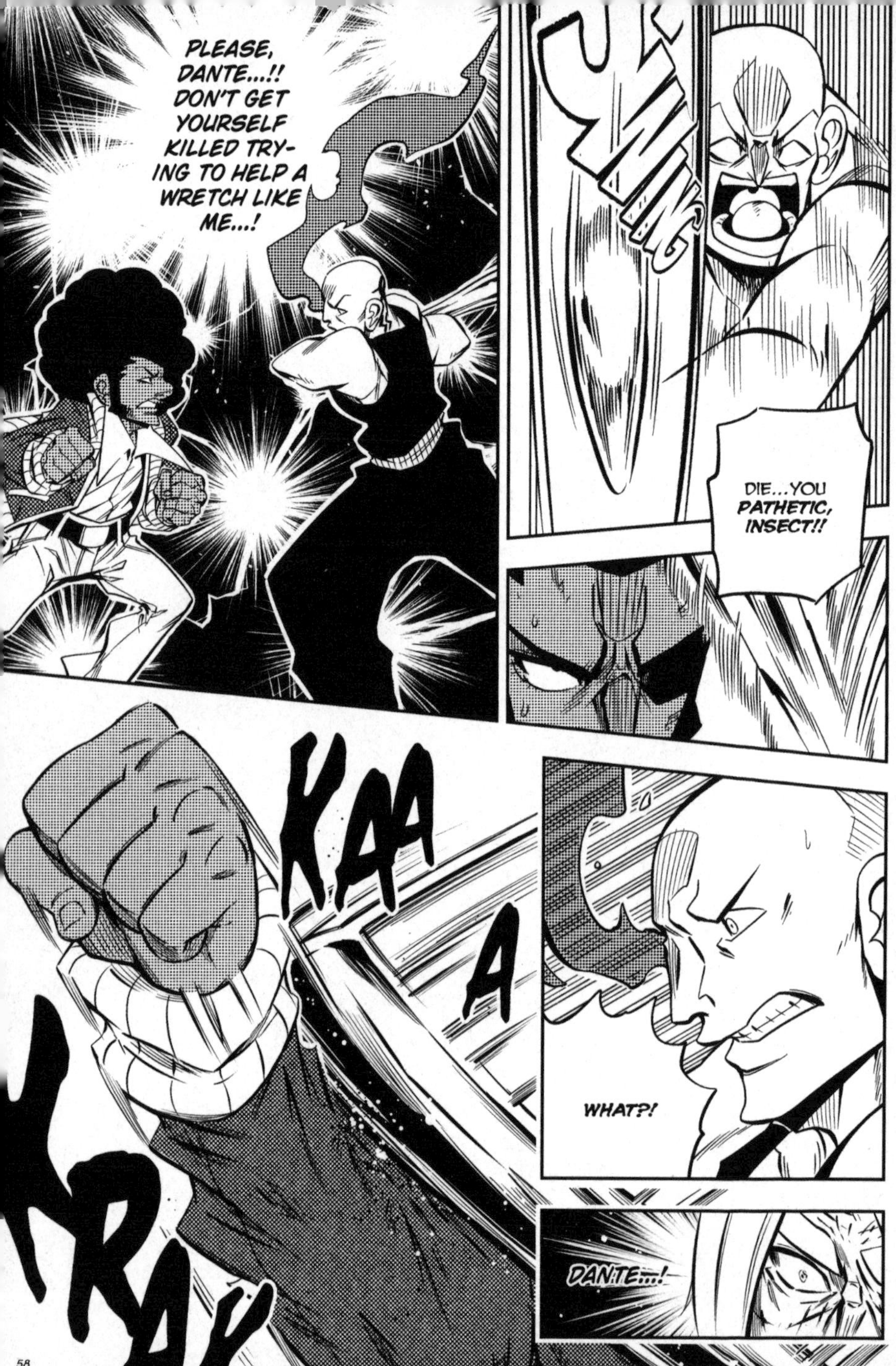
PLEASE, DANTE...!! DON'T GET YOURSELF KILLED TRYING TO HELP A WRETCH LIKE ME...!
DIE...YOU *PATHETIC, INSECT!!*
KAAA
TRAK
WHAT?!
DANTE...!

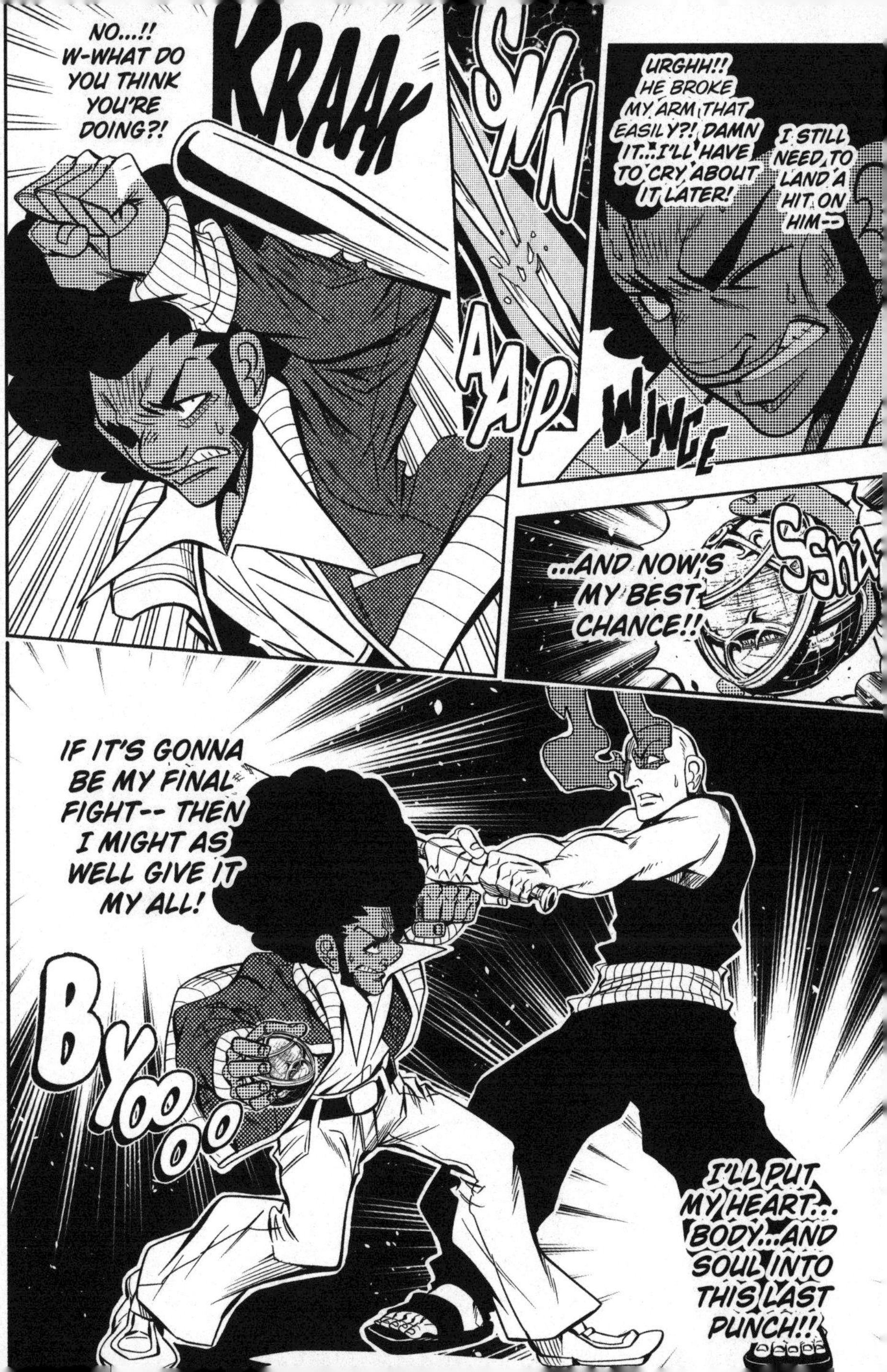
NO...!! W-WHAT DO YOU THINK YOU'RE DOING?!
KRAAK
SWN
AAP
URGHH!! HE BROKE MY ARM THAT EASILY?! DAMN IT...I'LL HAVE TO CRY ABOUT IT LATER!
I STILL NEED TO LAND A HIT ON HIM--
WINCE
...AND NOW'S MY BEST CHANCE!!
IF IT'S GONNA BE MY FINAL FIGHT-- THEN I MIGHT AS WELL GIVE IT MY ALL!
BYOOOOO
I'LL PUT MY HEART... BODY...AND SOUL INTO THIS LAST PUNCH!!

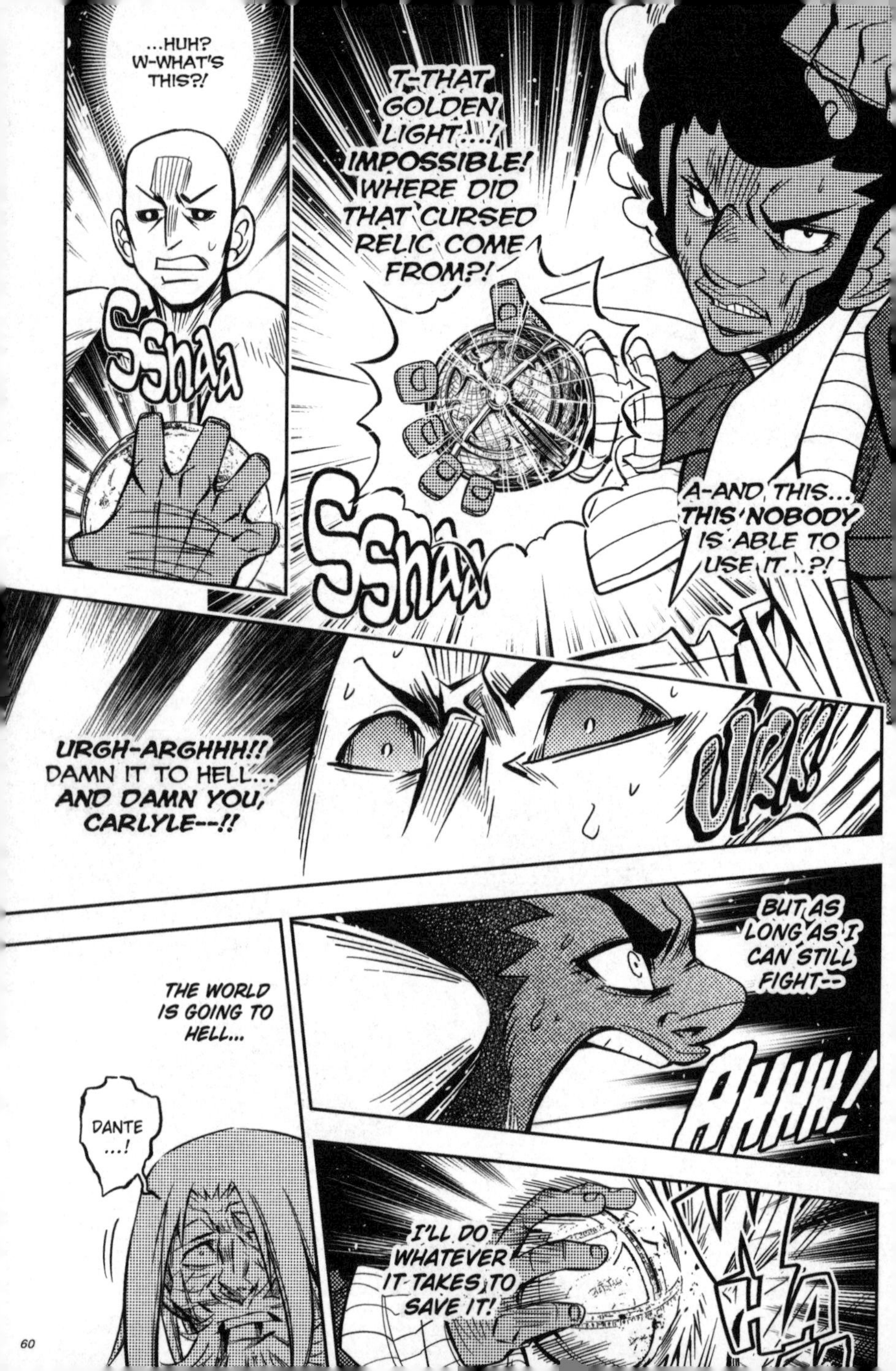
...HUH? W-WHAT'S THIS?!
SSHAA
T-THAT GOLDEN LIGHT...! IMPOSSIBLE! WHERE DID THAT CURSED RELIC COME FROM?!
SSHAA
A-AND THIS... THIS NOBODY IS ABLE TO USE IT...?!
URGH-ARGHHH!! DAMN IT TO HELL... AND DAMN YOU, CARLYLE--!!
THE WORLD IS GOING TO HELL...
DANTE ...!
BUT AS LONG AS I CAN STILL FIGHT--
AHHH!
I'LL DO WHATEVER IT TAKES TO SAVE IT!

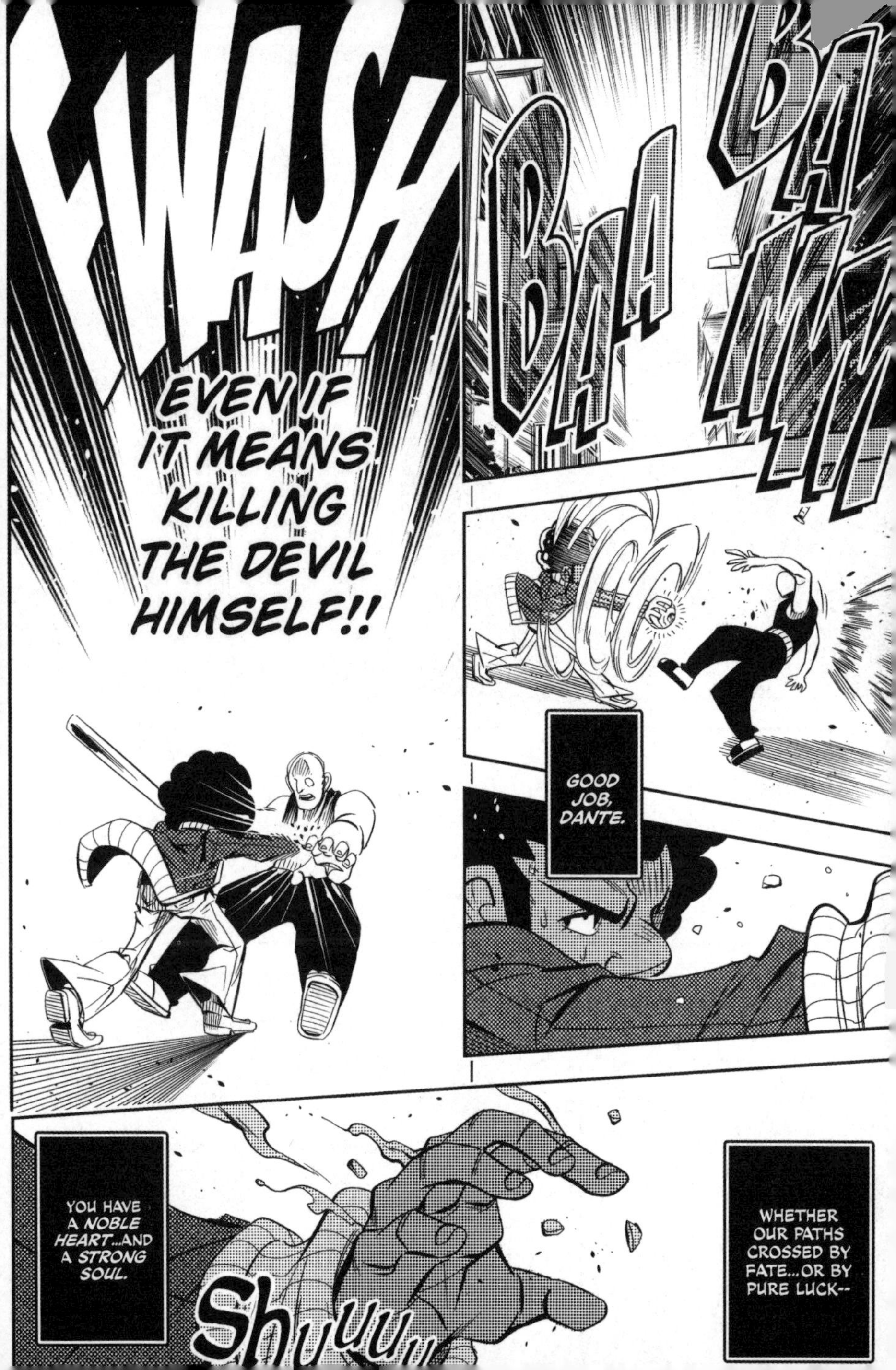
FWASH
EVEN IF IT MEANS KILLING THE DEVIL HIMSELF!!
GOOD JOB, DANTE.
YOU HAVE A *NOBLE HEART*...AND A *STRONG SOUL.*
Shuuu..
WHETHER OUR PATHS CROSSED BY FATE...OR BY PURE LUCK--

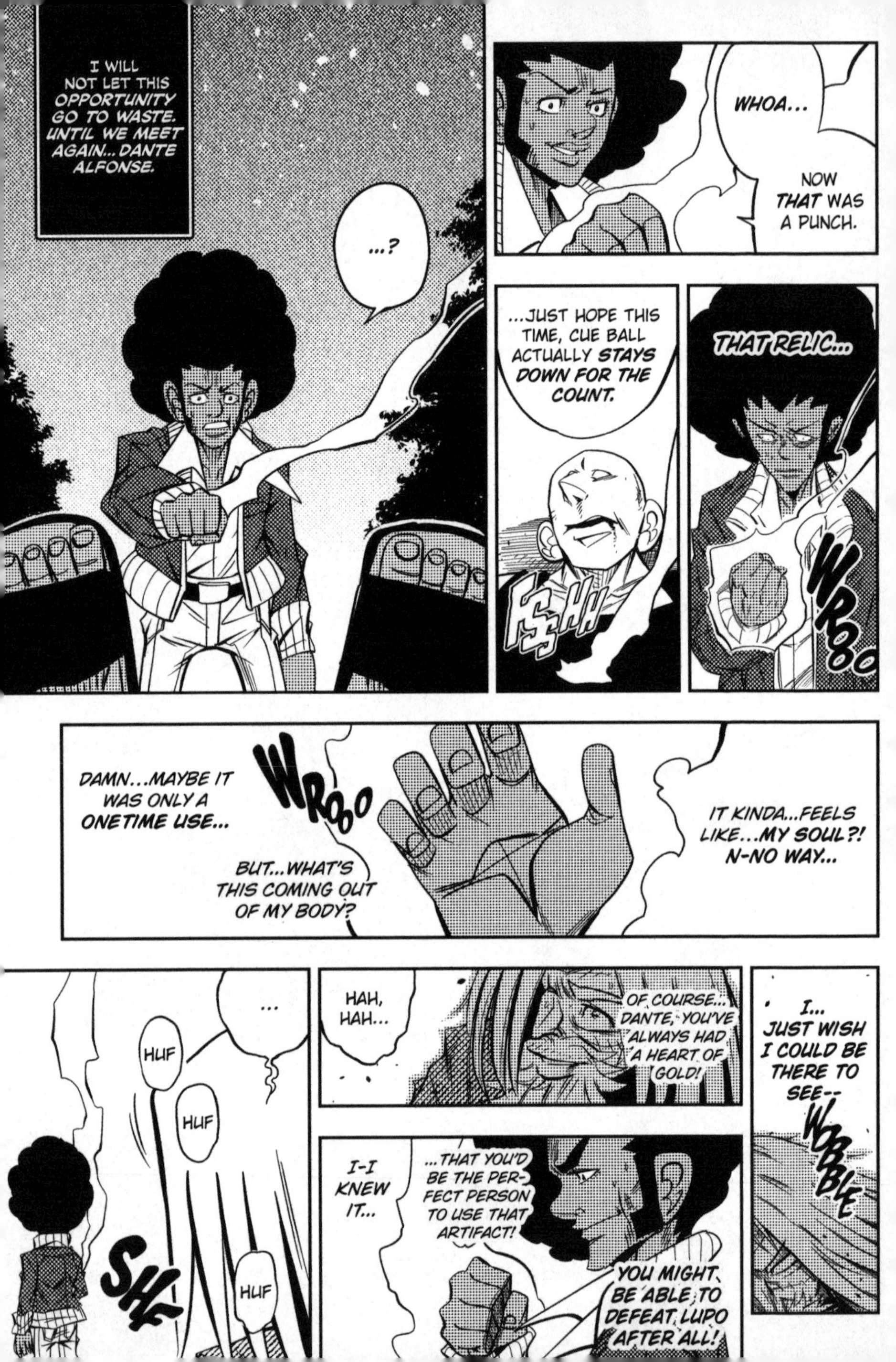
I WILL NOT LET THIS OPPORTUNITY GO TO WASTE. UNTIL WE MEET AGAIN...DANTE ALFONSE.
...?
WHOA...
NOW THAT WAS A PUNCH.
...JUST HOPE THIS TIME, CUE BALL ACTUALLY STAYS DOWN FOR THE COUNT.
FSSHH
THAT RELIC...
WROOO
DAMN...MAYBE IT WAS ONLY A ONETIME USE...
WROOO
BUT...WHAT'S THIS COMING OUT OF MY BODY?
IT KINDA...FEELS LIKE...MY SOUL?! N-NO WAY...
...
HUF
HUF
SHF
HUF
HAH, HAH...
OF COURSE... DANTE, YOU'VE ALWAYS HAD A HEART OF GOLD!
I... JUST WISH I COULD BE THERE TO SEE--
WOBBLE
I-I KNEW IT...
...THAT YOU'D BE THE PER-FECT PERSON TO USE THAT ARTIFACT!
YOU MIGHT BE ABLE TO DEFEAT LUPO AFTER ALL!

KATHUMP

ACK...! I-I NEARLY FORGOT ...!!

...?!

BEN...!! H-HANG IN THERE, OLD MAN!

DON'T LOSE CONSCIOUS-NESS, AND TRY TO--BEN?!

SKRRR

WHUP

H-HEY! YOU HEAR WHAT I'M SAYING?! STAY WITH ME, BEN!!

UNH...IT'S NO USE, KID...I CAN ALREADY FEEL THAT *INFERNAL COLD* CREEPING OVER ME.

SEEMS I COULDN'T OUTRUN MY FATE, AFTER ALL...*THAT BASTARD FINALLY WON.*

BUT NOT COMPLETELY!

AND, I'LL BE SURE TO REMIND HIM EVERY DAY HOW BAD HE LOST TO YOU!

SIGHH

AND, WHO KNOWS? MAYBE SOMEDAY YOU'LL STOP HIM FOR GOOD.

WELL, WHATEVER HAPPENS... *PROMISE ME ONE THING, DANTE--*

DON'T EVER GIVE UP HOPE.

GOOD LUCK, KID...

BEN!!

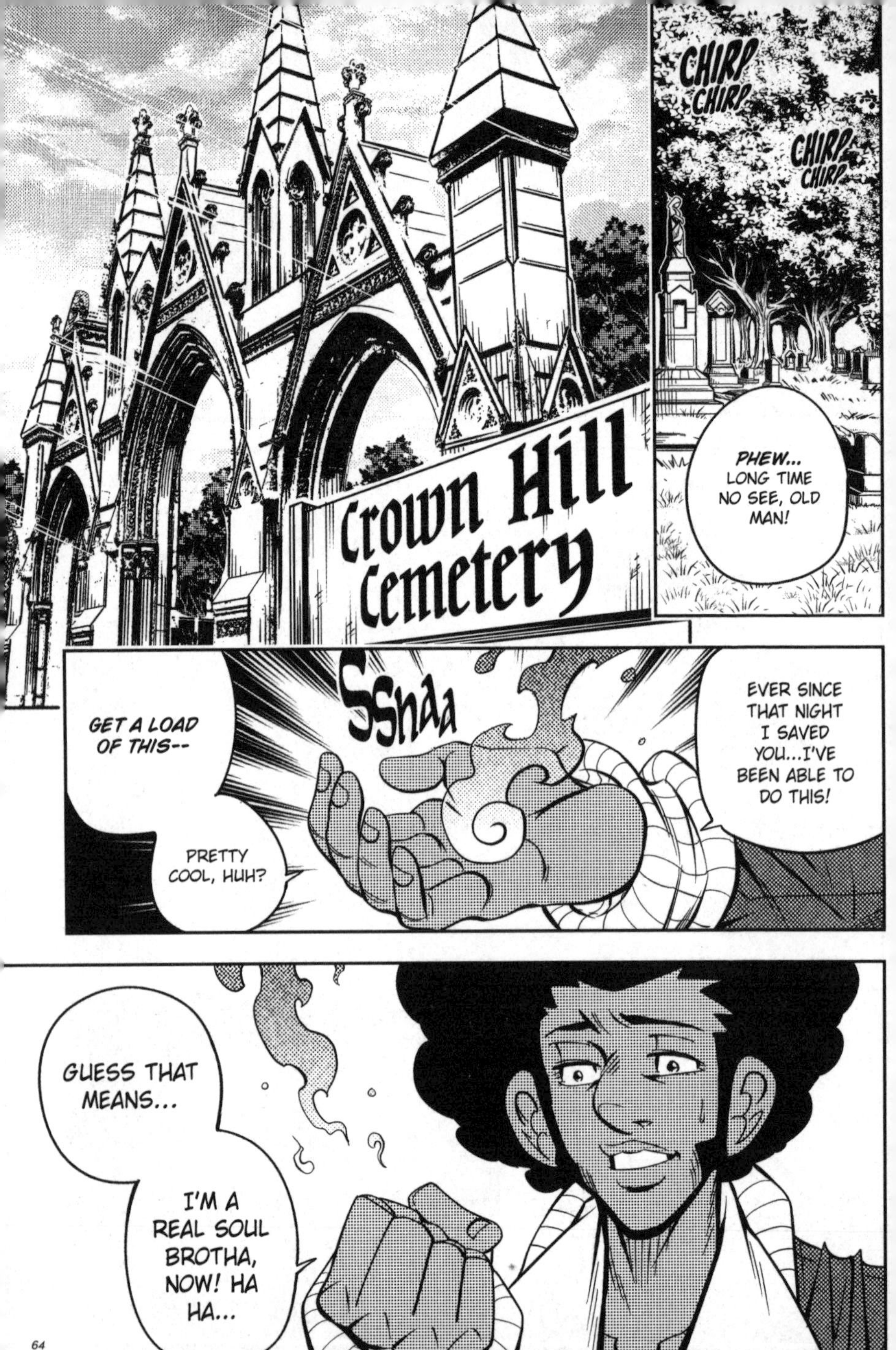

Crown Hill Cemetery
CHIRP CHIRP
CHIRP CHIRP
PHEW... LONG TIME NO SEE, OLD MAN!
GET A LOAD OF THIS--
SSHAA
PRETTY COOL, HUH?
EVER SINCE THAT NIGHT I SAVED YOU...I'VE BEEN ABLE TO DO THIS!
GUESS THAT MEANS...
I'M A REAL SOUL BROTHA, NOW! HA HA...

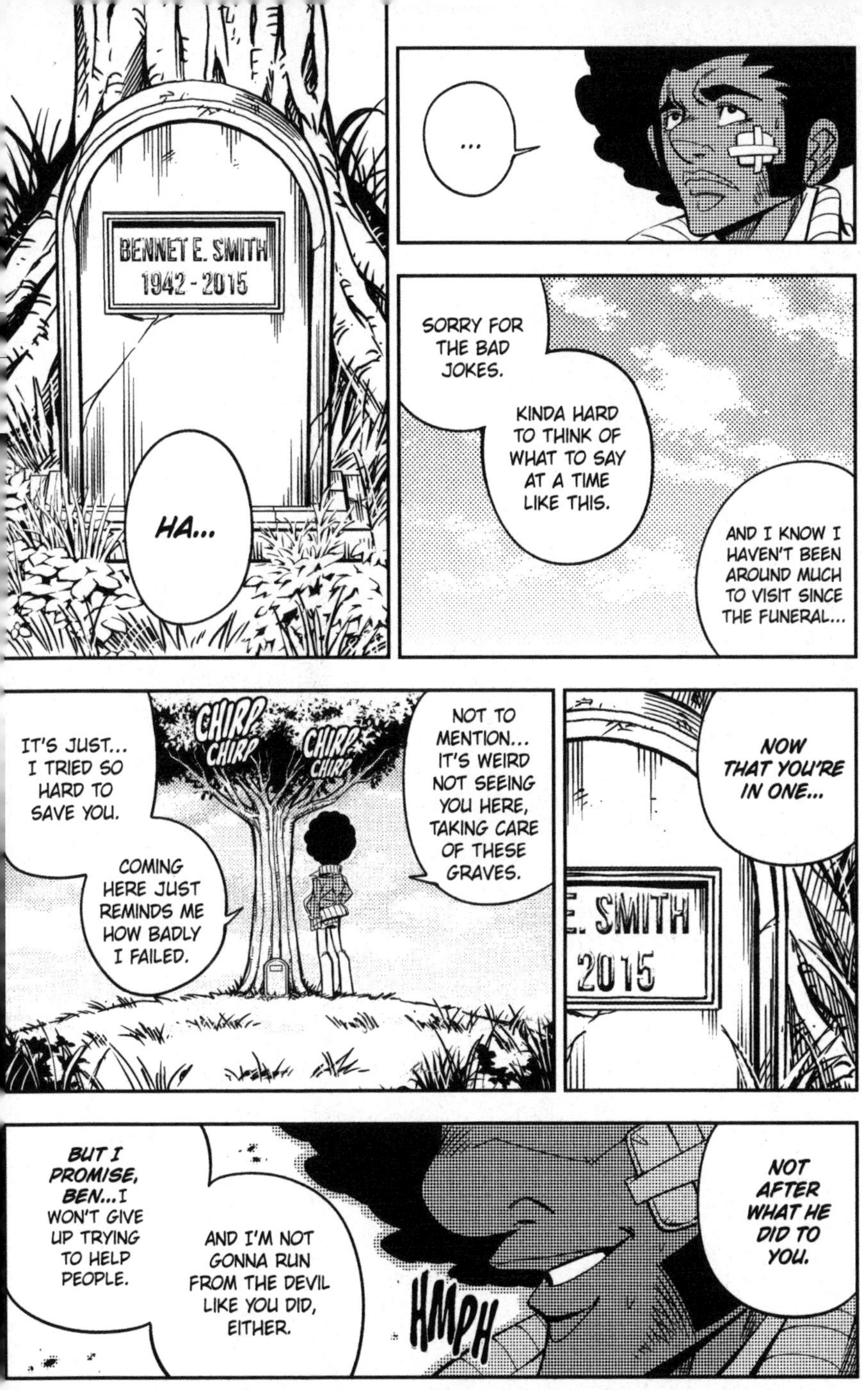
BENNET E. SMITH
1942 - 2015
HA...
...
SORRY FOR THE BAD JOKES.
KINDA HARD TO THINK OF WHAT TO SAY AT A TIME LIKE THIS.
AND I KNOW I HAVEN'T BEEN AROUND MUCH TO VISIT SINCE THE FUNERAL...
IT'S JUST... I TRIED SO HARD TO SAVE YOU.
CHIRP CHIRP
CHIRP CHIRP
COMING HERE JUST REMINDS ME HOW BADLY I FAILED.
NOT TO MENTION... IT'S WEIRD NOT SEEING YOU HERE, TAKING CARE OF THESE GRAVES.
NOW THAT YOU'RE IN ONE...
E. SMITH
2015
BUT I PROMISE, BEN...I WON'T GIVE UP TRYING TO HELP PEOPLE.
AND I'M NOT GONNA RUN FROM THE DEVIL LIKE YOU DID, EITHER.
HMPH
NOT AFTER WHAT HE DID TO YOU.

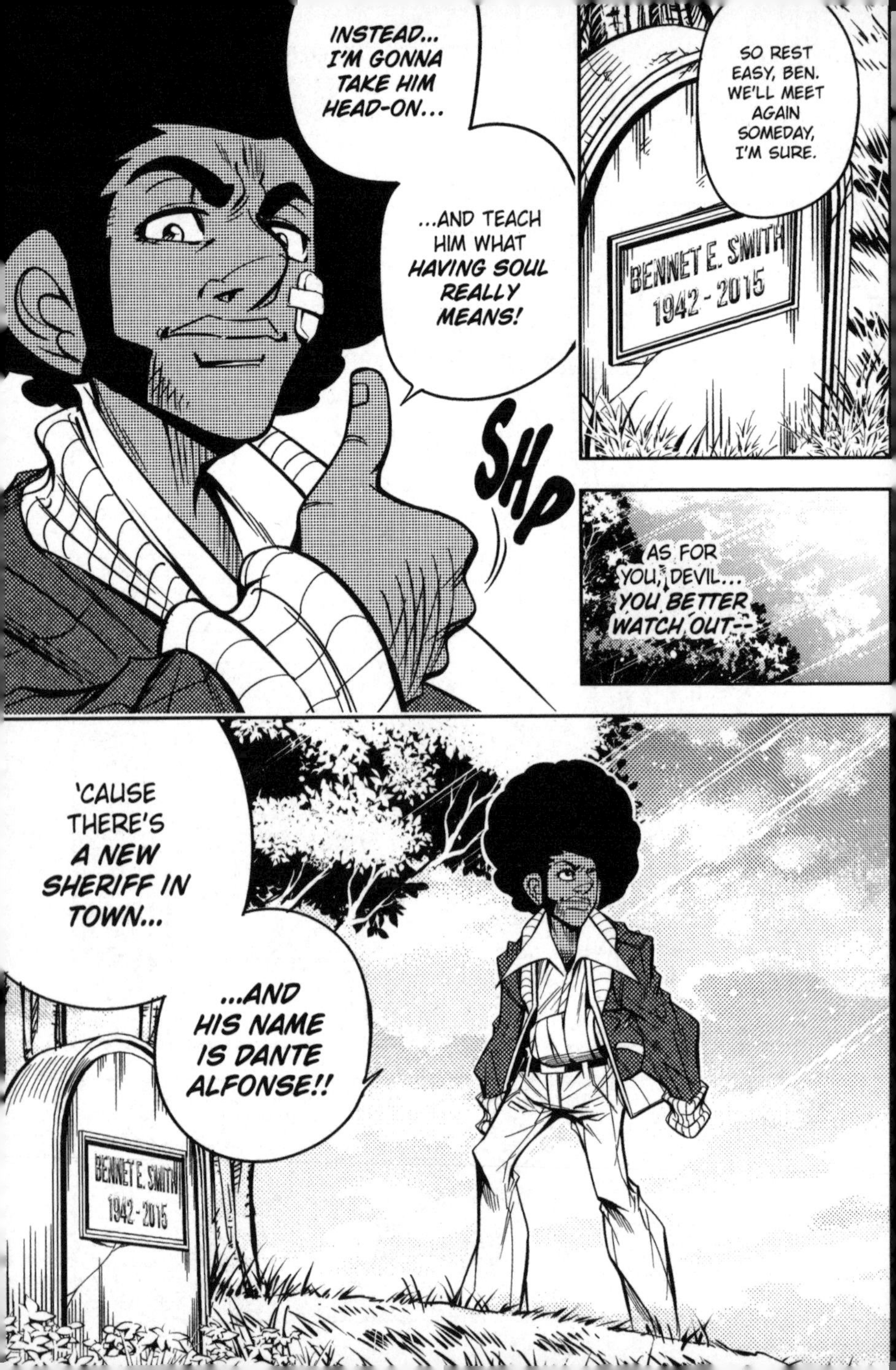

INSTEAD... I'M GONNA TAKE HIM HEAD-ON...
...AND TEACH HIM WHAT HAVING SOUL REALLY MEANS!
SHP
SO REST EASY, BEN. WE'LL MEET AGAIN SOMEDAY, I'M SURE.
BENNET E. SMITH 1942 - 2015
AS FOR YOU, DEVIL... YOU BETTER WATCH OUT--
'CAUSE THERE'S A NEW SHERIFF IN TOWN...
...AND HIS NAME IS DANTE ALFONSE!!
BENNET E. SMITH 1942 - 2015

SOUL BEAT

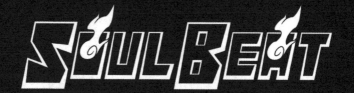

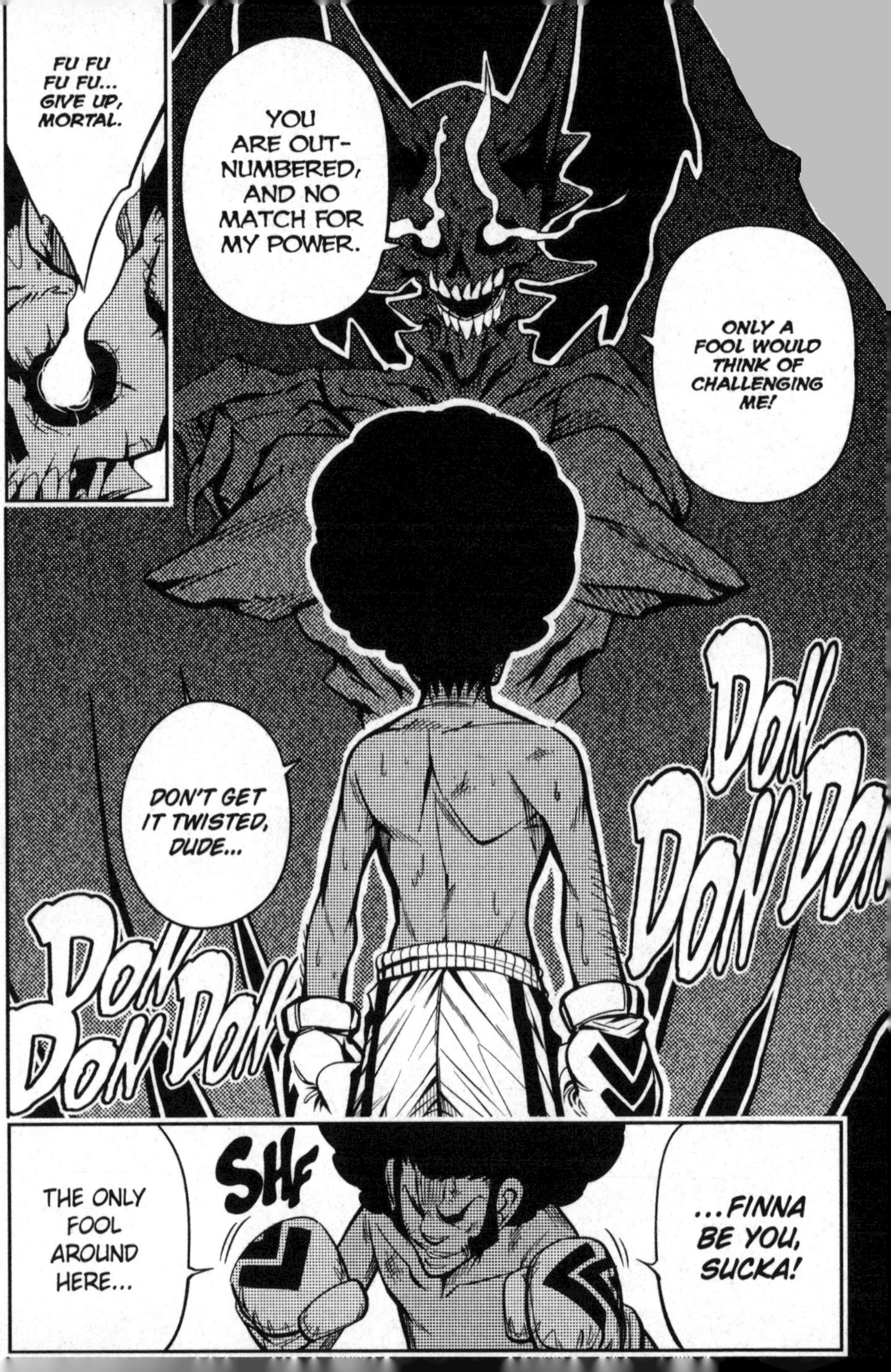
FU FU FU FU... GIVE UP, MORTAL.
YOU ARE OUT-NUMBERED, AND NO MATCH FOR MY POWER.
ONLY A FOOL WOULD THINK OF CHALLENGING ME!
DON'T GET IT TWISTED, DUDE...
DON DON DON
DON DON DON
THE ONLY FOOL AROUND HERE...
SHF
...FINNA BE YOU, SUCKA!

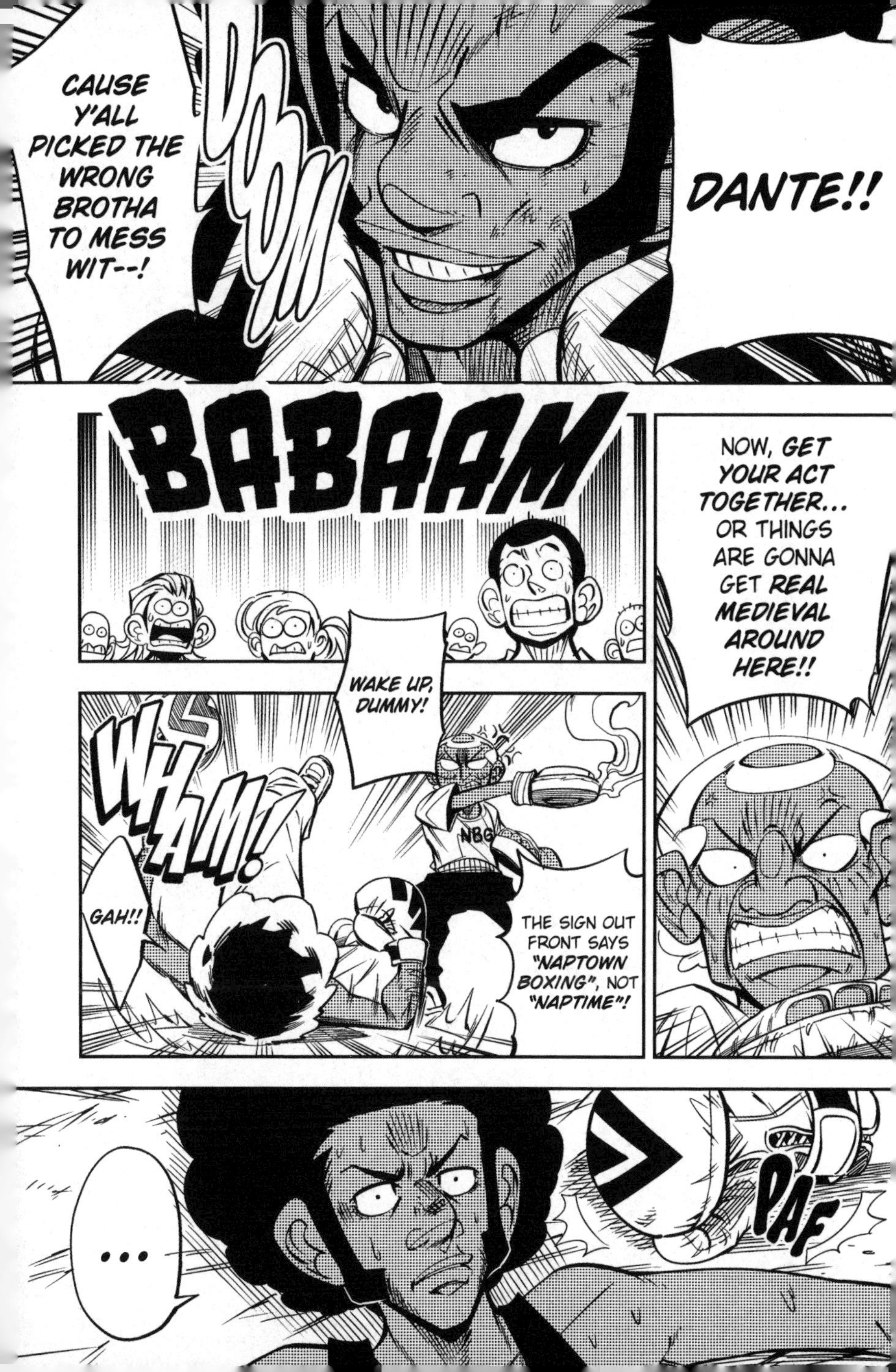

CAUSE Y'ALL PICKED THE WRONG BROTHA TO MESS WIT--!
DANTE!!
BABAAM
WAKE UP, DUMMY!
WHAM!
GAH!!
THE SIGN OUT FRONT SAYS "NAPTOWN BOXING", NOT "NAPTIME"!
NOW, GET YOUR ACT TOGETHER... OR THINGS ARE GONNA GET REAL MEDIEVAL AROUND HERE!!
...
PAF

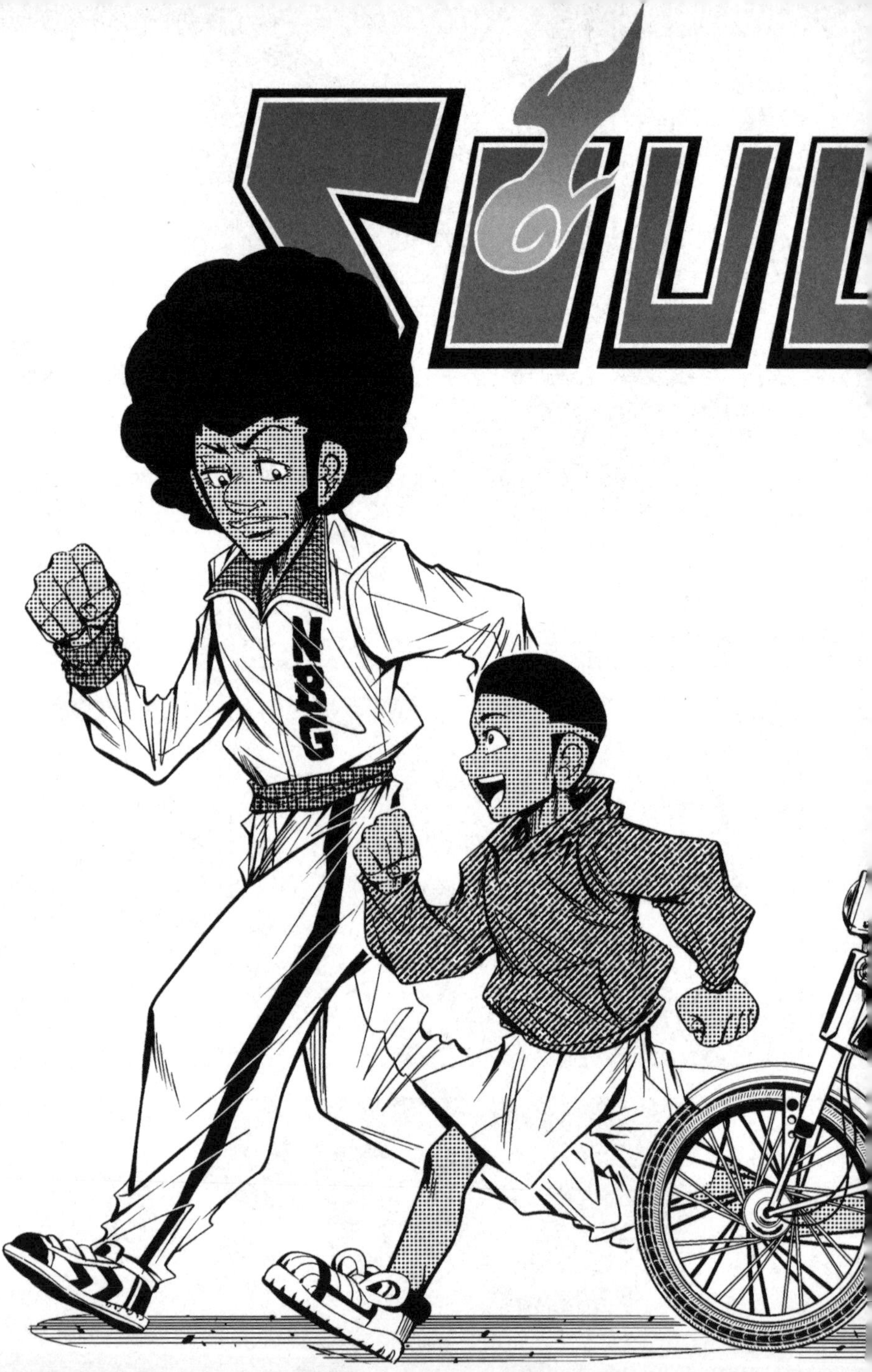

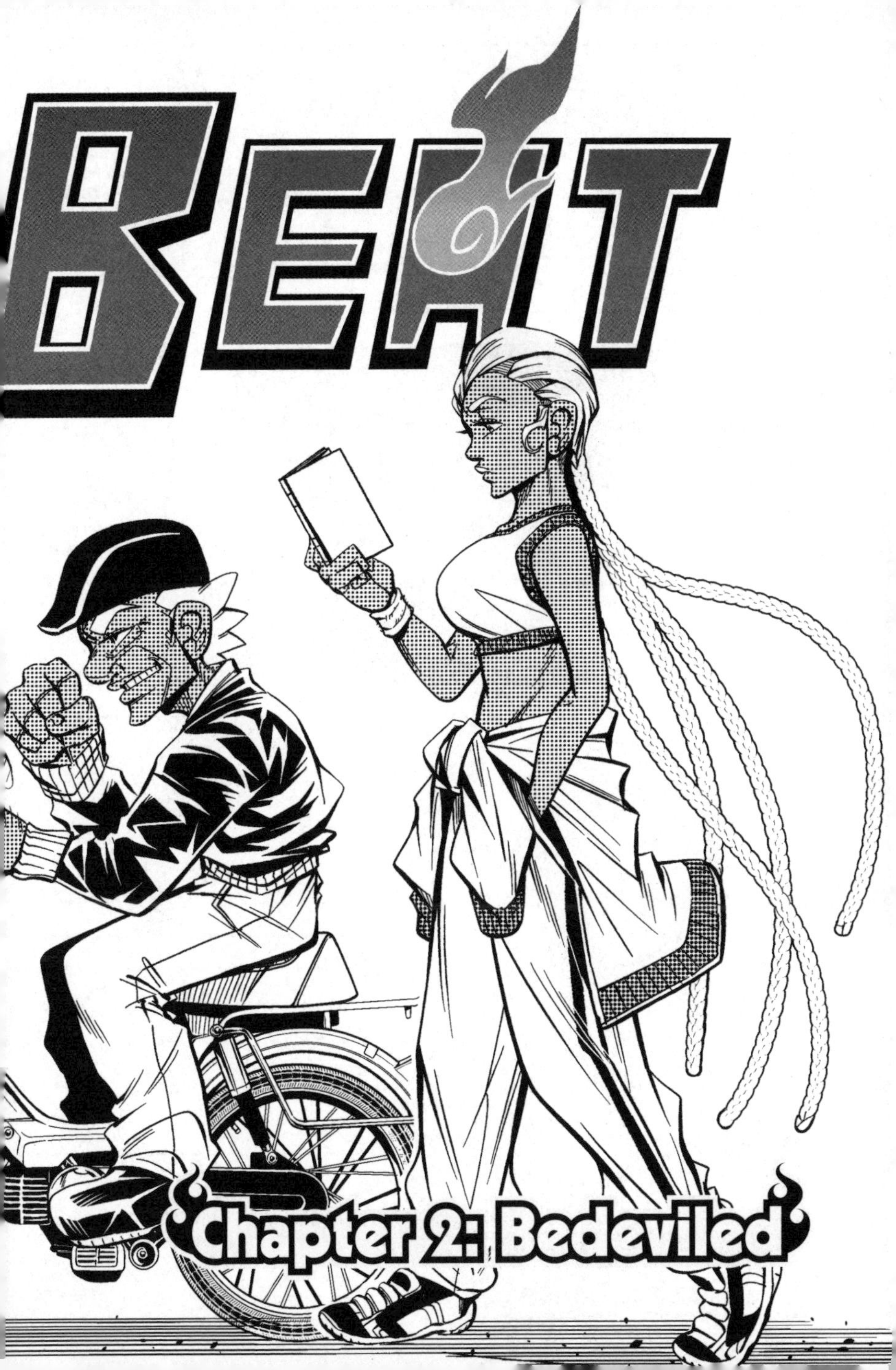
BEAT
Chapter 2: Bedeviled

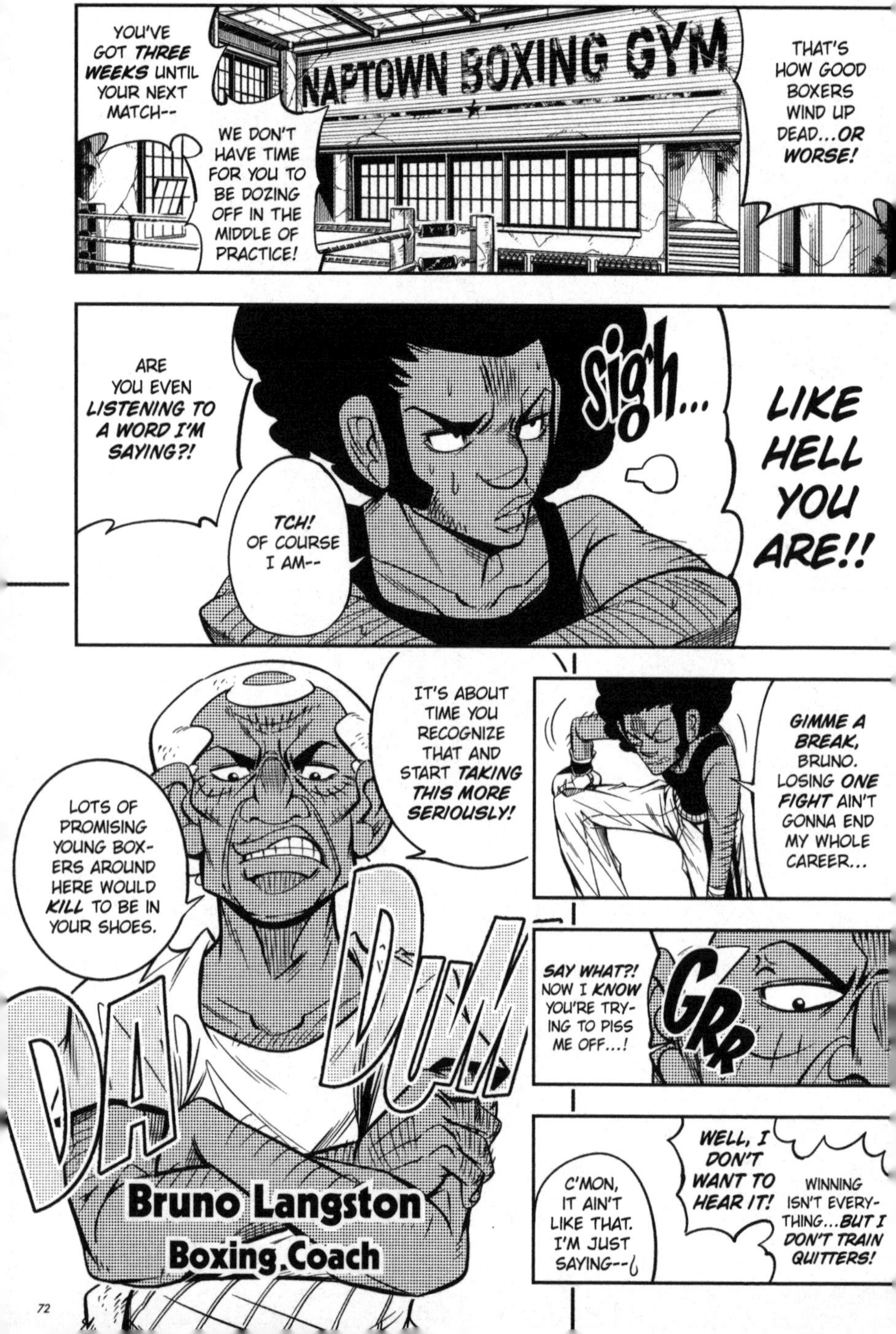

NAPTOWN BOXING GYM
YOU'VE GOT ***THREE WEEKS*** UNTIL YOUR NEXT MATCH--
WE DON'T HAVE TIME FOR YOU TO BE DOZING OFF IN THE MIDDLE OF PRACTICE!
THAT'S HOW GOOD BOXERS WIND UP DEAD...***OR WORSE!***
ARE YOU EVEN ***LISTENING TO A WORD I'M SAYING?!***
TCH! OF COURSE I AM--
sigh...
LIKE HELL YOU ARE!!
LOTS OF PROMISING YOUNG BOX-ERS AROUND HERE WOULD ***KILL*** TO BE IN YOUR SHOES.
IT'S ABOUT TIME YOU RECOGNIZE THAT AND START ***TAKING THIS MORE SERIOUSLY!***
DA DUM
Bruno Langston
Boxing Coach
GIMME A BREAK, BRUNO. LOSING ***ONE FIGHT*** AIN'T GONNA END MY WHOLE CAREER...
SAY WHAT?! NOW I ***KNOW*** YOU'RE TRY-ING TO PISS ME OFF...!
GRR
C'MON, IT AIN'T LIKE THAT. I'M JUST SAYING--
WELL, I DON'T WANT TO HEAR IT!
WINNING ISN'T EVERY-THING...***BUT I DON'T TRAIN QUITTERS!***

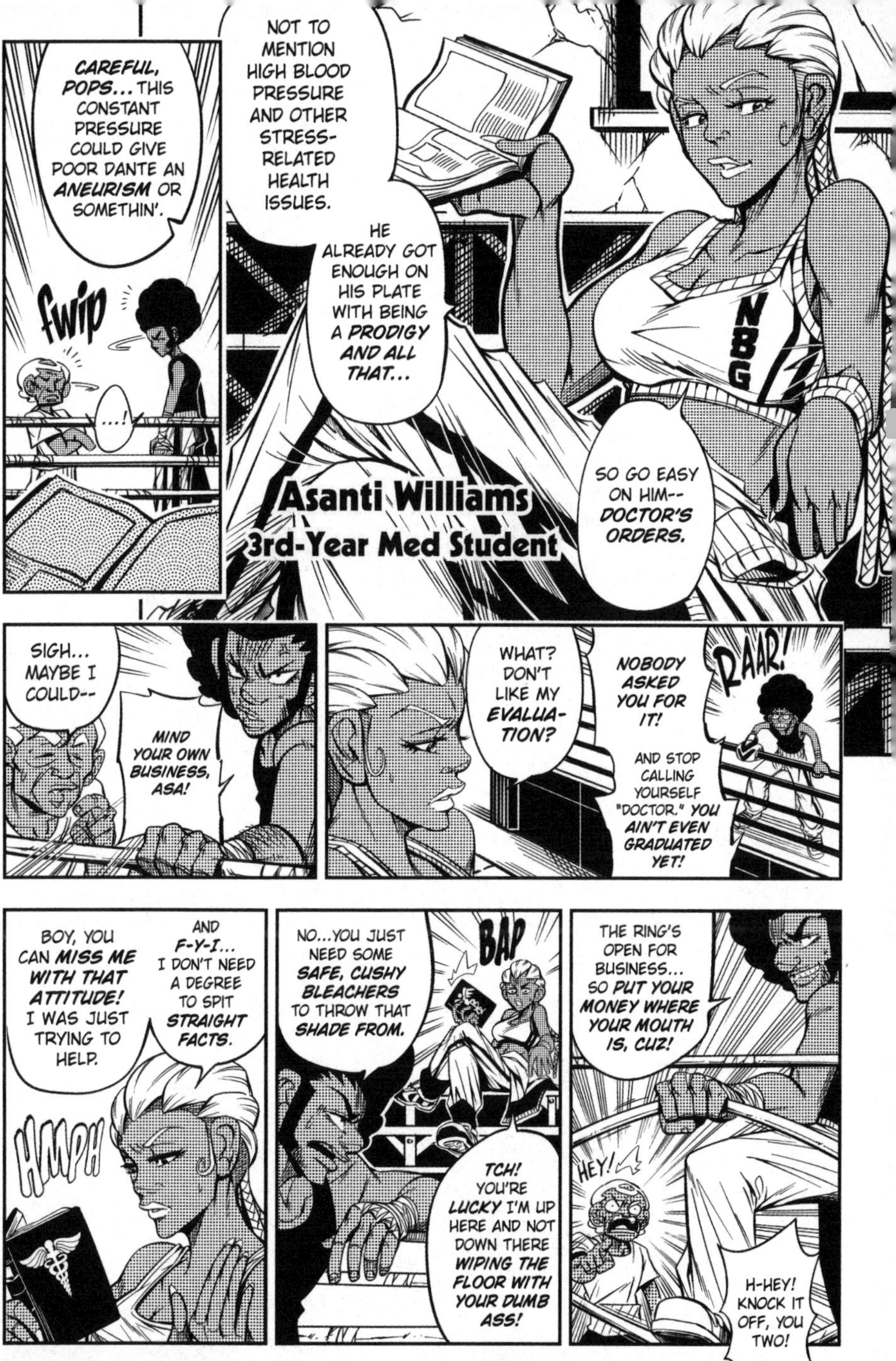
CAREFUL, POPS... THIS CONSTANT PRESSURE COULD GIVE POOR DANTE AN ANEURISM OR SOMETHIN'.
NOT TO MENTION HIGH BLOOD PRESSURE AND OTHER STRESS-RELATED HEALTH ISSUES.
fwip
...!
HE ALREADY GOT ENOUGH ON HIS PLATE WITH BEING A PRODIGY AND ALL THAT...
NBG
Asanti Williams
3rd-Year Med Student
SO GO EASY ON HIM-- DOCTOR'S ORDERS.
SIGH... MAYBE I COULD--
MIND YOUR OWN BUSINESS, ASA!
WHAT? DON'T LIKE MY EVALUATION?
RAAR!
NOBODY ASKED YOU FOR IT!
AND STOP CALLING YOURSELF "DOCTOR." YOU AIN'T EVEN GRADUATED YET!
BOY, YOU CAN MISS ME WITH THAT ATTITUDE! I WAS JUST TRYING TO HELP.
AND F-Y-I... I DON'T NEED A DEGREE TO SPIT STRAIGHT FACTS.
HMPH
NO...YOU JUST NEED SOME SAFE, CUSHY BLEACHERS TO THROW THAT SHADE FROM.
BAP
TCH! YOU'RE LUCKY I'M UP HERE AND NOT DOWN THERE WIPING THE FLOOR WITH YOUR DUMB ASS!
THE RING'S OPEN FOR BUSINESS... SO PUT YOUR MONEY WHERE YOUR MOUTH IS, CUZ!
HEY!
H-HEY! KNOCK IT OFF, YOU TWO!

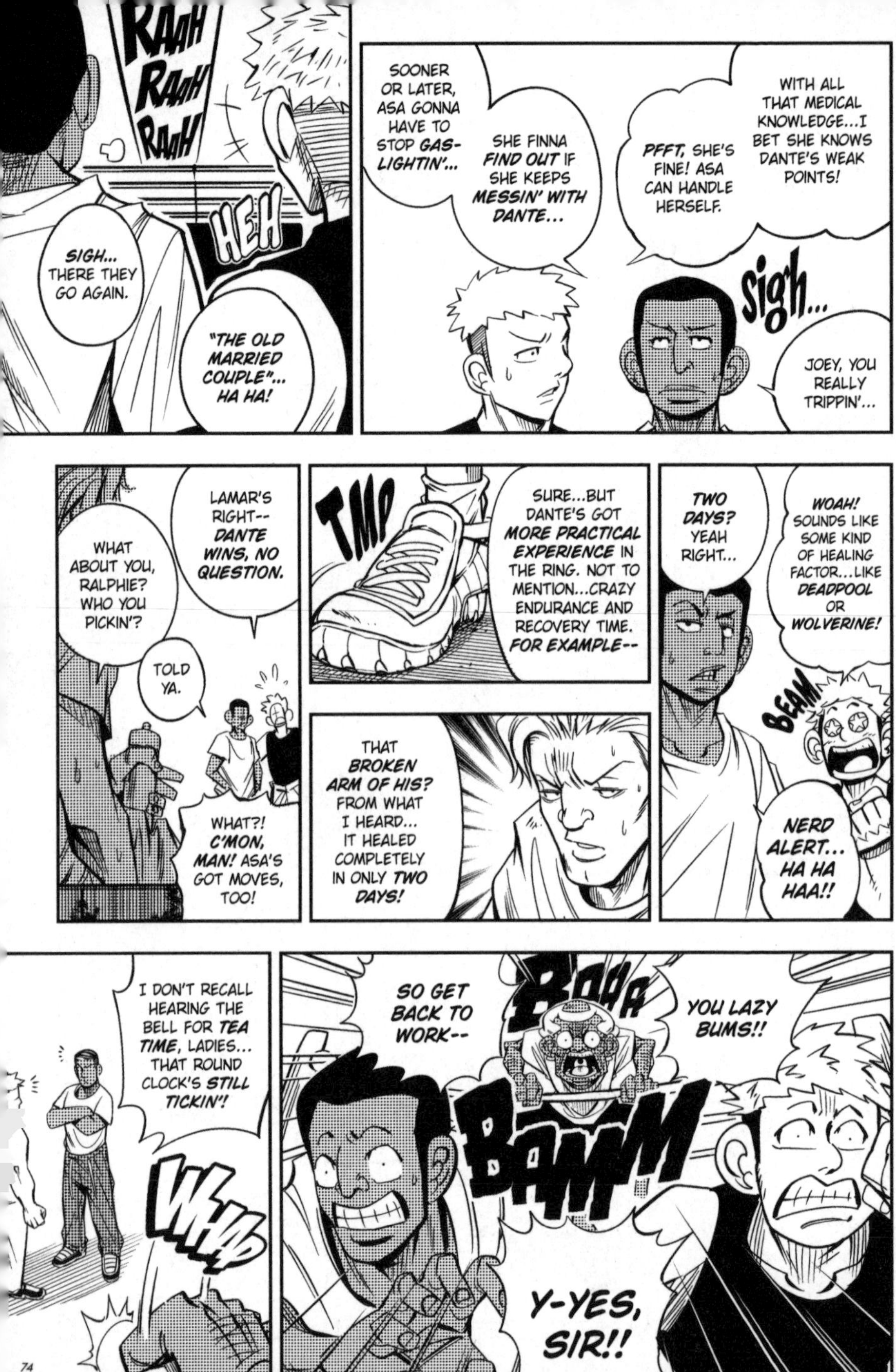
RAAH RAAH RAAH
HEH
SIGH... THERE THEY GO AGAIN.
"THE OLD MARRIED COUPLE"... HA HA!
SOONER OR LATER, ASA GONNA HAVE TO STOP GAS-LIGHTIN'...
SHE FINNA FIND OUT IF SHE KEEPS MESSIN' WITH DANTE...
PFFT, SHE'S FINE! ASA CAN HANDLE HERSELF.
WITH ALL THAT MEDICAL KNOWLEDGE...I BET SHE KNOWS DANTE'S WEAK POINTS!
Sigh...
JOEY, YOU REALLY TRIPPIN'...
WHAT ABOUT YOU, RALPHIE? WHO YOU PICKIN'?
LAMAR'S RIGHT-- DANTE WINS, NO QUESTION.
TOLD YA.
WHAT?! C'MON, MAN! ASA'S GOT MOVES, TOO!
TMP
SURE...BUT DANTE'S GOT MORE PRACTICAL EXPERIENCE IN THE RING. NOT TO MENTION...CRAZY ENDURANCE AND RECOVERY TIME. FOR EXAMPLE--
THAT BROKEN ARM OF HIS? FROM WHAT I HEARD... IT HEALED COMPLETELY IN ONLY TWO DAYS!
TWO DAYS? YEAH RIGHT...
WOAH! SOUNDS LIKE SOME KIND OF HEALING FACTOR...LIKE DEADPOOL OR WOLVERINE!
BEAM
NERD ALERT... HA HA HAA!!
I DON'T RECALL HEARING THE BELL FOR TEA TIME, LADIES... THAT ROUND CLOCK'S STILL TICKIN'!
WHAP
SO GET BACK TO WORK--
BAAA
YOU LAZY BUMS!!
BAMM
Y-YES, SIR!!

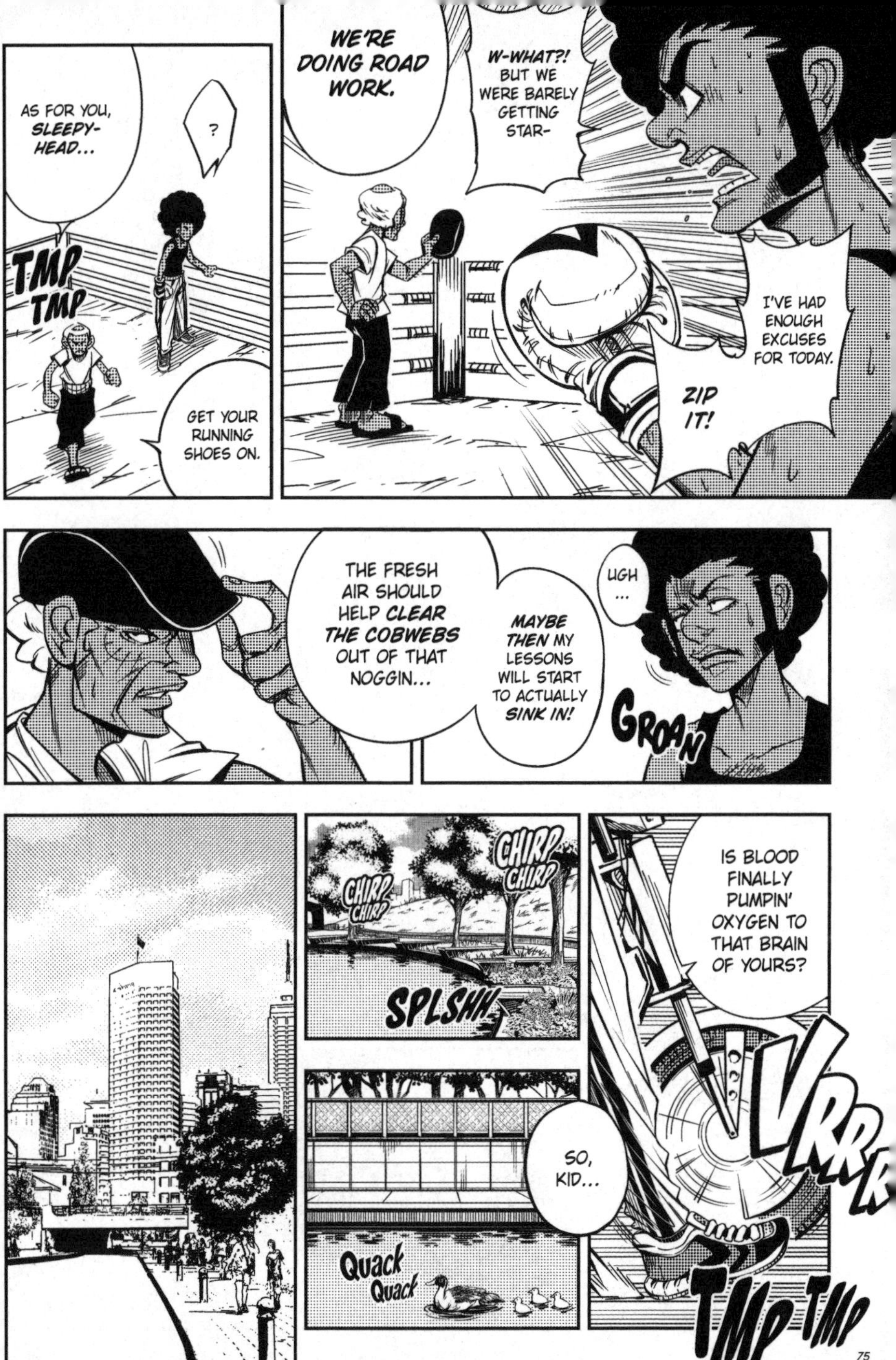
AS FOR YOU, SLEEPY-HEAD...
?
TMP TMP
GET YOUR RUNNING SHOES ON.
WE'RE DOING ROAD WORK.
W-WHAT?! BUT WE WERE BARELY GETTING STAR-
I'VE HAD ENOUGH EXCUSES FOR TODAY.
ZIP IT!
THE FRESH AIR SHOULD HELP CLEAR THE COBWEBS OUT OF THAT NOGGIN...
MAYBE THEN MY LESSONS WILL START TO ACTUALLY SINK IN!
UGH ...
GROAN
CHIRP CHIRP
CHIRP CHIRP
SPLSHH
Quack Quack
SO, KID...
IS BLOOD FINALLY PUMPIN' OXYGEN TO THAT BRAIN OF YOURS?
VRRRR
TMP TMP

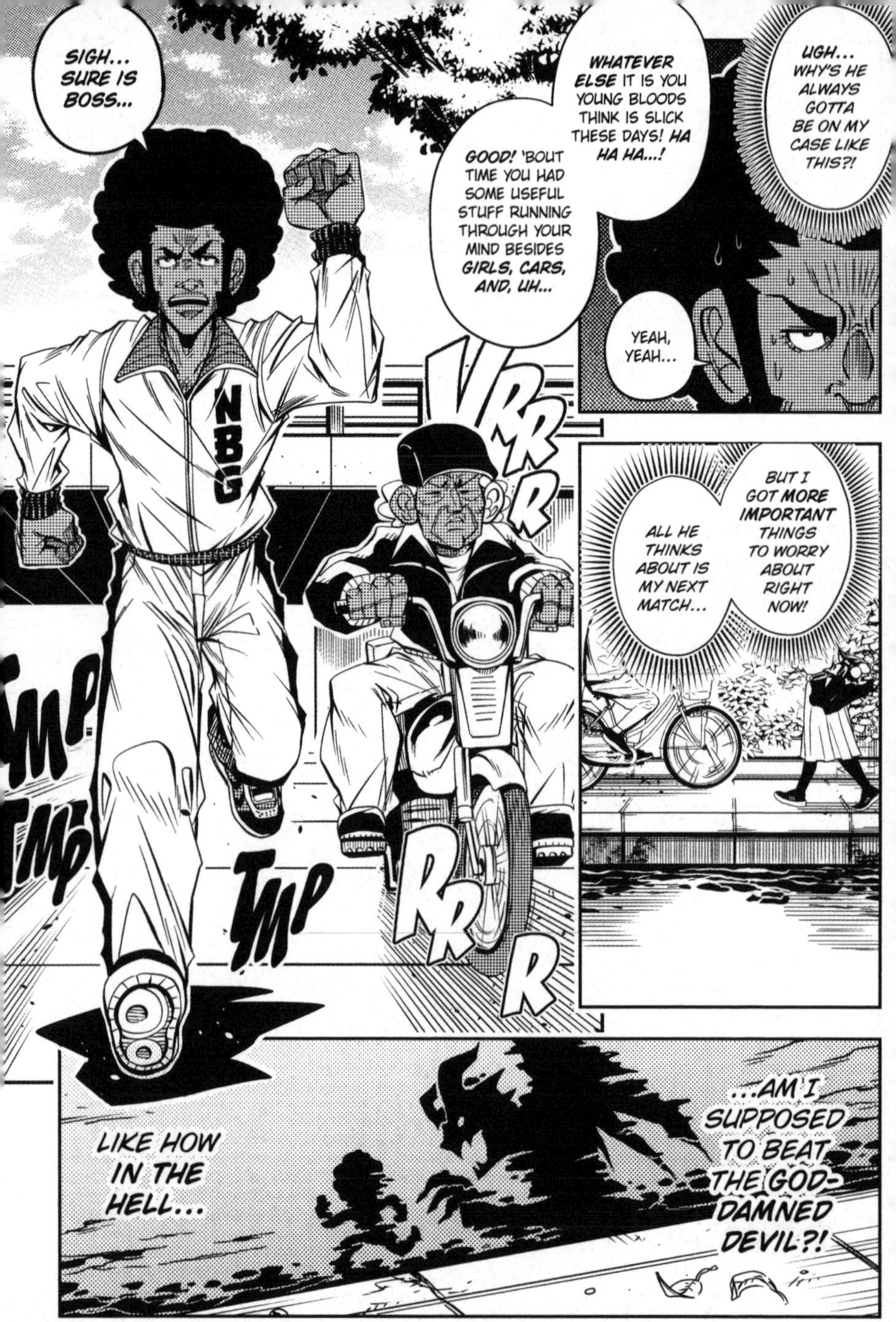
SIGH... SURE IS BOSS...
GOOD! 'BOUT TIME YOU HAD SOME USEFUL STUFF RUNNING THROUGH YOUR MIND BESIDES GIRLS, CARS, AND, UH...
WHATEVER ELSE IT IS YOU YOUNG BLOODS THINK IS SLICK THESE DAYS! HA HA HA...!
VRRRR
TMP TMP
TMP
RRR
UGH... WHY'S HE ALWAYS GOTTA BE ON MY CASE LIKE THIS?!
YEAH, YEAH...
ALL HE THINKS ABOUT IS MY NEXT MATCH...
BUT I GOT MORE IMPORTANT THINGS TO WORRY ABOUT RIGHT NOW!
LIKE HOW IN THE HELL...
...AM I SUPPOSED TO BEAT THE GOD-DAMNED DEVIL?!

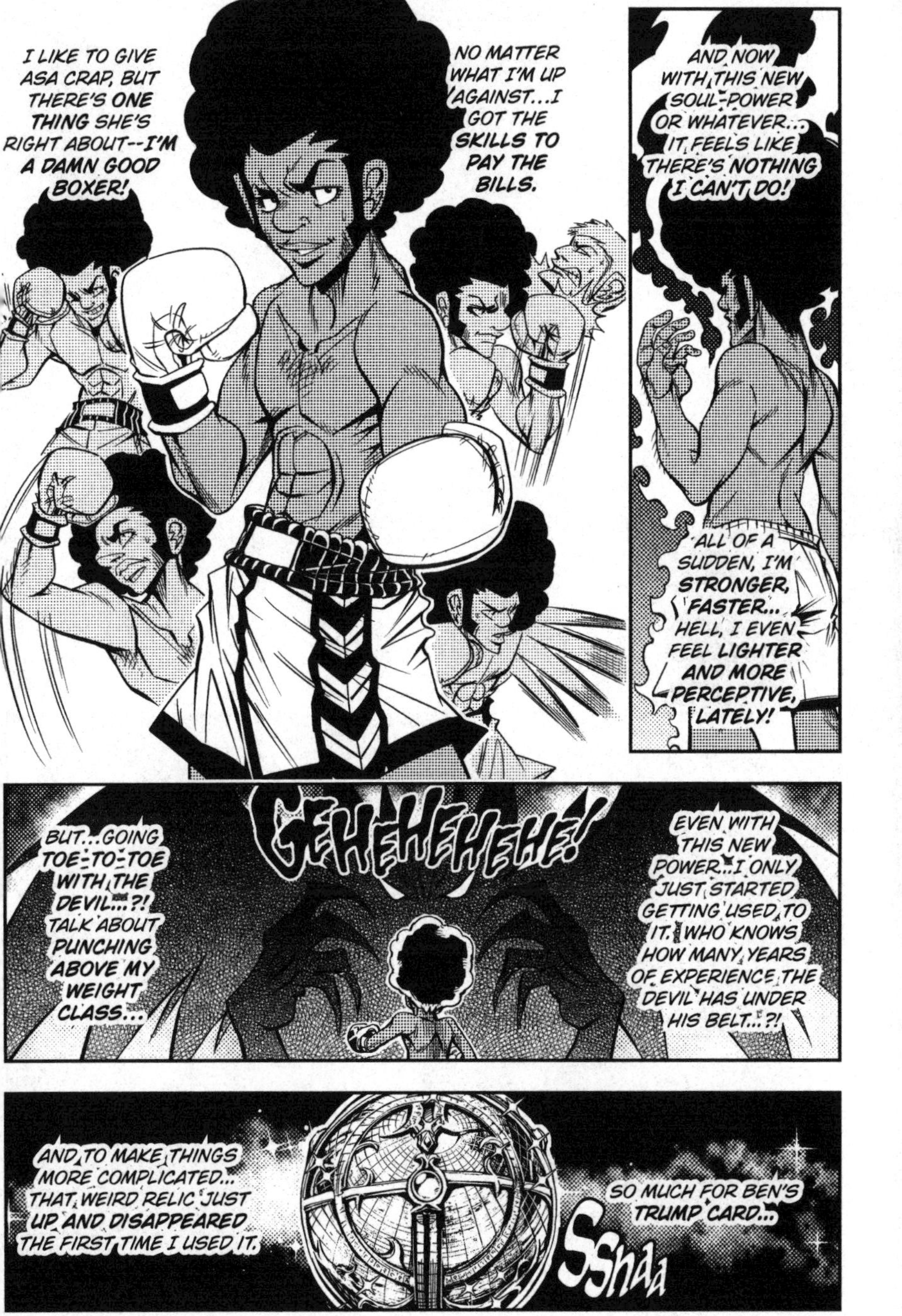
I LIKE TO GIVE ASA CRAP, BUT THERE'S ONE THING SHE'S RIGHT ABOUT--I'M A DAMN GOOD BOXER!
NO MATTER WHAT I'M UP AGAINST...I GOT THE SKILLS TO PAY THE BILLS.
AND NOW WITH THIS NEW SOUL-POWER OR WHATEVER... IT FEELS LIKE THERE'S NOTHING I CAN'T DO!
ALL OF A SUDDEN, I'M STRONGER, FASTER... HELL, I EVEN FEEL LIGHTER AND MORE PERCEPTIVE, LATELY!
GEHEHEHEHEHE!
BUT...GOING TOE-TO-TOE WITH THE DEVIL...?! TALK ABOUT PUNCHING ABOVE MY WEIGHT CLASS...
EVEN WITH THIS NEW POWER...I ONLY JUST STARTED GETTING USED TO IT. WHO KNOWS HOW MANY YEARS OF EXPERIENCE THE DEVIL HAS UNDER HIS BELT...?!
AND TO MAKE THINGS MORE COMPLICATED... THAT WEIRD RELIC JUST UP AND DISAPPEARED THE FIRST TIME I USED IT.
SO MUCH FOR BEN'S TRUMP CARD...
SSHAA

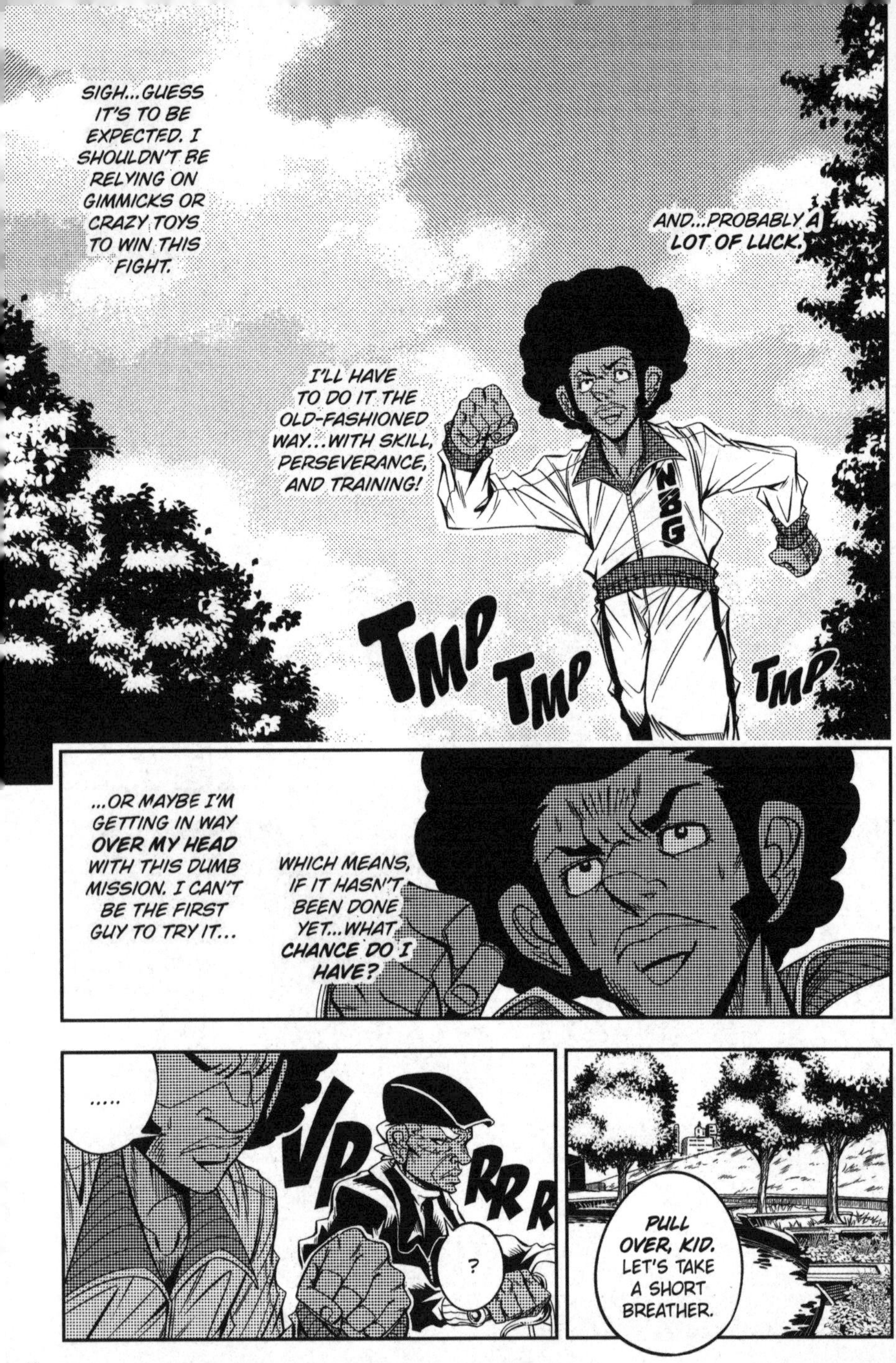
SIGH...GUESS IT'S TO BE EXPECTED. I SHOULDN'T BE RELYING ON GIMMICKS OR CRAZY TOYS TO WIN THIS FIGHT.
I'LL HAVE TO DO IT THE OLD-FASHIONED WAY...WITH SKILL, PERSEVERANCE, AND TRAINING!
AND...PROBABLY A LOT OF LUCK.
NBG
TMP TMP TMP
...OR MAYBE I'M GETTING IN WAY **OVER MY HEAD** WITH THIS DUMB MISSION. I CAN'T BE THE FIRST GUY TO TRY IT...
WHICH MEANS, IF IT HASN'T BEEN DONE YET...WHAT **CHANCE** DO I HAVE?
.....
VRRRR
?
PULL OVER, KID. LET'S TAKE A SHORT BREATHER.

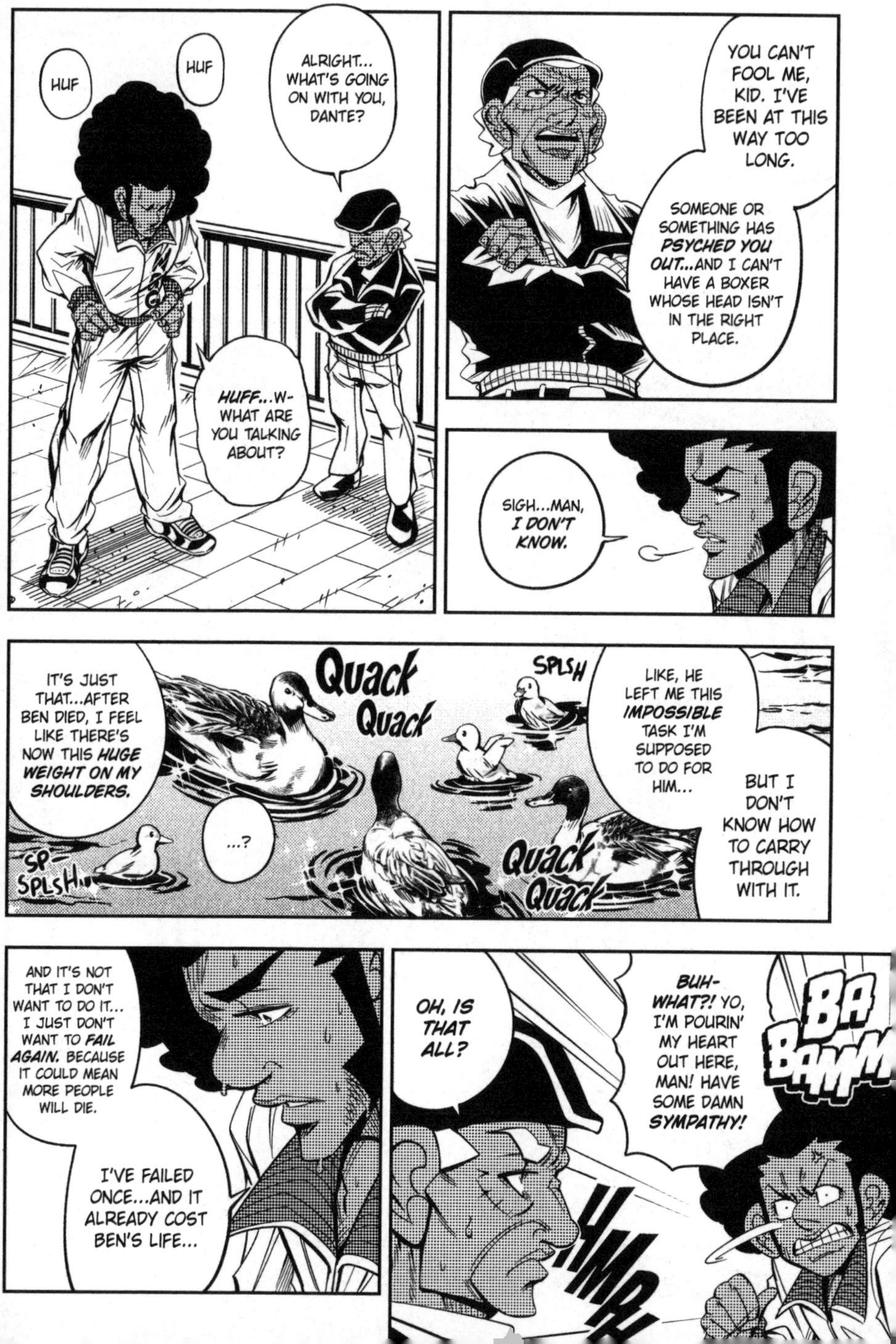
HUF
HUF
ALRIGHT... WHAT'S GOING ON WITH YOU, DANTE?
HUFF...W-WHAT ARE YOU TALKING ABOUT?
YOU CAN'T FOOL ME, KID. I'VE BEEN AT THIS WAY TOO LONG.
SOMEONE OR SOMETHING HAS PSYCHED YOU OUT...AND I CAN'T HAVE A BOXER WHOSE HEAD ISN'T IN THE RIGHT PLACE.
SIGH...MAN, I DON'T KNOW.
IT'S JUST THAT...AFTER BEN DIED, I FEEL LIKE THERE'S NOW THIS HUGE WEIGHT ON MY SHOULDERS.
Quack Quack
SPLSH
...?
SP-SPLSH
LIKE, HE LEFT ME THIS IMPOSSIBLE TASK I'M SUPPOSED TO DO FOR HIM...
BUT I DON'T KNOW HOW TO CARRY THROUGH WITH IT.
Quack Quack
AND IT'S NOT THAT I DON'T WANT TO DO IT... I JUST DON'T WANT TO FAIL AGAIN. BECAUSE IT COULD MEAN MORE PEOPLE WILL DIE.
I'VE FAILED ONCE...AND IT ALREADY COST BEN'S LIFE...
OH, IS THAT ALL?
BUH-WHAT?! YO, I'M POURIN' MY HEART OUT HERE, MAN! HAVE SOME DAMN SYMPATHY!

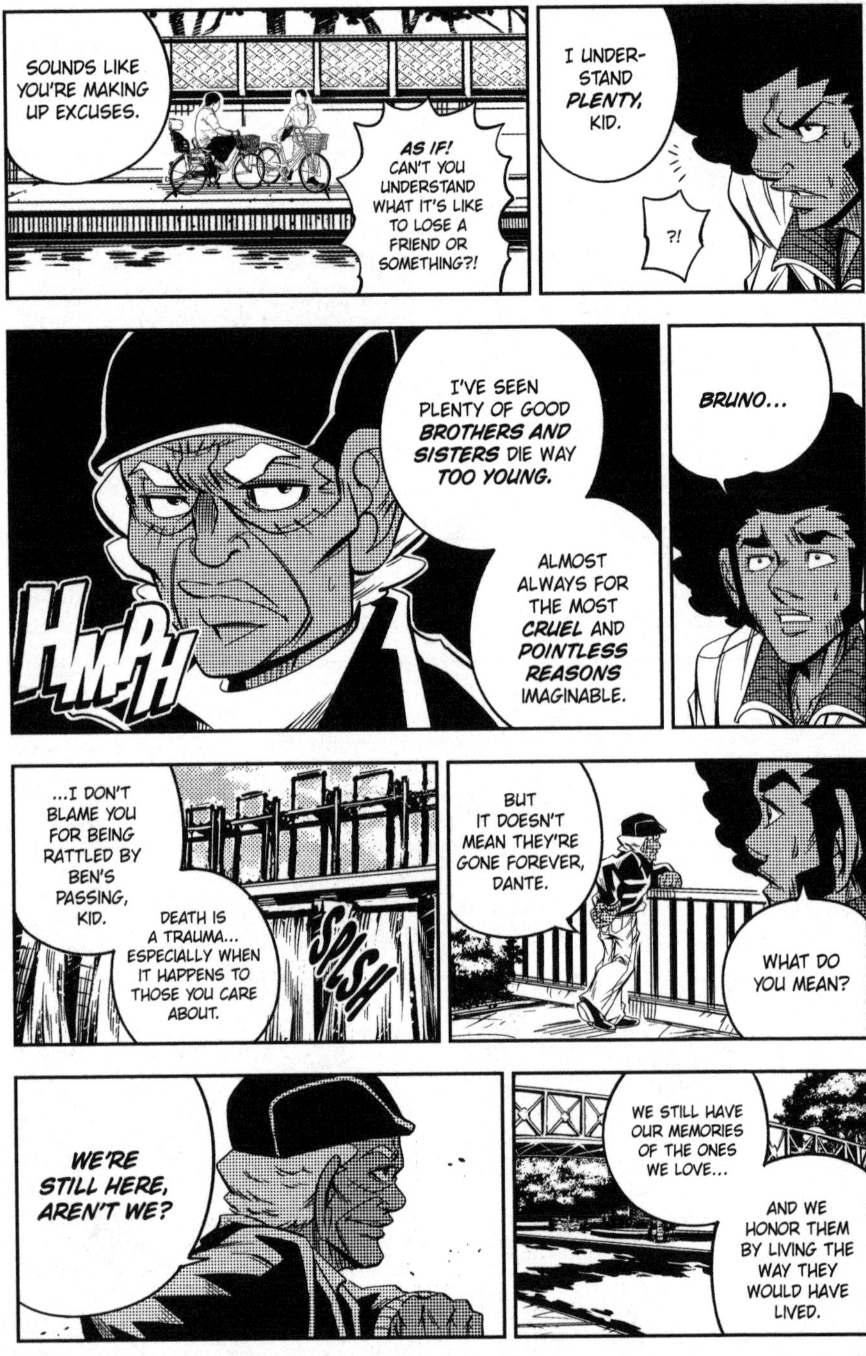
SOUNDS LIKE YOU'RE MAKING UP EXCUSES.
AS IF! CAN'T YOU UNDERSTAND WHAT IT'S LIKE TO LOSE A FRIEND OR SOMETHING?!
I UNDER-STAND PLENTY, KID.
?!
HMPH
I'VE SEEN PLENTY OF GOOD BROTHERS AND SISTERS DIE WAY TOO YOUNG.
ALMOST ALWAYS FOR THE MOST CRUEL AND POINTLESS REASONS IMAGINABLE.
BRUNO...
...I DON'T BLAME YOU FOR BEING RATTLED BY BEN'S PASSING, KID.
DEATH IS A TRAUMA... ESPECIALLY WHEN IT HAPPENS TO THOSE YOU CARE ABOUT.
SPLSH
BUT IT DOESN'T MEAN THEY'RE GONE FOREVER, DANTE.
WHAT DO YOU MEAN?
WE'RE STILL HERE, AREN'T WE?
WE STILL HAVE OUR MEMORIES OF THE ONES WE LOVE...
AND WE HONOR THEM BY LIVING THE WAY THEY WOULD HAVE LIVED.

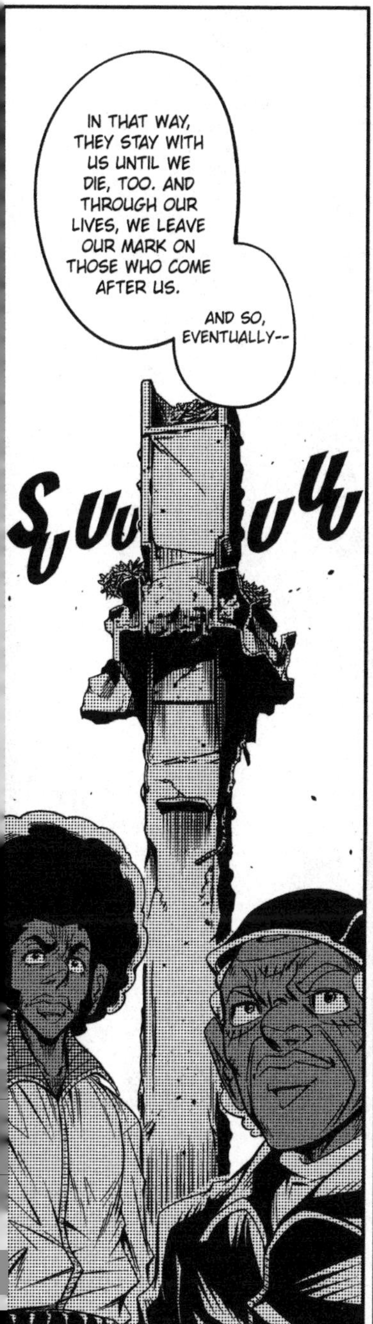
IN THAT WAY, THEY STAY WITH US UNTIL WE DIE, TOO. AND THROUGH OUR LIVES, WE LEAVE OUR MARK ON THOSE WHO COME AFTER US.
AND SO, EVENTUALLY--
SUUUUUU

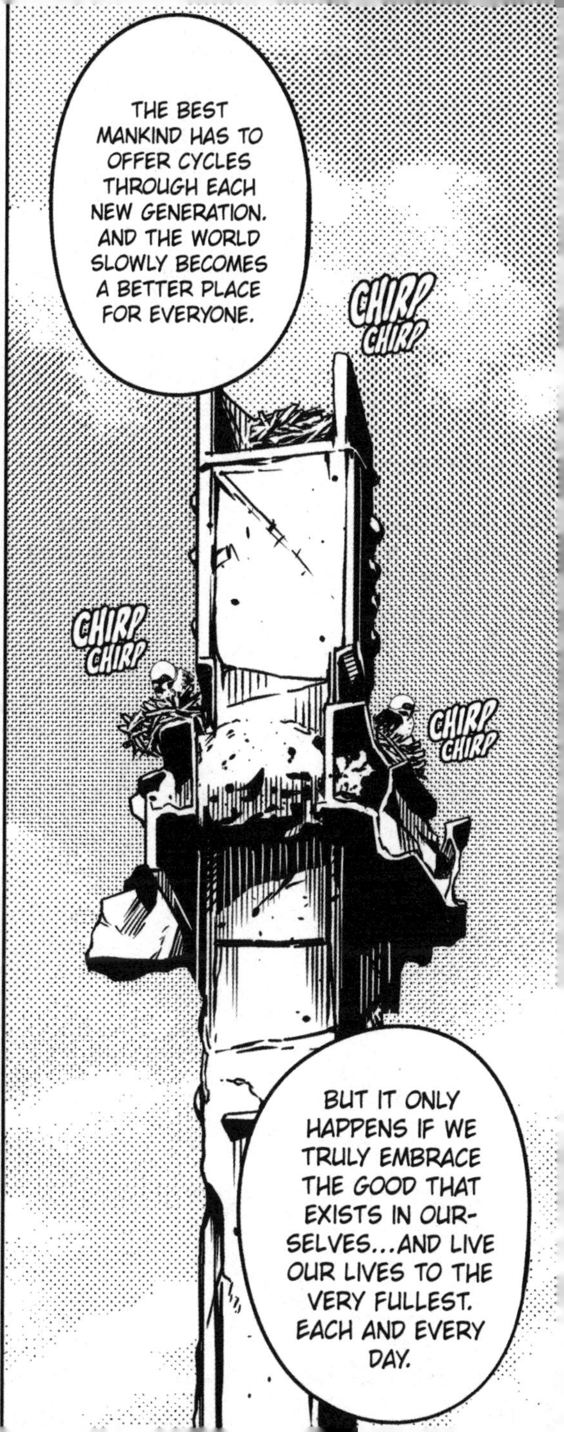
THE BEST MANKIND HAS TO OFFER CYCLES THROUGH EACH NEW GENERATION. AND THE WORLD SLOWLY BECOMES A BETTER PLACE FOR EVERYONE.
CHIRP CHIRP
CHIRP CHIRP
CHIRP CHIRP
BUT IT ONLY HAPPENS IF WE TRULY EMBRACE THE GOOD THAT EXISTS IN OUR-SELVES...AND LIVE OUR LIVES TO THE VERY FULLEST. EACH AND EVERY DAY.

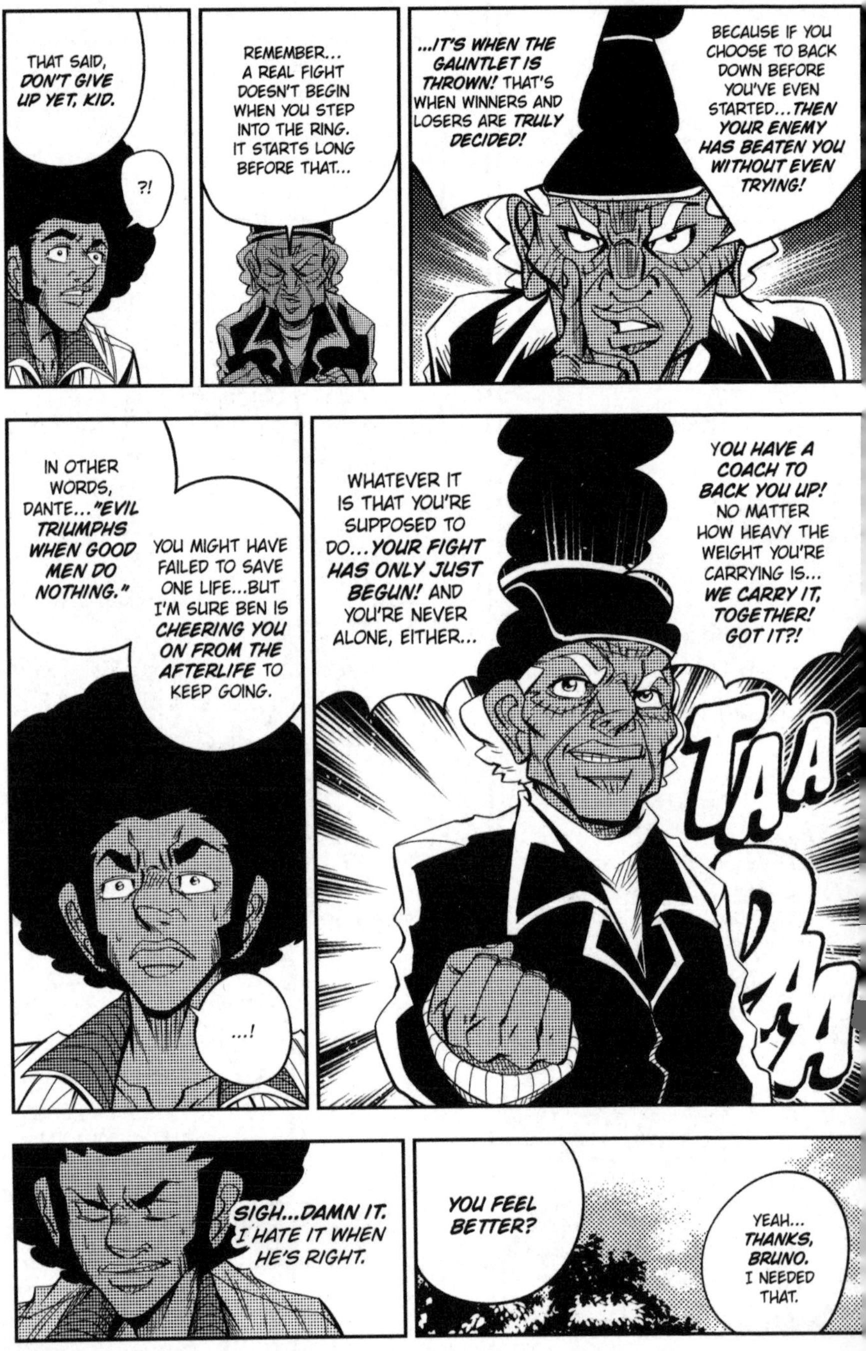
THAT SAID, DON'T GIVE UP YET, KID.
?!
REMEMBER... A REAL FIGHT DOESN'T BEGIN WHEN YOU STEP INTO THE RING. IT STARTS LONG BEFORE THAT...
...IT'S WHEN THE GAUNTLET IS THROWN! THAT'S WHEN WINNERS AND LOSERS ARE TRULY DECIDED!
BECAUSE IF YOU CHOOSE TO BACK DOWN BEFORE YOU'VE EVEN STARTED...THEN YOUR ENEMY HAS BEATEN YOU WITHOUT EVEN TRYING!
IN OTHER WORDS, DANTE..."EVIL TRIUMPHS WHEN GOOD MEN DO NOTHING."
YOU MIGHT HAVE FAILED TO SAVE ONE LIFE...BUT I'M SURE BEN IS CHEERING YOU ON FROM THE AFTERLIFE TO KEEP GOING.
...!
WHATEVER IT IS THAT YOU'RE SUPPOSED TO DO...YOUR FIGHT HAS ONLY JUST BEGUN! AND YOU'RE NEVER ALONE, EITHER...
YOU HAVE A COACH TO BACK YOU UP! NO MATTER HOW HEAVY THE WEIGHT YOU'RE CARRYING IS... WE CARRY IT, TOGETHER! GOT IT?!
TAA DAA
SIGH...DAMN IT. I HATE IT WHEN HE'S RIGHT.
YOU FEEL BETTER?
YEAH... THANKS, BRUNO. I NEEDED THAT.

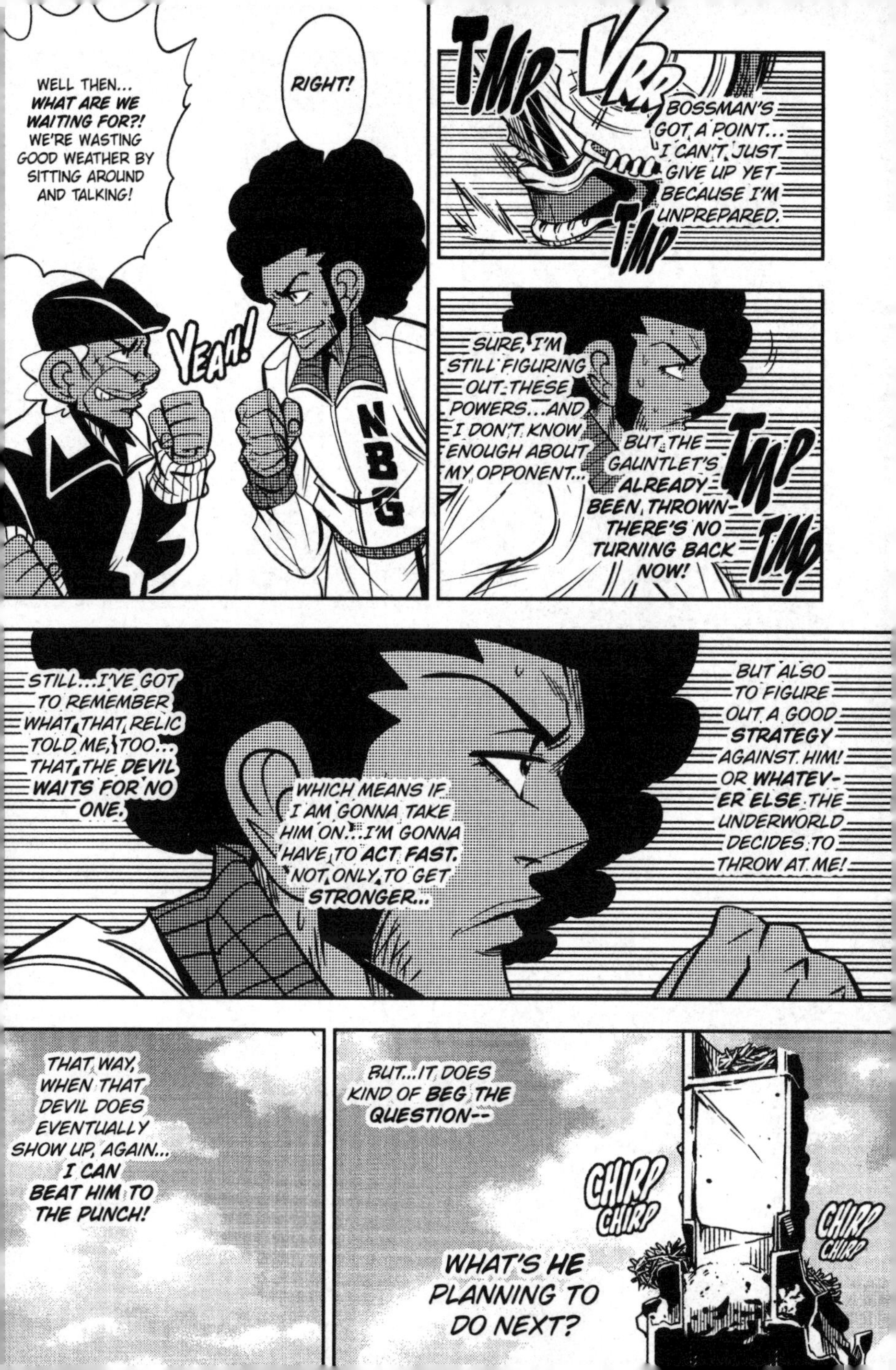
WELL THEN... WHAT ARE WE WAITING FOR?! WE'RE WASTING GOOD WEATHER BY SITTING AROUND AND TALKING!
RIGHT!
YEAH!
NBG
TMP
VRR
BOSSMAN'S GOT A POINT... I CAN'T JUST GIVE UP YET BECAUSE I'M UNPREPARED.
TMP
SURE, I'M STILL FIGURING OUT THESE POWERS...AND I DON'T KNOW ENOUGH ABOUT MY OPPONENT...
BUT THE GAUNTLET'S ALREADY BEEN THROWN-THERE'S NO TURNING BACK NOW!
TMP
TMP
STILL...I'VE GOT TO REMEMBER WHAT THAT RELIC TOLD ME, TOO... THAT THE DEVIL WAITS FOR NO ONE.
WHICH MEANS IF I AM GONNA TAKE HIM ON...I'M GONNA HAVE TO ACT FAST. NOT ONLY TO GET STRONGER...
BUT ALSO TO FIGURE OUT A GOOD STRATEGY AGAINST HIM! OR WHATEVER ELSE THE UNDERWORLD DECIDES TO THROW AT ME!
THAT WAY, WHEN THAT DEVIL DOES EVENTUALLY SHOW UP, AGAIN... I CAN BEAT HIM TO THE PUNCH!
BUT...IT DOES KIND OF BEG THE QUESTION--
CHIRP CHIRP
CHIRP CHIRP
WHAT'S HE PLANNING TO DO NEXT?

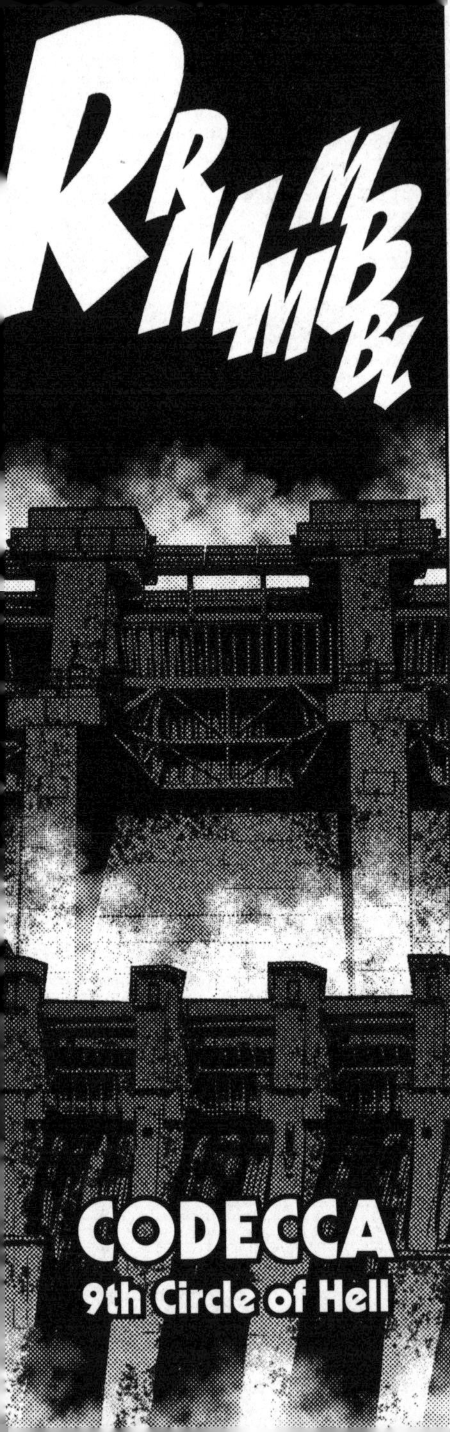
CODECCA
9th Circle of Hell

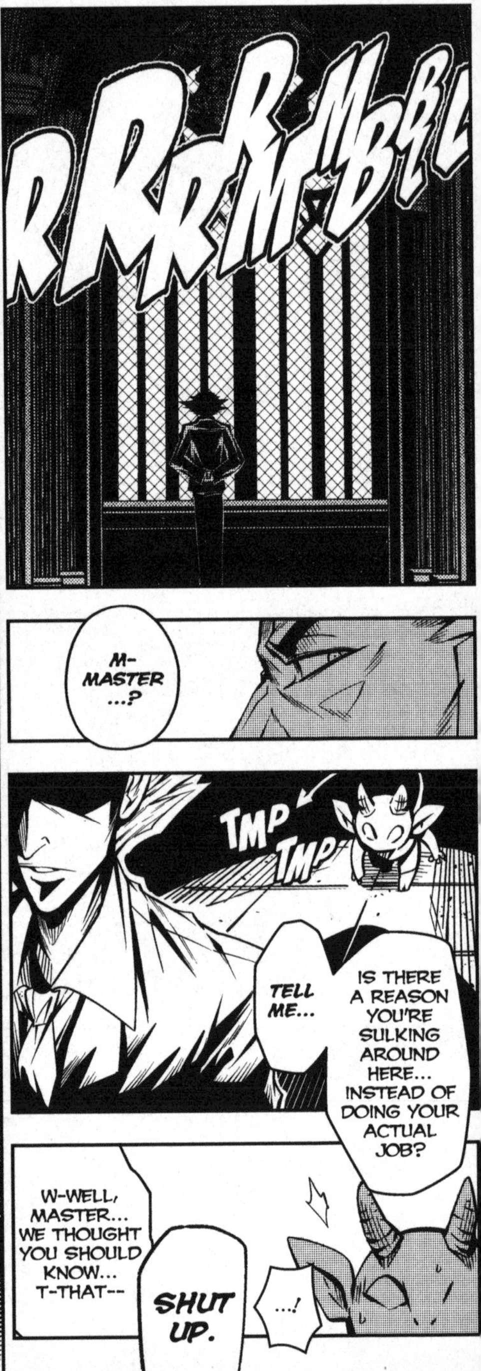
M-MASTER ...?
TMP TMP
TELL ME...
IS THERE A REASON YOU'RE SULKING AROUND HERE... INSTEAD OF DOING YOUR ACTUAL JOB?
W-WELL, MASTER... WE THOUGHT YOU SHOULD KNOW... T-THAT--
SHUT UP.
...!

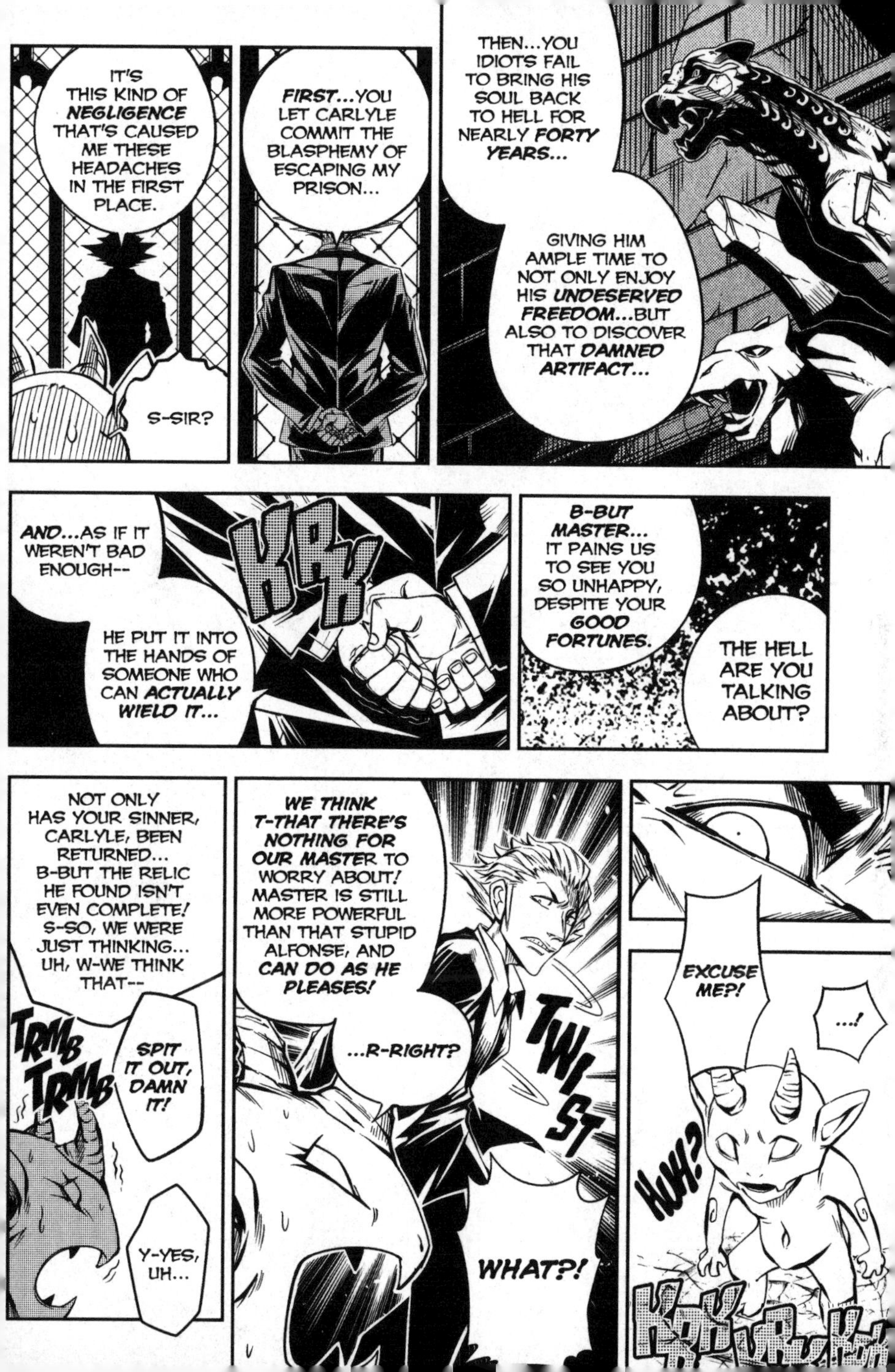
IT'S THIS KIND OF NEGLIGENCE THAT'S CAUSED ME THESE HEADACHES IN THE FIRST PLACE.
S-SIR?
FIRST...YOU LET CARLYLE COMMIT THE BLASPHEMY OF ESCAPING MY PRISON...
THEN...YOU IDIOTS FAIL TO BRING HIS SOUL BACK TO HELL FOR NEARLY FORTY YEARS...
GIVING HIM AMPLE TIME TO NOT ONLY ENJOY HIS UNDESERVED FREEDOM...BUT ALSO TO DISCOVER THAT DAMNED ARTIFACT...
AND...AS IF IT WEREN'T BAD ENOUGH--
KRK
HE PUT IT INTO THE HANDS OF SOMEONE WHO CAN ACTUALLY WIELD IT...
B-BUT MASTER... IT PAINS US TO SEE YOU SO UNHAPPY, DESPITE YOUR GOOD FORTUNES.
THE HELL ARE YOU TALKING ABOUT?
NOT ONLY HAS YOUR SINNER, CARLYLE, BEEN RETURNED... B-BUT THE RELIC HE FOUND ISN'T EVEN COMPLETE! S-SO, WE WERE JUST THINKING... UH, W-WE THINK THAT--
TRMB TRMB
SPIT IT OUT, DAMN IT!
Y-YES, UH...
WE THINK T-THAT THERE'S NOTHING FOR OUR MASTER TO WORRY ABOUT! MASTER IS STILL MORE POWERFUL THAN THAT STUPID ALFONSE, AND CAN DO AS HE PLEASES!
...R-RIGHT?
TWIST
WHAT?!
EXCUSE ME?!
...!
HUH?

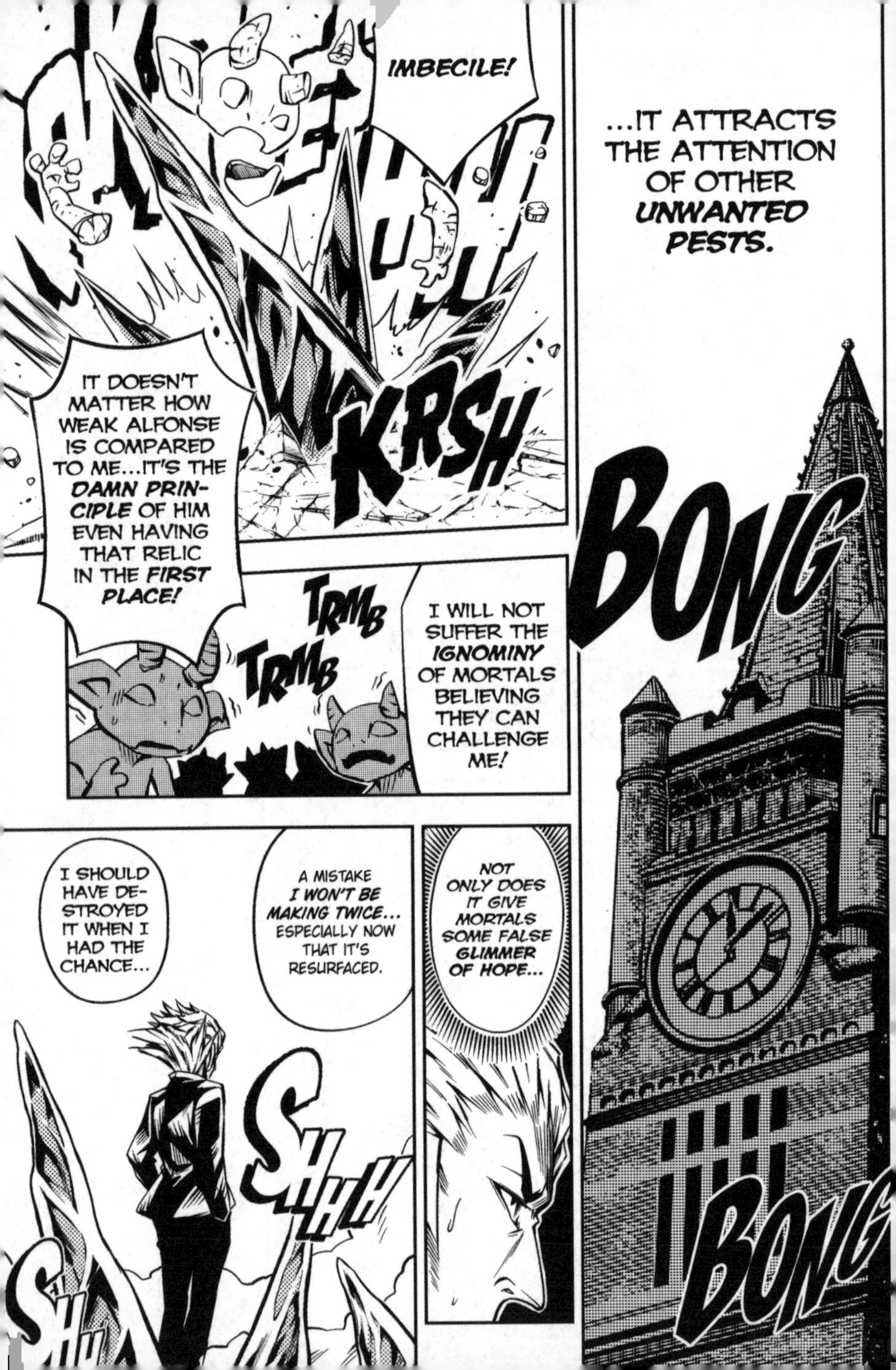
IMBECILE!
KRSH
IT DOESN'T MATTER HOW WEAK ALFONSE IS COMPARED TO ME...IT'S THE DAMN PRINCIPLE OF HIM EVEN HAVING THAT RELIC IN THE FIRST PLACE!
TRMB
TRMB
I WILL NOT SUFFER THE IGNOMINY OF MORTALS BELIEVING THEY CAN CHALLENGE ME!
I SHOULD HAVE DESTROYED IT WHEN I HAD THE CHANCE...
A MISTAKE I WON'T BE MAKING TWICE... ESPECIALLY NOW THAT IT'S RESURFACED.
NOT ONLY DOES IT GIVE MORTALS SOME FALSE GLIMMER OF HOPE...
...IT ATTRACTS THE ATTENTION OF OTHER UNWANTED PESTS.
BONG
BONG

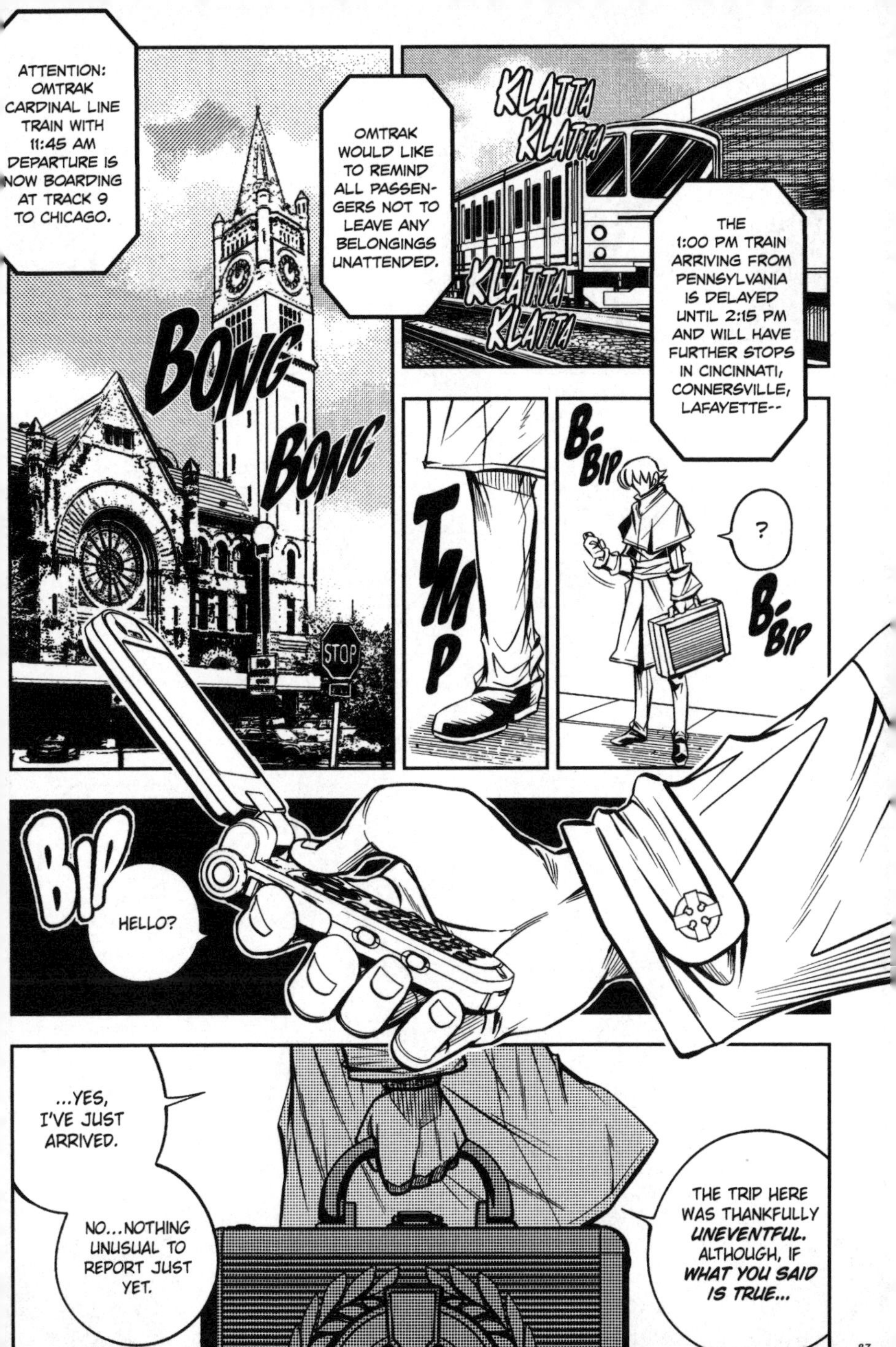

ATTENTION: OMTRAK CARDINAL LINE TRAIN WITH 11:45 AM DEPARTURE IS NOW BOARDING AT TRACK 9 TO CHICAGO.
OMTRAK WOULD LIKE TO REMIND ALL PASSEN-GERS NOT TO LEAVE ANY BELONGINGS UNATTENDED.
BONG
BONG
STOP
KLATTA KLATTA
KLATTA KLATTA
THE 1:00 PM TRAIN ARRIVING FROM PENNSYLVANIA IS DELAYED UNTIL 2:15 PM AND WILL HAVE FURTHER STOPS IN CINCINNATI, CONNERSVILLE, LAFAYETTE--
TMP
B-BIP
?
B-BIP
BIP
HELLO?
...YES, I'VE JUST ARRIVED.
NO...NOTHING UNUSUAL TO REPORT JUST YET.
THE TRIP HERE WAS THANKFULLY ***UNEVENTFUL.*** ALTHOUGH, IF ***WHAT YOU SAID IS TRUE...***

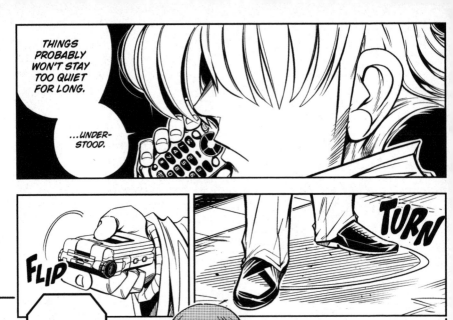

THINGS PROBABLY WON'T STAY TOO QUIET FOR LONG.

...UNDER-STOOD.

FLIP

TURN

FINAL CALL FOR THE 12:00 PM SERVICE TO NEW YORK ON PLATFORM 5. FINAL CALL FOR 12:00 PM TO NEW YORK.

PLEASE WATCH YOUR STEP WHEN APPROACHING PLATFORMS FOR ARRIVING OR DEPARTING TRAINS, AND THANK YOU FOR TRAVELING WITH OMTRAK--

TMP

TMP

SOULBEAT

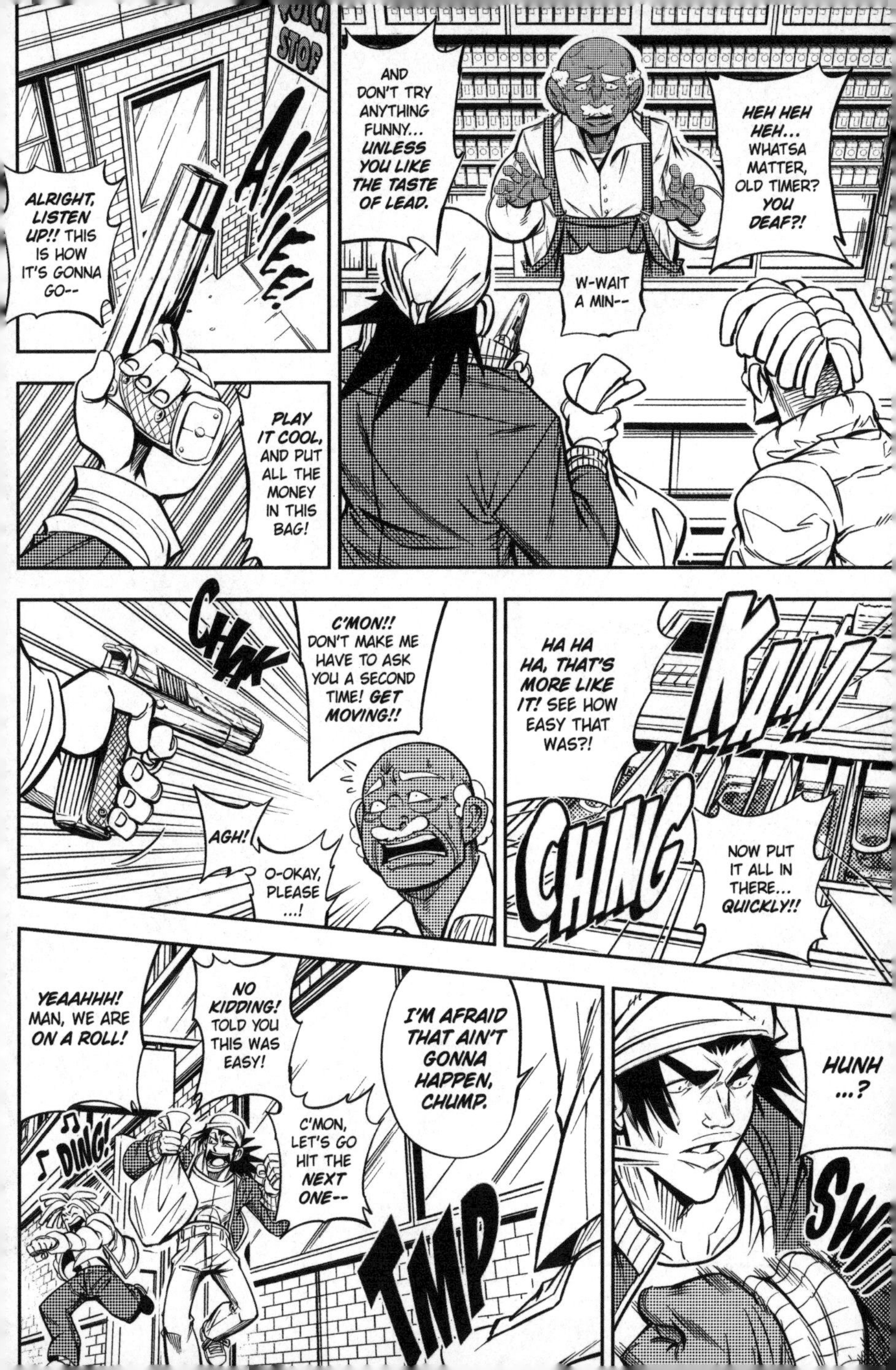
ALRIGHT, LISTEN UP!! THIS IS HOW IT'S GONNA GO--
PLAY IT COOL, AND PUT ALL THE MONEY IN THIS BAG!
AND DON'T TRY ANYTHING FUNNY... UNLESS YOU LIKE THE TASTE OF LEAD.
W-WAIT A MIN--
HEH HEH HEH... WHATSA MATTER, OLD TIMER? YOU DEAF?!
C'MON!! DON'T MAKE ME HAVE TO ASK YOU A SECOND TIME! GET MOVING!!
AGH!
O-OKAY, PLEASE ...!
HA HA HA, THAT'S MORE LIKE IT! SEE HOW EASY THAT WAS?!
CHING
NOW PUT IT ALL IN THERE... QUICKLY!!
YEAAHHH! MAN, WE ARE ON A ROLL!
NO KIDDING! TOLD YOU THIS WAS EASY!
DING!
C'MON, LET'S GO HIT THE NEXT ONE--
I'M AFRAID THAT AIN'T GONNA HAPPEN, CHUMP.
TMP
HUNH ...?

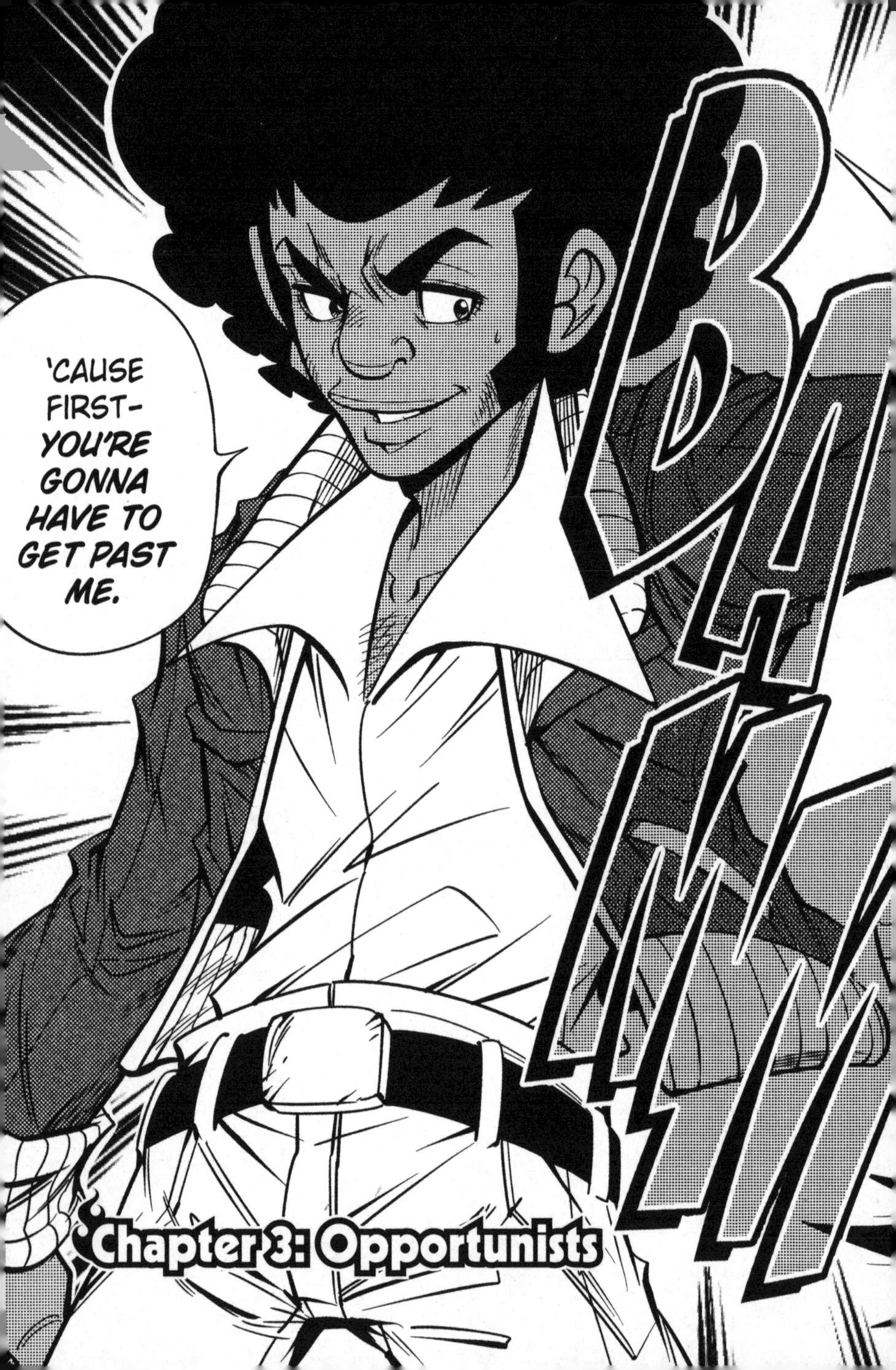
'CAUSE FIRST- YOU'RE GONNA HAVE TO GET PAST ME.

Chapter 3: Opportunists

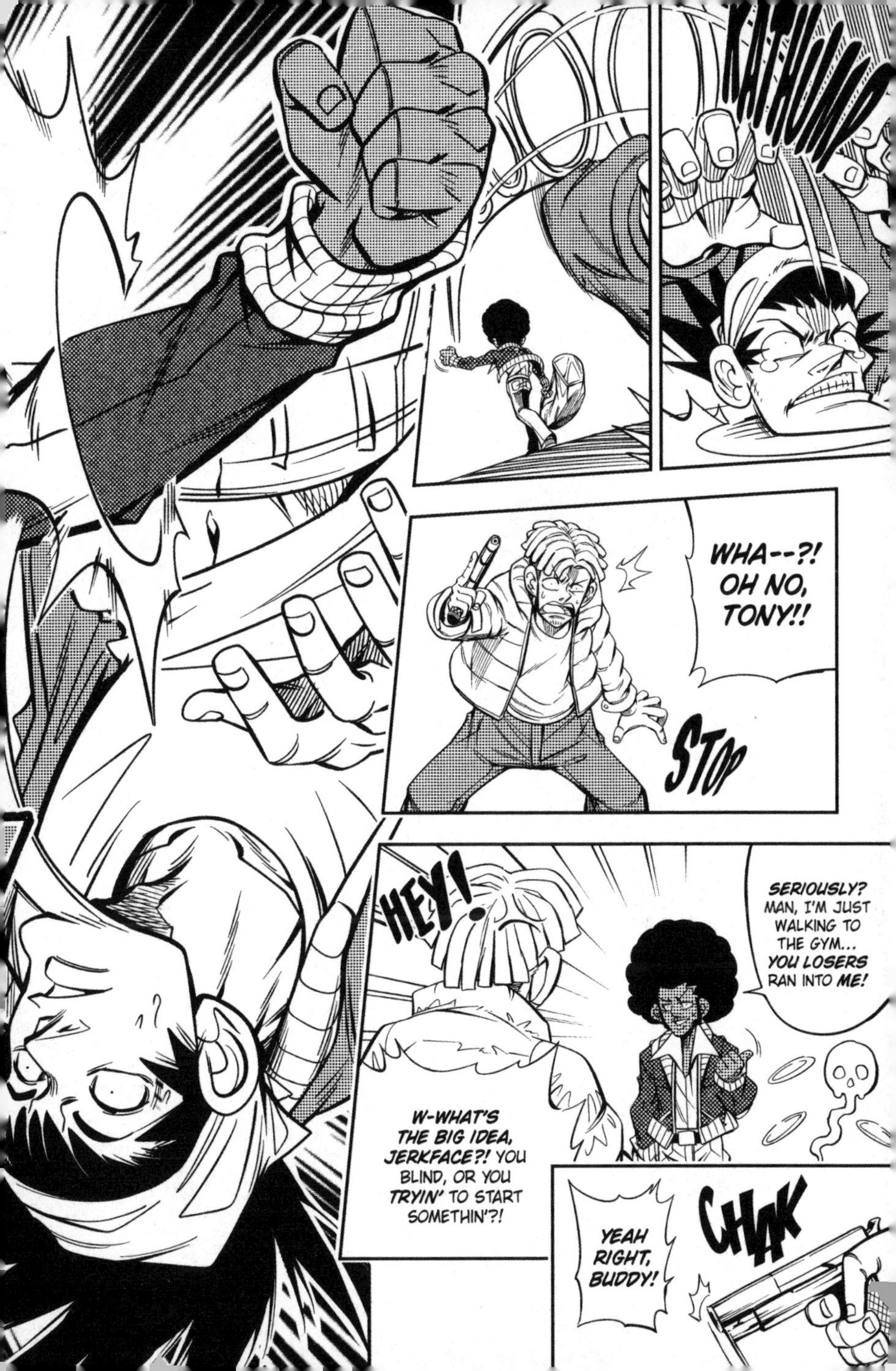
KATHUMP
WHA--?! OH NO, TONY!!
STOP
HEY!
W-WHAT'S THE BIG IDEA, JERKFACE?! YOU BLIND, OR YOU TRYIN' TO START SOMETHIN'?!
SERIOUSLY? MAN, I'M JUST WALKING TO THE GYM... YOU LOSERS RAN INTO ME!
YEAH RIGHT, BUDDY!
CHAK

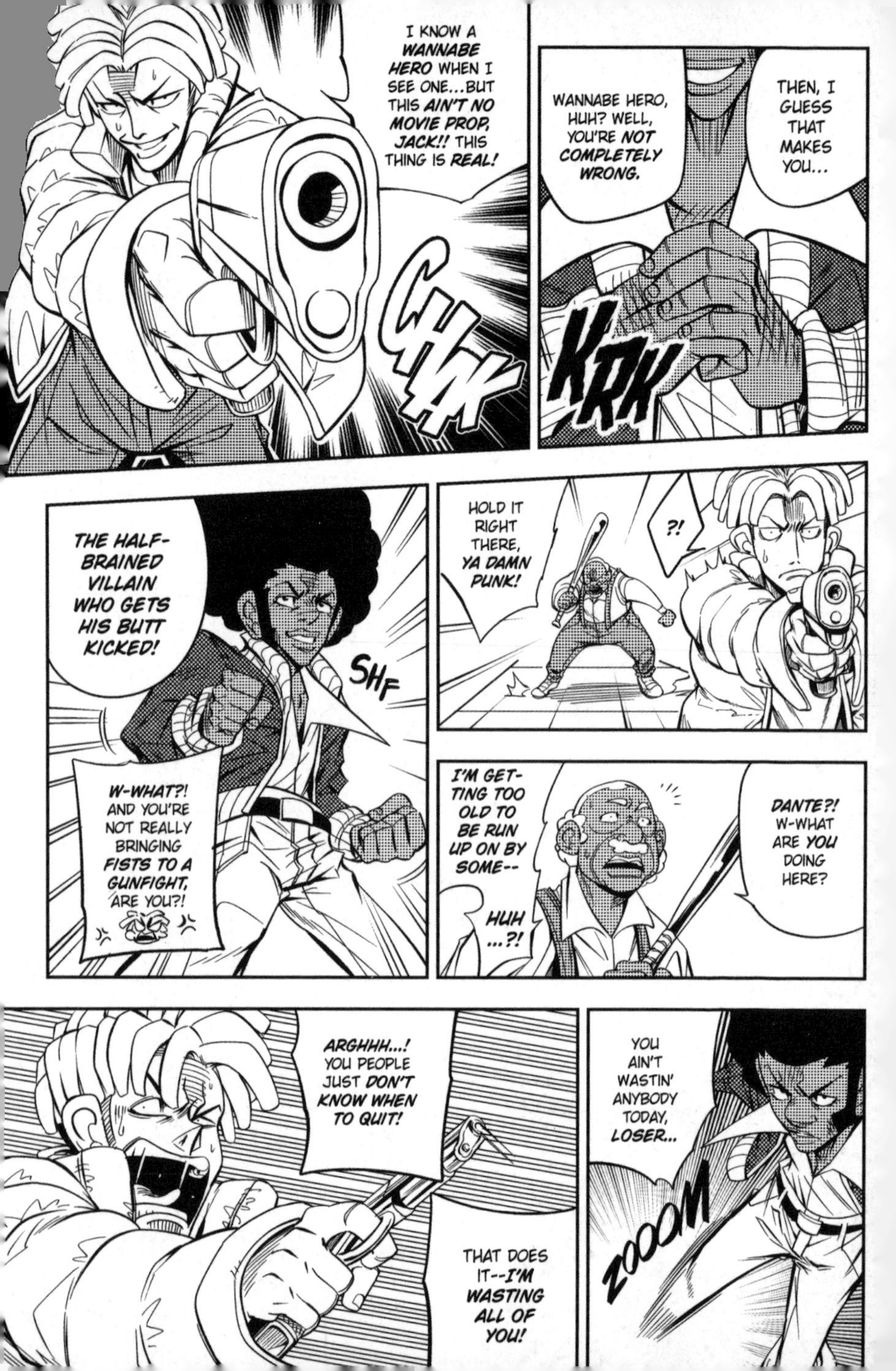

I KNOW A WANNABE HERO WHEN I SEE ONE...BUT THIS AIN'T NO MOVIE PROP, JACK!! THIS THING IS REAL!
CHAK
WANNABE HERO, HUH? WELL, YOU'RE NOT COMPLETELY WRONG.
THEN, I GUESS THAT MAKES YOU...
KRK
THE HALF-BRAINED VILLAIN WHO GETS HIS BUTT KICKED!
SHF
W-WHAT?! AND YOU'RE NOT REALLY BRINGING FISTS TO A GUNFIGHT, ARE YOU?!
HOLD IT RIGHT THERE, YA DAMN PUNK!
?!
I'M GETTING TOO OLD TO BE RUN UP ON BY SOME--
HUH ...?!
DANTE?! W-WHAT ARE YOU DOING HERE?
ARGHHH...! YOU PEOPLE JUST DON'T KNOW WHEN TO QUIT!
THAT DOES IT--I'M WASTING ALL OF YOU!
YOU AIN'T WASTIN' ANYBODY TODAY, LOSER...
ZOOOM

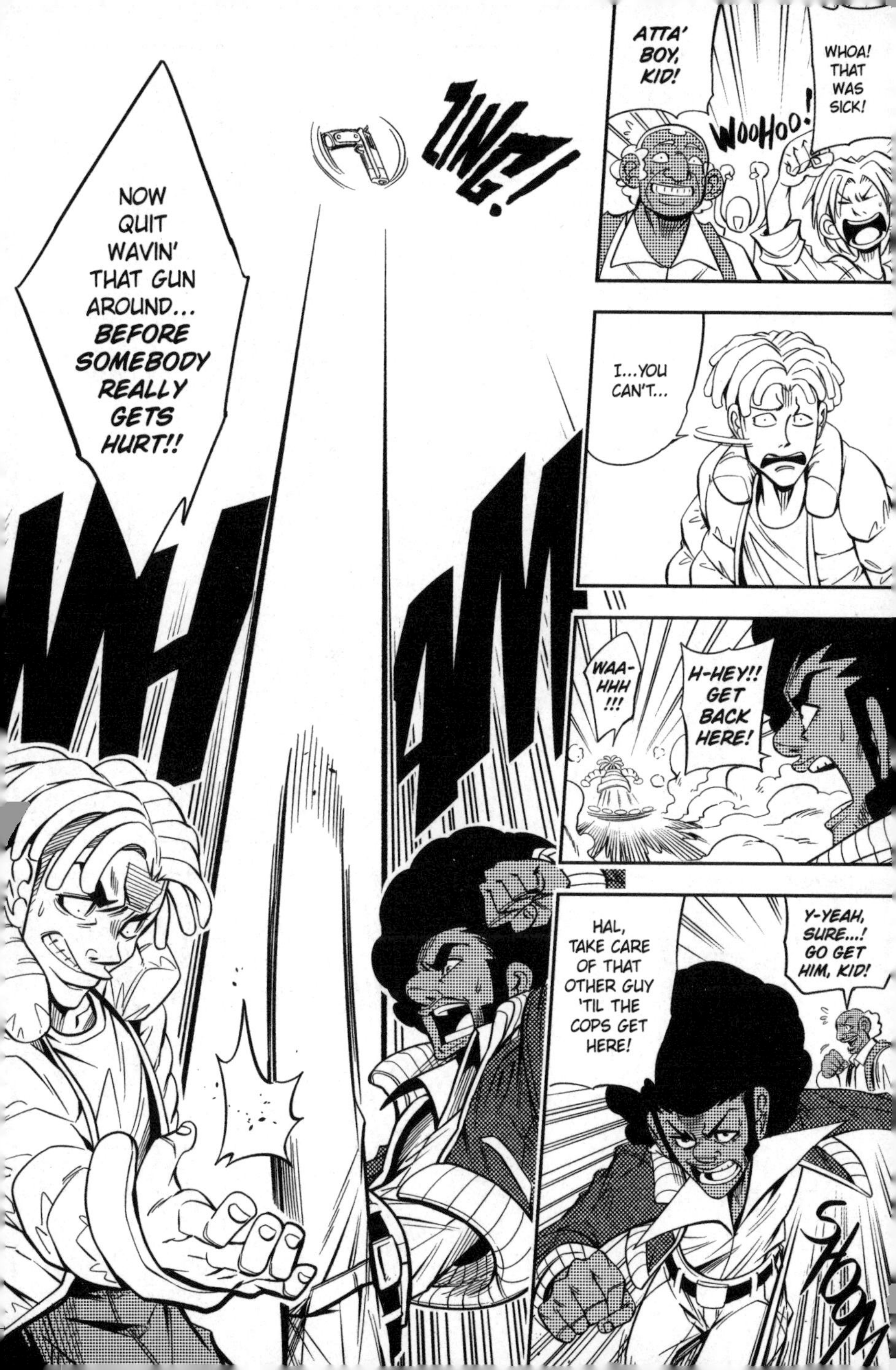
NOW QUIT WAVIN' THAT GUN AROUND... BEFORE SOMEBODY REALLY GETS HURT!!
ZING!
ATTA' BOY, KID!
WOOHOO!
WHOA! THAT WAS SICK!
I...YOU CAN'T...
WAA-HHH!!!
H-HEY!! GET BACK HERE!
HAL, TAKE CARE OF THAT OTHER GUY 'TIL THE COPS GET HERE!
Y-YEAH, SURE...! GO GET HIM, KID!
SHOOM

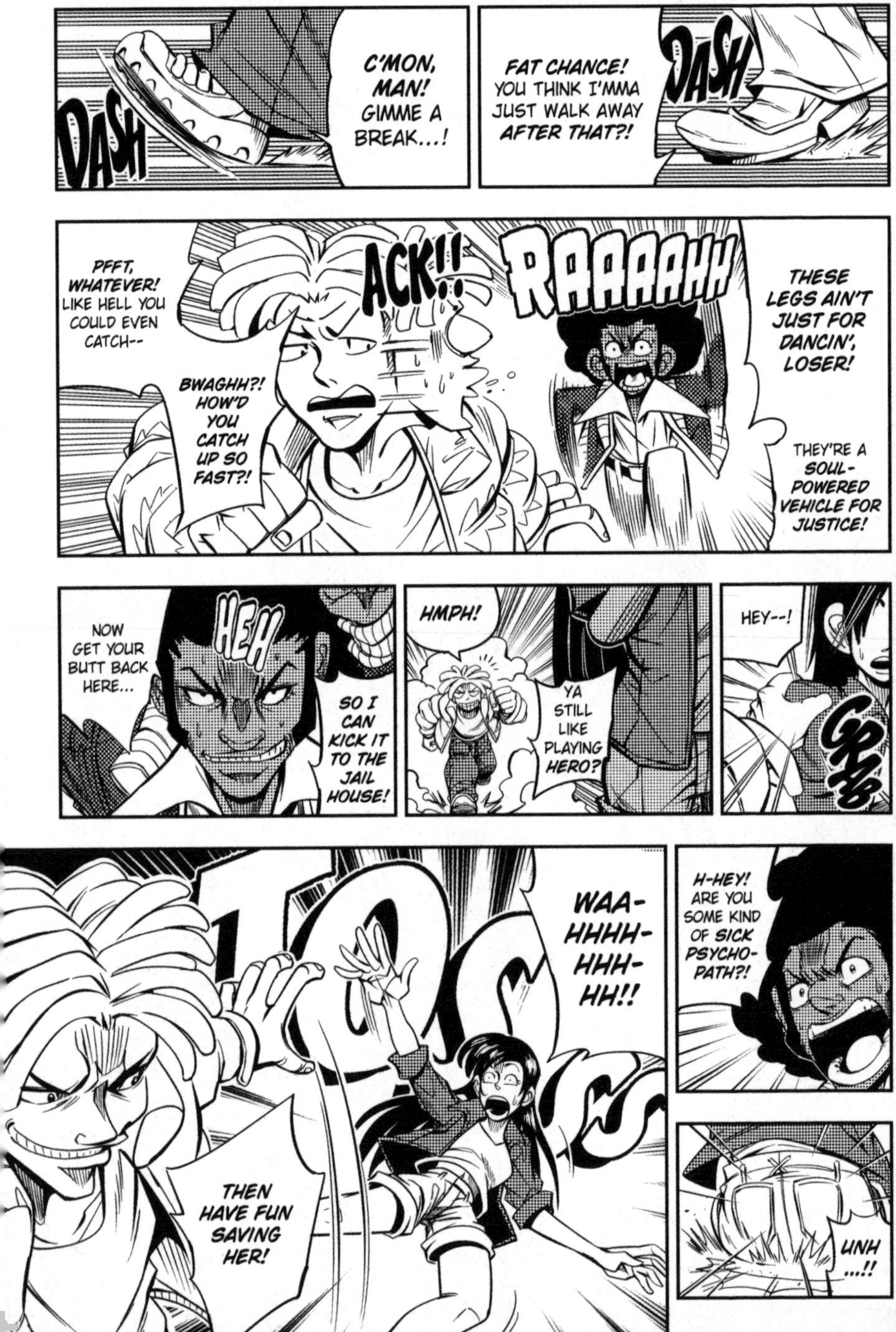
DASH
C'MON, MAN! GIMME A BREAK...!
FAT CHANCE! YOU THINK I'MMA JUST WALK AWAY AFTER THAT?!
DASH
PFFT, WHATEVER! LIKE HELL YOU COULD EVEN CATCH--
BWAGHH?! HOW'D YOU CATCH UP SO FAST?!
ACK!!
RAAAAAHH
THESE LEGS AIN'T JUST FOR DANCIN', LOSER!
THEY'RE A SOUL-POWERED VEHICLE FOR JUSTICE!
NOW GET YOUR BUTT BACK HERE...
HEH
SO I CAN KICK IT TO THE JAIL HOUSE!
HMPH!
YA STILL LIKE PLAYING HERO?
HEY--!
GRAB
WAA-HHHH-HHH-HH!!
THEN HAVE FUN SAVING HER!
H-HEY! ARE YOU SOME KIND OF SICK PSYCHO-PATH?!
UNH ...!!

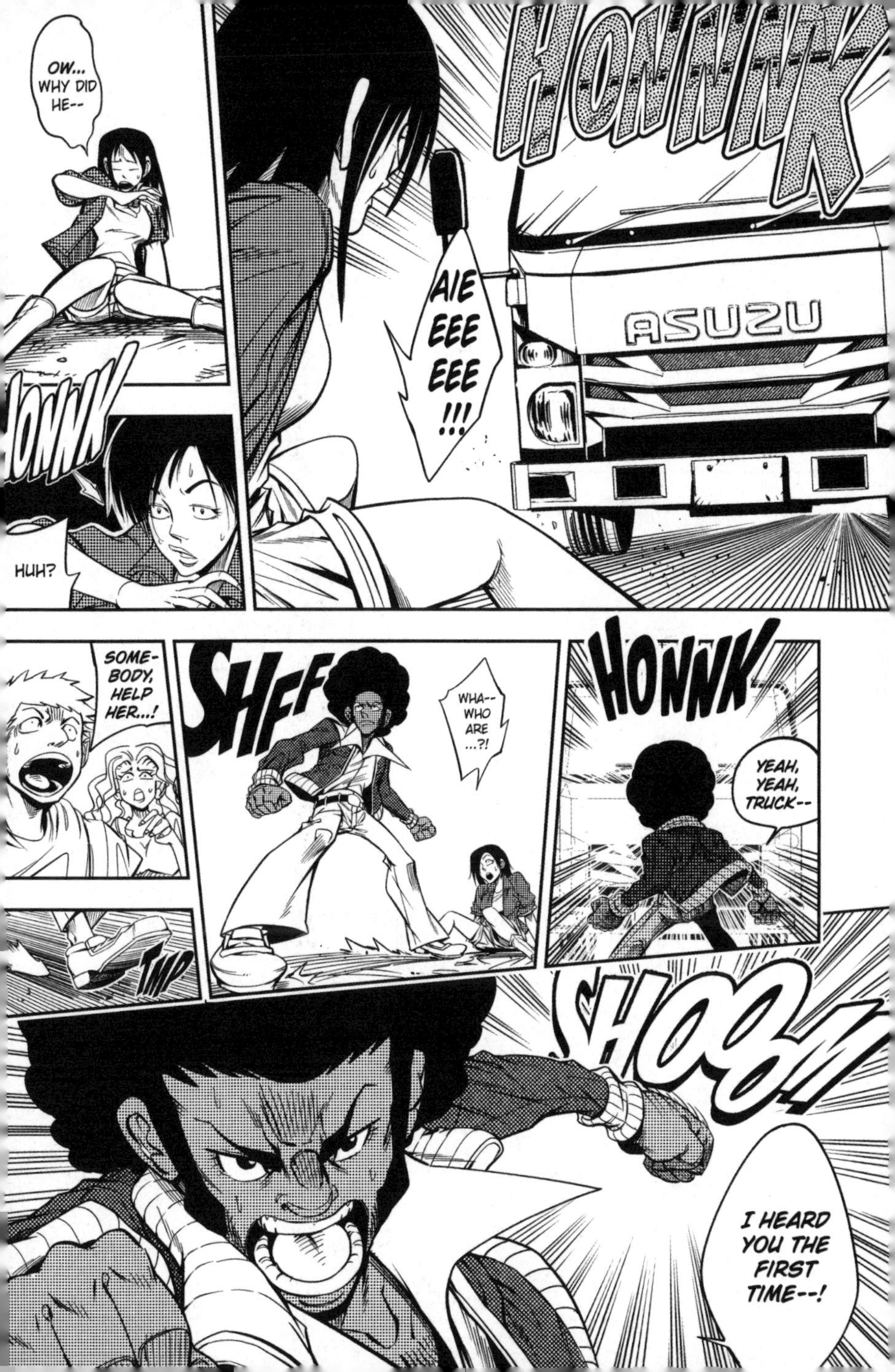
OW... WHY DID HE--
HONNK
HUH?
HONNNK
AIE EEE EEE!!!
ASUZU
SOME-BODY, HELP HER...!
TMP
SHFF
WHA-- WHO ARE ...?!
HONNK
YEAH, YEAH, TRUCK--
SHOOM
I HEARD YOU THE FIRST TIME--!

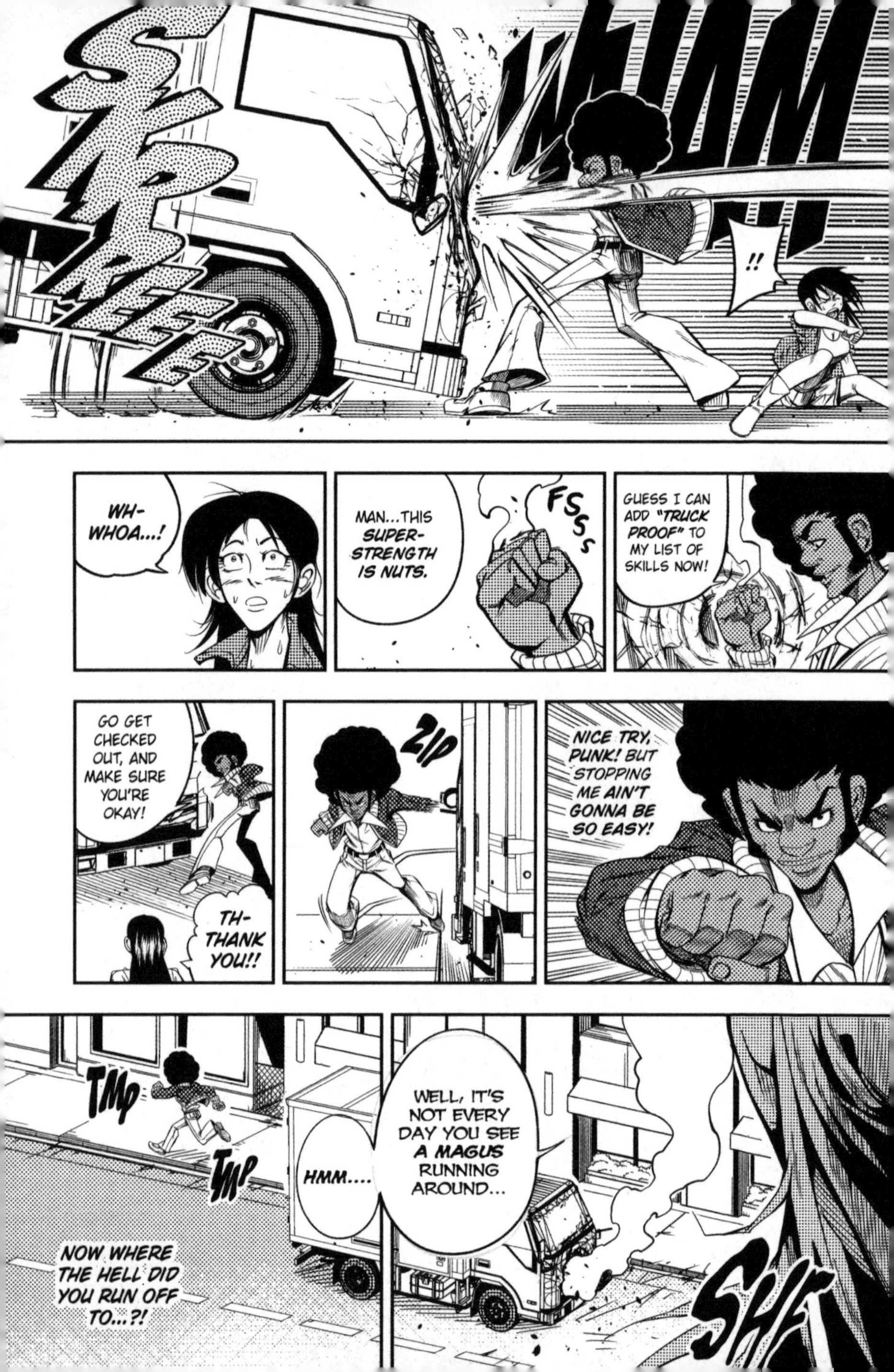
SKREEE
WHAM
!!
WH- WHOA...!
MAN...THIS SUPER-STRENGTH IS NUTS.
FSSS
GUESS I CAN ADD "TRUCK PROOF" TO MY LIST OF SKILLS NOW!
GO GET CHECKED OUT, AND MAKE SURE YOU'RE OKAY!
TH- THANK YOU!!
ZIP
NICE TRY, PUNK! BUT STOPPING ME AIN'T GONNA BE SO EASY!
TMP
TMP
NOW WHERE THE HELL DID YOU RUN OFF TO...?!
HMM....
WELL, IT'S NOT EVERY DAY YOU SEE A MAGUS RUNNING AROUND...
SHF

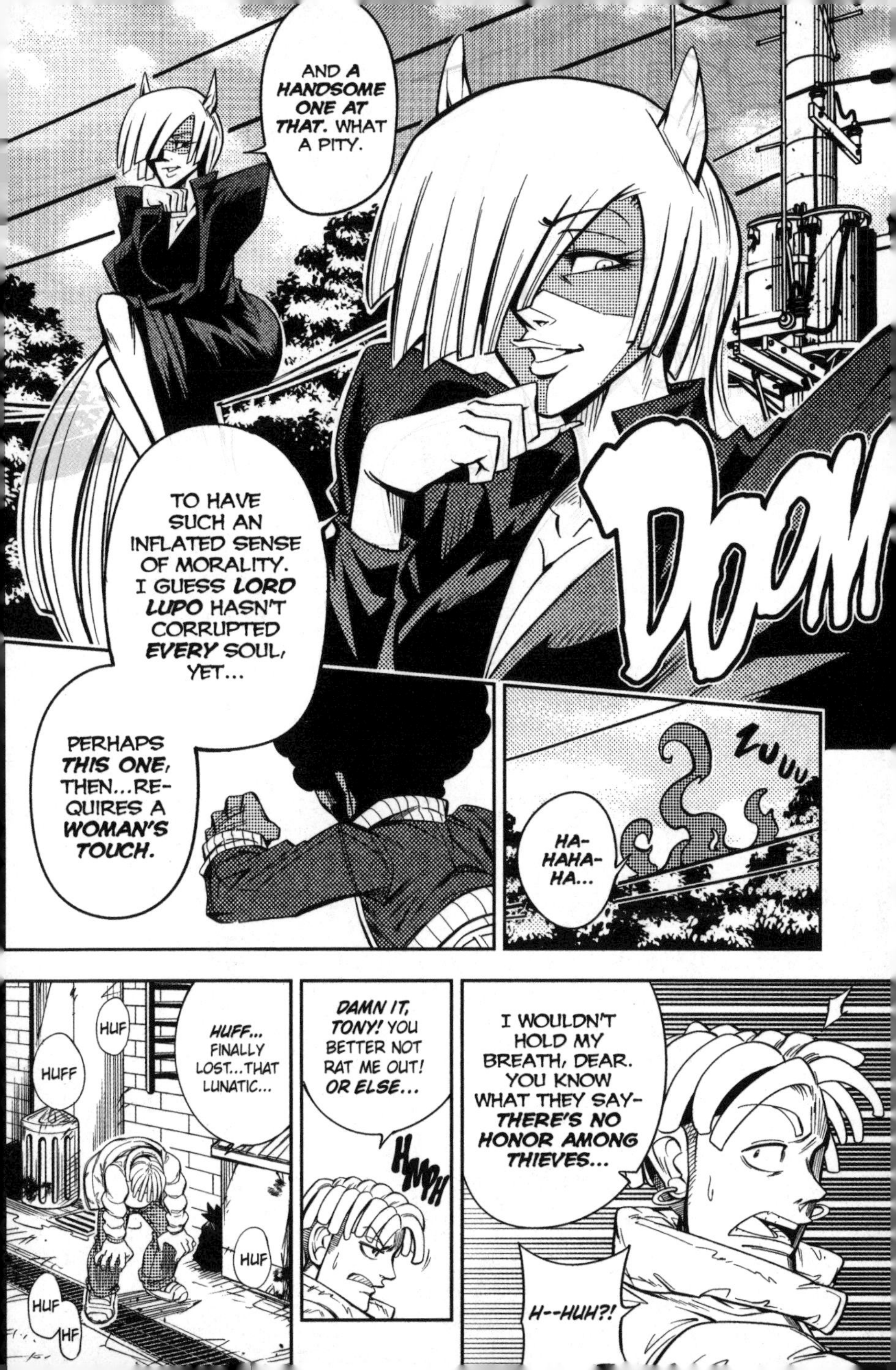
AND A HANDSOME ONE AT THAT. WHAT A PITY.
TO HAVE SUCH AN INFLATED SENSE OF MORALITY. I GUESS LORD LUPO HASN'T CORRUPTED EVERY SOUL, YET...
DOOM
PERHAPS THIS ONE, THEN...REQUIRES A WOMAN'S TOUCH.
ZUUU
HA-HAHAHA-HA...
HUF
HUFF
HUFF... FINALLY LOST...THAT LUNATIC...
HUF
HUF
HF
DAMN IT, TONY! YOU BETTER NOT RAT ME OUT! OR ELSE...
HMPH
I WOULDN'T HOLD MY BREATH, DEAR. YOU KNOW WHAT THEY SAY- THERE'S NO HONOR AMONG THIEVES...
H--HUH?!

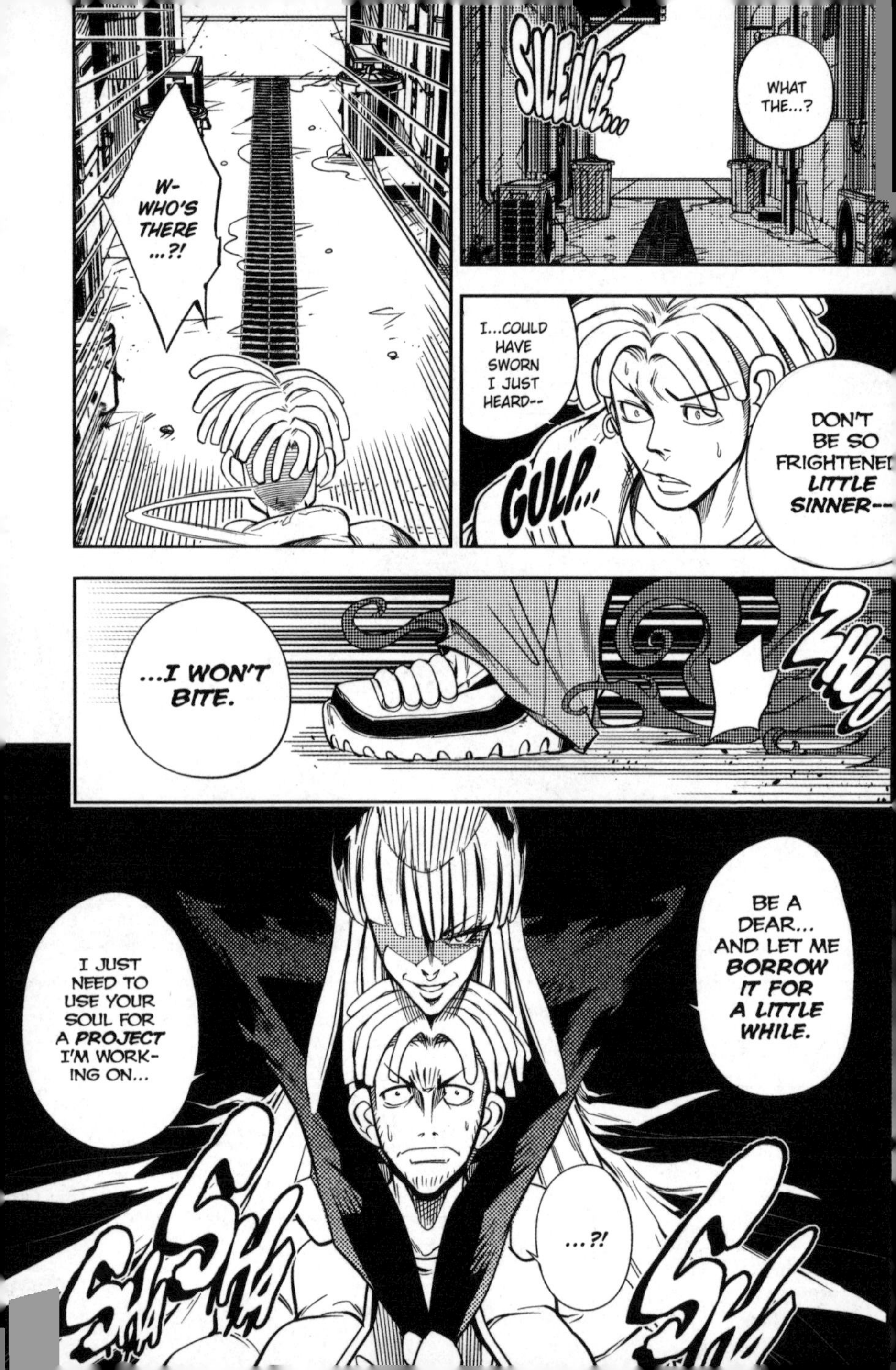

W- WHO'S THERE ...?!
SILENCE...
WHAT THE...?
I...COULD HAVE SWORN I JUST HEARD--
GULP...
DON'T BE SO FRIGHTENE LITTLE SINNER--
...I WON'T BITE.
I JUST NEED TO USE YOUR SOUL FOR A PROJECT I'M WORKING ON...
BE A DEAR... AND LET ME BORROW IT FOR A LITTLE WHILE.
...?!

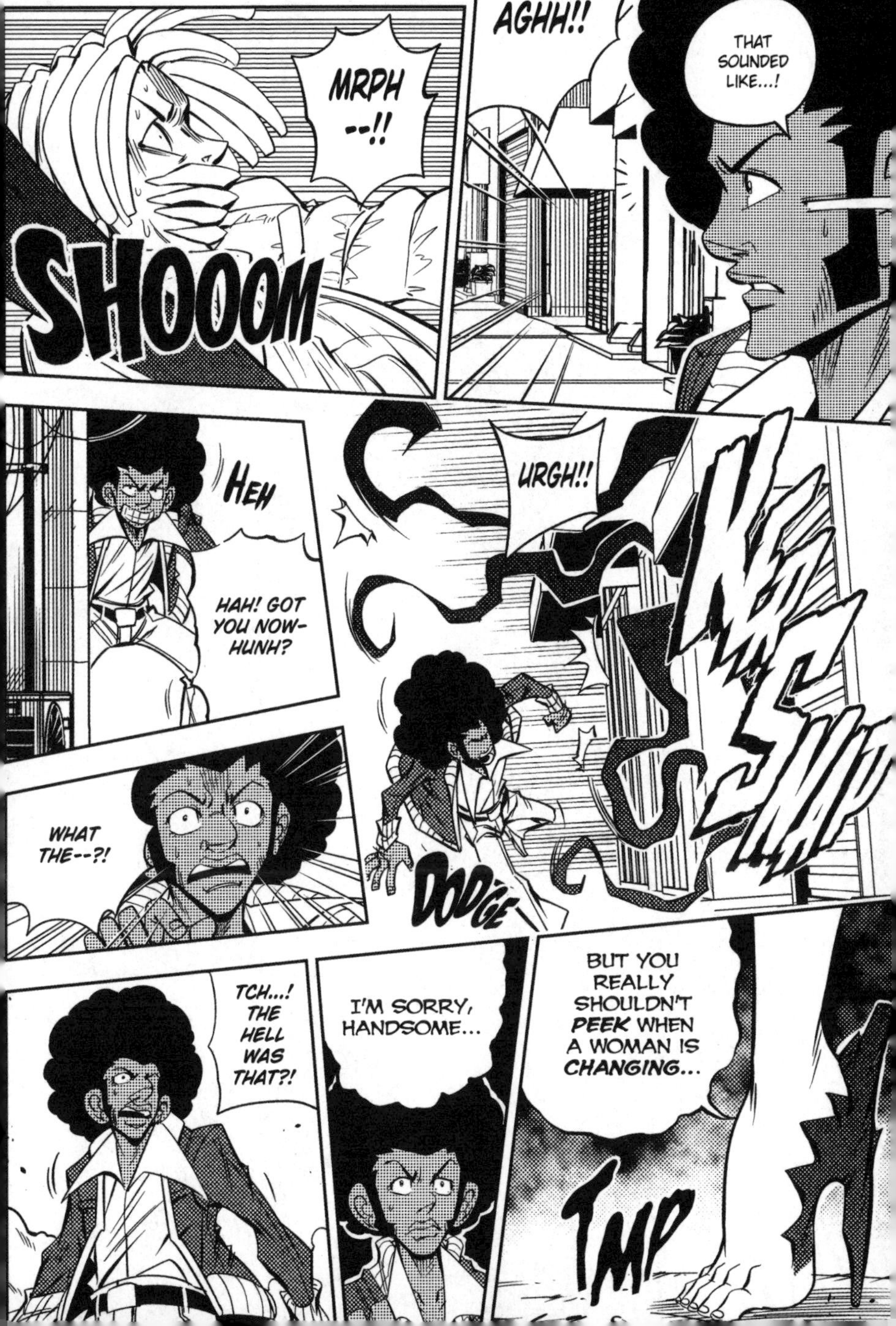
MRPH --!!
SHOOOM
AGHH!!
THAT SOUNDED LIKE...!
HEH
HAH! GOT YOU NOW-HUNH?
WHAT THE--?!
URGH!!
DODGE
TCH...! THE HELL WAS THAT?!
I'M SORRY, HANDSOME...
BUT YOU REALLY SHOULDN'T PEEK WHEN A WOMAN IS CHANGING...
TMP

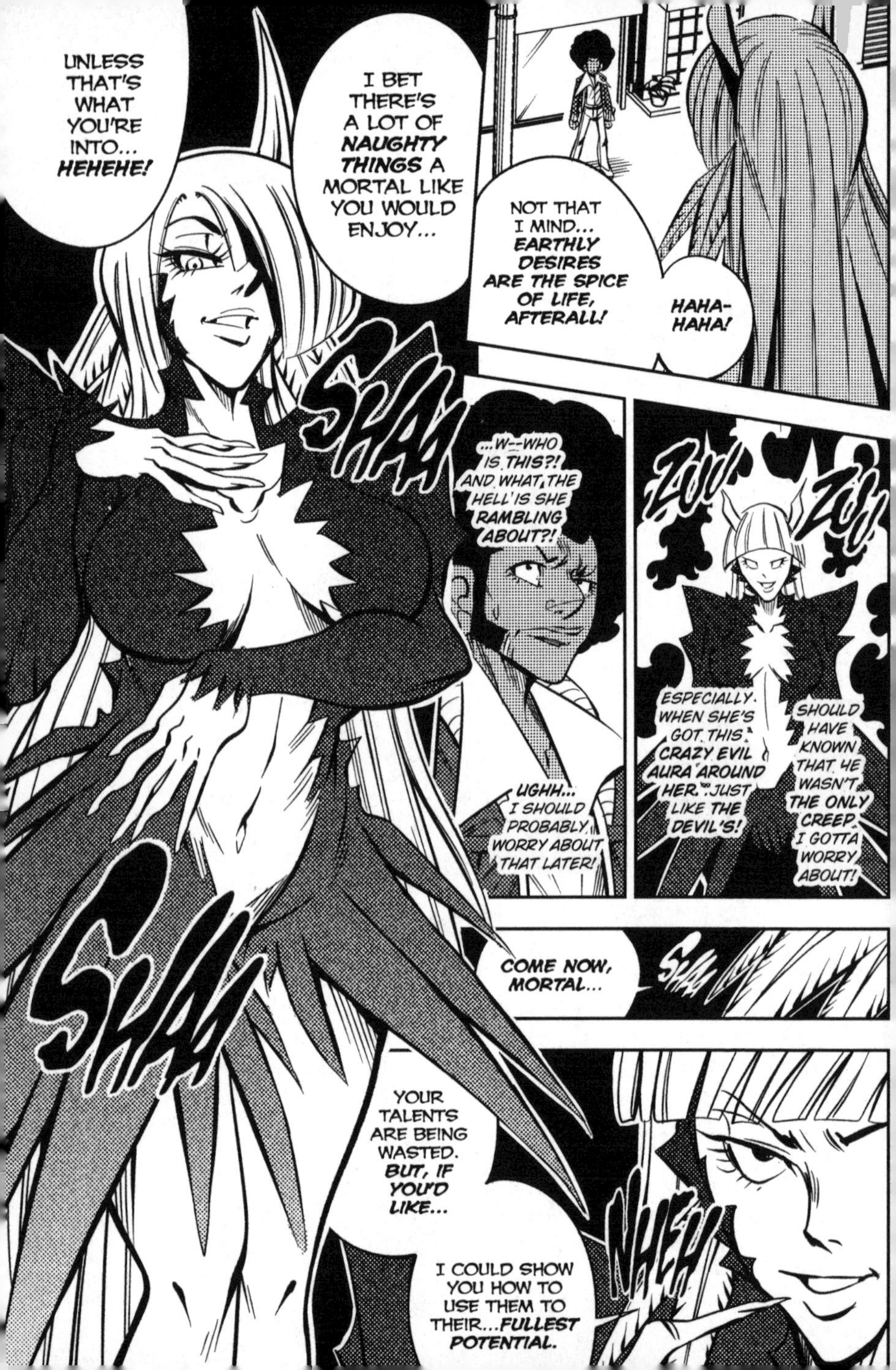
UNLESS THAT'S WHAT YOU'RE INTO... HEHEHE!
I BET THERE'S A LOT OF NAUGHTY THINGS A MORTAL LIKE YOU WOULD ENJOY...
SHAA
SHAA
NOT THAT I MIND... EARTHLY DESIRES ARE THE SPICE OF LIFE, AFTERALL!
HAHA-HAHA!
...W--WHO IS THIS?! AND WHAT THE HELL IS SHE RAMBLING ABOUT?!
UGHH... I SHOULD PROBABLY WORRY ABOUT THAT LATER!
ZOU
ZOU
ESPECIALLY WHEN SHE'S GOT THIS CRAZY EVIL AURA AROUND HER... JUST LIKE THE DEVIL'S!
SHOULD HAVE KNOWN THAT HE WASN'T THE ONLY CREEP I GOTTA WORRY ABOUT!
COME NOW, MORTAL...
SHA
YOUR TALENTS ARE BEING WASTED. BUT, IF YOU'D LIKE...
I COULD SHOW YOU HOW TO USE THEM TO THEIR...FULLEST POTENTIAL.
NHEH

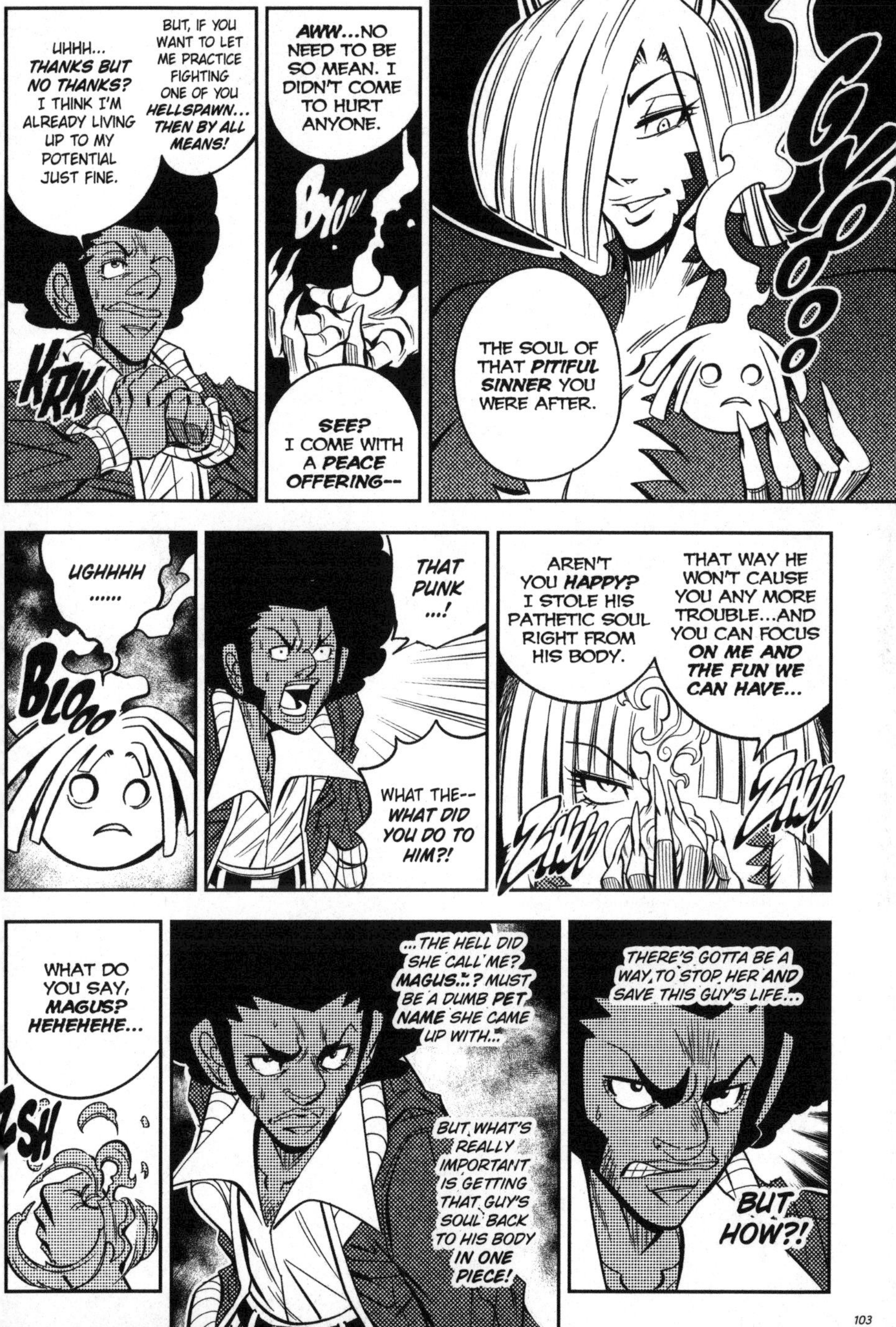

UHHH... THANKS BUT NO THANKS? I THINK I'M ALREADY LIVING UP TO MY POTENTIAL JUST FINE.
BUT, IF YOU WANT TO LET ME PRACTICE FIGHTING ONE OF YOU HELLSPAWN... THEN BY ALL MEANS!
KRK
AWW...NO NEED TO BE SO MEAN. I DIDN'T COME TO HURT ANYONE.
SEE? I COME WITH A PEACE OFFERING--
THE SOUL OF THAT PITIFUL SINNER YOU WERE AFTER.
UGHHHH ......
BLOOO
THAT PUNK ...!
WHAT THE-- WHAT DID YOU DO TO HIM?!
AREN'T YOU HAPPY? I STOLE HIS PATHETIC SOUL RIGHT FROM HIS BODY.
THAT WAY HE WON'T CAUSE YOU ANY MORE TROUBLE...AND YOU CAN FOCUS ON ME AND THE FUN WE CAN HAVE...
WHAT DO YOU SAY, MAGUS? HEHEHEHE...
...THE HELL DID SHE CALL ME? MAGUS...? MUST BE A DUMB PET NAME SHE CAME UP WITH...
BUT WHAT'S REALLY IMPORTANT IS GETTING THAT GUY'S SOUL BACK TO HIS BODY IN ONE PIECE!
THERE'S GOTTA BE A WAY TO STOP HER AND SAVE THIS GUY'S LIFE...
BUT HOW?!

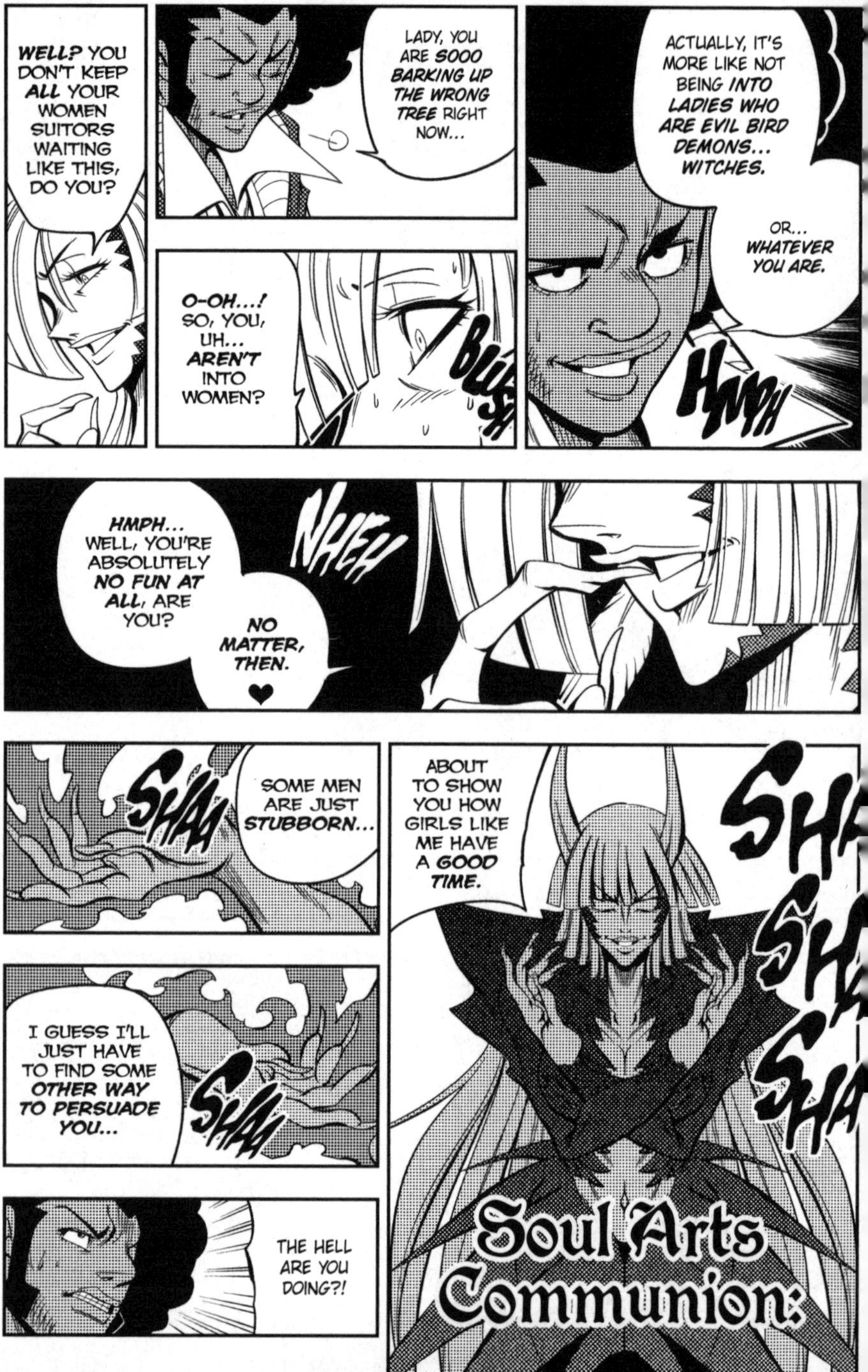
WELL? YOU DON'T KEEP ALL YOUR WOMEN SUITORS WAITING LIKE THIS, DO YOU?
LADY, YOU ARE SOOO BARKING UP THE WRONG TREE RIGHT NOW...
O-OH...! SO, YOU, UH... AREN'T INTO WOMEN?
BLUSH
ACTUALLY, IT'S MORE LIKE NOT BEING INTO LADIES WHO ARE EVIL BIRD DEMONS... WITCHES.
OR... WHATEVER YOU ARE.
HMMPH
HMPH... WELL, YOU'RE ABSOLUTELY NO FUN AT ALL, ARE YOU?
NHEH
NO MATTER, THEN. ❤
SHAA
SOME MEN ARE JUST STUBBORN...
I GUESS I'LL JUST HAVE TO FIND SOME OTHER WAY TO PERSUADE YOU...
SHAA
THE HELL ARE YOU DOING?!
ABOUT TO SHOW YOU HOW GIRLS LIKE ME HAVE A GOOD TIME.
Soul Arts Communion:

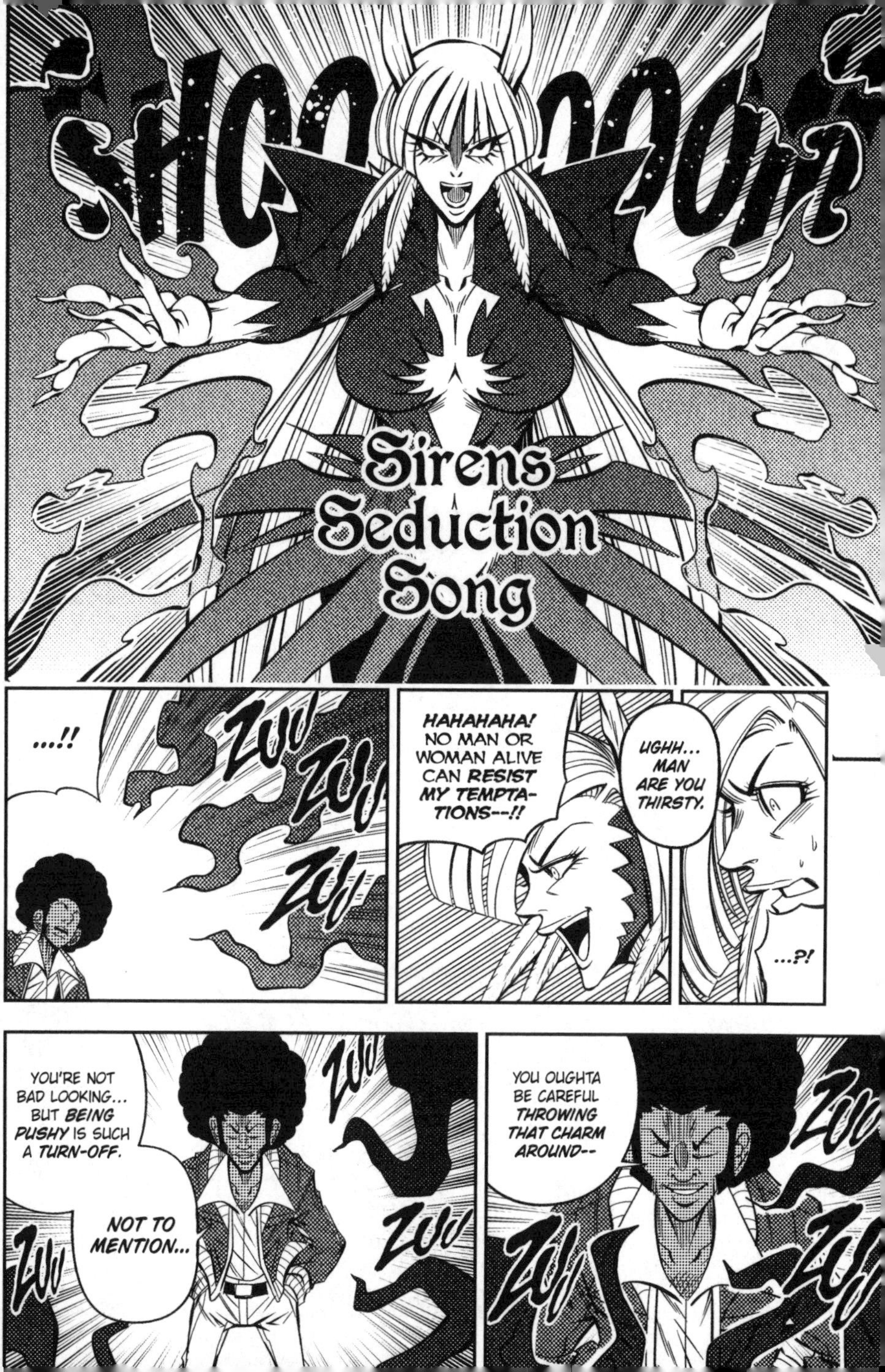
SHOO
OOOM
Sirens Seduction Song
...!!
ZUU
ZUU
ZUU
HAHAHAHA! NO MAN OR WOMAN ALIVE CAN RESIST MY TEMPTATIONS--!!
UGHH... MAN ARE YOU THIRSTY.
...?!
YOU'RE NOT BAD LOOKING... BUT BEING PUSHY IS SUCH A TURN-OFF.
ZUU
NOT TO MENTION...
ZUU
ZUU
YOU OUGHTA BE CAREFUL THROWING THAT CHARM AROUND--
ZUU
ZUU
ZUU

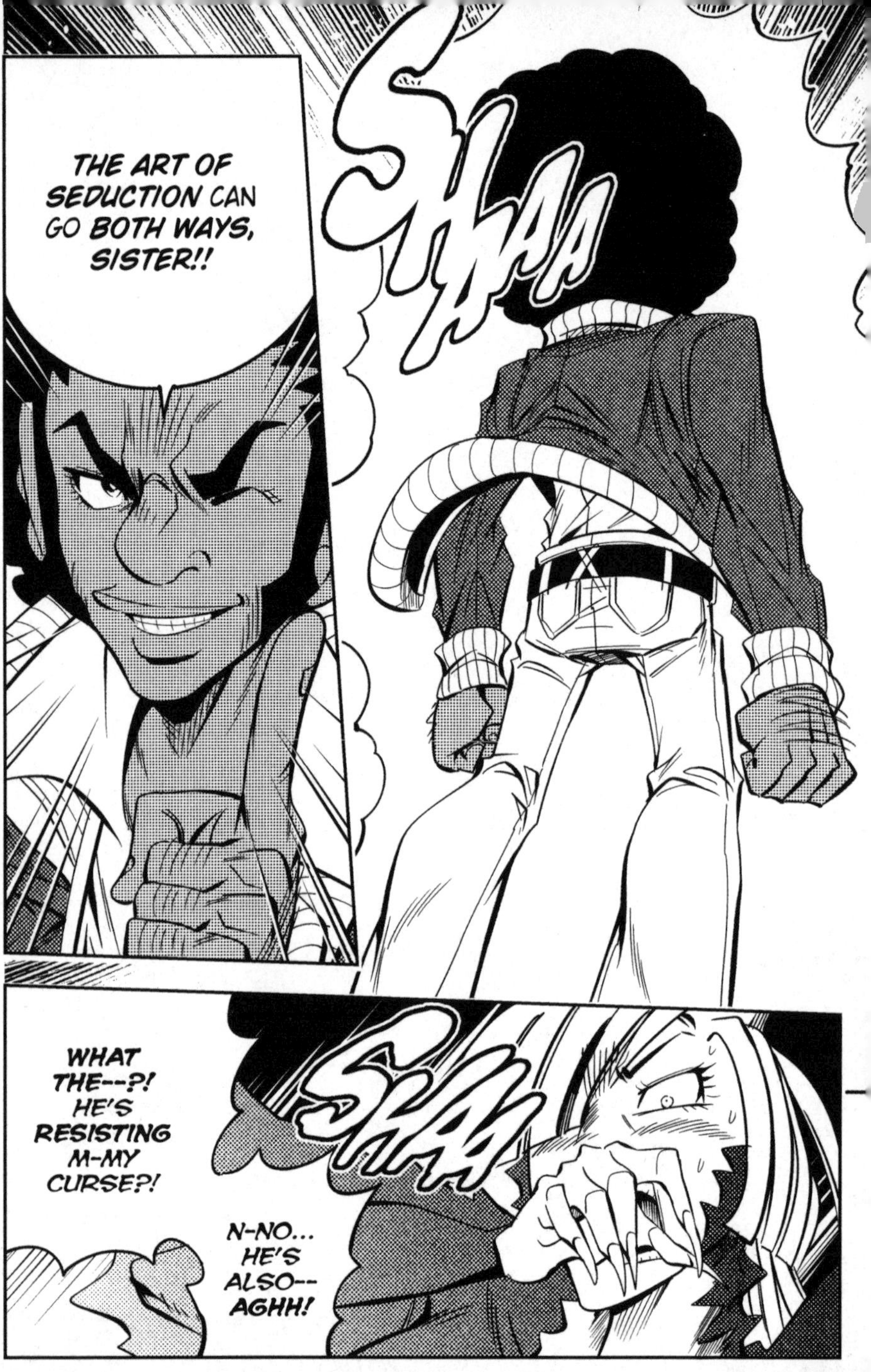
THE ART OF SEDUCTION CAN GO BOTH WAYS, SISTER!!
SHAAA
SHAA
WHAT THE--?! HE'S RESISTING M-MY CURSE?!
N-NO... HE'S ALSO-- AGHH!

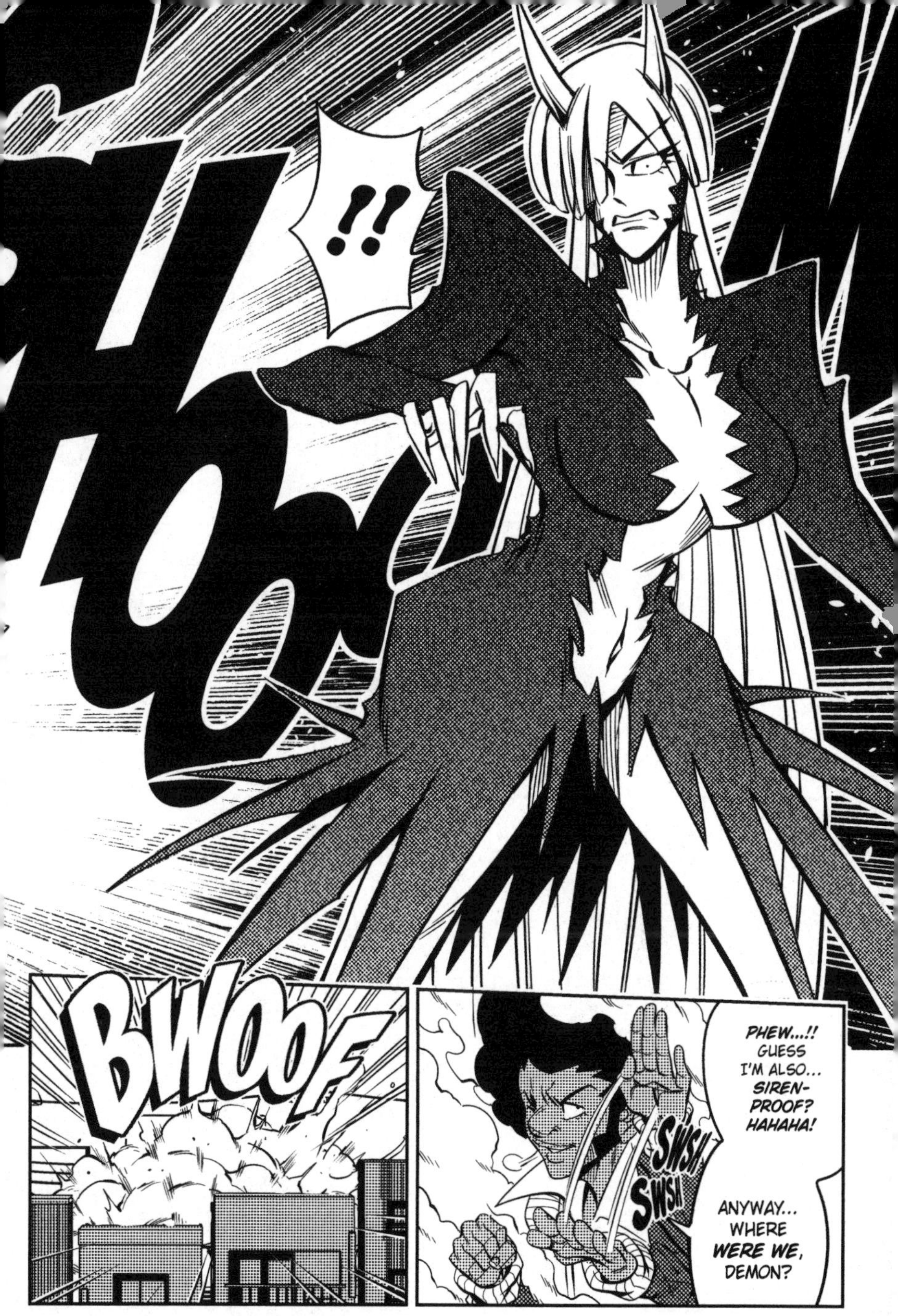
!!
BWOOF
PHEW...!! GUESS I'M ALSO... SIREN-PROOF? HAHAHA!
SWSH SWSH
ANYWAY... WHERE WERE WE, DEMON?

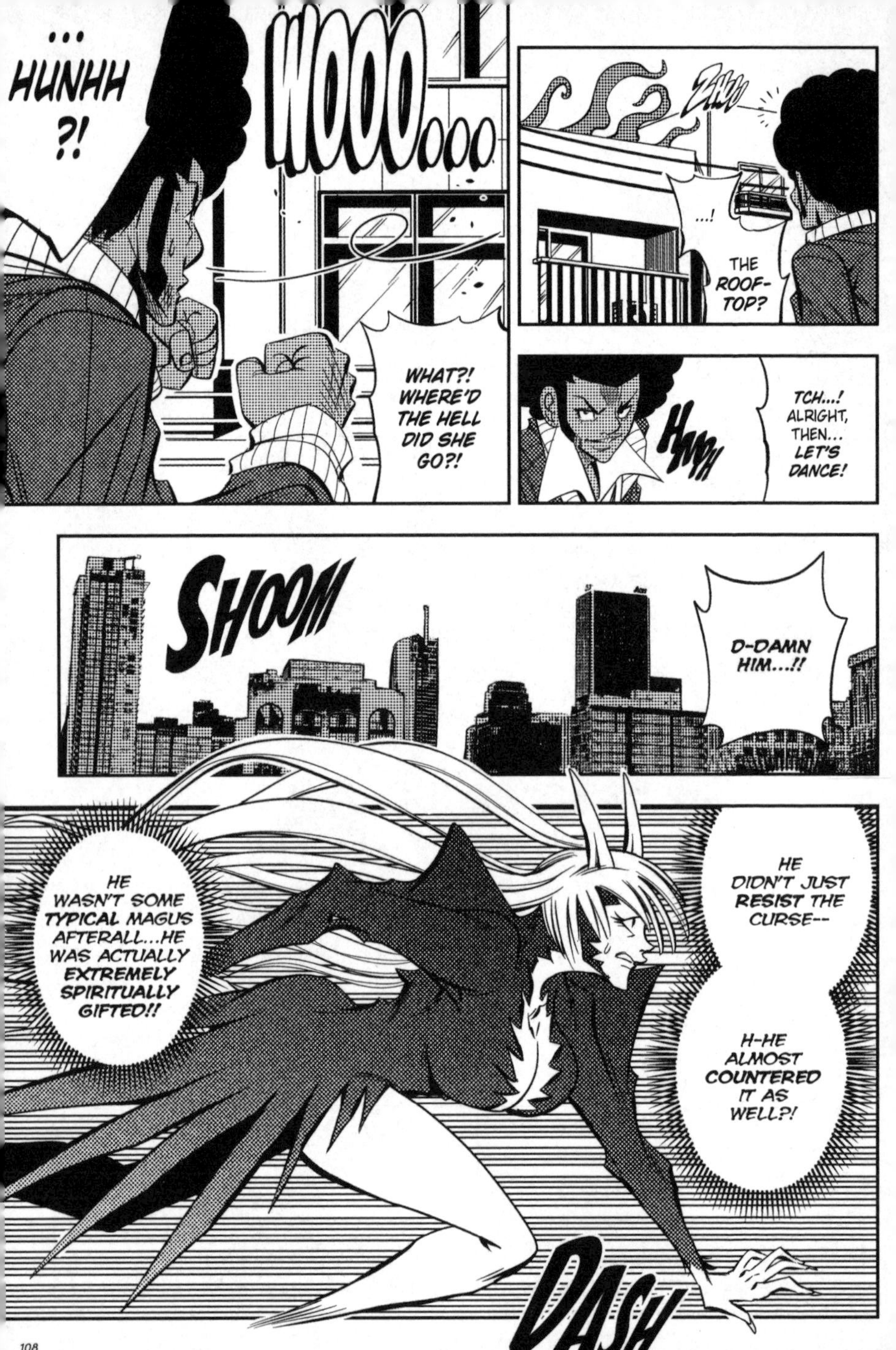
...HUNNH?!
WOOOooo
WHAT?! WHERE'D THE HELL DID SHE GO?!
...!
THE ROOF-TOP?
TCH...! ALRIGHT, THEN... LET'S DANCE!
SHOOM
D-DAMN HIM...!!
HE WASN'T SOME TYPICAL MAGUS AFTERALL...HE WAS ACTUALLY EXTREMELY SPIRITUALLY GIFTED!!
HE DIDN'T JUST RESIST THE CURSE--
H-HE ALMOST COUNTERED IT AS WELL?!
DASH

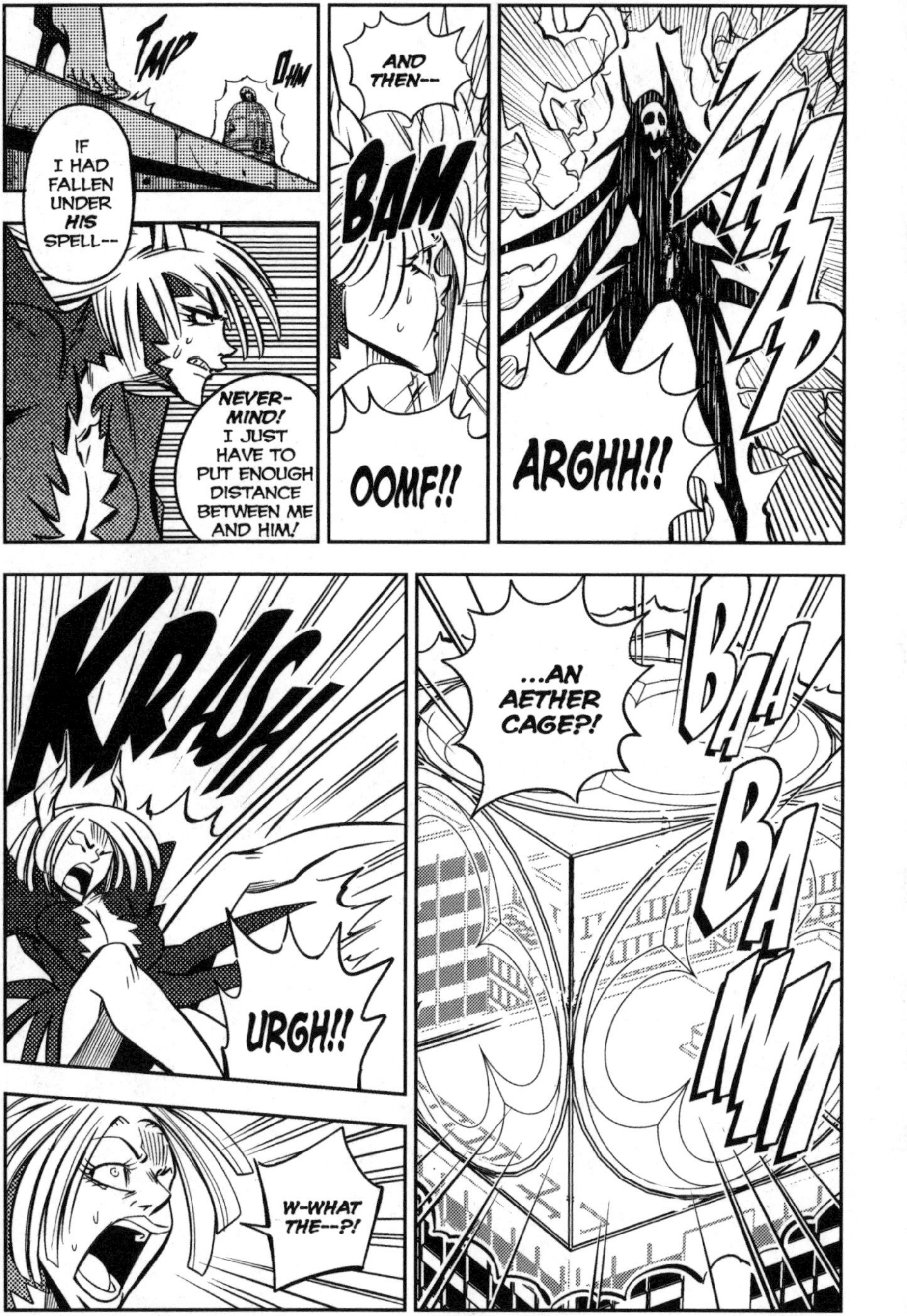
TMP
OHM
IF I HAD FALLEN UNDER HIS SPELL--
NEVERMIND! I JUST HAVE TO PUT ENOUGH DISTANCE BETWEEN ME AND HIM!
AND THEN--
BAM
OOMF!!
ZAAP
ARGHH!!
KRASH
URGH!!
W-WHAT THE--?!
...AN AETHER CAGE?!
BAABAAMM

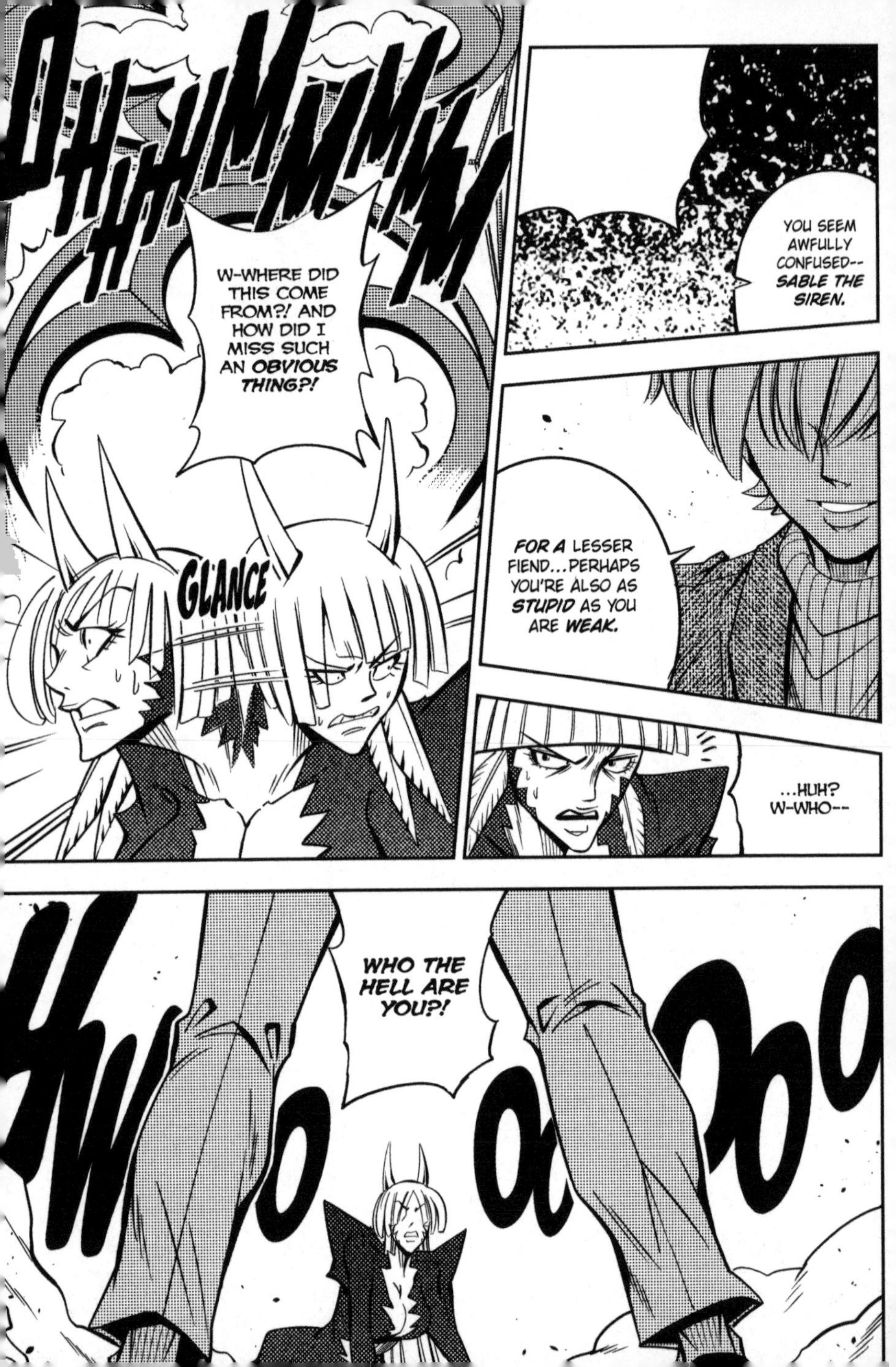
W-WHERE DID THIS COME FROM?! AND HOW DID I MISS SUCH AN OBVIOUS THING?!
GLANCE
YOU SEEM AWFULLY CONFUSED-- SABLE THE SIREN.
FOR A LESSER FIEND...PERHAPS YOU'RE ALSO AS STUPID AS YOU ARE WEAK.
...HUH? W-WHO--
WHO THE HELL ARE YOU?!

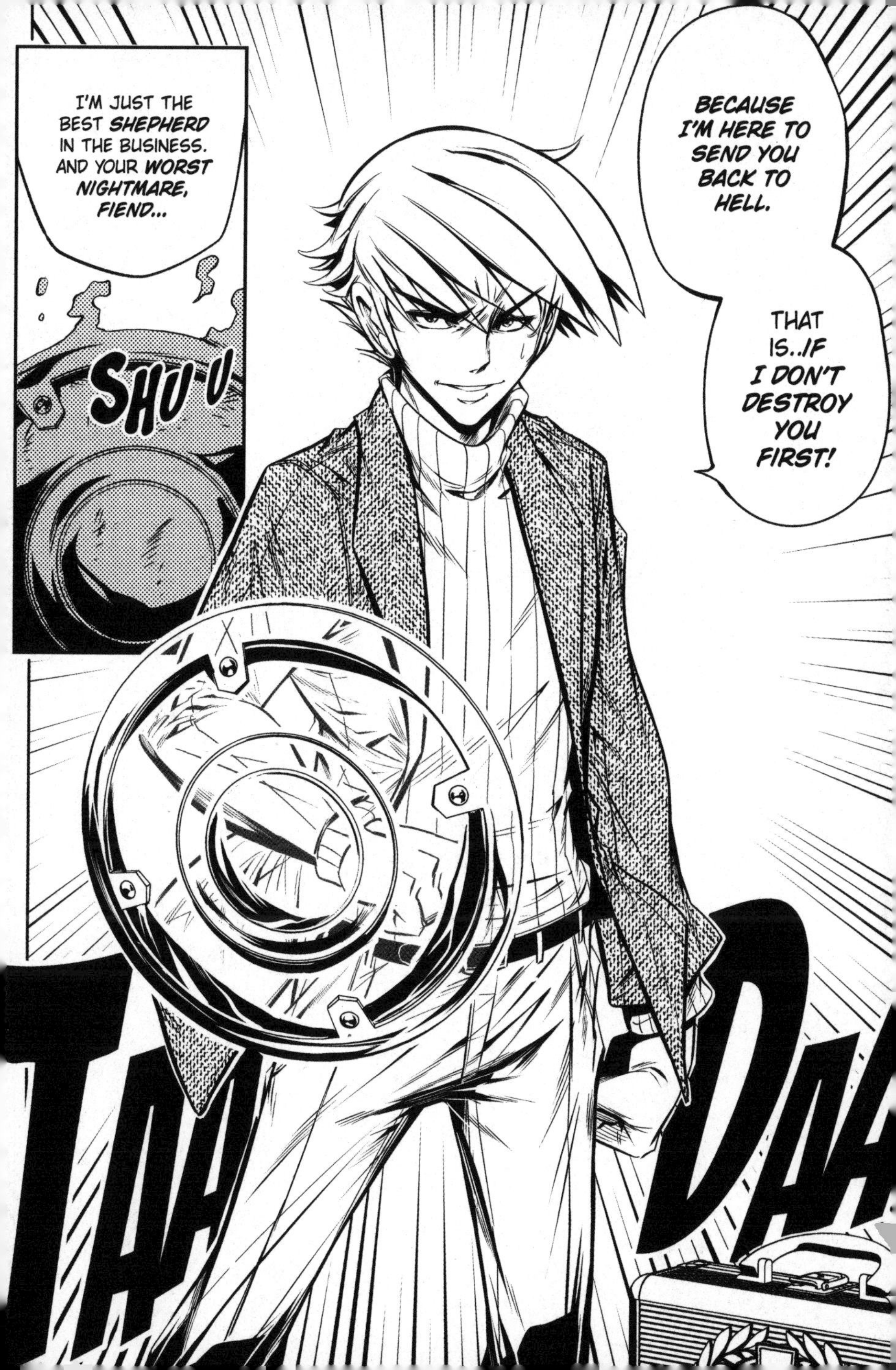
I'M JUST THE BEST SHEPHERD IN THE BUSINESS. AND YOUR WORST NIGHTMARE, FIEND...
SHUU
BECAUSE I'M HERE TO SEND YOU BACK TO HELL.
THAT IS..IF I DON'T DESTROY YOU FIRST!
TA
DA

SOUL BEAT

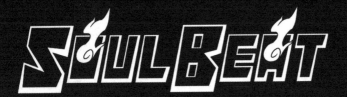

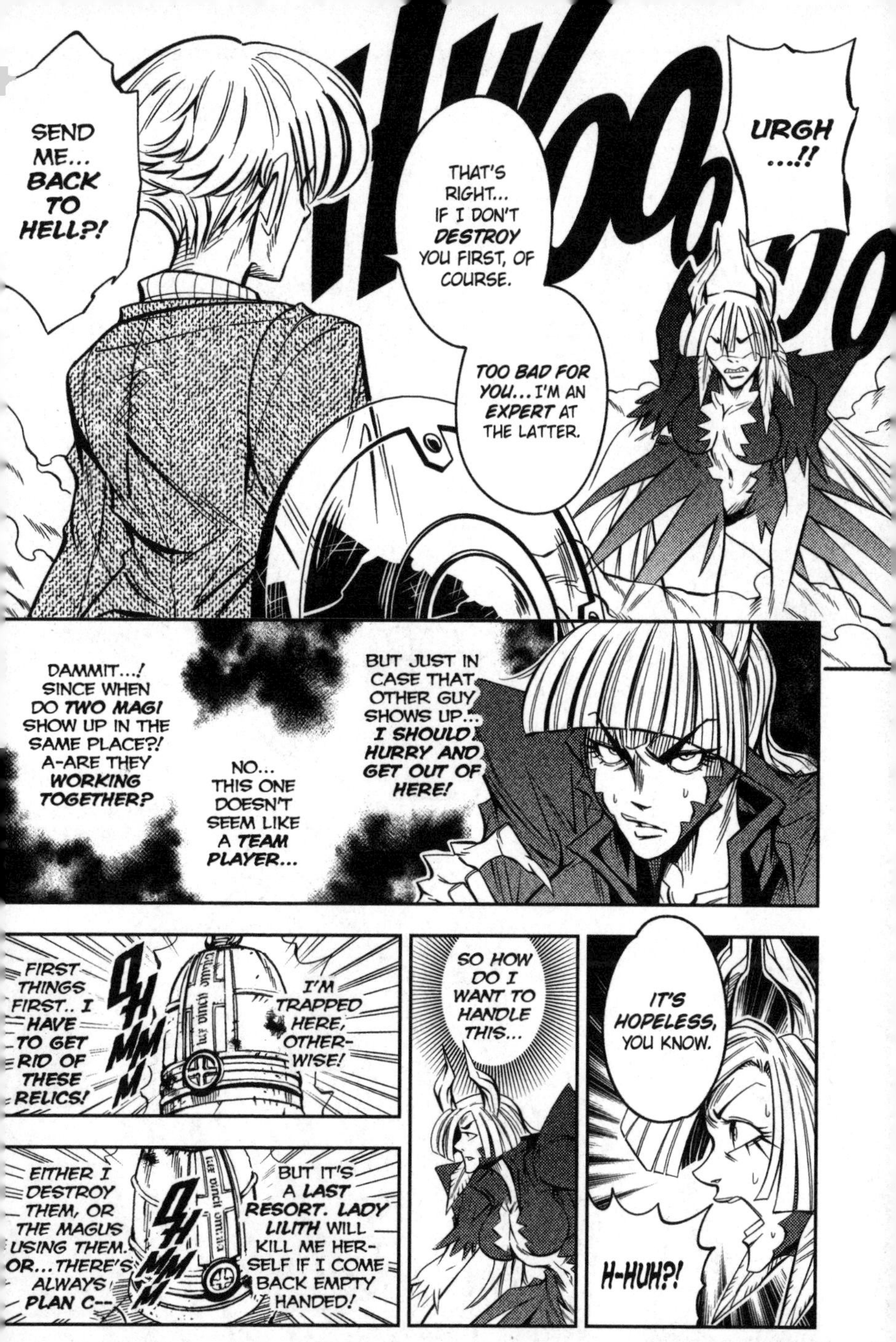
SEND ME... BACK TO HELL?!
THAT'S RIGHT... IF I DON'T DESTROY YOU FIRST, OF COURSE.
TOO BAD FOR YOU... I'M AN EXPERT AT THE LATTER.
URGH ...!!
DAMMIT...! SINCE WHEN DO TWO MAGI SHOW UP IN THE SAME PLACE?! A-ARE THEY WORKING TOGETHER?
NO... THIS ONE DOESN'T SEEM LIKE A TEAM PLAYER...
BUT JUST IN CASE THAT OTHER GUY SHOWS UP... I SHOULD HURRY AND GET OUT OF HERE!
FIRST THINGS FIRST.. I HAVE TO GET RID OF THESE RELICS!
I'M TRAPPED HERE, OTHER-WISE!
EITHER I DESTROY THEM, OR THE MAGUS USING THEM. OR...THERE'S ALWAYS PLAN C--
BUT IT'S A LAST RESORT. LADY LILITH WILL KILL ME HER-SELF IF I COME BACK EMPTY HANDED!
SO HOW DO I WANT TO HANDLE THIS...
IT'S HOPELESS, YOU KNOW.
H-HUH?!

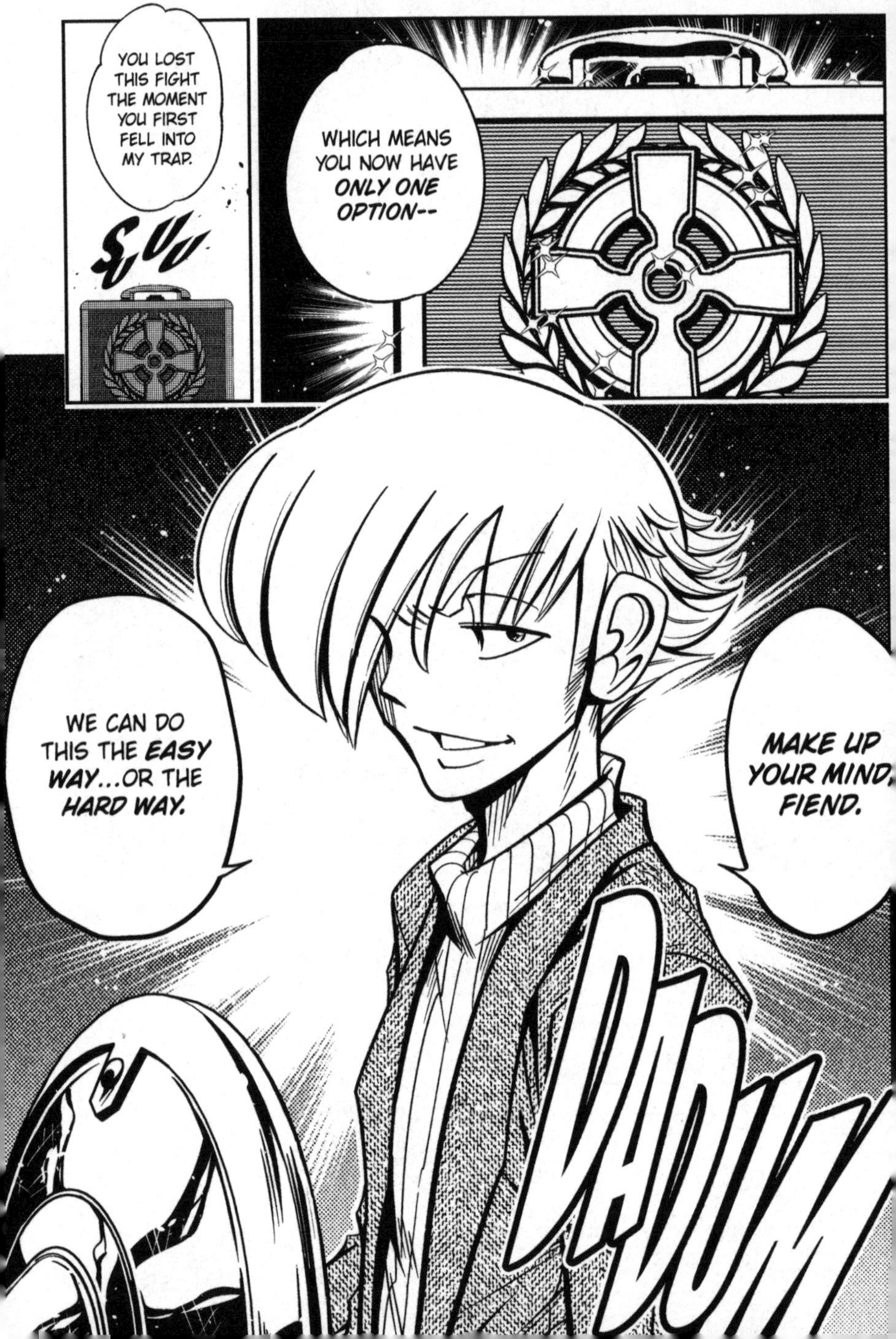
YOU LOST THIS FIGHT THE MOMENT YOU FIRST FELL INTO MY TRAP.
WHICH MEANS YOU NOW HAVE *ONLY ONE OPTION*--
WE CAN DO THIS THE *EASY WAY*...OR THE *HARD WAY.*
MAKE UP YOUR MIND, FIEND.

Chapter 4: Divine Intervention

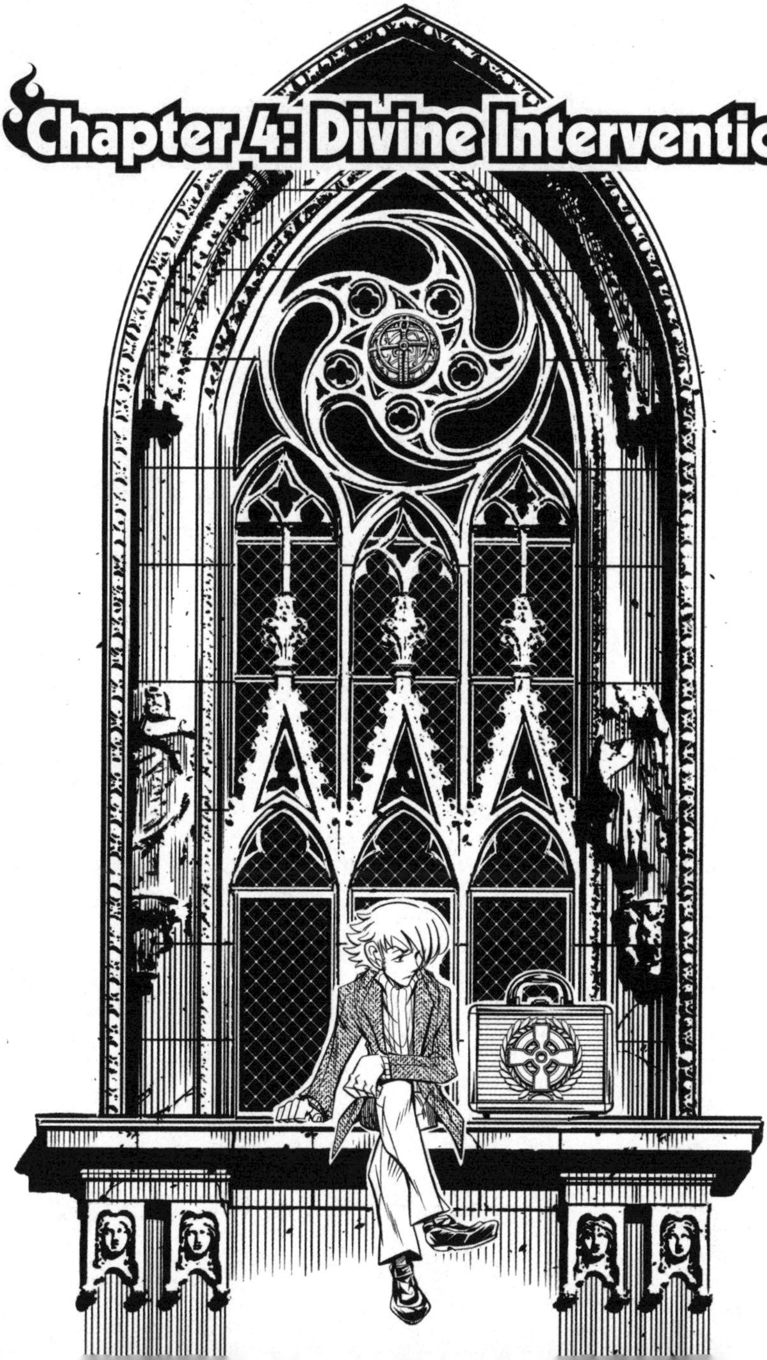

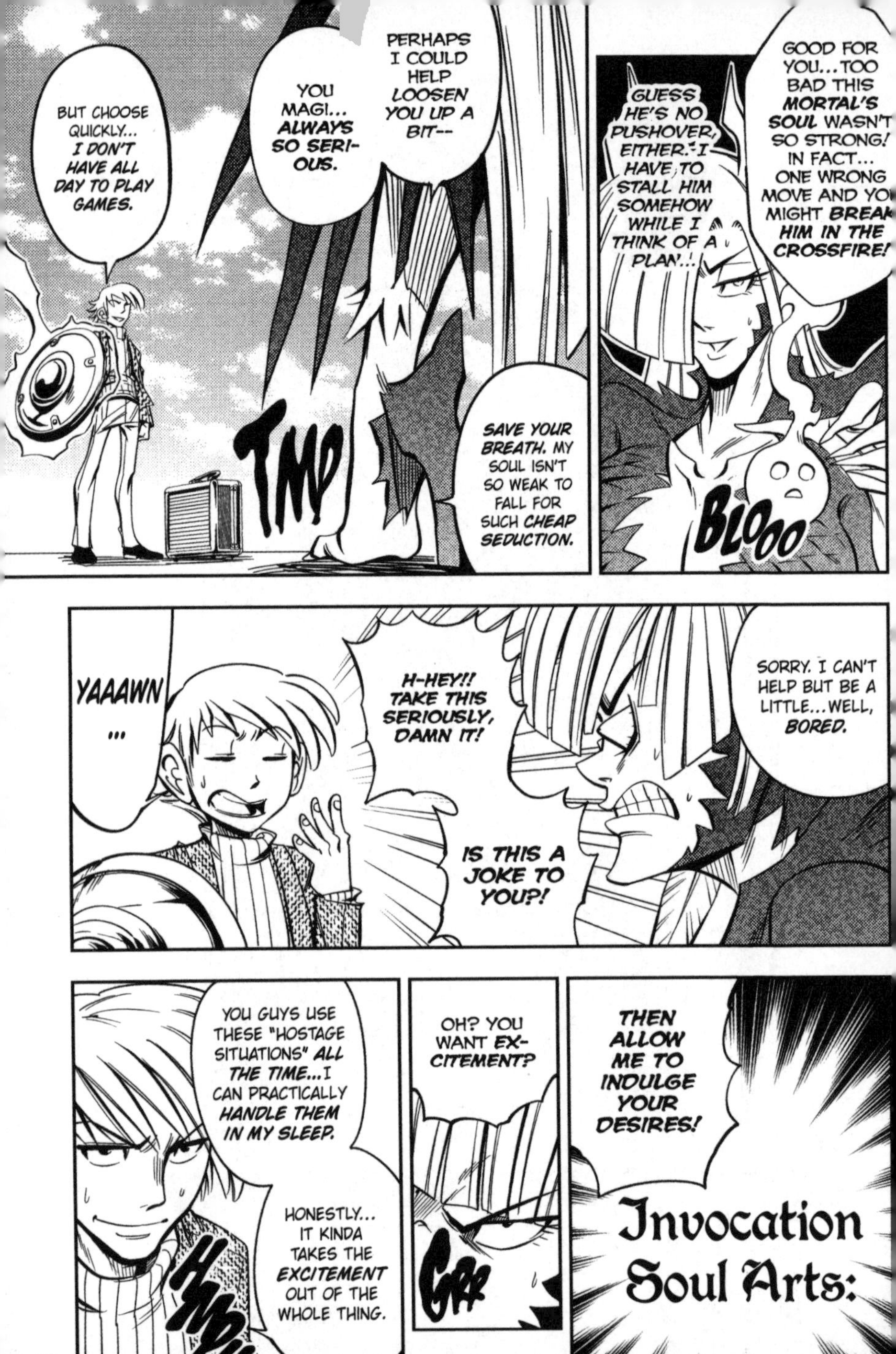
BUT CHOOSE QUICKLY... I DON'T HAVE ALL DAY TO PLAY GAMES.
YOU MAGI... ALWAYS SO SERI-OUS.
PERHAPS I COULD HELP LOOSEN YOU UP A BIT--
TMP
SAVE YOUR BREATH. MY SOUL ISN'T SO WEAK TO FALL FOR SUCH CHEAP SEDUCTION.
GUESS HE'S NO PUSHOVER, EITHER... I HAVE TO STALL HIM SOMEHOW WHILE I THINK OF A PLAN...
GOOD FOR YOU...TOO BAD THIS MORTAL'S SOUL WASN'T SO STRONG! IN FACT... ONE WRONG MOVE AND YOU MIGHT BREAK HIM IN THE CROSSFIRE!
BLOOO
YAAAWN...
H-HEY!! TAKE THIS SERIOUSLY, DAMN IT!
IS THIS A JOKE TO YOU?!
SORRY. I CAN'T HELP BUT BE A LITTLE...WELL, BORED.
YOU GUYS USE THESE "HOSTAGE SITUATIONS" ALL THE TIME...I CAN PRACTICALLY HANDLE THEM IN MY SLEEP.
HONESTLY... IT KINDA TAKES THE EXCITEMENT OUT OF THE WHOLE THING.
OH? YOU WANT EX-CITEMENT?
GRR
THEN ALLOW ME TO INDULGE YOUR DESIRES!
Invocation Soul Arts:

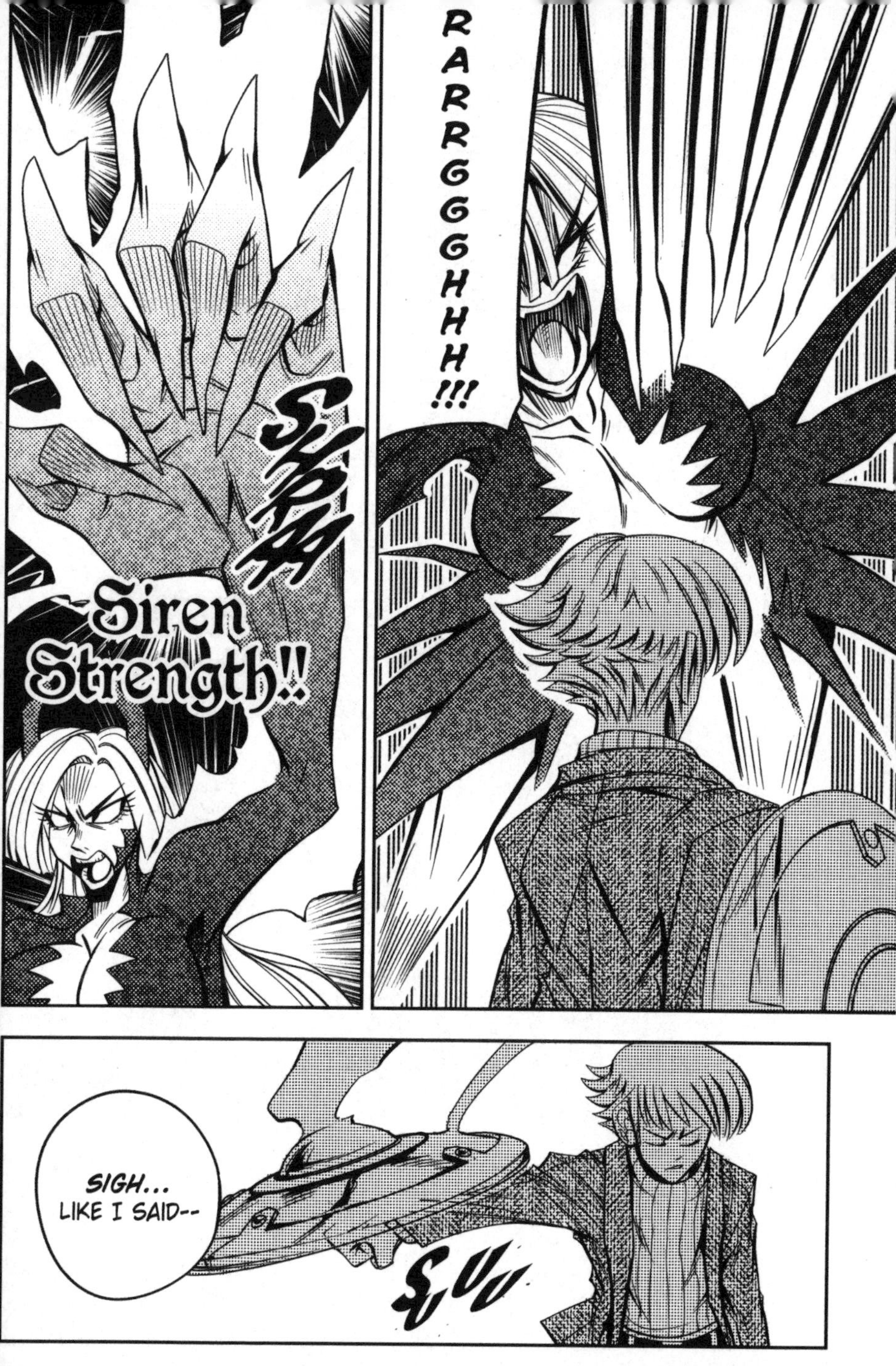

Siren Strength!!
RARRGGGHHH!!!
SIGH...
LIKE I SAID--

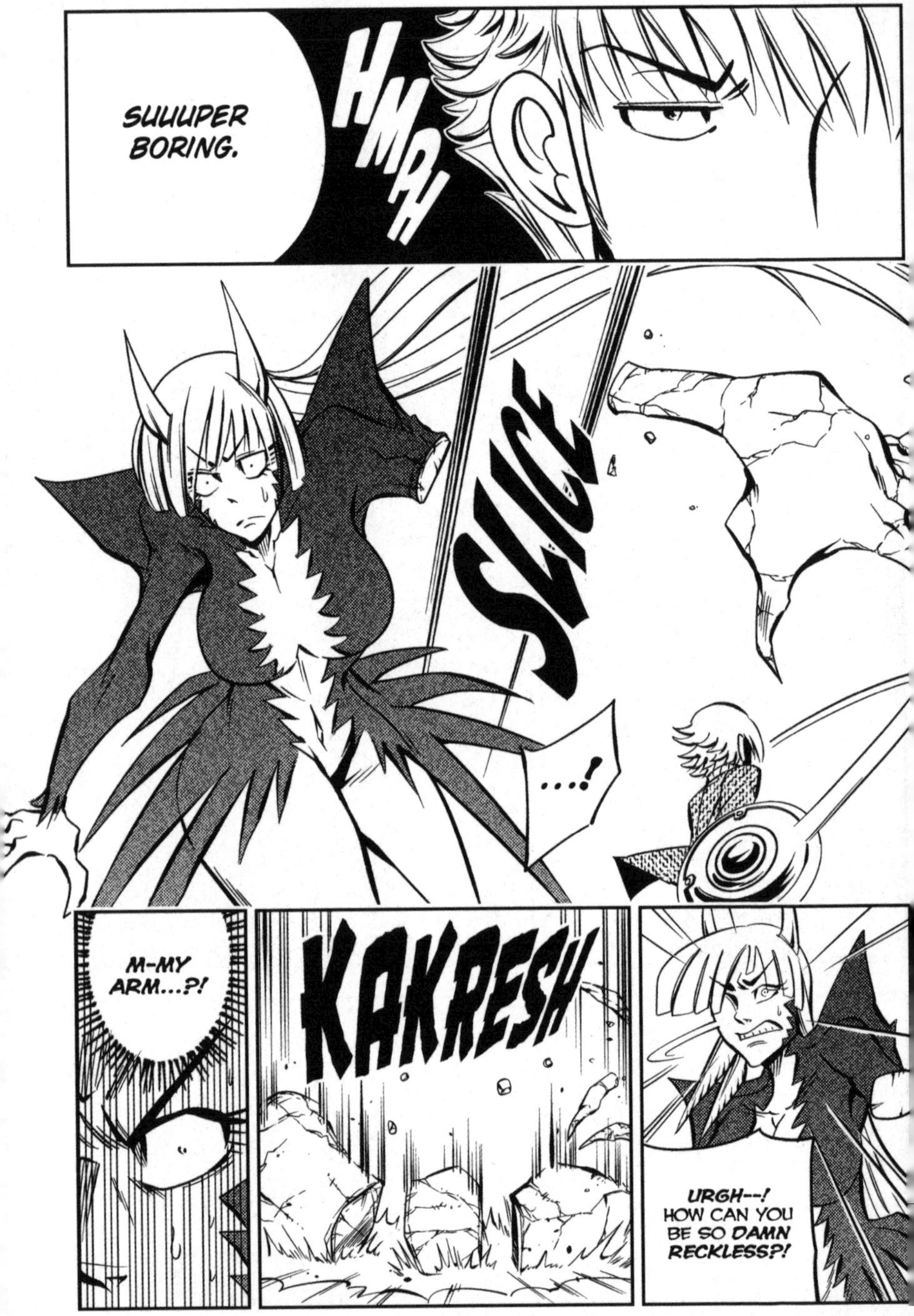
SUUUPER BORING.
HMPH
SLICE
...!
M-MY ARM...?!
KAKRESH
URGH--! HOW CAN YOU BE SO DAMN RECKLESS?!

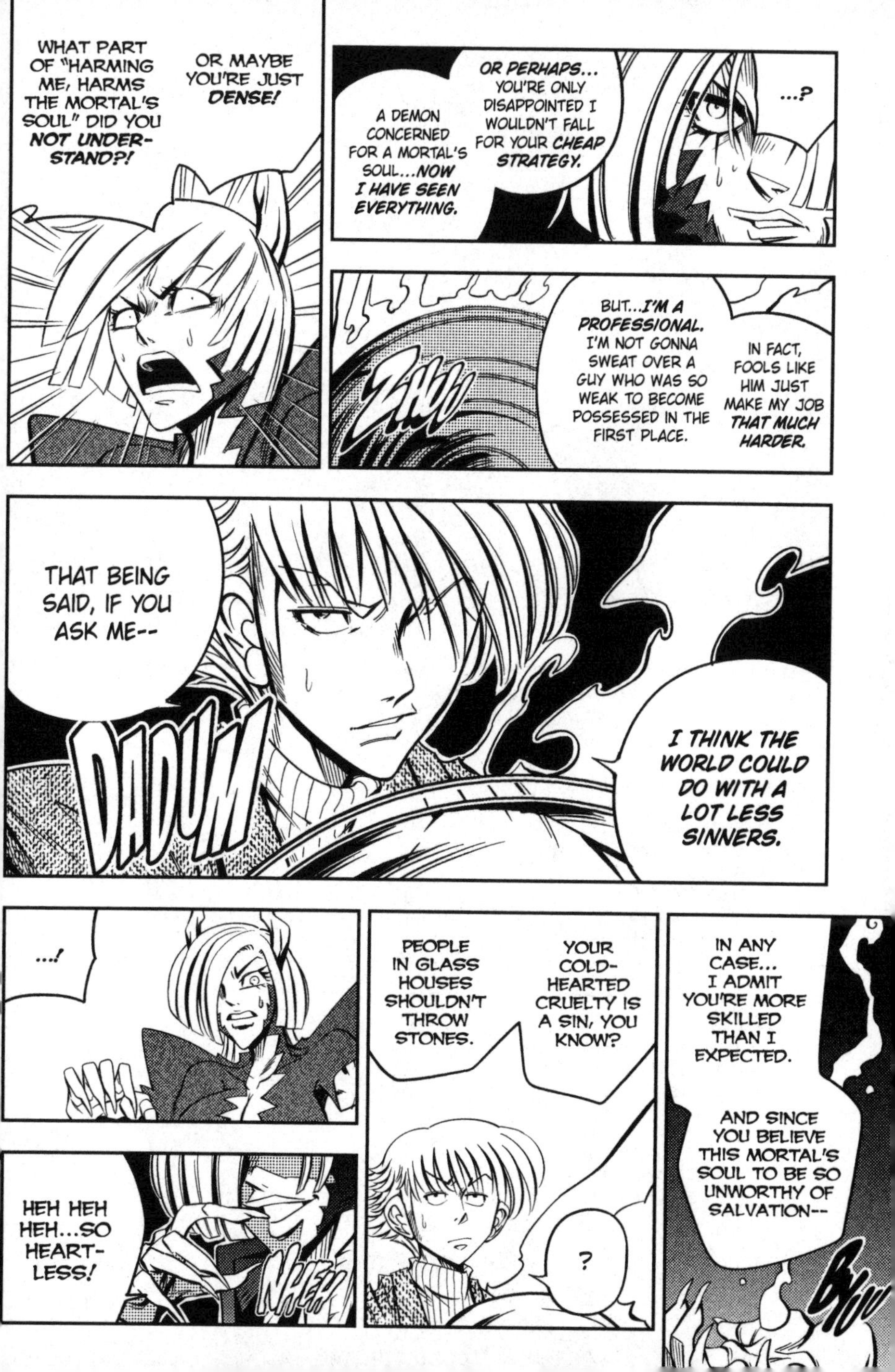
WHAT PART OF "HARMING ME, HARMS THE MORTAL'S SOUL" DID YOU NOT UNDER-STAND?!
OR MAYBE YOU'RE JUST DENSE!
A DEMON CONCERNED FOR A MORTAL'S SOUL...NOW I HAVE SEEN EVERYTHING.
OR PERHAPS... YOU'RE ONLY DISAPPOINTED I WOULDN'T FALL FOR YOUR CHEAP STRATEGY.
...?
BUT...I'M A PROFESSIONAL. I'M NOT GONNA SWEAT OVER A GUY WHO WAS SO WEAK TO BECOME POSSESSED IN THE FIRST PLACE.
IN FACT, FOOLS LIKE HIM JUST MAKE MY JOB THAT MUCH HARDER.
THAT BEING SAID, IF YOU ASK ME--
DADUM
I THINK THE WORLD COULD DO WITH A LOT LESS SINNERS.
...!
HEH HEH HEH...SO HEART-LESS!
NHEH
PEOPLE IN GLASS HOUSES SHOULDN'T THROW STONES.
YOUR COLD-HEARTED CRUELTY IS A SIN, YOU KNOW?
?
IN ANY CASE... I ADMIT YOU'RE MORE SKILLED THAN I EXPECTED.
AND SINCE YOU BELIEVE THIS MORTAL'S SOUL TO BE SO UNWORTHY OF SALVATION--

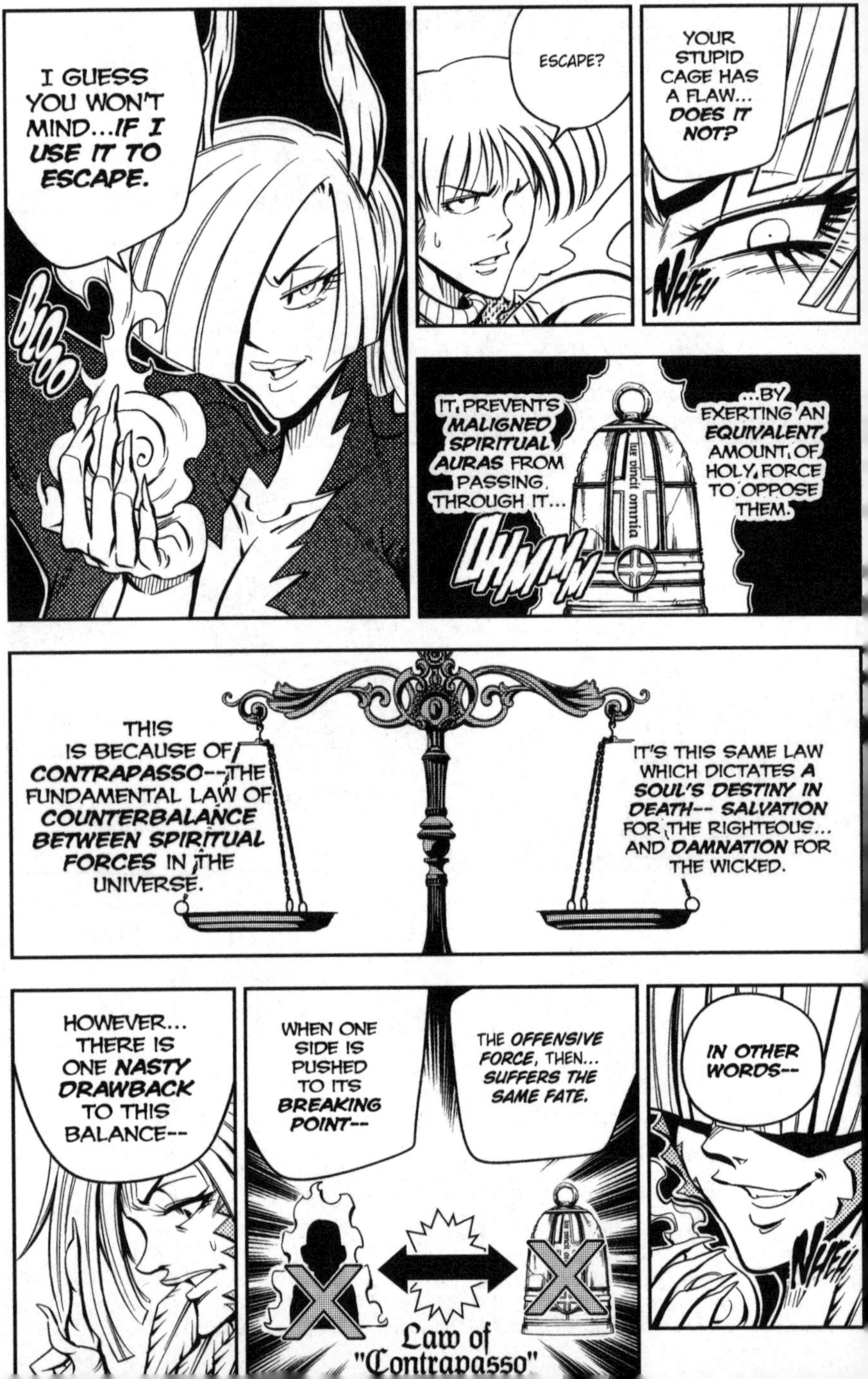

I GUESS YOU WON'T MIND...IF I USE IT TO ESCAPE.
BLOOO
ESCAPE?
YOUR STUPID CAGE HAS A FLAW... DOES IT NOT?
NHEH
IT PREVENTS MALIGNED SPIRITUAL AURAS FROM PASSING THROUGH IT...
lux vincit omnia
OHMMM
...BY EXERTING AN EQUIVALENT AMOUNT OF HOLY FORCE TO OPPOSE THEM.
THIS IS BECAUSE OF CONTRAPASSO--THE FUNDAMENTAL LAW OF COUNTERBALANCE BETWEEN SPIRITUAL FORCES IN THE UNIVERSE.
IT'S THIS SAME LAW WHICH DICTATES A SOUL'S DESTINY IN DEATH-- SALVATION FOR THE RIGHTEOUS... AND DAMNATION FOR THE WICKED.
HOWEVER... THERE IS ONE NASTY DRAWBACK TO THIS BALANCE--
WHEN ONE SIDE IS PUSHED TO ITS BREAKING POINT--
THE OFFENSIVE FORCE, THEN... SUFFERS THE SAME FATE.
Law of "Contrapasso"
IN OTHER WORDS--
NHEH

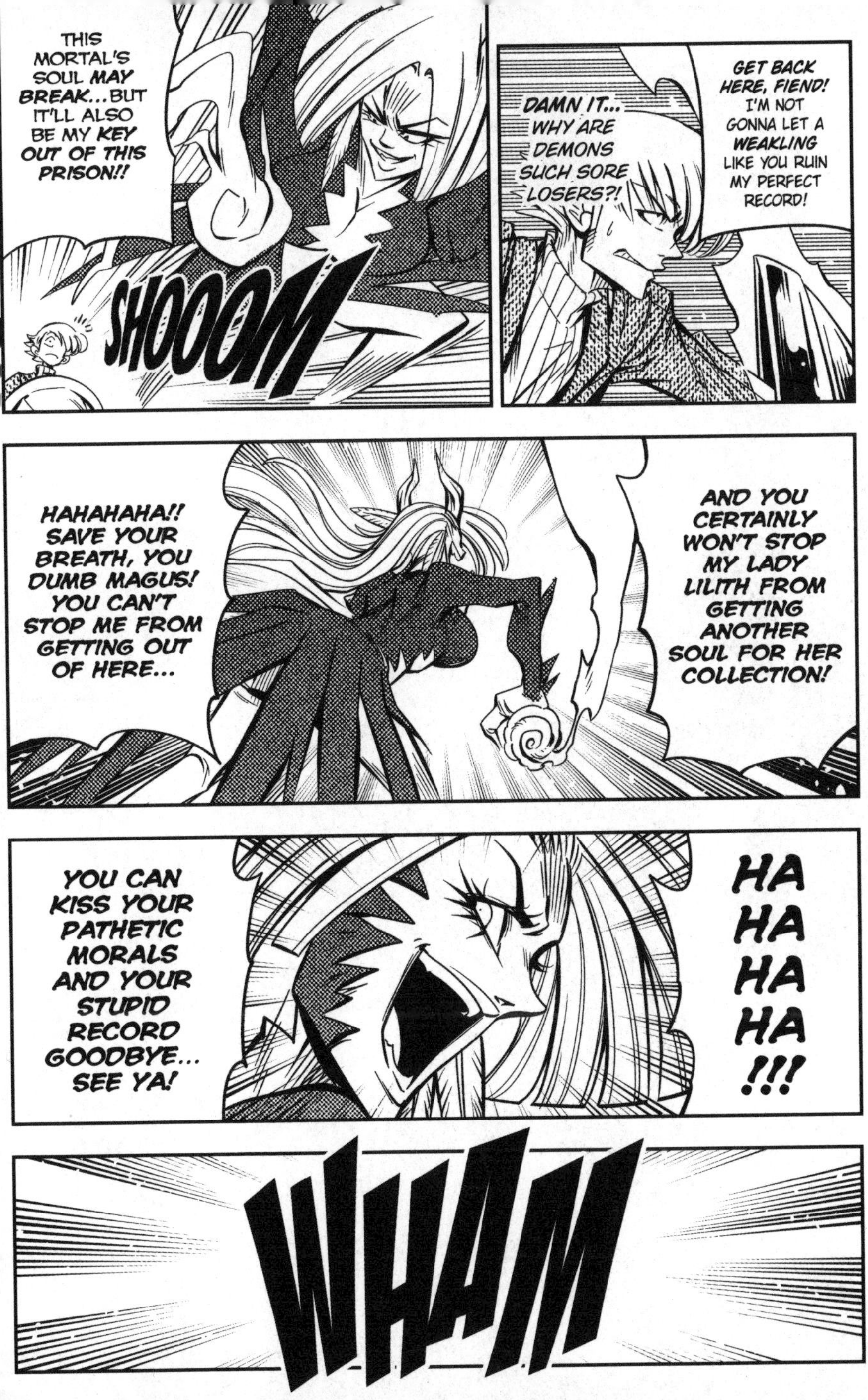
THIS MORTAL'S SOUL MAY BREAK... BUT IT'LL ALSO BE MY KEY OUT OF THIS PRISON!!
SHOOOM
DAMN IT... WHY ARE DEMONS SUCH SORE LOSERS?!
GET BACK HERE, FIEND! I'M NOT GONNA LET A WEAKLING LIKE YOU RUIN MY PERFECT RECORD!
HAHAHAHA!! SAVE YOUR BREATH, YOU DUMB MAGUS! YOU CAN'T STOP ME FROM GETTING OUT OF HERE...
AND YOU CERTAINLY WON'T STOP MY LADY LILITH FROM GETTING ANOTHER SOUL FOR HER COLLECTION!
YOU CAN KISS YOUR PATHETIC MORALS AND YOUR STUPID RECORD GOODBYE... SEE YA!
HA HA HA HA HA !!!
WHAM

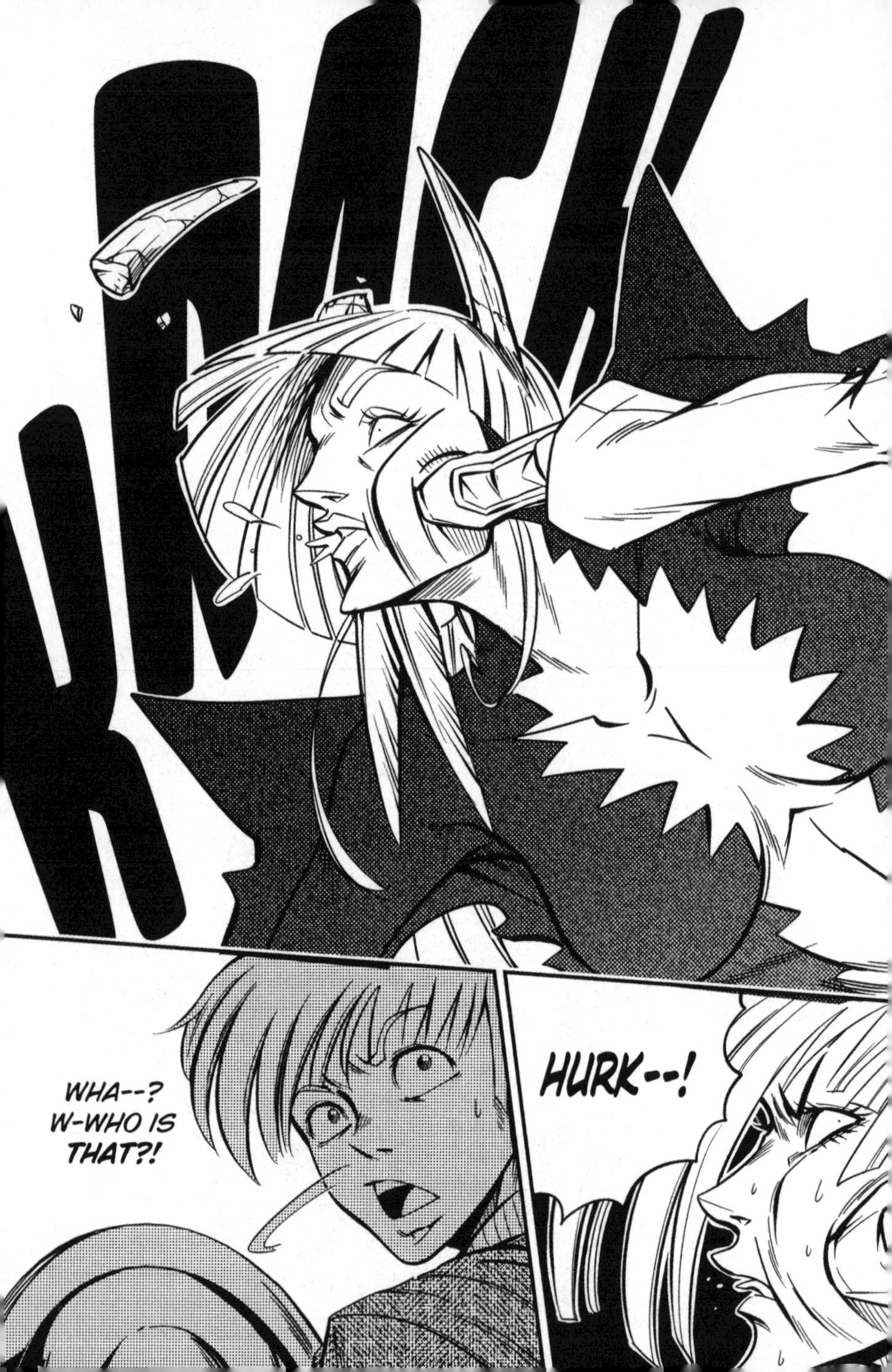
WHA--? W-WHO IS THAT?!
HURK--!

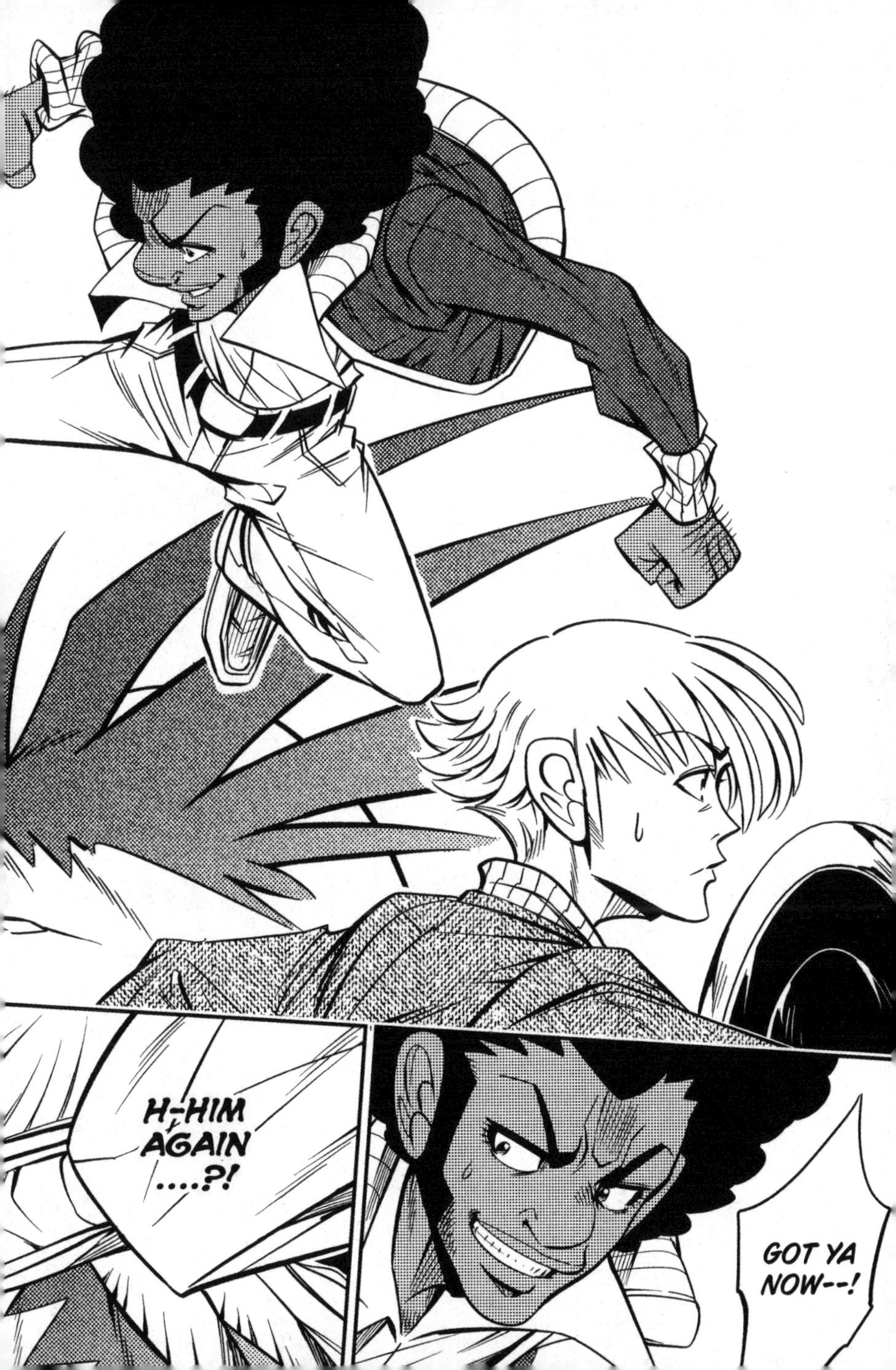
H-HIM AGAIN ....?!
GOT YA NOW--!

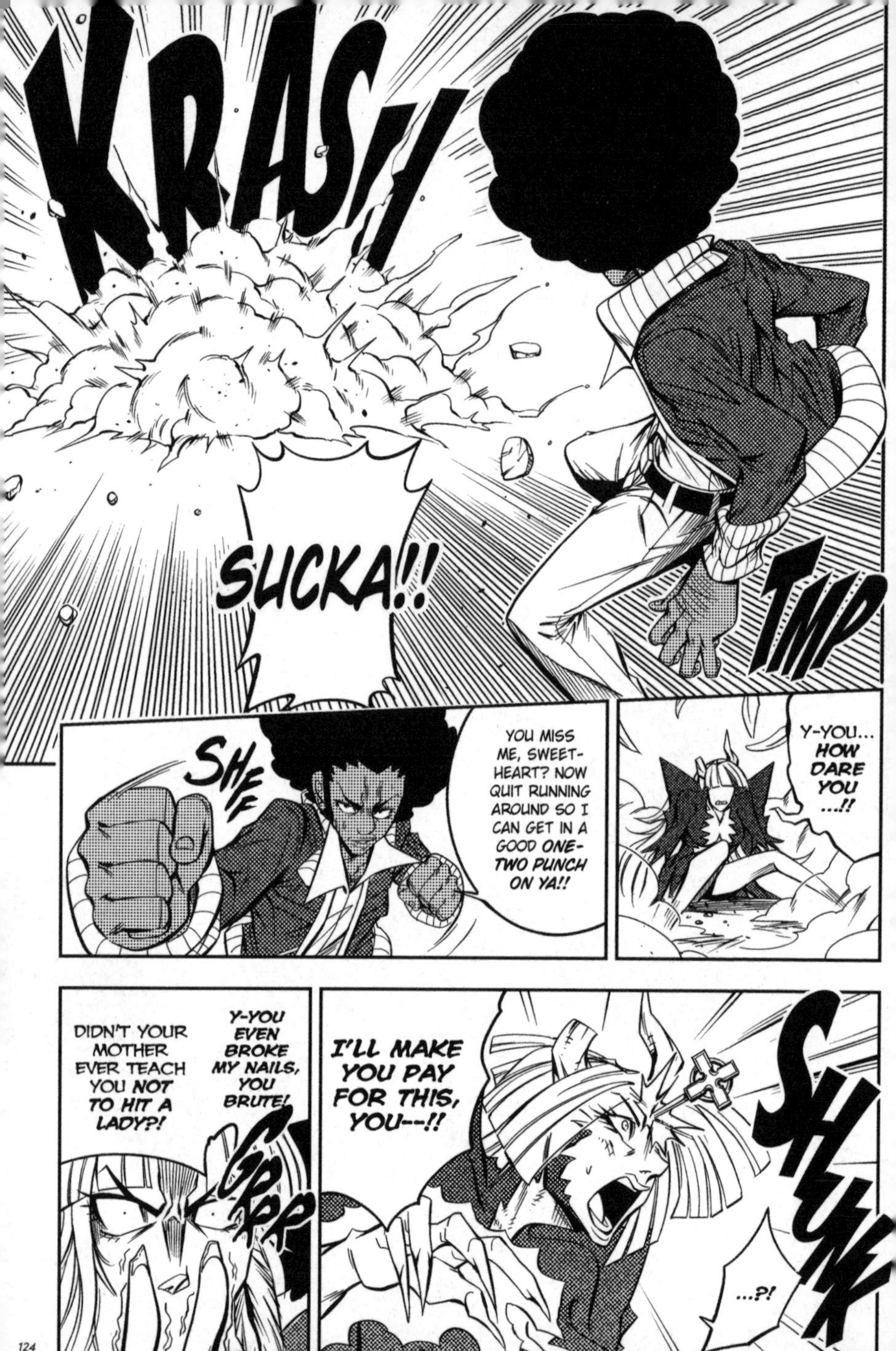
KRASH
SUCKA!!
TMP
SHFF
YOU MISS ME, SWEET-HEART? NOW QUIT RUNNING AROUND SO I CAN GET IN A GOOD *ONE-TWO PUNCH* ON YA!!
Y-YOU... *HOW DARE YOU ...!!*
DIDN'T YOUR MOTHER EVER TEACH YOU *NOT TO HIT A LADY?!*
Y-YOU EVEN BROKE MY NAILS, YOU BRUTE!
GRRR
I'LL MAKE YOU PAY FOR THIS, YOU--!!
SHUNK
...?!

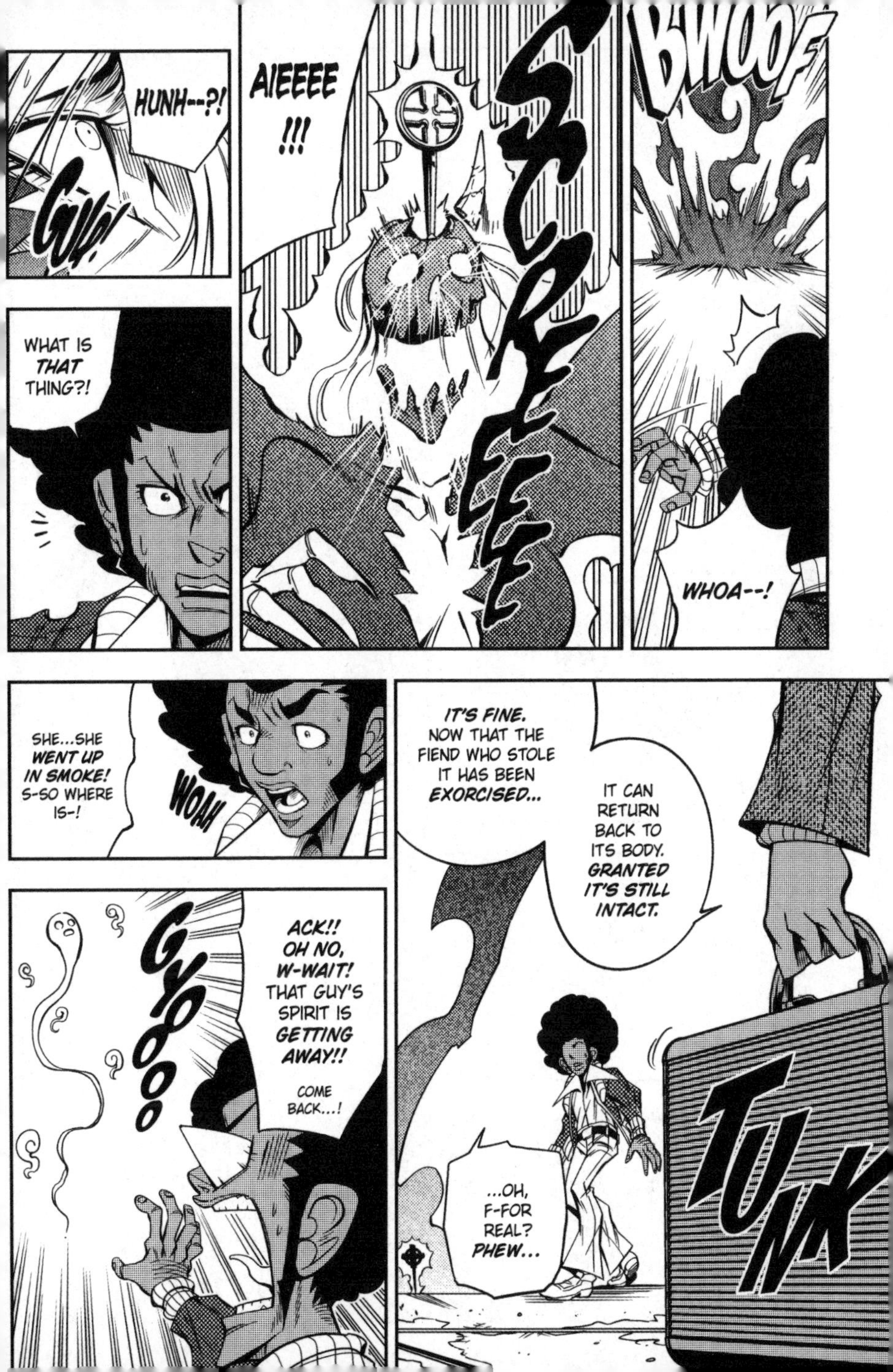
HUNH--?!
GULP
WHAT IS THAT THING?!
AIEEEE !!!
SCREEEEEEE
BWOOF
WHOA--!
SHE...SHE WENT UP IN SMOKE! S-SO WHERE IS-!
WOAH
ACK!! OH NO, W-WAIT! THAT GUY'S SPIRIT IS GETTING AWAY!!
COME BACK...!
GYOOOO
IT'S FINE. NOW THAT THE FIEND WHO STOLE IT HAS BEEN EXORCISED...
IT CAN RETURN BACK TO ITS BODY. GRANTED IT'S STILL INTACT.
...OH, F-FOR REAL? PHEW...
TUNK

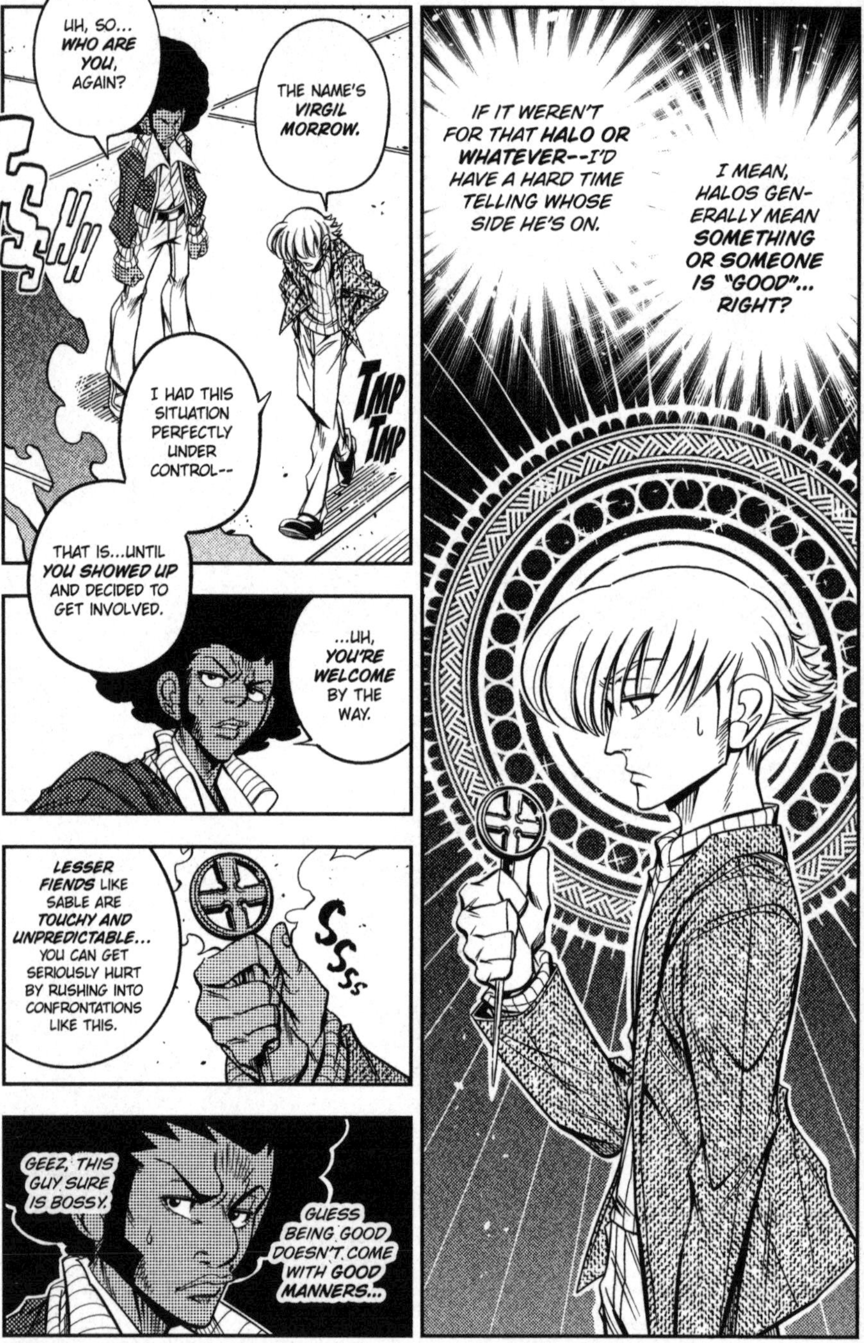

UH, SO... WHO ARE YOU, AGAIN?
FSSHH
THE NAME'S VIRGIL MORROW.
I HAD THIS SITUATION PERFECTLY UNDER CONTROL--
TMP TMP
THAT IS...UNTIL YOU SHOWED UP AND DECIDED TO GET INVOLVED.
...UH, YOU'RE WELCOME BY THE WAY.
LESSER FIENDS LIKE SABLE ARE TOUCHY AND UNPREDICTABLE... YOU CAN GET SERIOUSLY HURT BY RUSHING INTO CONFRONTATIONS LIKE THIS.
SSSS
GEEZ, THIS GUY SURE IS BOSSY.
GUESS BEING GOOD DOESN'T COME WITH GOOD MANNERS...
IF IT WEREN'T FOR THAT HALO OR WHATEVER--I'D HAVE A HARD TIME TELLING WHOSE SIDE HE'S ON.
I MEAN, HALOS GEN-ERALLY MEAN SOMETHING OR SOMEONE IS "GOOD"... RIGHT?

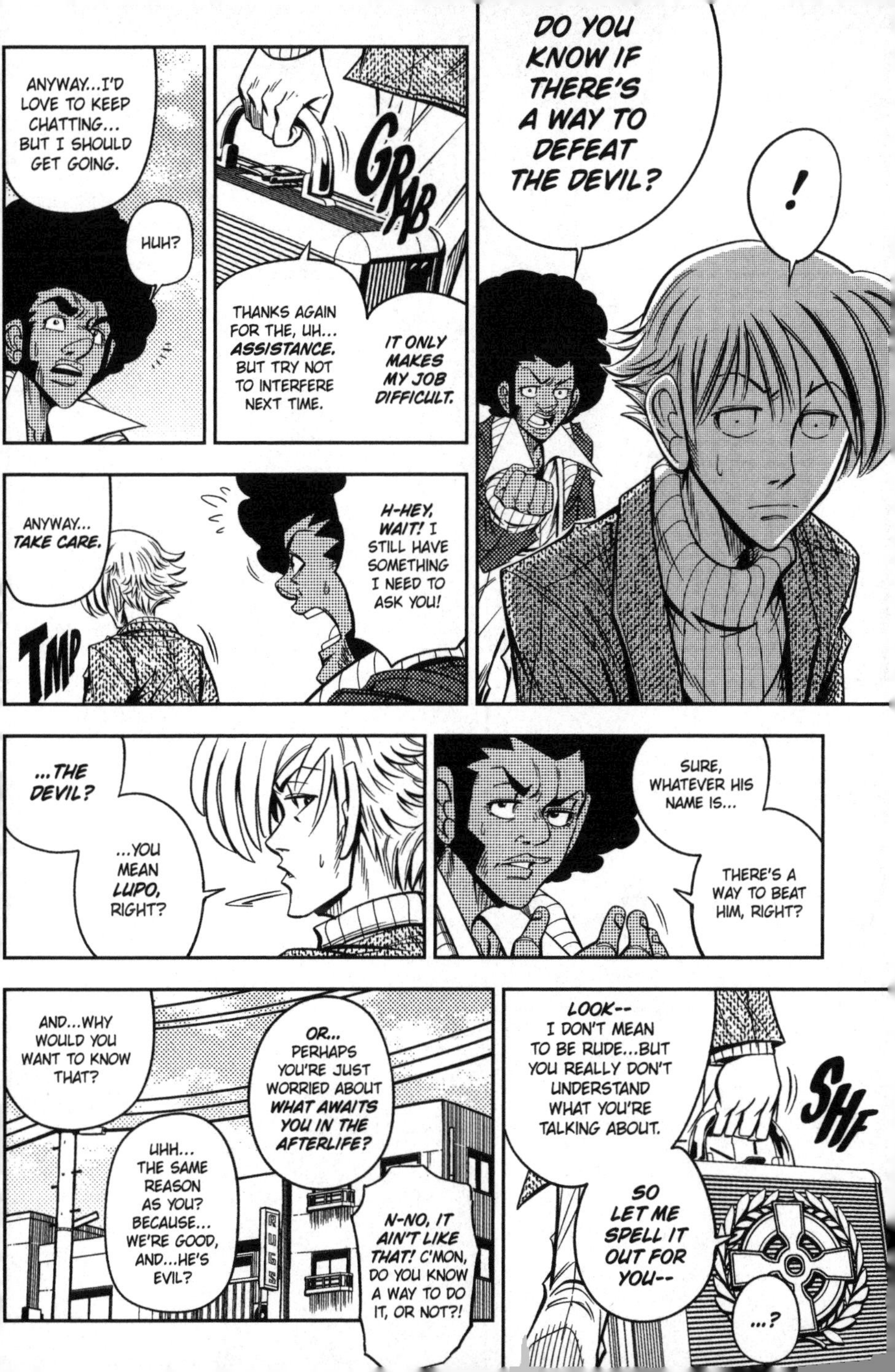
ANYWAY...I'D LOVE TO KEEP CHATTING... BUT I SHOULD GET GOING.
HUH?
GRAB
THANKS AGAIN FOR THE, UH... ASSISTANCE. BUT TRY NOT TO INTERFERE NEXT TIME.
IT ONLY MAKES MY JOB DIFFICULT.
ANYWAY... TAKE CARE.
TMP
H-HEY, WAIT! I STILL HAVE SOMETHING I NEED TO ASK YOU!
DO YOU KNOW IF THERE'S A WAY TO DEFEAT THE DEVIL?
!
...THE DEVIL?
...YOU MEAN LUPO, RIGHT?
SURE, WHATEVER HIS NAME IS...
THERE'S A WAY TO BEAT HIM, RIGHT?
AND...WHY WOULD YOU WANT TO KNOW THAT?
UHH... THE SAME REASON AS YOU? BECAUSE... WE'RE GOOD, AND...HE'S EVIL?
OR... PERHAPS YOU'RE JUST WORRIED ABOUT WHAT AWAITS YOU IN THE AFTERLIFE?
N-NO, IT AIN'T LIKE THAT! C'MON, DO YOU KNOW A WAY TO DO IT, OR NOT?!
RUGS
LOOK-- I DON'T MEAN TO BE RUDE...BUT YOU REALLY DON'T UNDERSTAND WHAT YOU'RE TALKING ABOUT.
SHF
SO LET ME SPELL IT OUT FOR YOU--
...?

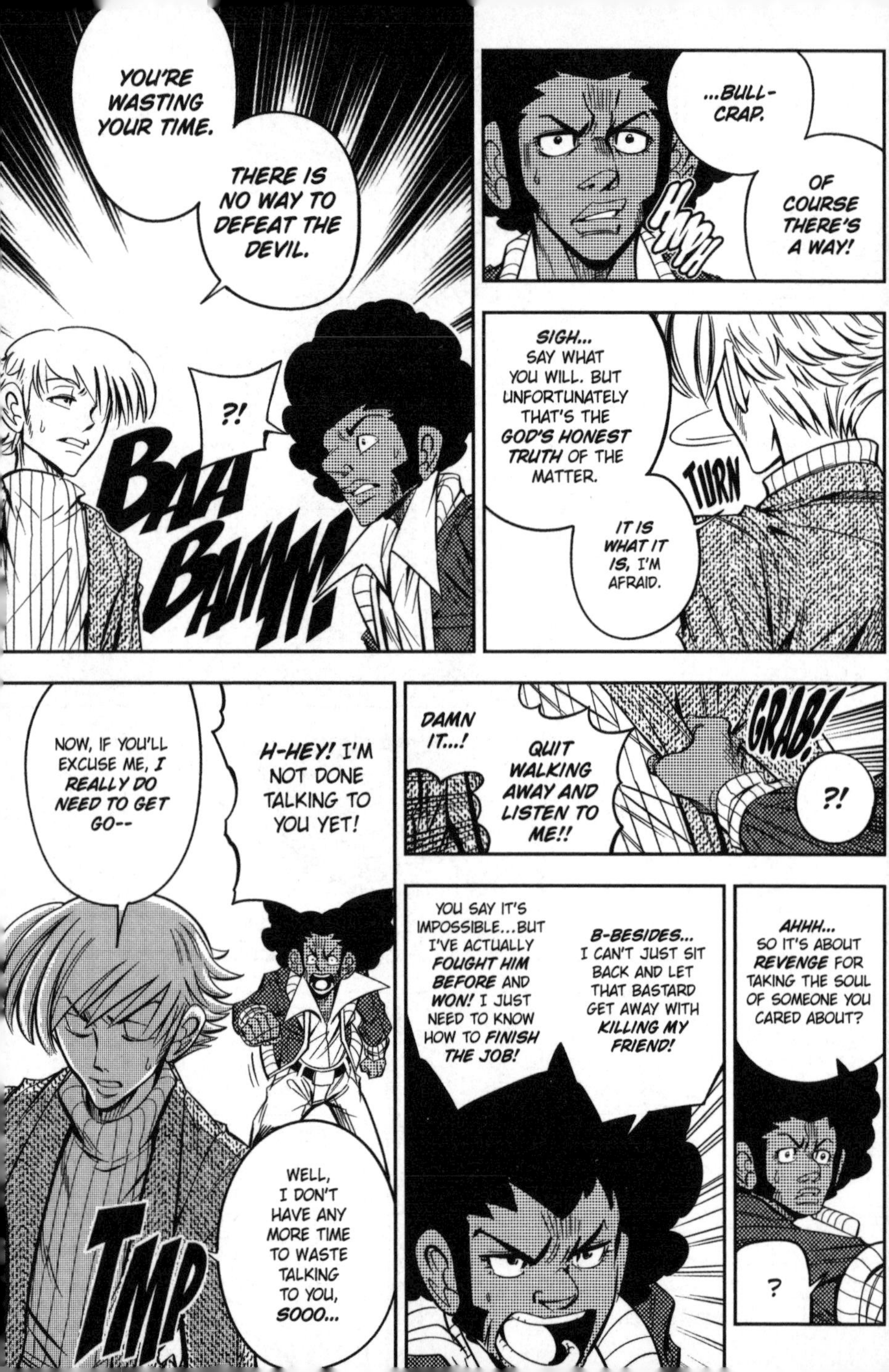
YOU'RE WASTING YOUR TIME.
THERE IS NO WAY TO DEFEAT THE DEVIL.
?!
BAA BAMM!
...BULL-CRAP.
OF COURSE THERE'S A WAY!
SIGH... SAY WHAT YOU WILL. BUT UNFORTUNATELY THAT'S THE GOD'S HONEST TRUTH OF THE MATTER.
TURN
IT IS WHAT IT IS, I'M AFRAID.
NOW, IF YOU'LL EXCUSE ME, I REALLY DO NEED TO GET GO--
H-HEY! I'M NOT DONE TALKING TO YOU YET!
WELL, I DON'T HAVE ANY MORE TIME TO WASTE TALKING TO YOU, SOOO...
TMP
DAMN IT...!
QUIT WALKING AWAY AND LISTEN TO ME!!
GRAB!
?!
YOU SAY IT'S IMPOSSIBLE...BUT I'VE ACTUALLY FOUGHT HIM BEFORE AND WON! I JUST NEED TO KNOW HOW TO FINISH THE JOB!
B-BESIDES... I CAN'T JUST SIT BACK AND LET THAT BASTARD GET AWAY WITH KILLING MY FRIEND!
AHHH... SO IT'S ABOUT REVENGE FOR TAKING THE SOUL OF SOMEONE YOU CARED ABOUT?
?

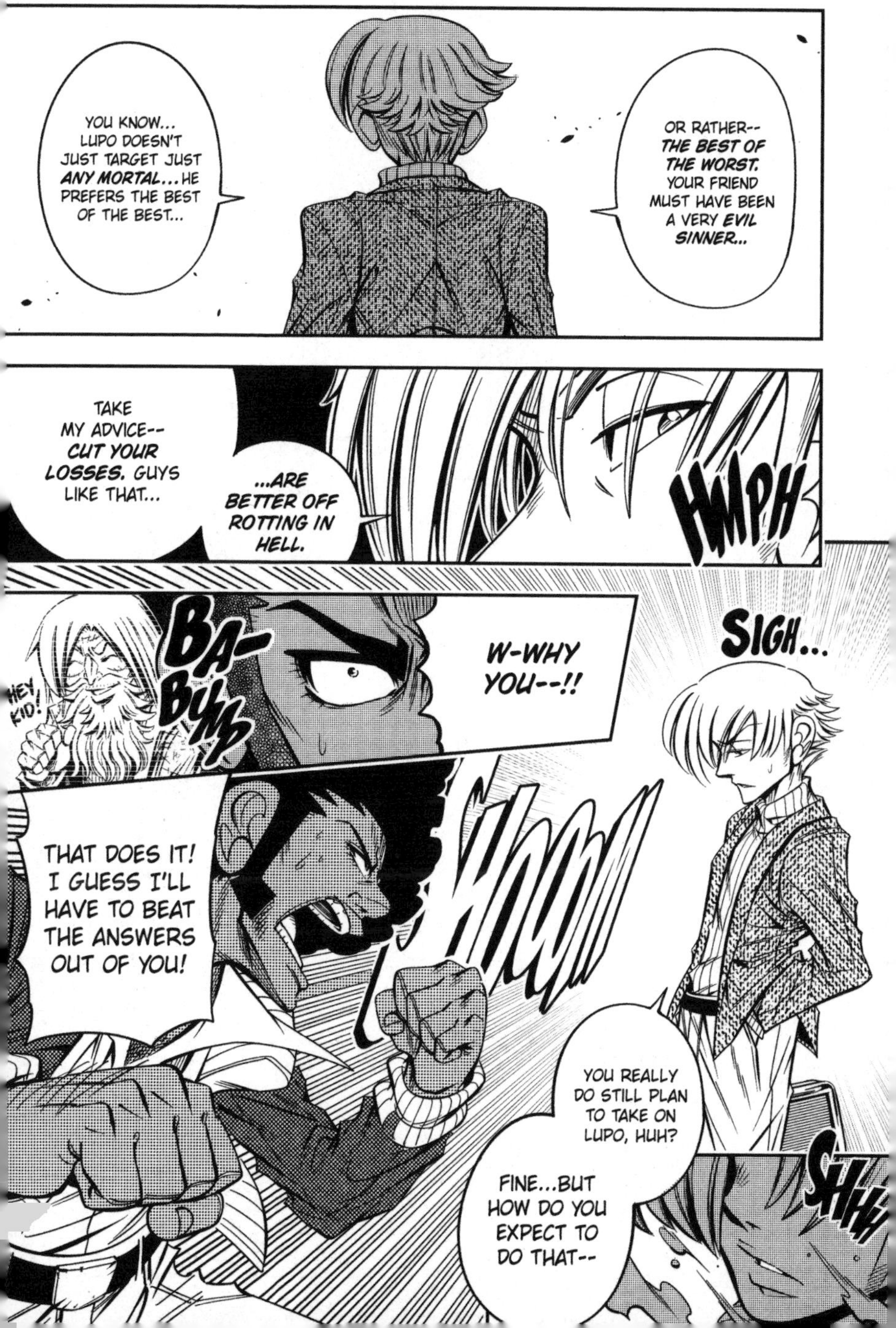
YOU KNOW... LUPO DOESN'T JUST TARGET JUST ANY MORTAL... HE PREFERS THE BEST OF THE BEST...
OR RATHER-- THE BEST OF THE WORST. YOUR FRIEND MUST HAVE BEEN A VERY EVIL SINNER...
TAKE MY ADVICE-- CUT YOUR LOSSES. GUYS LIKE THAT...
...ARE BETTER OFF ROTTING IN HELL.
HMPH
SIGH...
W-WHY YOU--!!
BA-BUMP
HEY KID!
THAT DOES IT! I GUESS I'LL HAVE TO BEAT THE ANSWERS OUT OF YOU!
YOU REALLY DO STILL PLAN TO TAKE ON LUPO, HUH?
FINE...BUT HOW DO YOU EXPECT TO DO THAT--
SHHK

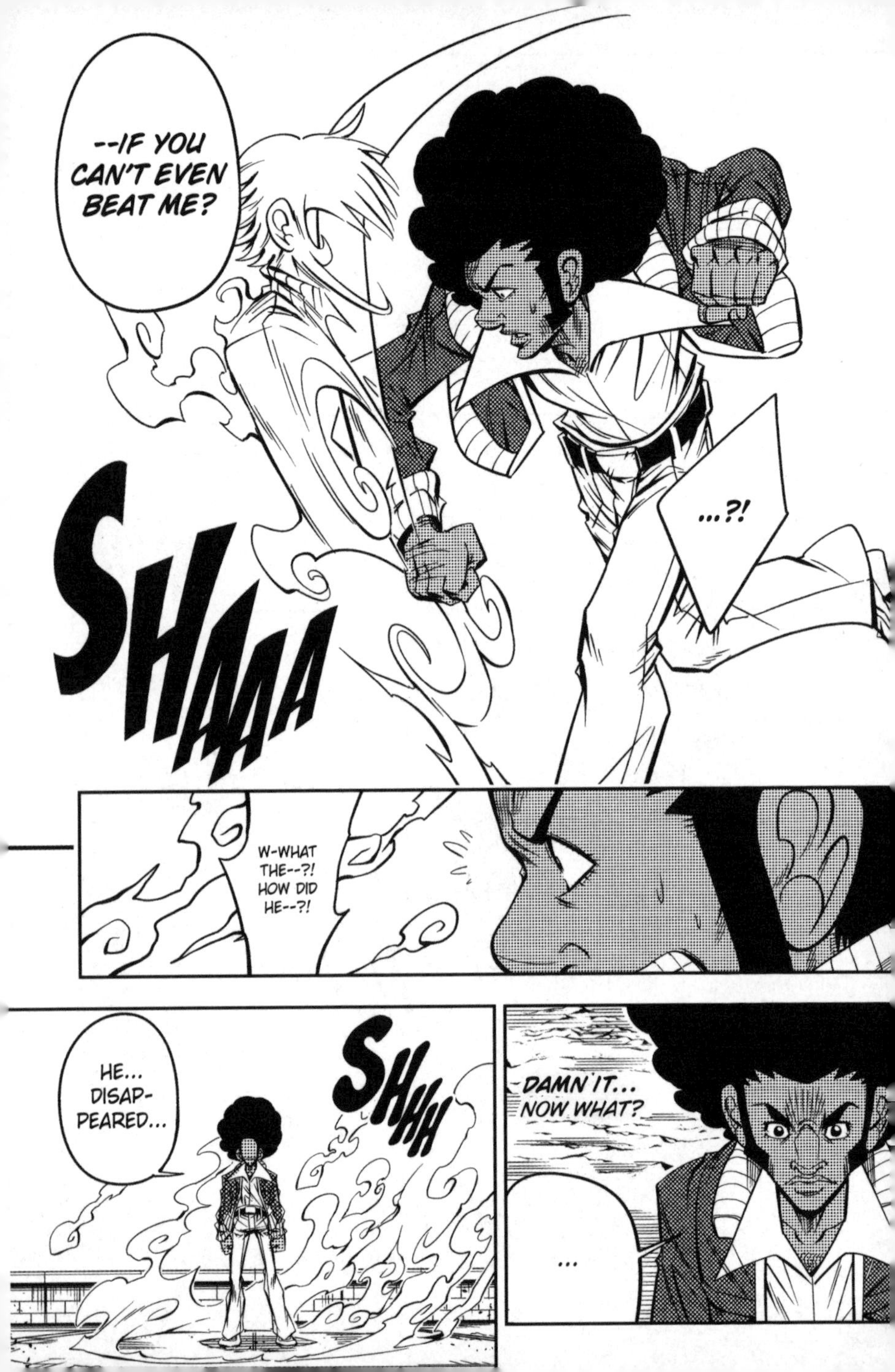
--IF YOU CAN'T EVEN BEAT ME?
SHAAAA
...?!
W-WHAT THE--?! HOW DID HE--?!
HE... DISAP-PEARED...
SHHH
DAMN IT... NOW WHAT?
...

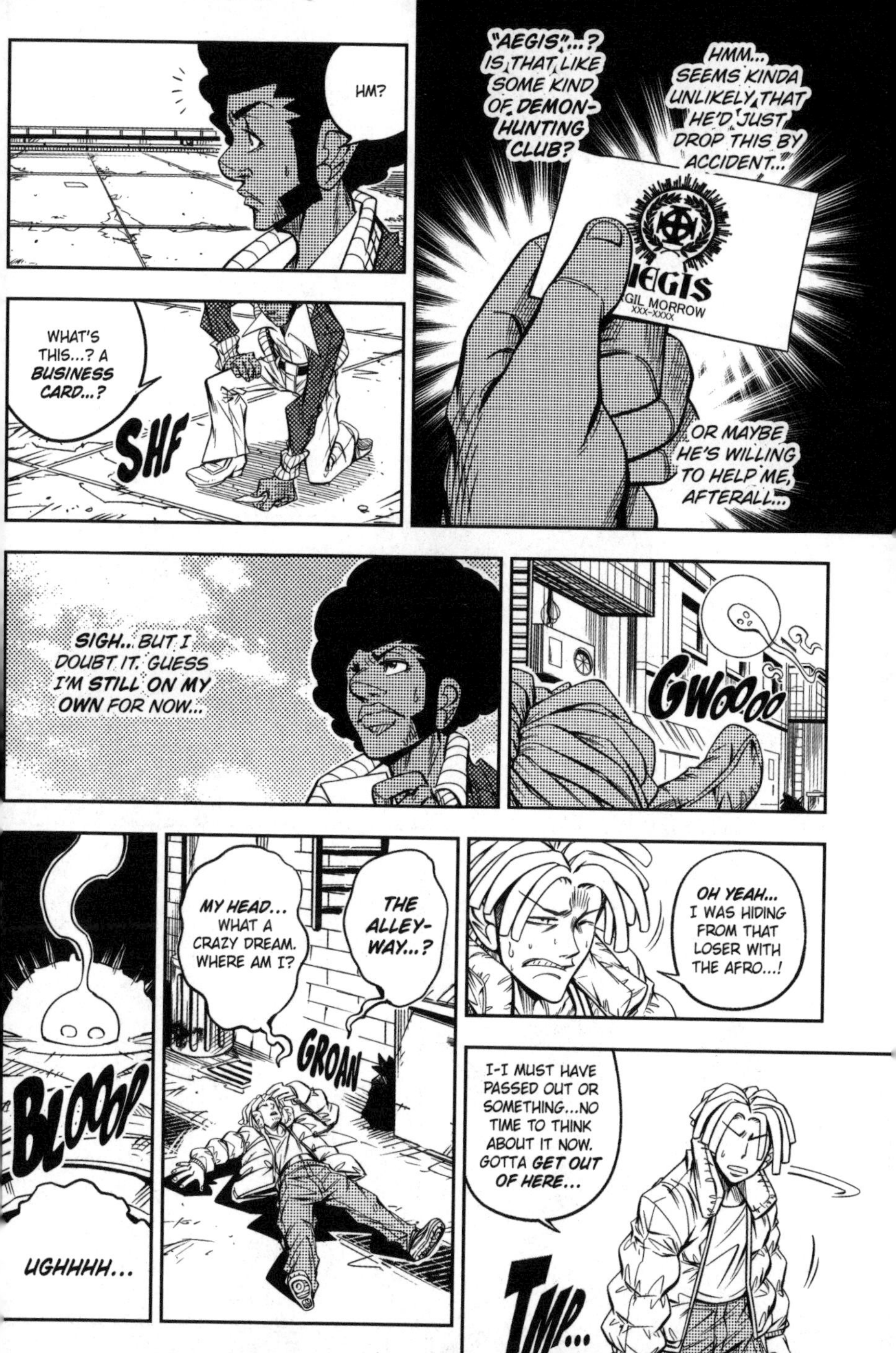
HM?
WHAT'S THIS...? A BUSINESS CARD...?
SHF
"AEGIS"...? IS THAT LIKE SOME KIND OF DEMON-HUNTING CLUB?
HMM... SEEMS KINDA UNLIKELY THAT HE'D JUST DROP THIS BY ACCIDENT...
OR MAYBE HE'S WILLING TO HELP ME, AFTERALL...
SIGH... BUT I DOUBT IT. GUESS I'M STILL ON MY OWN FOR NOW...
GWOOOOO
BLOOOP
UGHHHH...
MY HEAD... WHAT A CRAZY DREAM. WHERE AM I?
THE ALLEY-WAY...?
GROAN
OH YEAH... I WAS HIDING FROM THAT LOSER WITH THE AFRO...!
I-I MUST HAVE PASSED OUT OR SOMETHING...NO TIME TO THINK ABOUT IT NOW. GOTTA GET OUT OF HERE...
TMP...

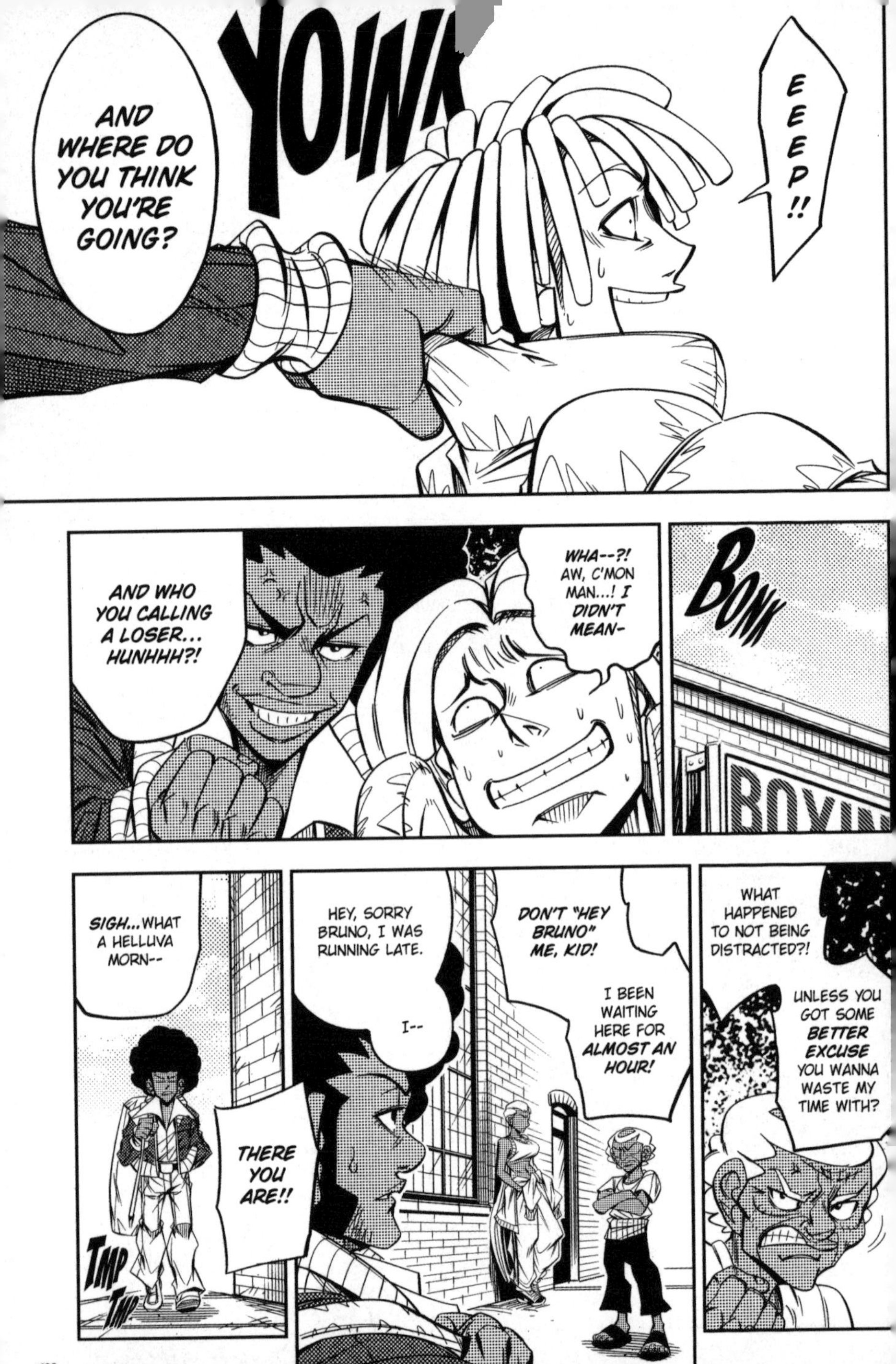
YOINK
AND WHERE DO YOU THINK YOU'RE GOING?
EEEEP!!
AND WHO YOU CALLING A LOSER... HUNHHH?!
WHA--?! AW, C'MON MAN...! I DIDN'T MEAN-
BONK
SIGH...WHAT A HELLUVA MORN--
TMP TMP
THERE YOU ARE!!
HEY, SORRY BRUNO, I WAS RUNNING LATE.
I--
DON'T "HEY BRUNO" ME, KID!
I BEEN WAITING HERE FOR ALMOST AN HOUR!
WHAT HAPPENED TO NOT BEING DISTRACTED?!
UNLESS YOU GOT SOME BETTER EXCUSE YOU WANNA WASTE MY TIME WITH?

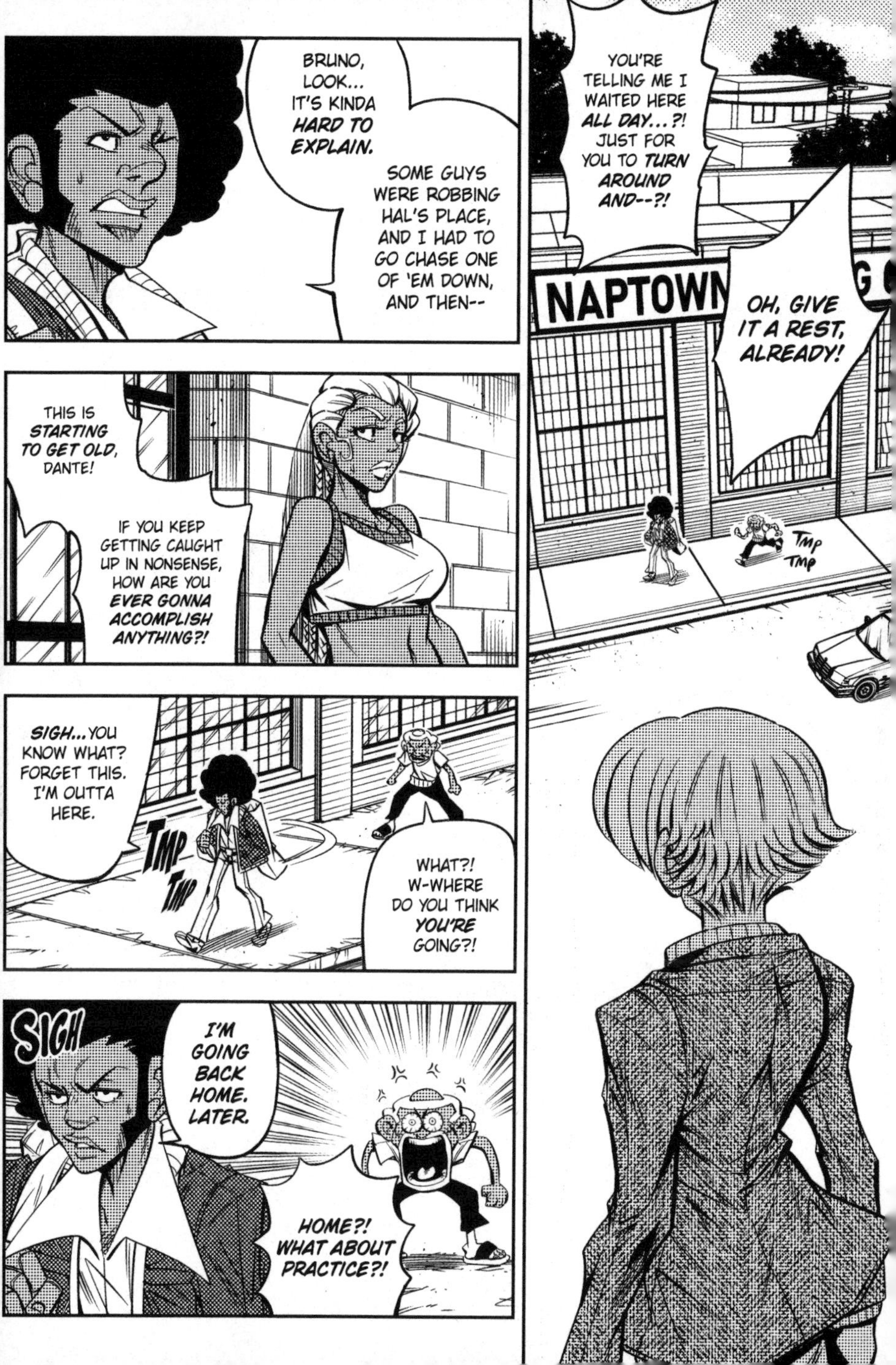
BRUNO, LOOK... IT'S KINDA HARD TO EXPLAIN.
SOME GUYS WERE ROBBING HAL'S PLACE, AND I HAD TO GO CHASE ONE OF 'EM DOWN, AND THEN--
THIS IS STARTING TO GET OLD, DANTE!
IF YOU KEEP GETTING CAUGHT UP IN NONSENSE, HOW ARE YOU EVER GONNA ACCOMPLISH ANYTHING?!
SIGH...YOU KNOW WHAT? FORGET THIS. I'M OUTTA HERE.
TMP TMP
WHAT?! W-WHERE DO YOU THINK YOU'RE GOING?!
SIGH
I'M GOING BACK HOME. LATER.
HOME?! WHAT ABOUT PRACTICE?!
YOU'RE TELLING ME I WAITED HERE ALL DAY...?! JUST FOR YOU TO TURN AROUND AND--?!
NAPTOWN
OH, GIVE IT A REST, ALREADY!
TMP TMP

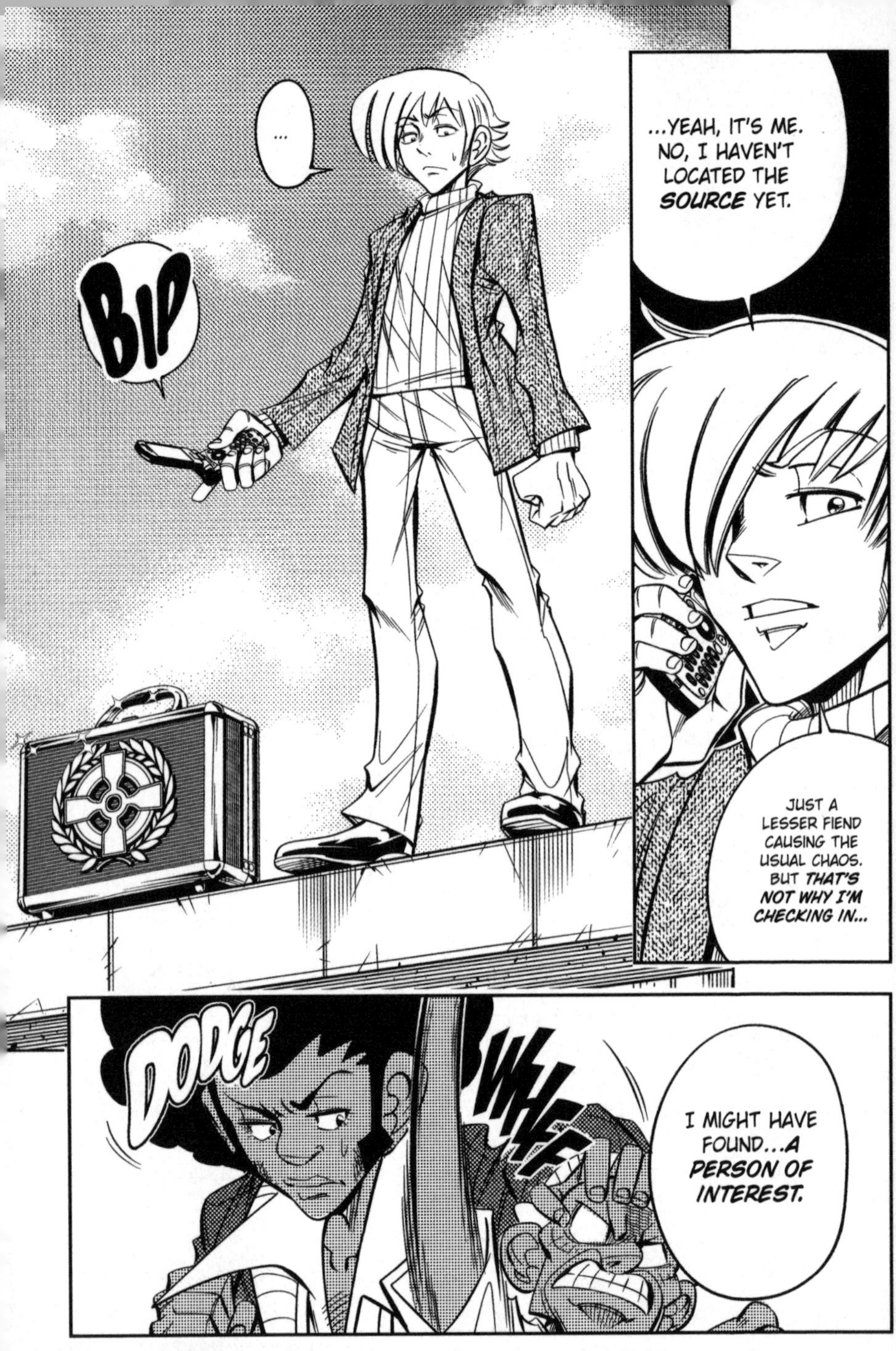

...
BIP
...YEAH, IT'S ME. NO, I HAVEN'T LOCATED THE SOURCE YET.
JUST A LESSER FIEND CAUSING THE USUAL CHAOS. BUT THAT'S NOT WHY I'M CHECKING IN...
DODGE
WHF
I MIGHT HAVE FOUND...A PERSON OF INTEREST.

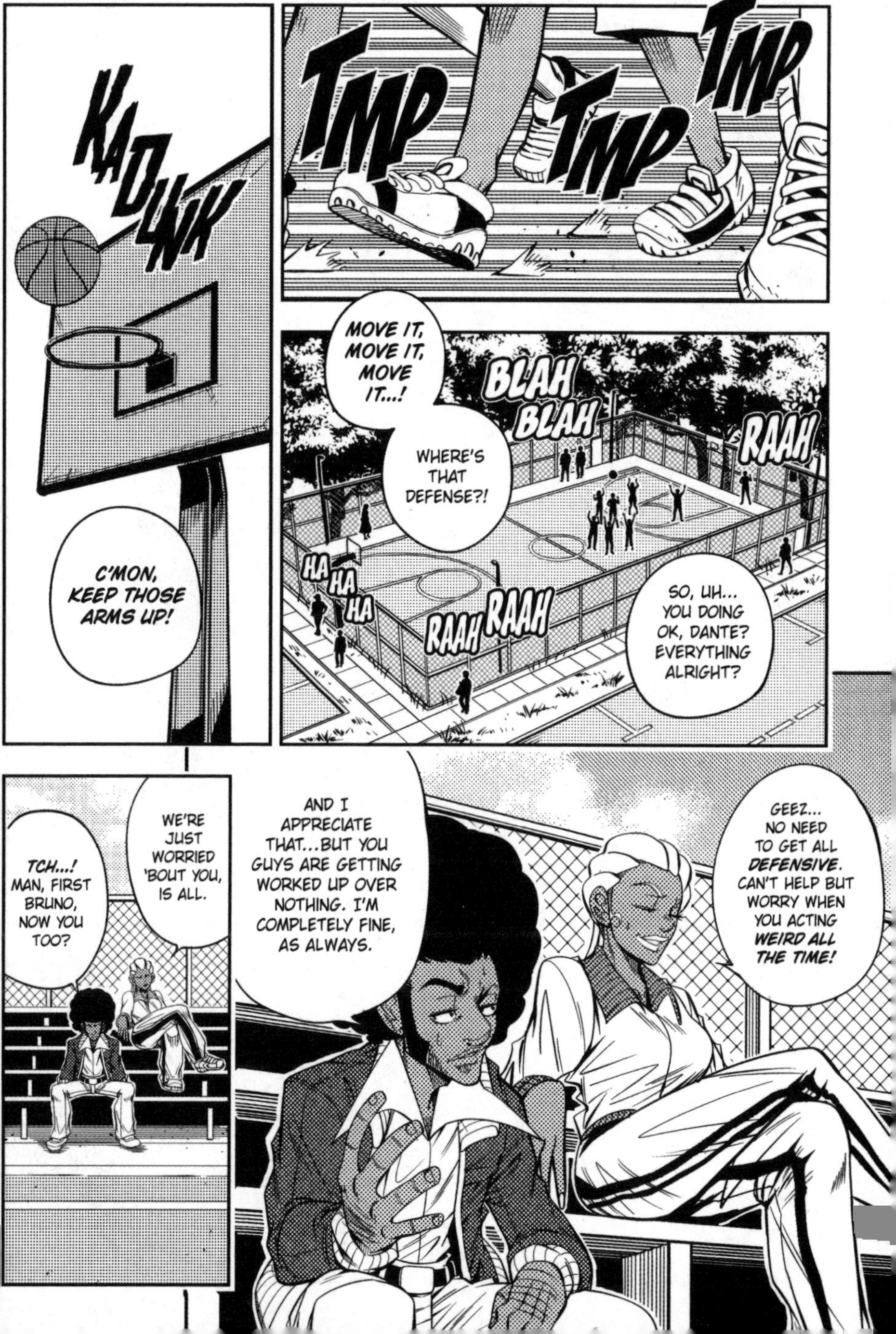
KADUNK
C'MON, KEEP THOSE ARMS UP!
TMP
TMP
TMP
MOVE IT, MOVE IT, MOVE IT...!
BLAH BLAH
WHERE'S THAT DEFENSE?!
RAAH
HA HA HA
RAAH RAAH
SO, UH... YOU DOING OK, DANTE? EVERYTHING ALRIGHT?
TCH...! MAN, FIRST BRUNO, NOW YOU TOO?
WE'RE JUST WORRIED 'BOUT YOU, IS ALL.
AND I APPRECIATE THAT...BUT YOU GUYS ARE GETTING WORKED UP OVER NOTHING. I'M COMPLETELY FINE, AS ALWAYS.
GEEZ... NO NEED TO GET ALL DEFENSIVE. CAN'T HELP BUT WORRY WHEN YOU ACTING WEIRD ALL THE TIME!

A GOOD DOCTOR'S GOTTA LOOK OUT FOR EMOTIONAL DISTRESS...AND BOY, IT IS WRITTEN *ALL OVER YOU,* LATELY.

A-AND WHAT MAKES YOU THINK THAT?

ASIDE FROM THE *OBVIOUS?* YOU'RE ALWAYS LATE TO PRACTICE, NOW...

AND IT KINDA FEELS LIKE YOU BEEN *AVOIDIN'* SOME OF US, LATELY...

AND THEN THERE'S THESE *WEIRDLY SPECIFIC BOOKS* YOU BEEN READING...WHAT'S UP WITH THAT?

NOT EVERYTHING IN MY LIFE IS ABOUT BOXING, YOU KNOW?

ANGE
DEMO
AND the
AFTER LIFE

YEAH, BUT LIKE...*DEMONS AND STUFF?* I NEVER HEARD YOU TALK ABOUT THOSE THINGS BEFORE...

WELL, IT NEVER INTERESTED ME BEFORE. NOW IT DOES.

BUT I GUESS AFTER BEN DIED...I JUST FEEL LIKE I SHOULD BE MORE PREPARED.

KA-DAWK

PREPARED FOR *WHAT?*

SIGH... WHO REALLY KNOWS?

I CAN'T TELL HER THE TRUTH JUST YET--

--BUT IT'S SO I CAN BE READY FOR THE NEXT DAMN DEMON WHO DECIDES TO SHOW UP AROUND HERE!

Chapter 5: Flashpoint

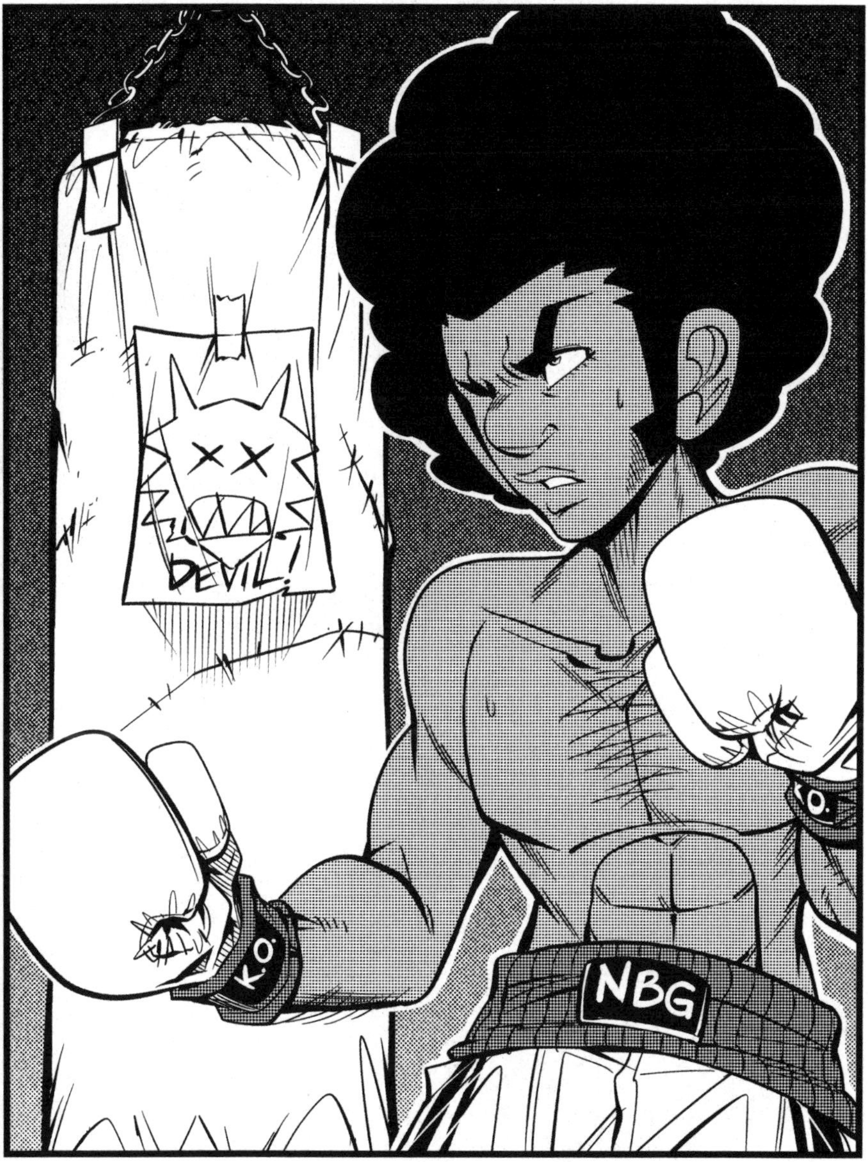
DEVIL!
K.O.
K.O.
NBG

FWEET!

ALRIGHT, EVERYONE, GOOD HUSTLE TODAY!

YO, DANTE!!

HEY, ELI!

WERE YOU WATCHING ME?

I SCORED LIKE TWENTY POINTS!

TMP TMP

TMP

Eli Williams
Little Brother

YOU BET I WAS WATCHING! THAT OFFENSE IS LOOKIN' REAL SOLID!

THAT'S 'CAUSE I'VE BEEN PRACTICING EVERY DAY... JUST LIKE YOU TOLD ME TO!

SEE! I'VE BEEN DRIBBLIN' SO MUCH...I CAN PRACTICALLY DO IT WITH MY EYES CLOSED!

NOW NOBODY CAN TAKE IT FROM ME!

DRBL DRBL DRBL

YEAH!

WAY TO GO, ELI!

YOU'RE GONNA BE PRO IN NO TIME!

OF COURSE HE WILL! SPORTS EXCELLENCE RUNS IN OUR FAMILY'S DNA!

BUT DAD SAYS SOMETIMES IT SKIPS A GENERATION...

YEAAAH...

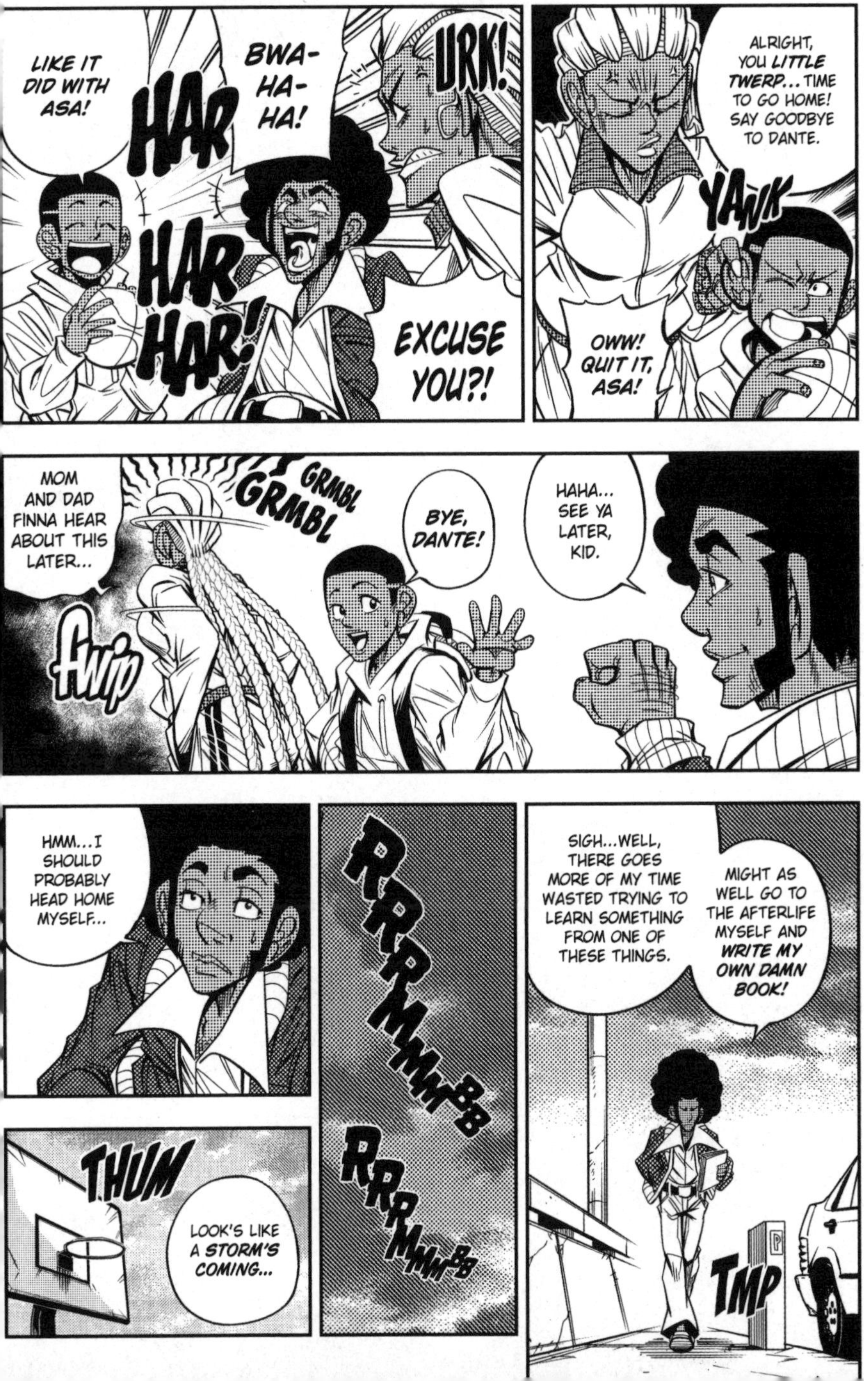

LIKE IT DID WITH ASA!
HAR HAR HAR!
BWA-HA-HA!
URK!
EXCUSE YOU?!
ALRIGHT, YOU LITTLE TWERP... TIME TO GO HOME! SAY GOODBYE TO DANTE.
YANK
OWW! QUIT IT, ASA!
MOM AND DAD FINNA HEAR ABOUT THIS LATER...
GRMBL GRMBL
fwip
BYE, DANTE!
HAHA... SEE YA LATER, KID.
HMM... I SHOULD PROBABLY HEAD HOME MYSELF...
T.THUM
LOOK'S LIKE A STORM'S COMING...
RRRMMMBB
RRRMMMBB
SIGH...WELL, THERE GOES MORE OF MY TIME WASTED TRYING TO LEARN SOMETHING FROM ONE OF THESE THINGS.
MIGHT AS WELL GO TO THE AFTERLIFE MYSELF AND WRITE MY OWN DAMN BOOK!
TMP

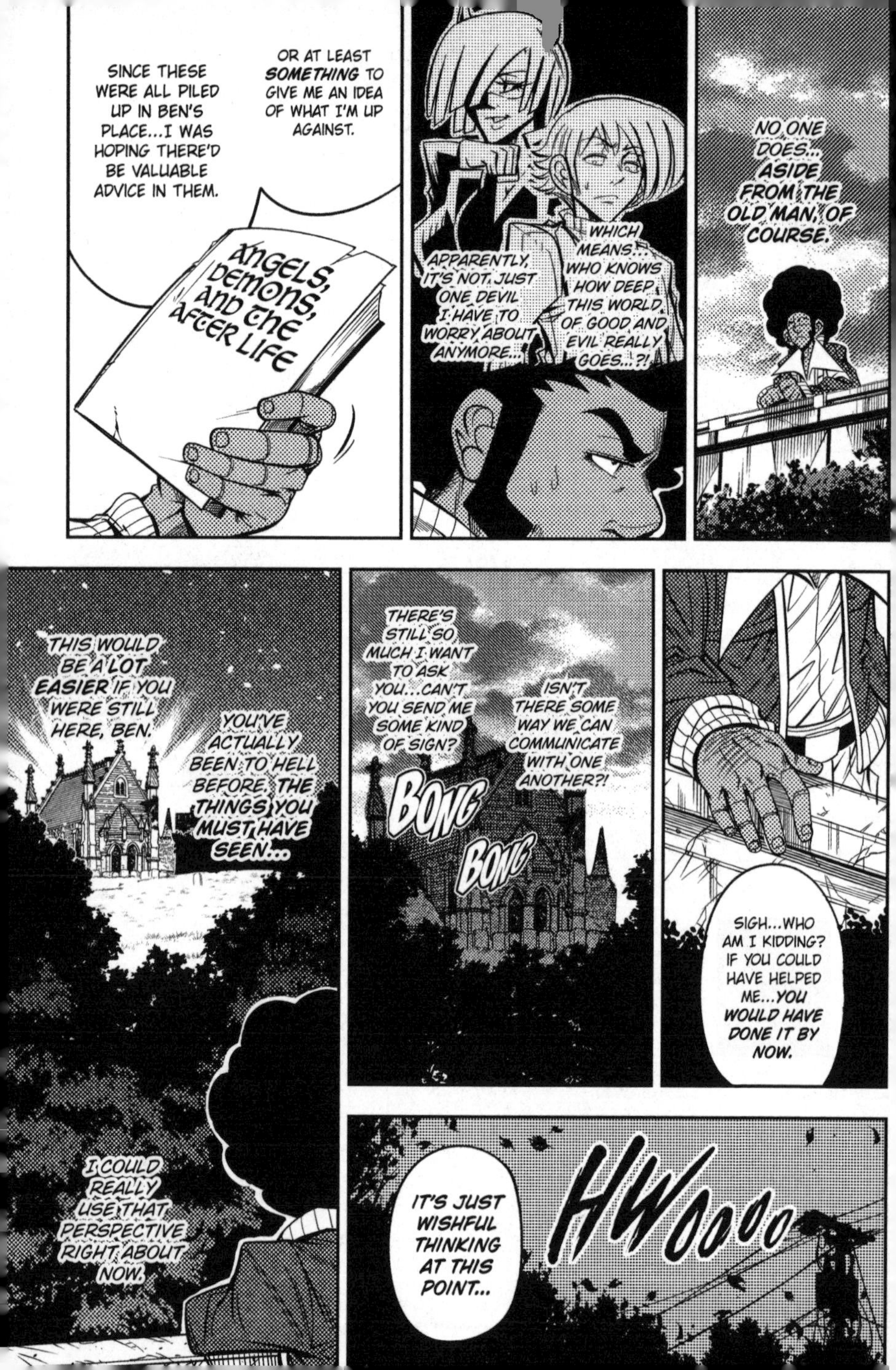
SINCE THESE WERE ALL PILED UP IN BEN'S PLACE...I WAS HOPING THERE'D BE VALUABLE ADVICE IN THEM.
OR AT LEAST SOMETHING TO GIVE ME AN IDEA OF WHAT I'M UP AGAINST.
ANGELS, DEMONS, AND THE AFTER LIFE
APPARENTLY, IT'S NOT JUST ONE DEVIL I HAVE TO WORRY ABOUT ANYMORE...
WHICH MEANS... WHO KNOWS HOW DEEP THIS WORLD OF GOOD AND EVIL REALLY GOES...?!
NO ONE DOES... ASIDE FROM THE OLD MAN, OF COURSE.
THIS WOULD BE A LOT EASIER IF YOU WERE STILL HERE, BEN.
YOU'VE ACTUALLY BEEN TO HELL BEFORE. THE THINGS YOU MUST HAVE SEEN...
I COULD REALLY USE THAT PERSPECTIVE RIGHT ABOUT NOW.
THERE'S STILL SO MUCH I WANT TO ASK YOU...CAN'T YOU SEND ME SOME KIND OF SIGN?
ISN'T THERE SOME WAY WE CAN COMMUNICATE WITH ONE ANOTHER?!
BONG
BONG
SIGH...WHO AM I KIDDING? IF YOU COULD HAVE HELPED ME...YOU WOULD HAVE DONE IT BY NOW.
IT'S JUST WISHFUL THINKING AT THIS POINT...
HWOOOO

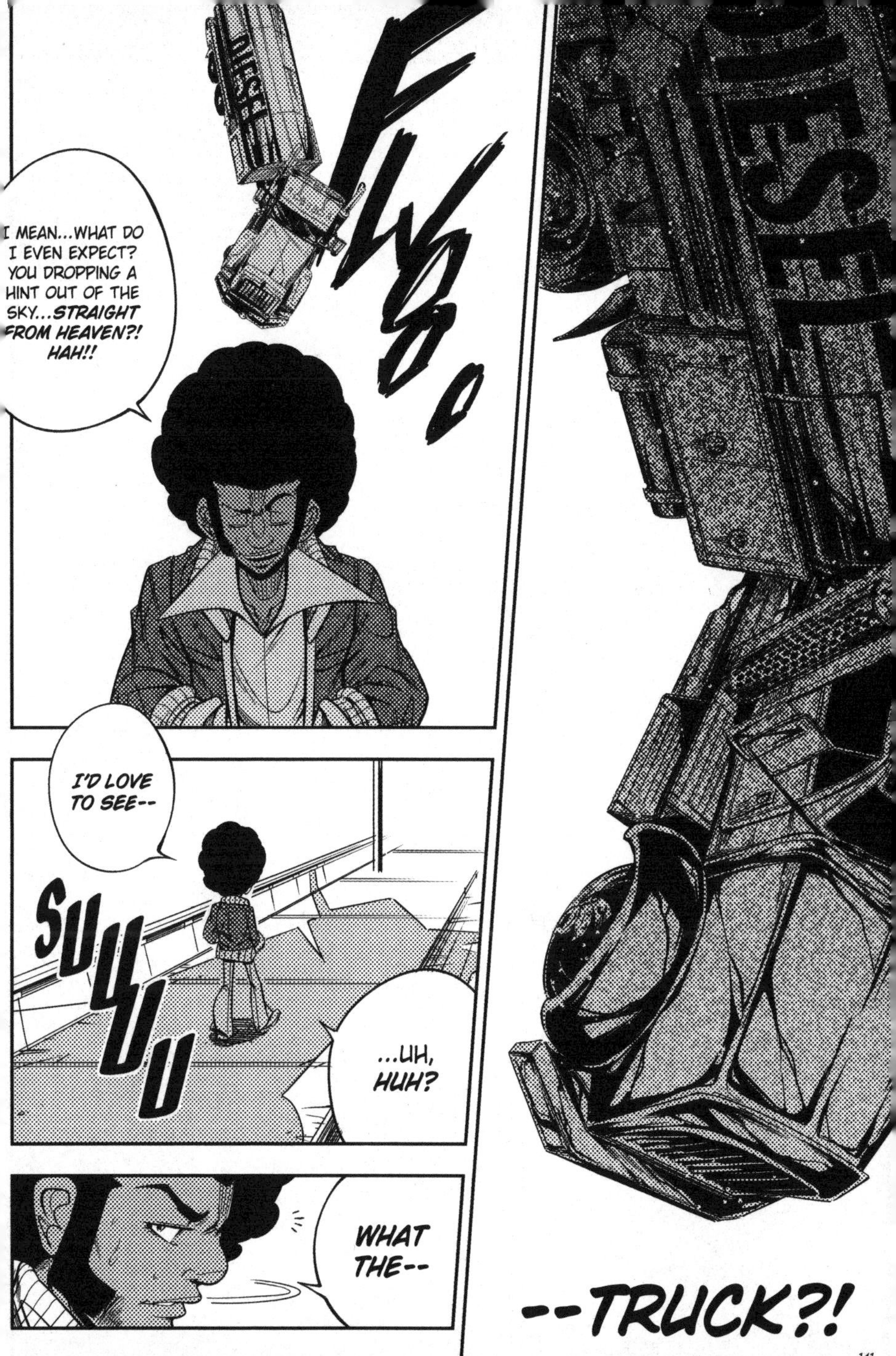
DIESEL
I MEAN...WHAT DO I EVEN EXPECT? YOU DROPPING A HINT OUT OF THE SKY...STRAIGHT FROM HEAVEN?! HAH!!
I'D LOVE TO SEE--
...UH, HUH?
WHAT THE--
DIESEL
--TRUCK?!

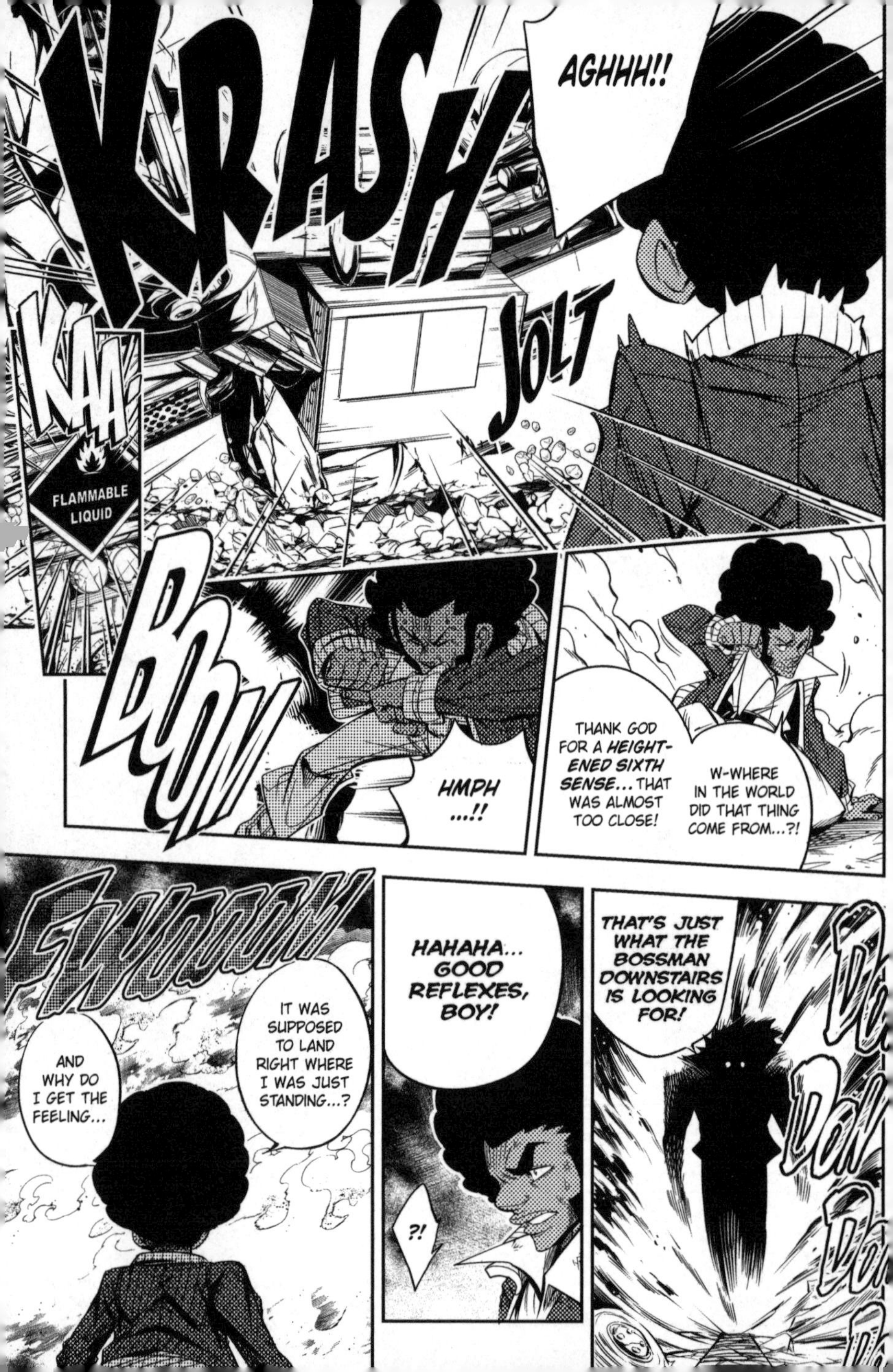
KRASH
AGHHH!!
KAA
FLAMMABLE LIQUID
JOLT
BOOM
HMPH ...!!
THANK GOD FOR A HEIGHT-ENED SIXTH SENSE... THAT WAS ALMOST TOO CLOSE!
W-WHERE IN THE WORLD DID THAT THING COME FROM...?!
AND WHY DO I GET THE FEELING...
IT WAS SUPPOSED TO LAND RIGHT WHERE I WAS JUST STANDING...?
HAHAHA... GOOD REFLEXES, BOY!
?!
THAT'S JUST WHAT THE BOSSMAN DOWNSTAIRS IS LOOKING FOR!

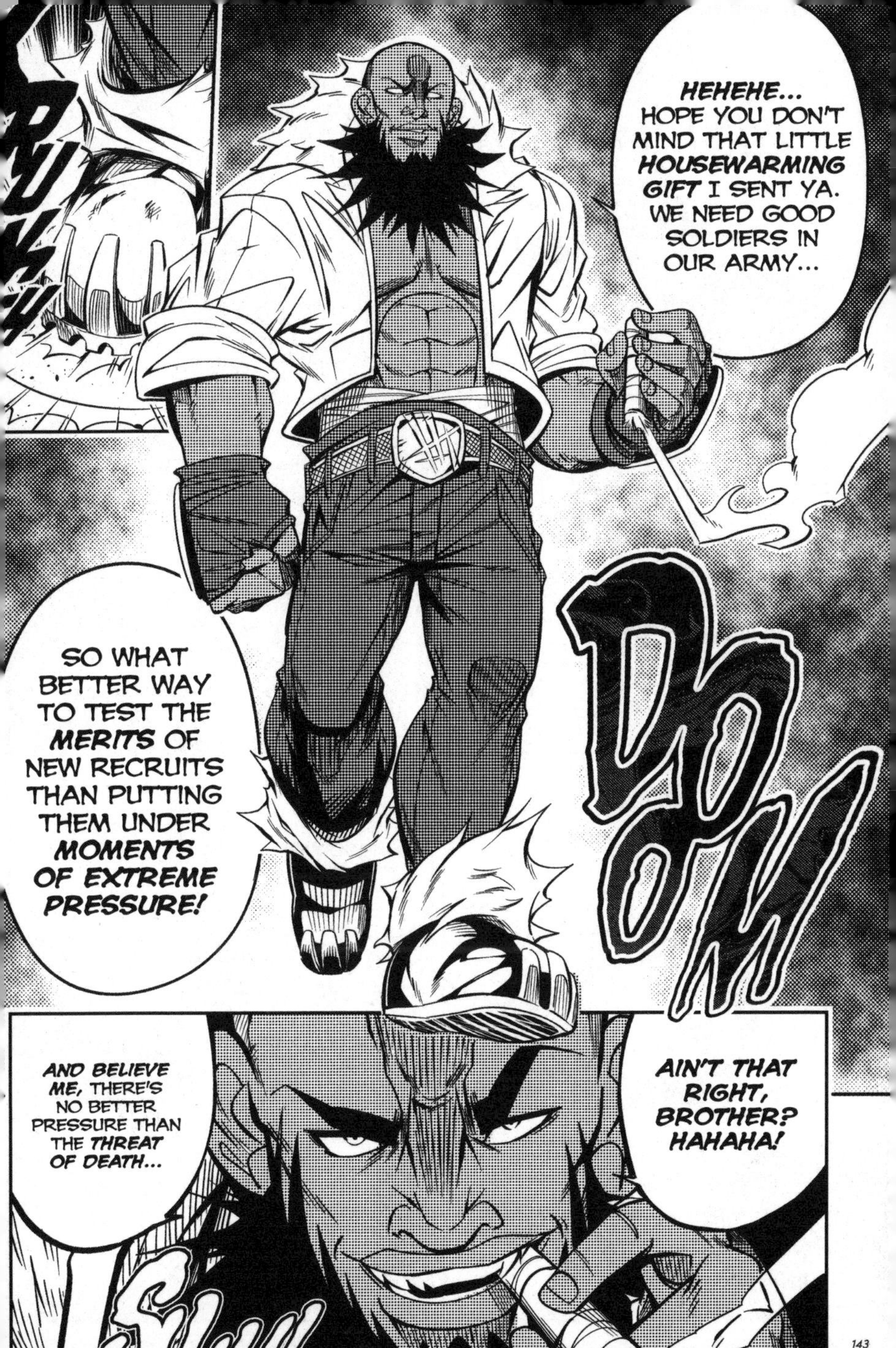
HEHEHE... HOPE YOU DON'T MIND THAT LITTLE HOUSEWARMING GIFT I SENT YA. WE NEED GOOD SOLDIERS IN OUR ARMY...
SO WHAT BETTER WAY TO TEST THE MERITS OF NEW RECRUITS THAN PUTTING THEM UNDER MOMENTS OF EXTREME PRESSURE!
DOOM
AND BELIEVE ME, THERE'S NO BETTER PRESSURE THAN THE THREAT OF DEATH...
AIN'T THAT RIGHT, BROTHER? HAHAHA!

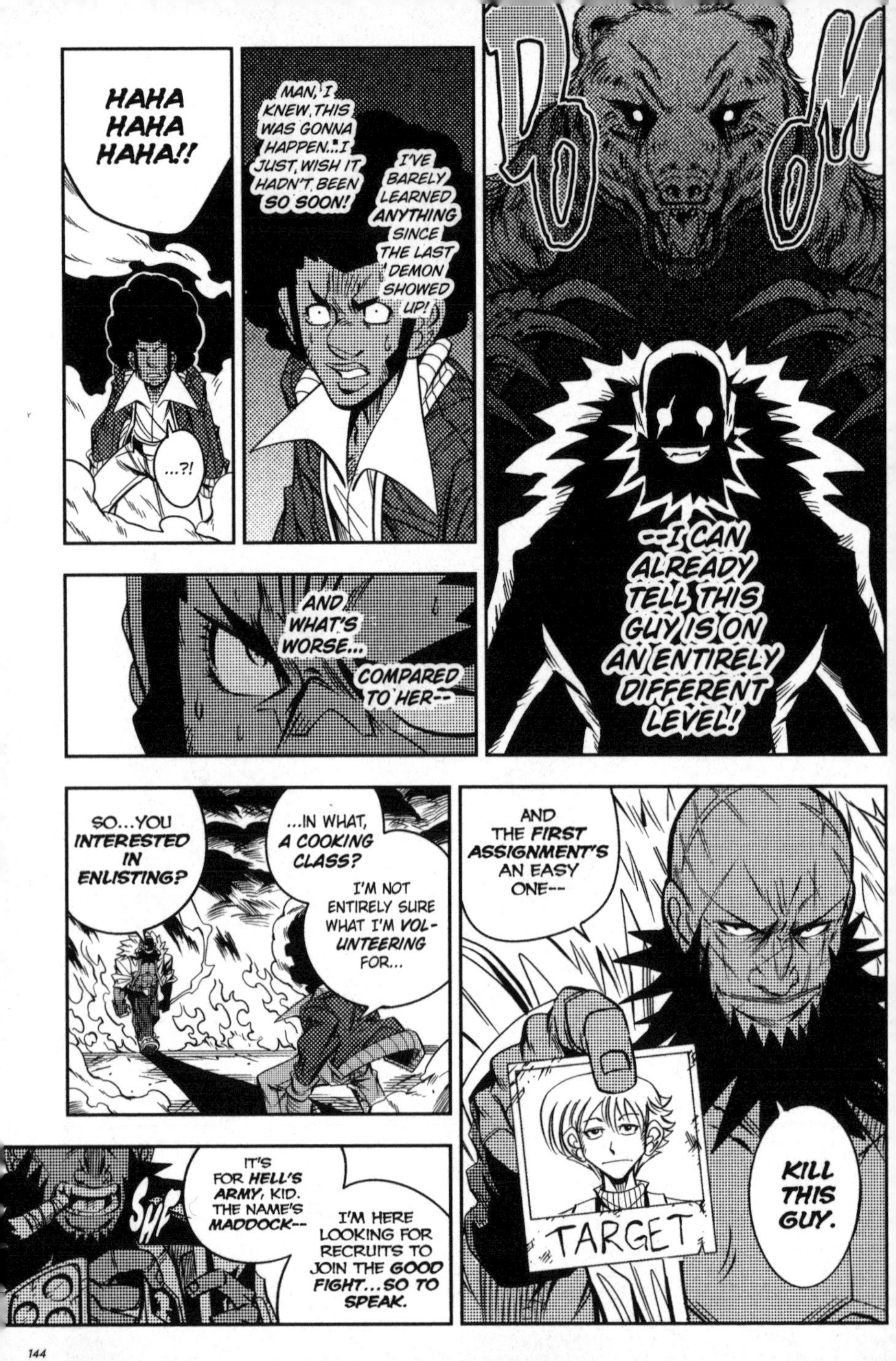
HAHA HAHA HAHA!!
...?!
MAN, I KNEW THIS WAS GONNA HAPPEN...I JUST WISH IT HADN'T BEEN SO SOON!
I'VE BARELY LEARNED ANYTHING SINCE THE LAST DEMON SHOWED UP!
AND WHAT'S WORSE...
COMPARED TO HER--
DOOM
--I CAN ALREADY TELL THIS GUY IS ON AN ENTIRELY DIFFERENT LEVEL!
SO...YOU INTERESTED IN ENLISTING?
...IN WHAT, A COOKING CLASS?
I'M NOT ENTIRELY SURE WHAT I'M VOL-UNTEERING FOR...
SHF
IT'S FOR HELL'S ARMY, KID. THE NAME'S MADDOCK--
I'M HERE LOOKING FOR RECRUITS TO JOIN THE GOOD FIGHT...SO TO SPEAK.
AND THE FIRST ASSIGNMENT'S AN EASY ONE--
TARGET
KILL THIS GUY.

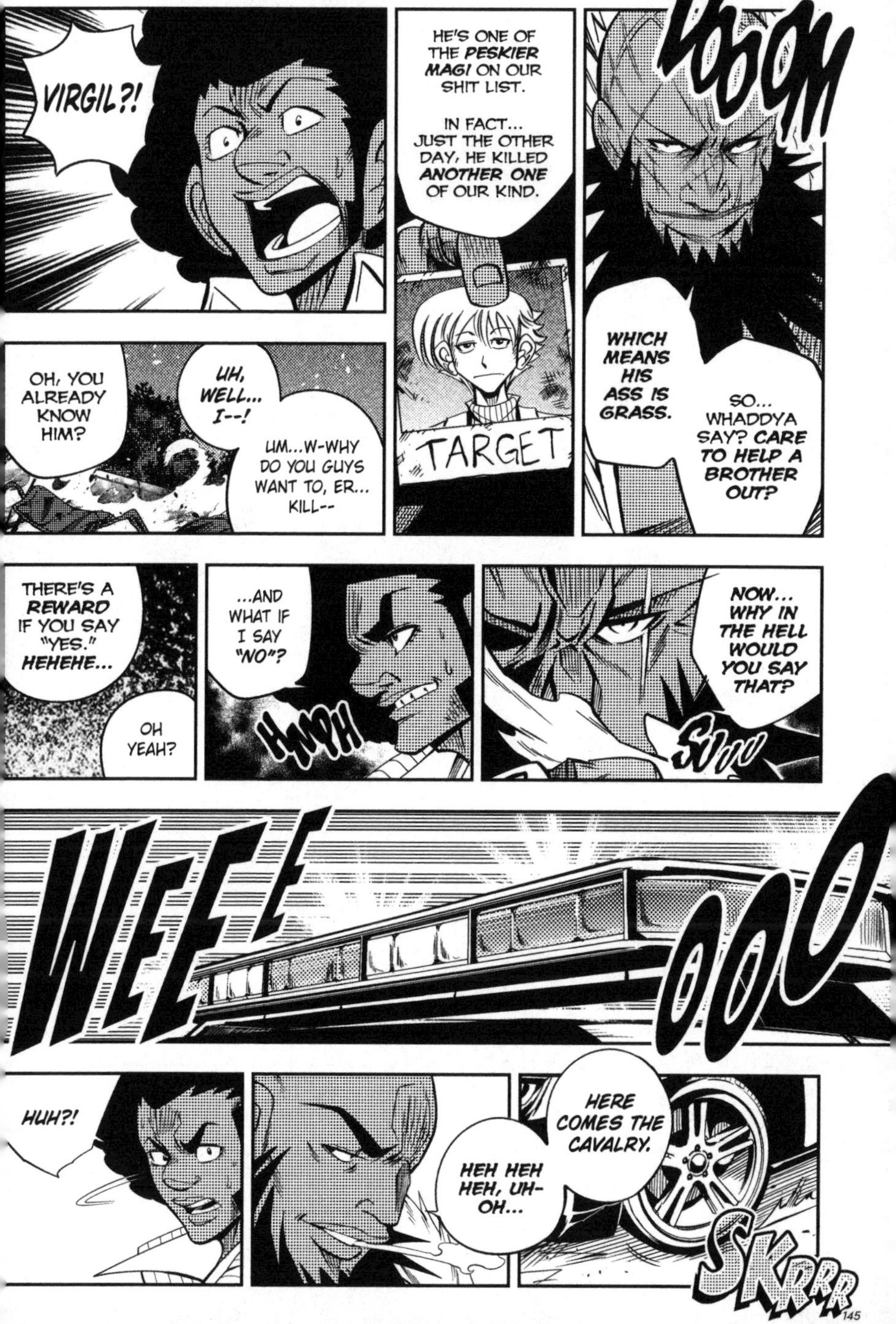
VIRGIL?!
OH, YOU ALREADY KNOW HIM?
UH, WELL... I--!
UM...W-WHY DO YOU GUYS WANT TO, ER... KILL--
HE'S ONE OF THE PESKIER MAGI ON OUR SHIT LIST.
IN FACT... JUST THE OTHER DAY, HE KILLED ANOTHER ONE OF OUR KIND.
TARGET
LOOOM
WHICH MEANS HIS ASS IS GRASS.
SO... WHADDYA SAY? CARE TO HELP A BROTHER OUT?
THERE'S A REWARD IF YOU SAY "YES." HEHEHE...
OH YEAH?
...AND WHAT IF I SAY "NO"?
NOW... WHY IN THE HELL WOULD YOU SAY THAT?
WEEEOOOO
HUH?!
HEH HEH HEH, UH-OH...
HERE COMES THE CAVALRY.
SKRRR

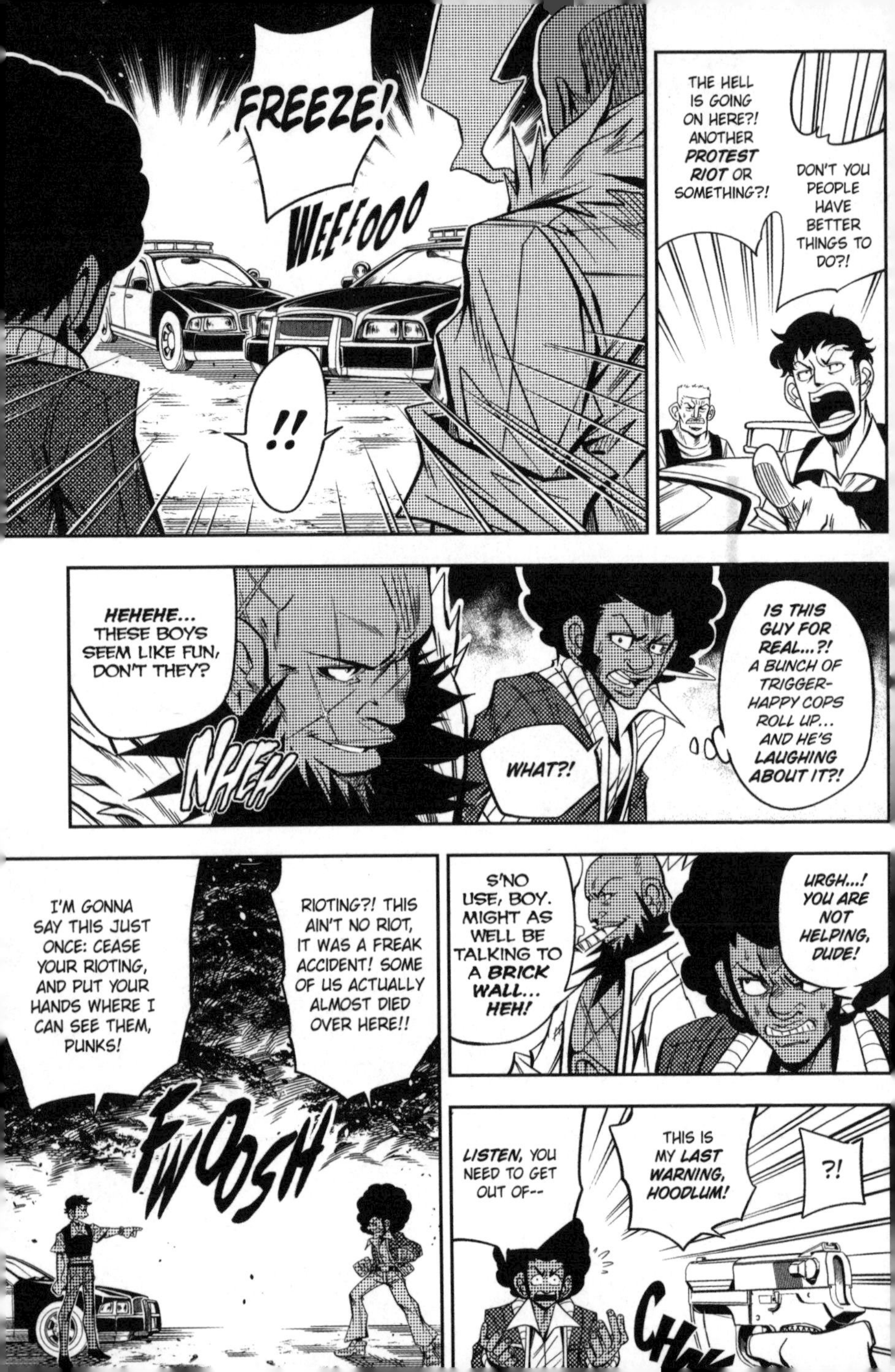
FREEZE!
WEEEOOO
!!
THE HELL IS GOING ON HERE?! ANOTHER PROTEST RIOT OR SOMETHING?!
DON'T YOU PEOPLE HAVE BETTER THINGS TO DO?!
HEHEHE... THESE BOYS SEEM LIKE FUN, DON'T THEY?
NHEH
WHAT?!
IS THIS GUY FOR REAL...?! A BUNCH OF TRIGGER-HAPPY COPS ROLL UP... AND HE'S LAUGHING ABOUT IT?!
I'M GONNA SAY THIS JUST ONCE: CEASE YOUR RIOTING, AND PUT YOUR HANDS WHERE I CAN SEE THEM, PUNKS!
RIOTING?! THIS AIN'T NO RIOT, IT WAS A FREAK ACCIDENT! SOME OF US ACTUALLY ALMOST DIED OVER HERE!!
FWOOSH
S'NO USE, BOY. MIGHT AS WELL BE TALKING TO A BRICK WALL... HEH!
URGH...! YOU ARE NOT HELPING, DUDE!
LISTEN, YOU NEED TO GET OUT OF--
THIS IS MY LAST WARNING, HOODLUM!
?!
CHAK

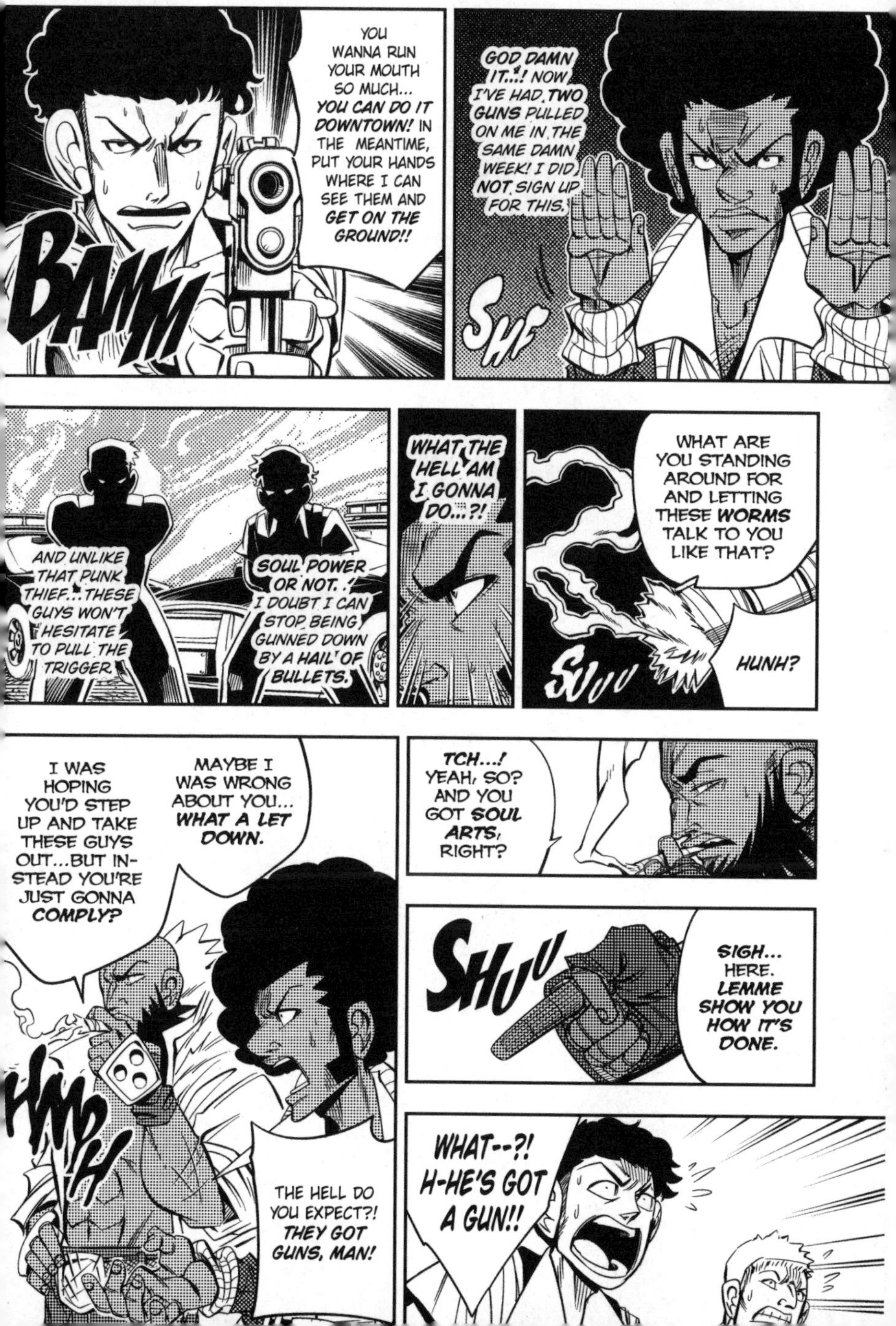

YOU WANNA RUN YOUR MOUTH SO MUCH... YOU CAN DO IT DOWNTOWN! IN THE MEANTIME, PUT YOUR HANDS WHERE I CAN SEE THEM AND GET ON THE GROUND!!
BAMM
GOD DAMN IT...! NOW I'VE HAD TWO GUNS PULLED ON ME IN THE SAME DAMN WEEK! I DID NOT SIGN UP FOR THIS.
SHF
AND UNLIKE THAT PUNK THIEF... THESE GUYS WON'T HESITATE TO PULL THE TRIGGER.
SOUL POWER OR NOT...! I DOUBT I CAN STOP BEING GUNNED DOWN BY A HAIL OF BULLETS.
WHAT THE HELL AM I GONNA DO...?!
WHAT ARE YOU STANDING AROUND FOR AND LETTING THESE WORMS TALK TO YOU LIKE THAT?
SUUU
HUNH?
I WAS HOPING YOU'D STEP UP AND TAKE THESE GUYS OUT...BUT IN-STEAD YOU'RE JUST GONNA COMPLY?
MAYBE I WAS WRONG ABOUT YOU... WHAT A LET DOWN.
HMPH
THE HELL DO YOU EXPECT?! THEY GOT GUNS, MAN!
TCH...! YEAH, SO? AND YOU GOT SOUL ARTS, RIGHT?
SHUU
SIGH... HERE. LEMME SHOW YOU HOW IT'S DONE.
WHAT--?! H-HE'S GOT A GUN!!

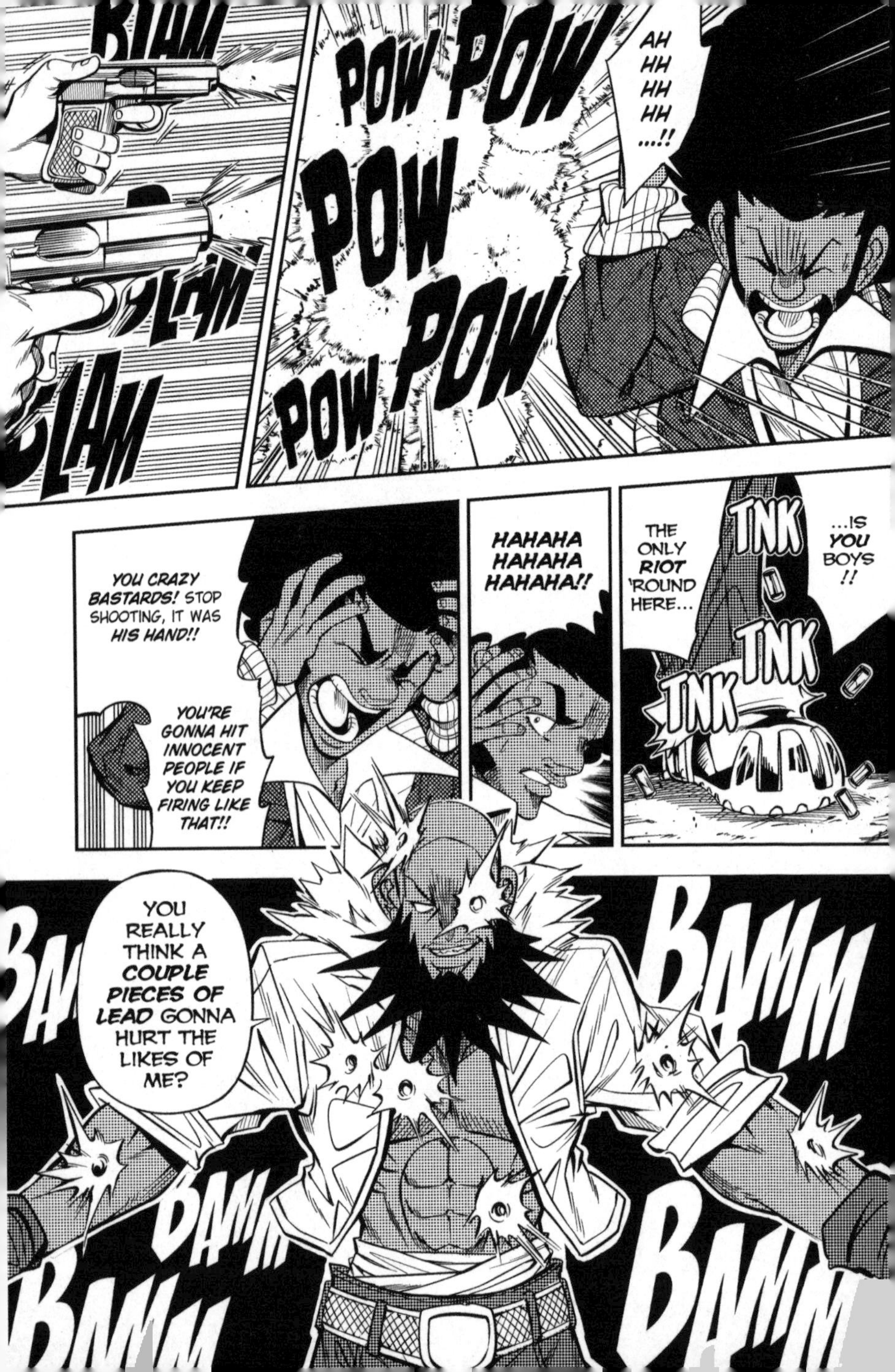
BLAM
BLAM BLAM
BLAM
POW POW
POW
POW POW
AHHHHHHHH...!!
YOU CRAZY BASTARDS! STOP SHOOTING, IT WAS HIS HAND!!
YOU'RE GONNA HIT INNOCENT PEOPLE IF YOU KEEP FIRING LIKE THAT!!
HAHAHA HAHAHA HAHAHA!!
THE ONLY RIOT 'ROUND HERE...
TNK
TNK
TNK
...IS YOU BOYS!!
YOU REALLY THINK A COUPLE PIECES OF LEAD GONNA HURT THE LIKES OF ME?
BAMM
BAMM
BAMM
BAMM
BAMM

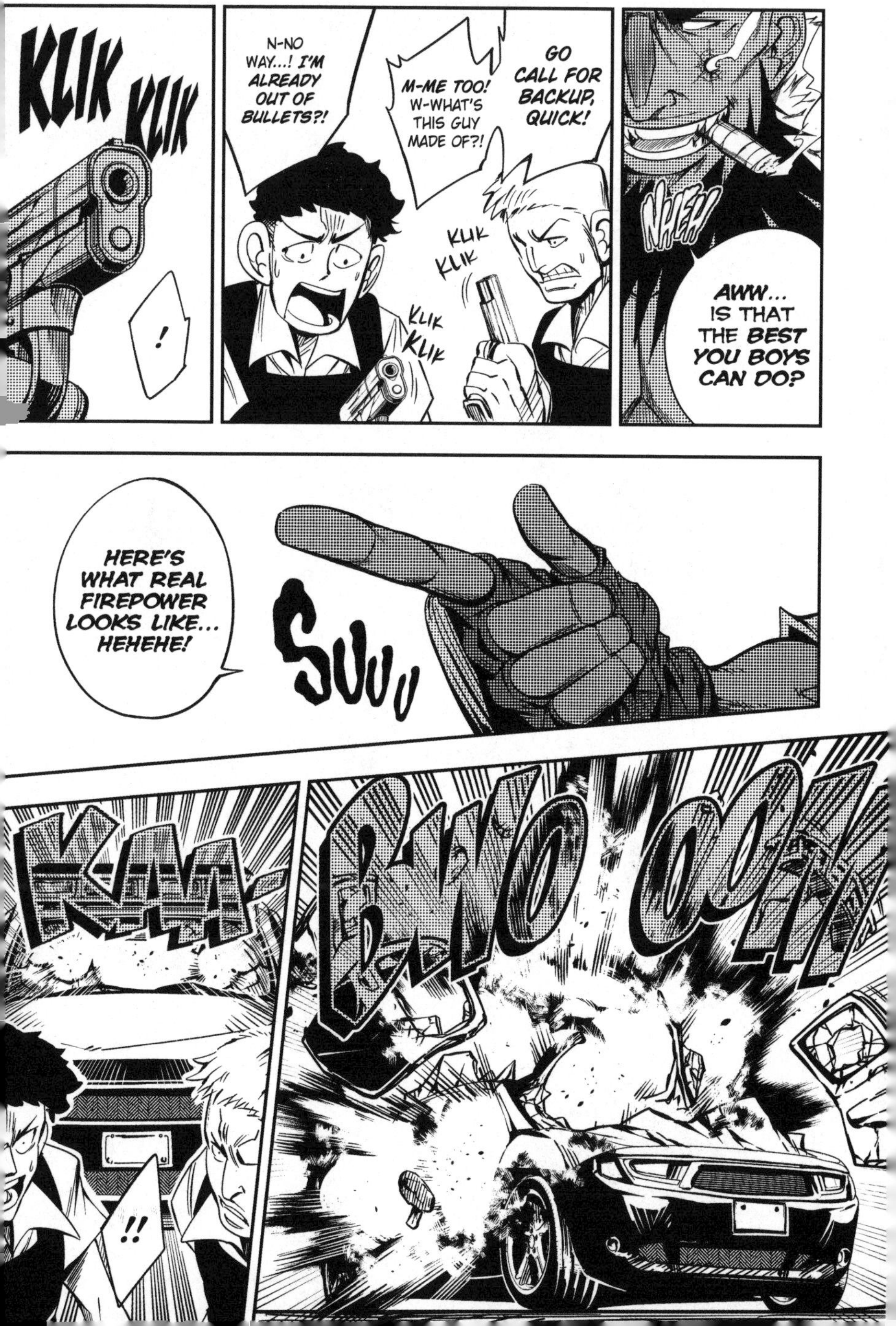
KLIK KLIK
!
N-NO WAY...! I'M ALREADY OUT OF BULLETS?!
M-ME TOO! W-WHAT'S THIS GUY MADE OF?!
GO CALL FOR BACKUP, QUICK!
KLIK KLIK
KLIK KLIK
NHEH
AWW... IS THAT THE BEST YOU BOYS CAN DO?
HERE'S WHAT REAL FIREPOWER LOOKS LIKE... HEHEHE!
SUUU
KAM
!!
BWOOOM

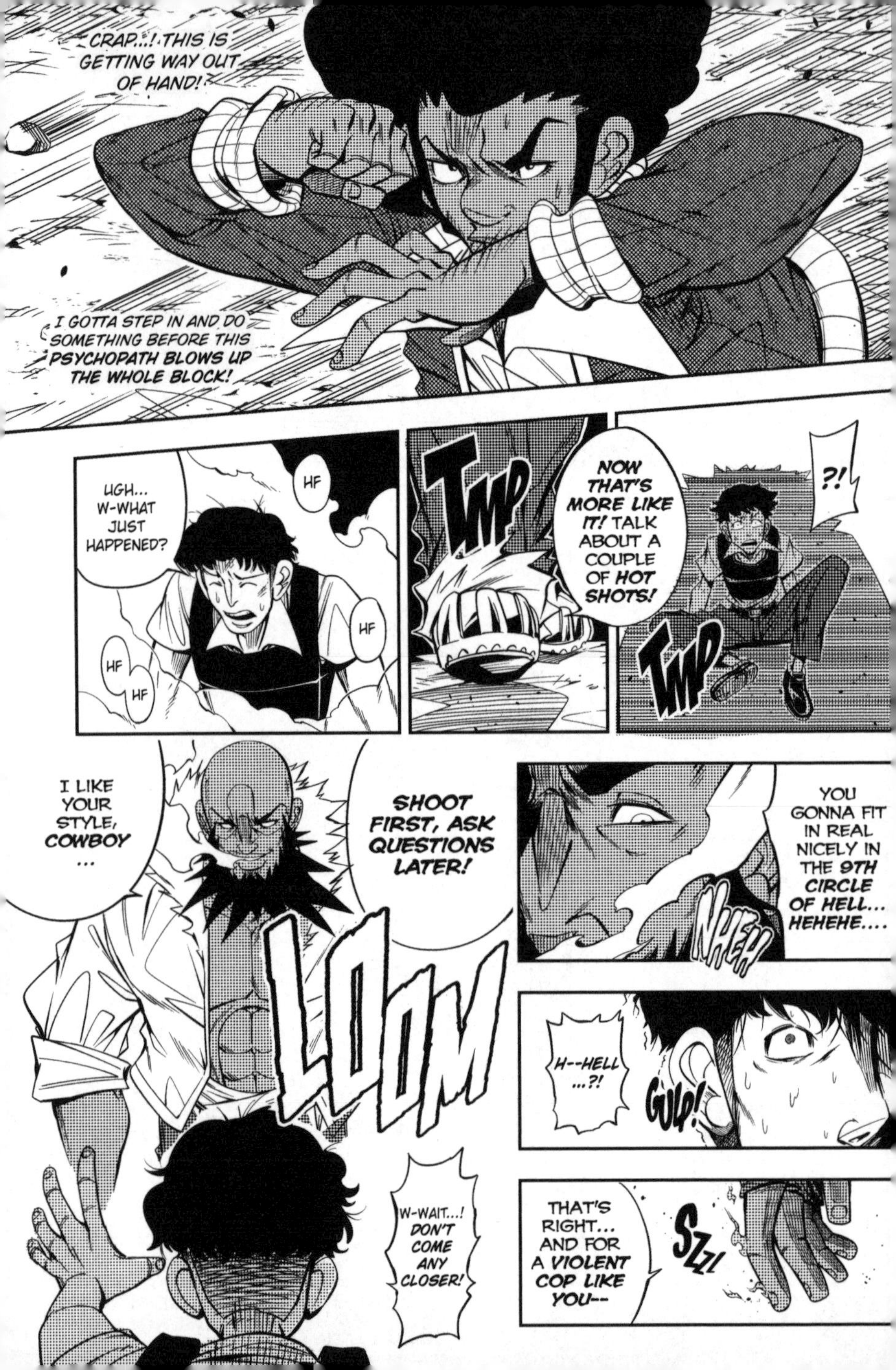
CRAP...! THIS IS GETTING WAY OUT OF HAND!
I GOTTA STEP IN AND DO SOMETHING BEFORE THIS PSYCHOPATH BLOWS UP THE WHOLE BLOCK!
UGH... W-WHAT JUST HAPPENED?
HF
HF
HF
HF
TMP
NOW THAT'S MORE LIKE IT! TALK ABOUT A COUPLE OF HOT SHOTS!
?!
TMP
I LIKE YOUR STYLE, COWBOY ...
SHOOT FIRST, ASK QUESTIONS LATER!
LOOM
W-WAIT...! DON'T COME ANY CLOSER!
YOU GONNA FIT IN REAL NICELY IN THE 9TH CIRCLE OF HELL... HEHEHE....
NHEH
H--HELL ...?!
GULP!
THAT'S RIGHT... AND FOR A VIOLENT COP LIKE YOU--
SZZZ

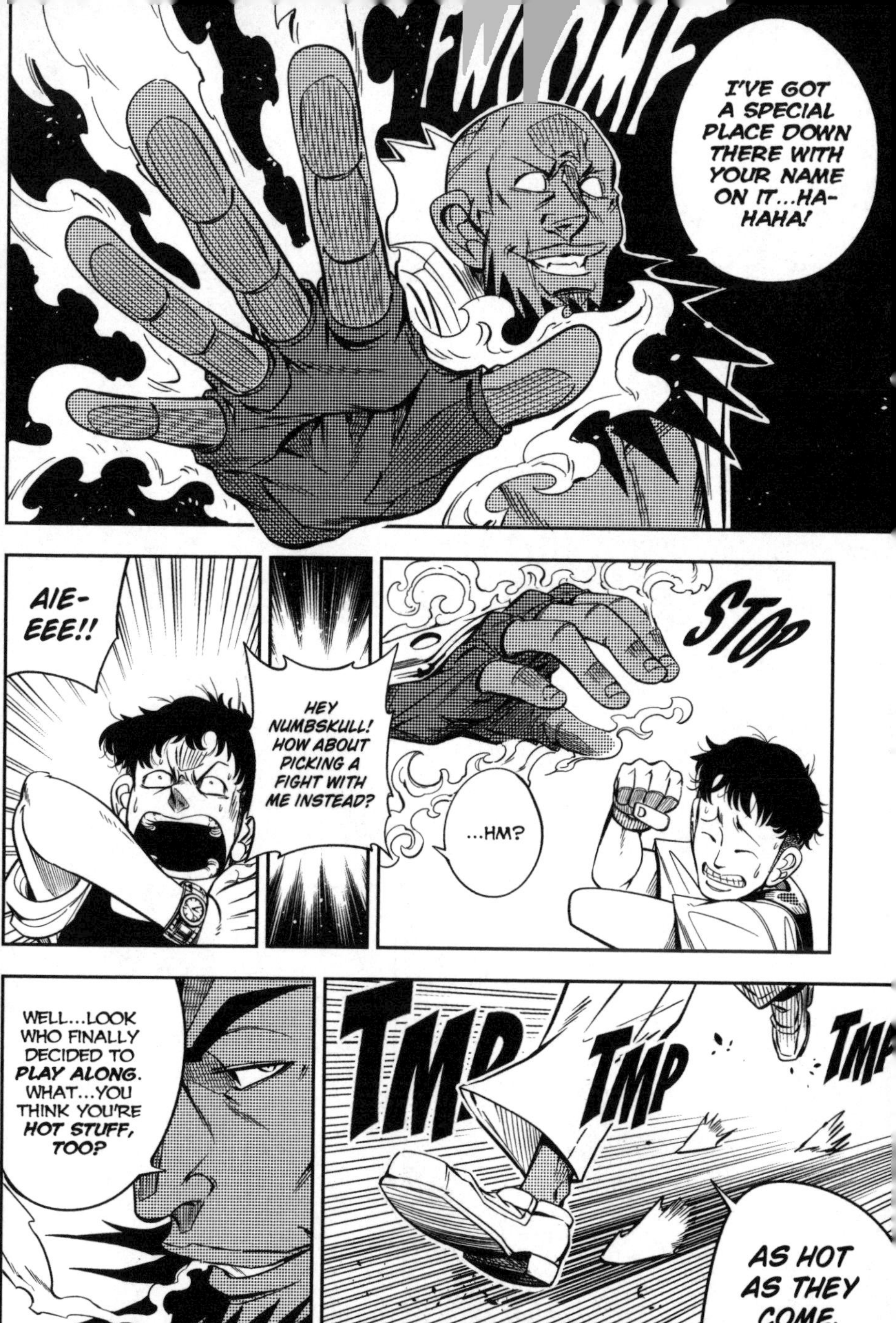
FWOOM!
I'VE GOT A SPECIAL PLACE DOWN THERE WITH YOUR NAME ON IT...HA-HAHA!
AIE-EEE!!
HEY NUMBSKULL! HOW ABOUT PICKING A FIGHT WITH ME INSTEAD?
STOP
...HM?
WELL...LOOK WHO FINALLY DECIDED TO PLAY ALONG. WHAT...YOU THINK YOU'RE HOT STUFF, TOO?
TMP
TMP
AS HOT AS THEY COME, SUCKA!

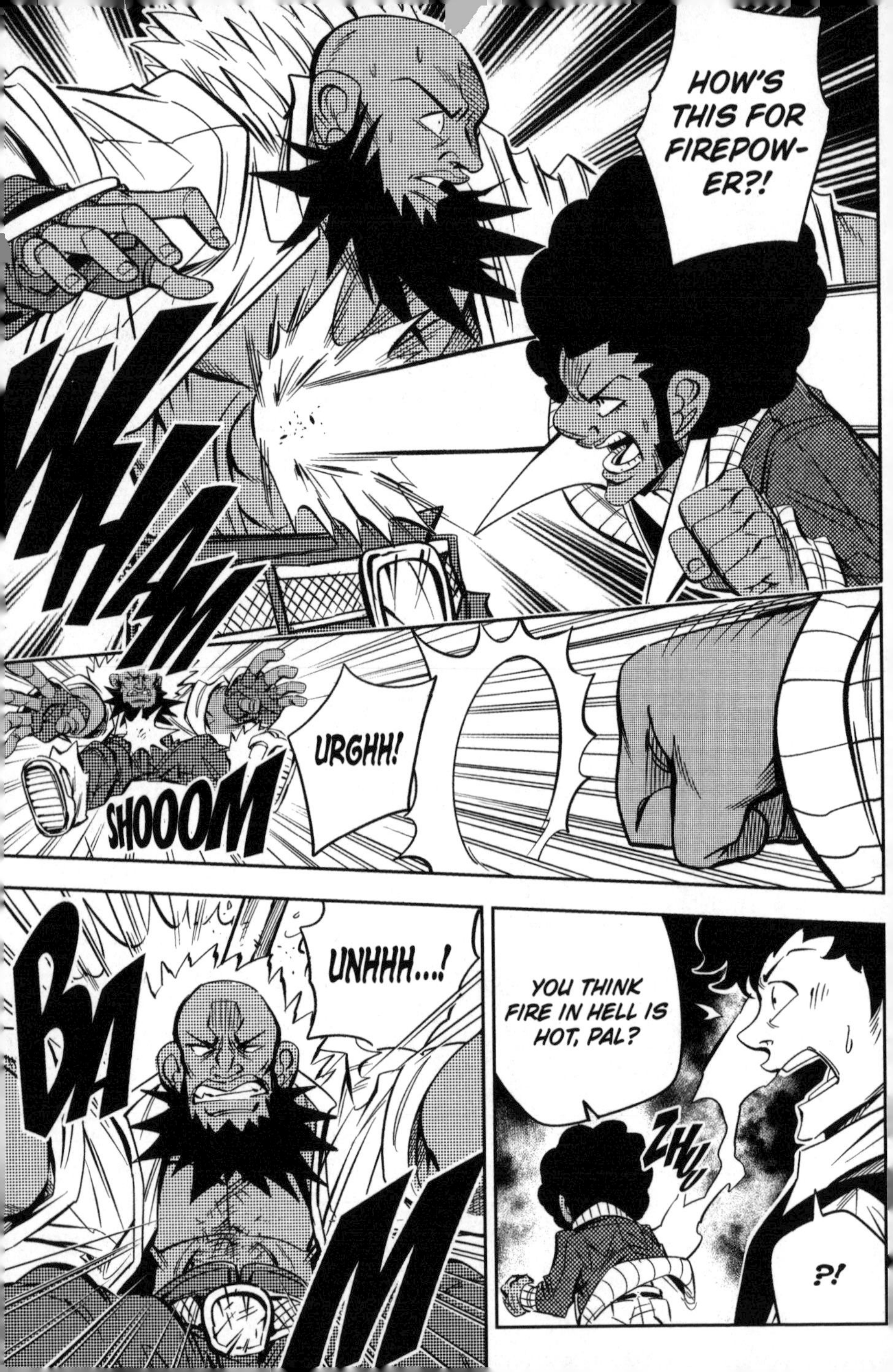
HOW'S THIS FOR FIREPOW-ER?!
WHAM
URGHH!
SHOOOM
BAM
UNHHH...!
YOU THINK FIRE IN HELL IS HOT, PAL?
ZHU
?!

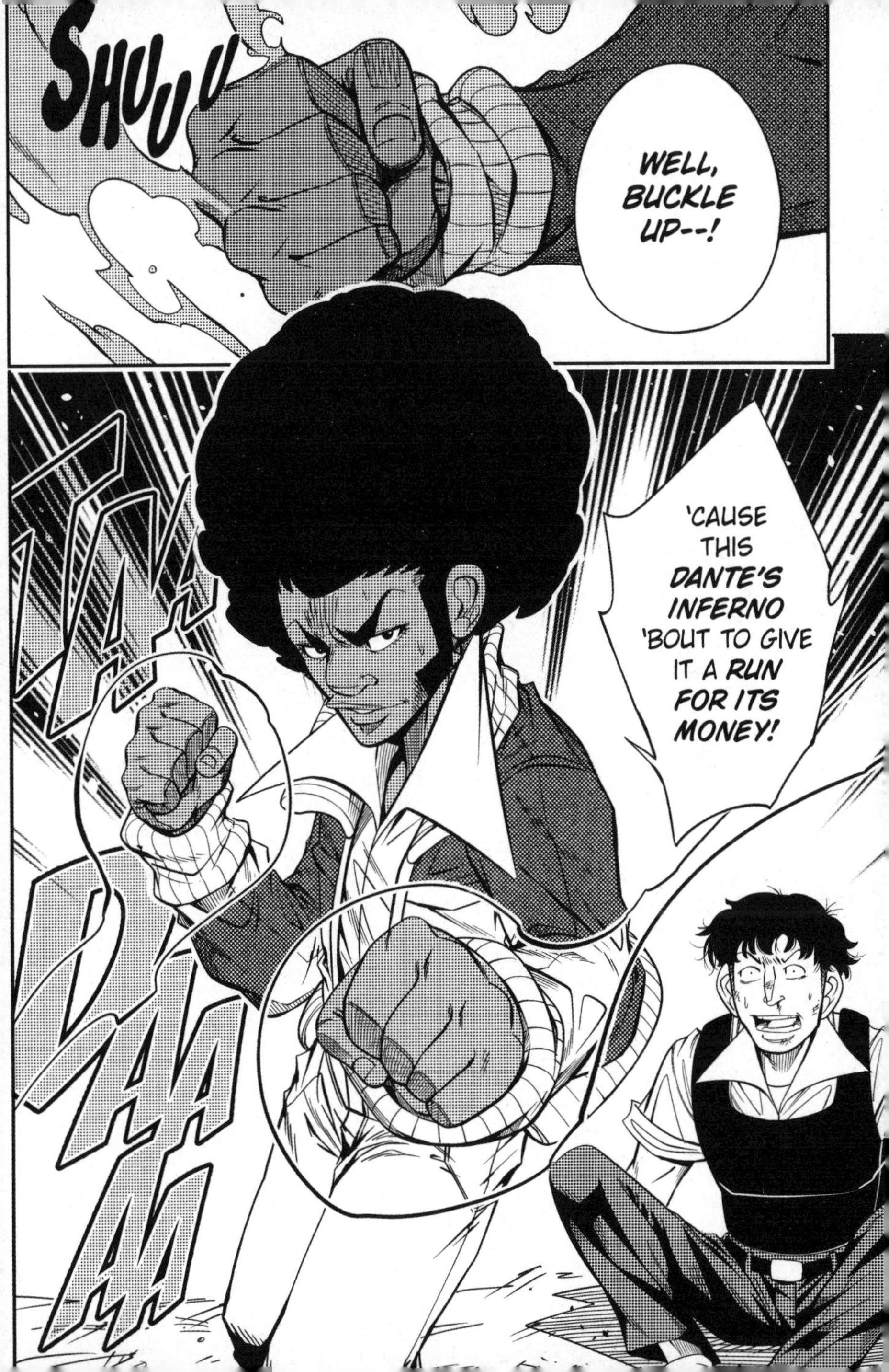
SHUUU
WELL, BUCKLE UP--!
'CAUSE THIS *DANTE'S INFERNO* 'BOUT TO GIVE IT A *RUN FOR ITS MONEY!*

SOUL BEAT

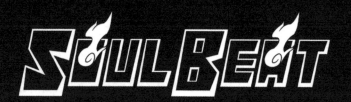

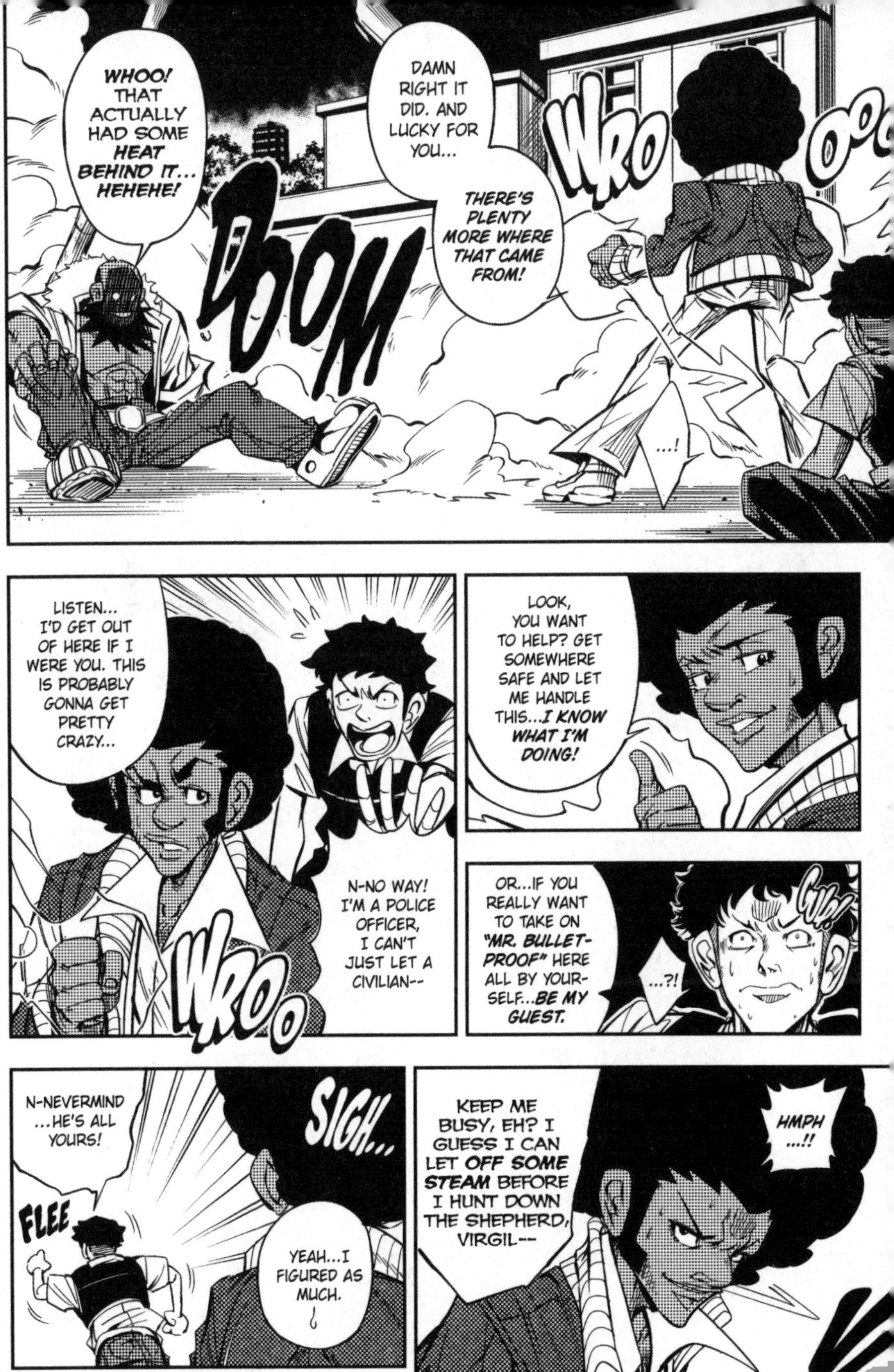
WHOO! THAT ACTUALLY HAD SOME HEAT BEHIND IT... HEHEHE!
DOOM
DAMN RIGHT IT DID. AND LUCKY FOR YOU...
THERE'S PLENTY MORE WHERE THAT CAME FROM!
WROOO
...!
LISTEN... I'D GET OUT OF HERE IF I WERE YOU. THIS IS PROBABLY GONNA GET PRETTY CRAZY...
N-NO WAY! I'M A POLICE OFFICER, I CAN'T JUST LET A CIVILIAN--
WROOO
LOOK, YOU WANT TO HELP? GET SOMEWHERE SAFE AND LET ME HANDLE THIS...I KNOW WHAT I'M DOING!
OR...IF YOU REALLY WANT TO TAKE ON "MR. BULLET-PROOF" HERE ALL BY YOUR-SELF...BE MY GUEST.
...?!
GULP
N-NEVERMIND ...HE'S ALL YOURS!
SIGH...
FLEE
YEAH...I FIGURED AS MUCH.
KEEP ME BUSY, EH? I GUESS I CAN LET OFF SOME STEAM BEFORE I HUNT DOWN THE SHEPHERD, VIRGIL--
HMPH ...!!

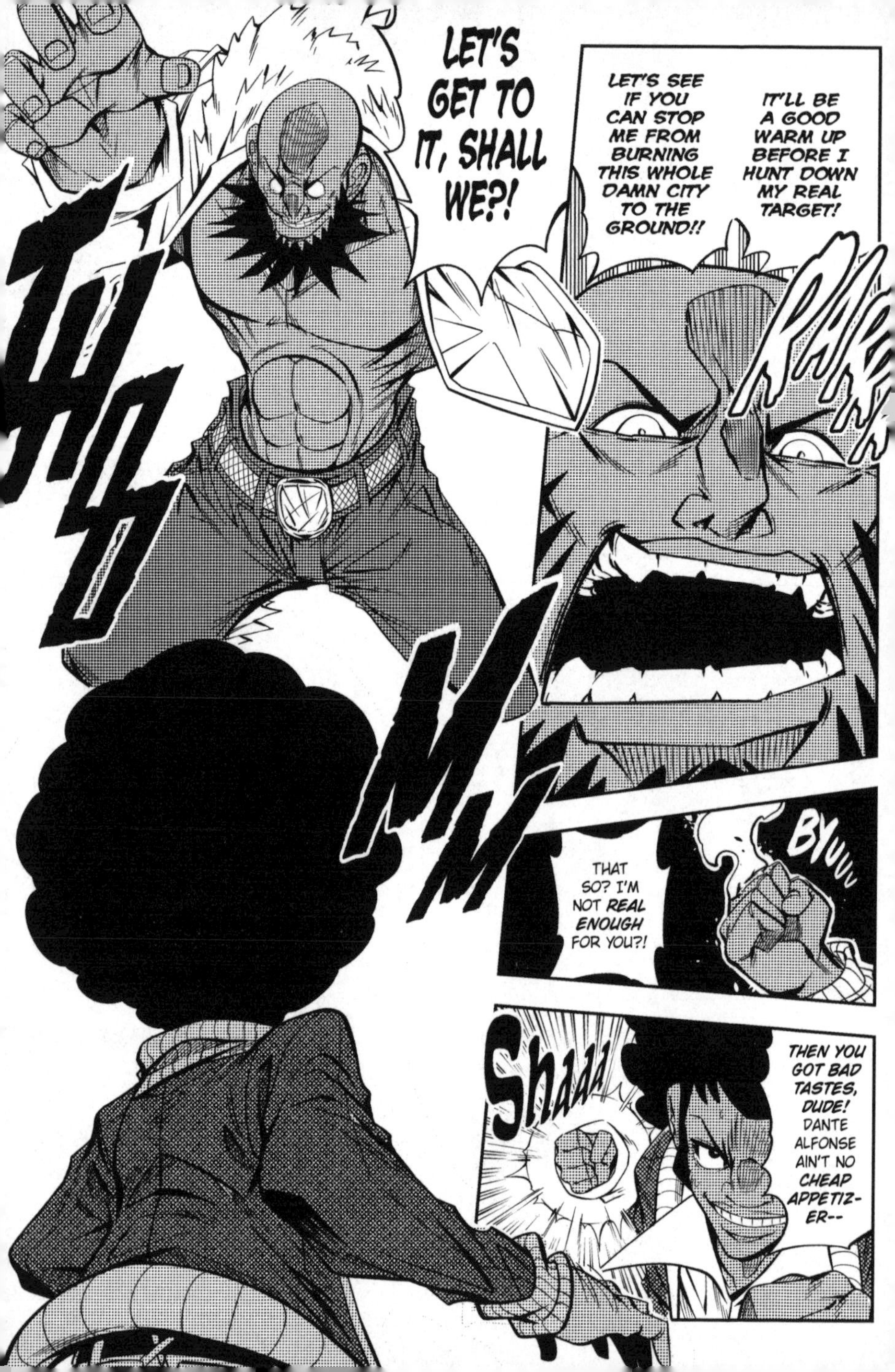
LET'S GET TO IT, SHALL WE?!
LET'S SEE IF YOU CAN STOP ME FROM BURNING THIS WHOLE DAMN CITY TO THE GROUND!!
IT'LL BE A GOOD WARM UP BEFORE I HUNT DOWN MY REAL TARGET!
THAT SO? I'M NOT *REAL ENOUGH* FOR YOU?!
THEN YOU GOT BAD TASTES, DUDE! DANTE ALFONSE AIN'T NO *CHEAP APPETIZ-ER--*

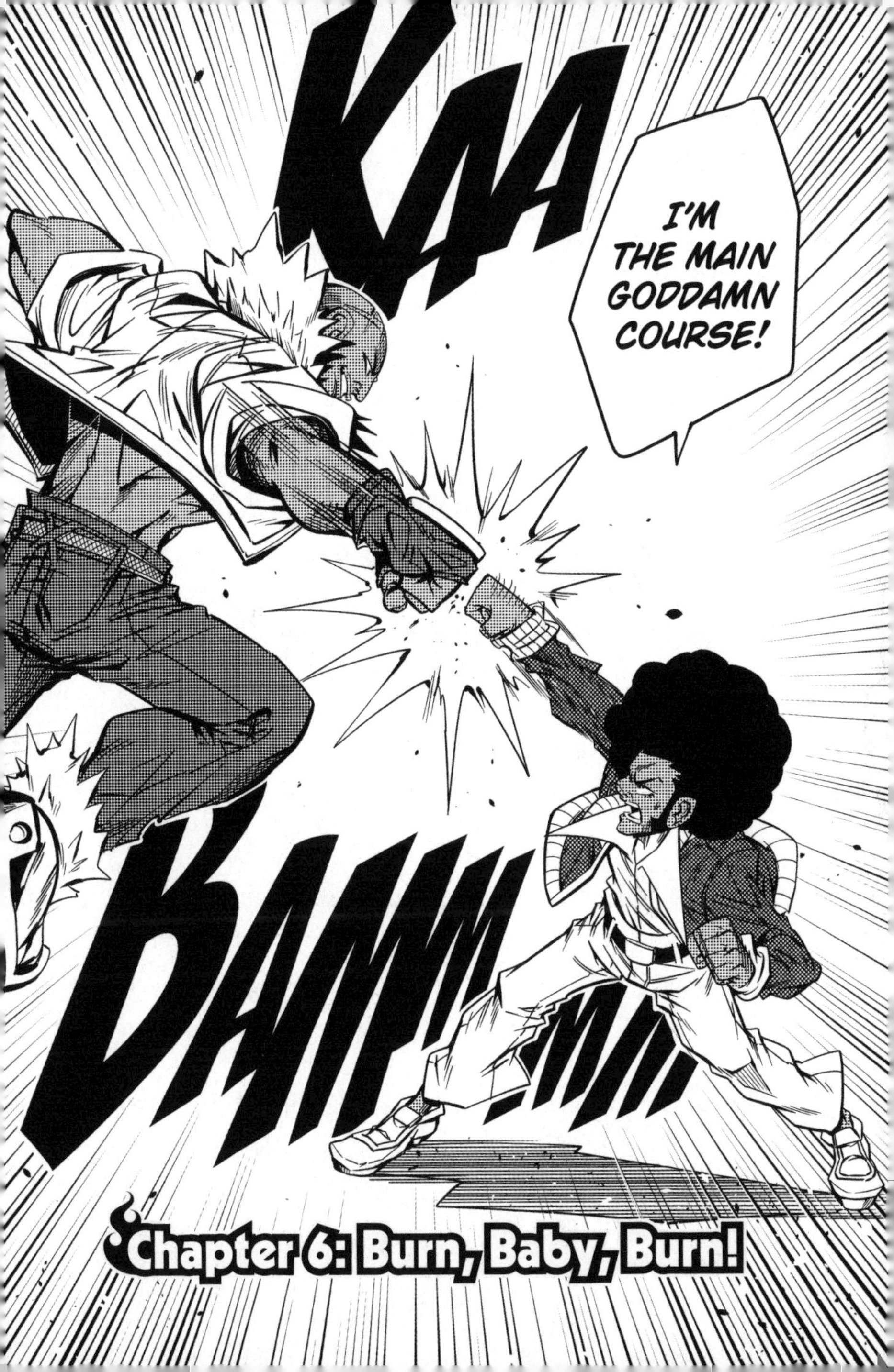
KAA
I'M THE MAIN GODDAMN COURSE!
BAMM...

Chapter 6: Burn, Baby, Burn!

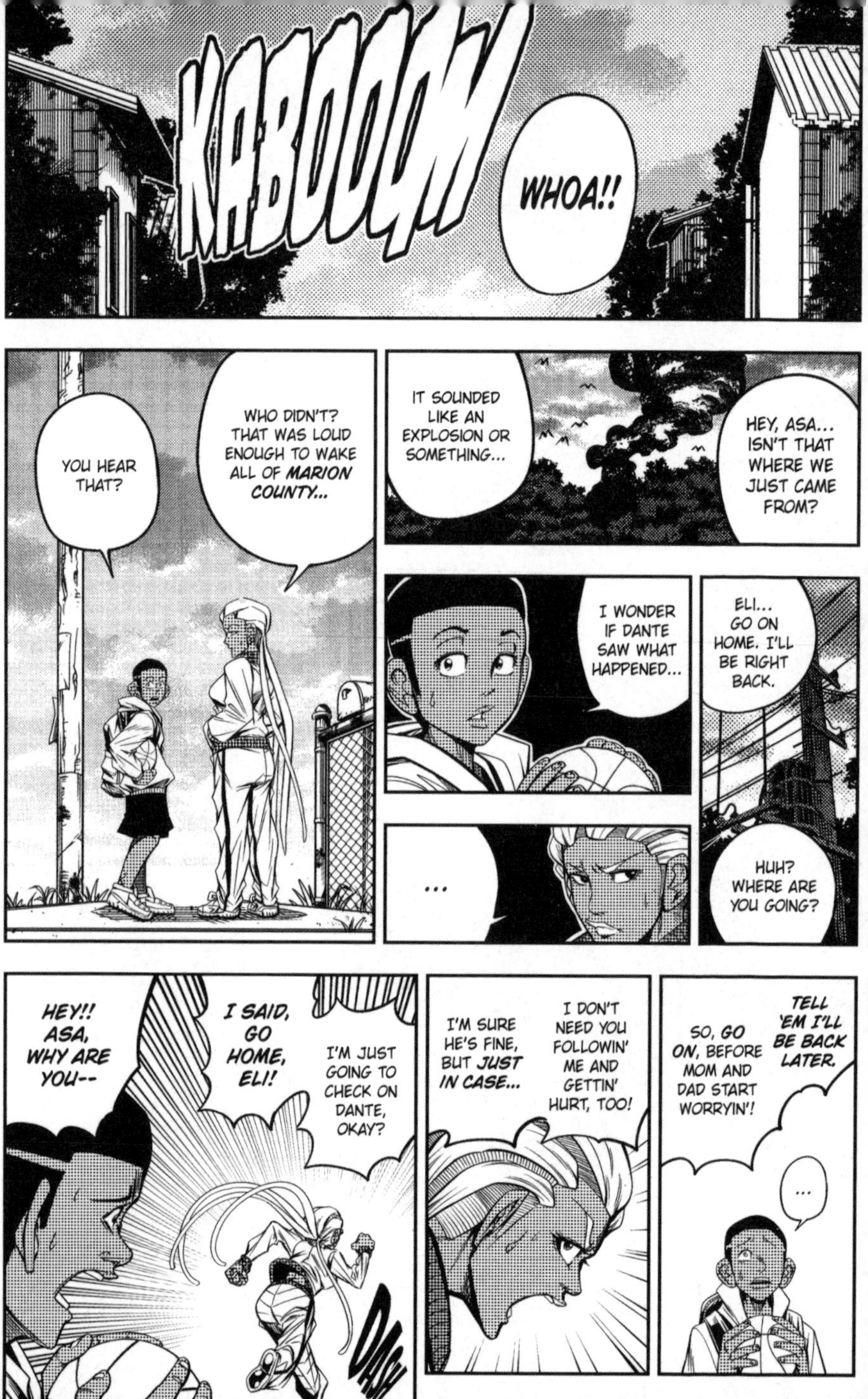
KABOOOM
WHOA!!
YOU HEAR THAT?
WHO DIDN'T? THAT WAS LOUD ENOUGH TO WAKE ALL OF MARION COUNTY...
IT SOUNDED LIKE AN EXPLOSION OR SOMETHING...
HEY, ASA... ISN'T THAT WHERE WE JUST CAME FROM?
I WONDER IF DANTE SAW WHAT HAPPENED...
...
ELI... GO ON HOME. I'LL BE RIGHT BACK.
HUH? WHERE ARE YOU GOING?
HEY!! ASA, WHY ARE YOU--
I SAID, GO HOME, ELI!
I'M JUST GOING TO CHECK ON DANTE, OKAY?
DASH
I'M SURE HE'S FINE, BUT JUST IN CASE...
I DON'T NEED YOU FOLLOWIN' ME AND GETTIN' HURT, TOO!
SO, GO ON, BEFORE MOM AND DAD START WORRYIN'!
TELL 'EM I'LL BE BACK LATER.
...

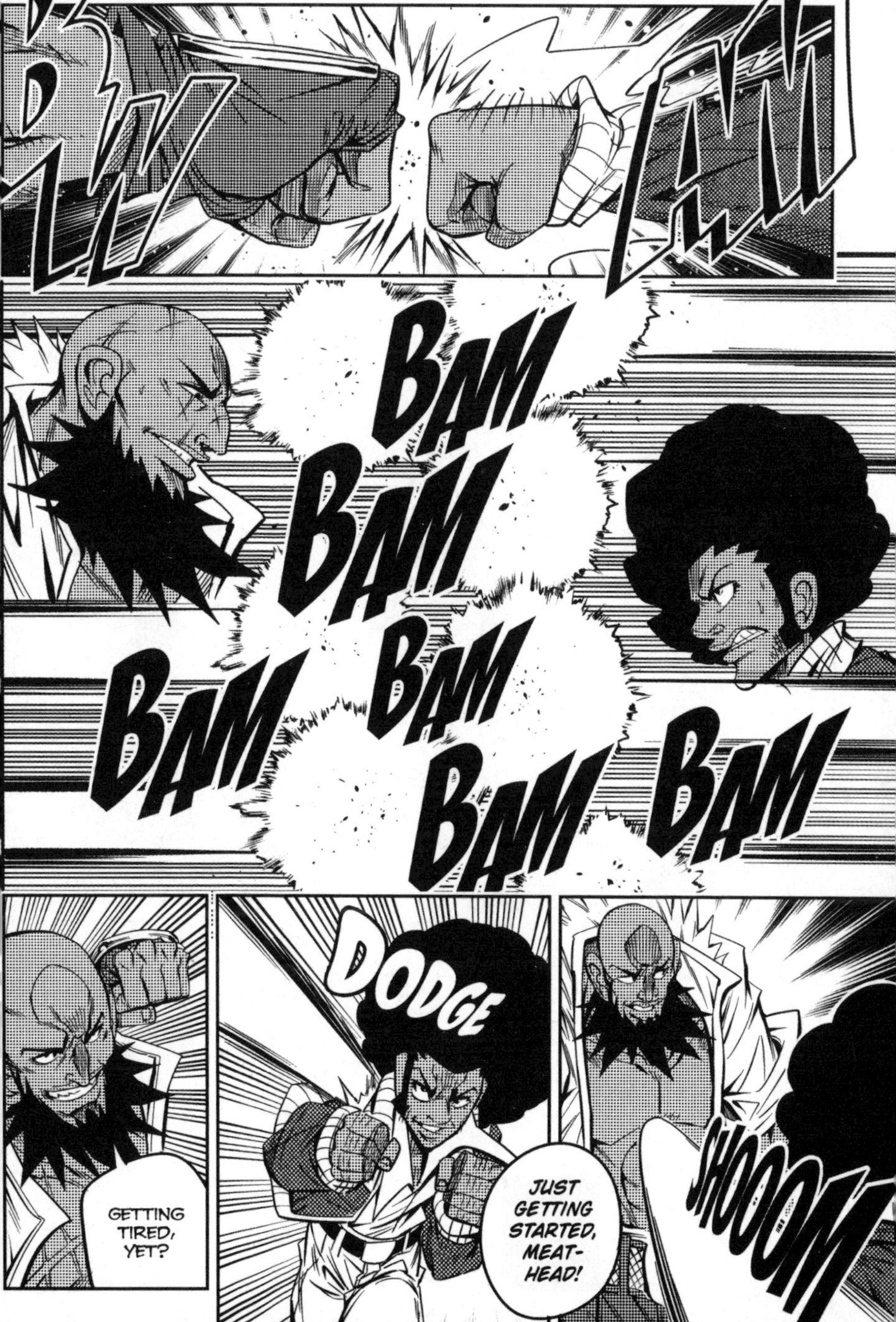
BAM
BAM
BAM
BAM
BAM
BAM
GETTING TIRED, YET?
DODGE
JUST GETTING STARTED, MEAT-HEAD!
SHOOOM

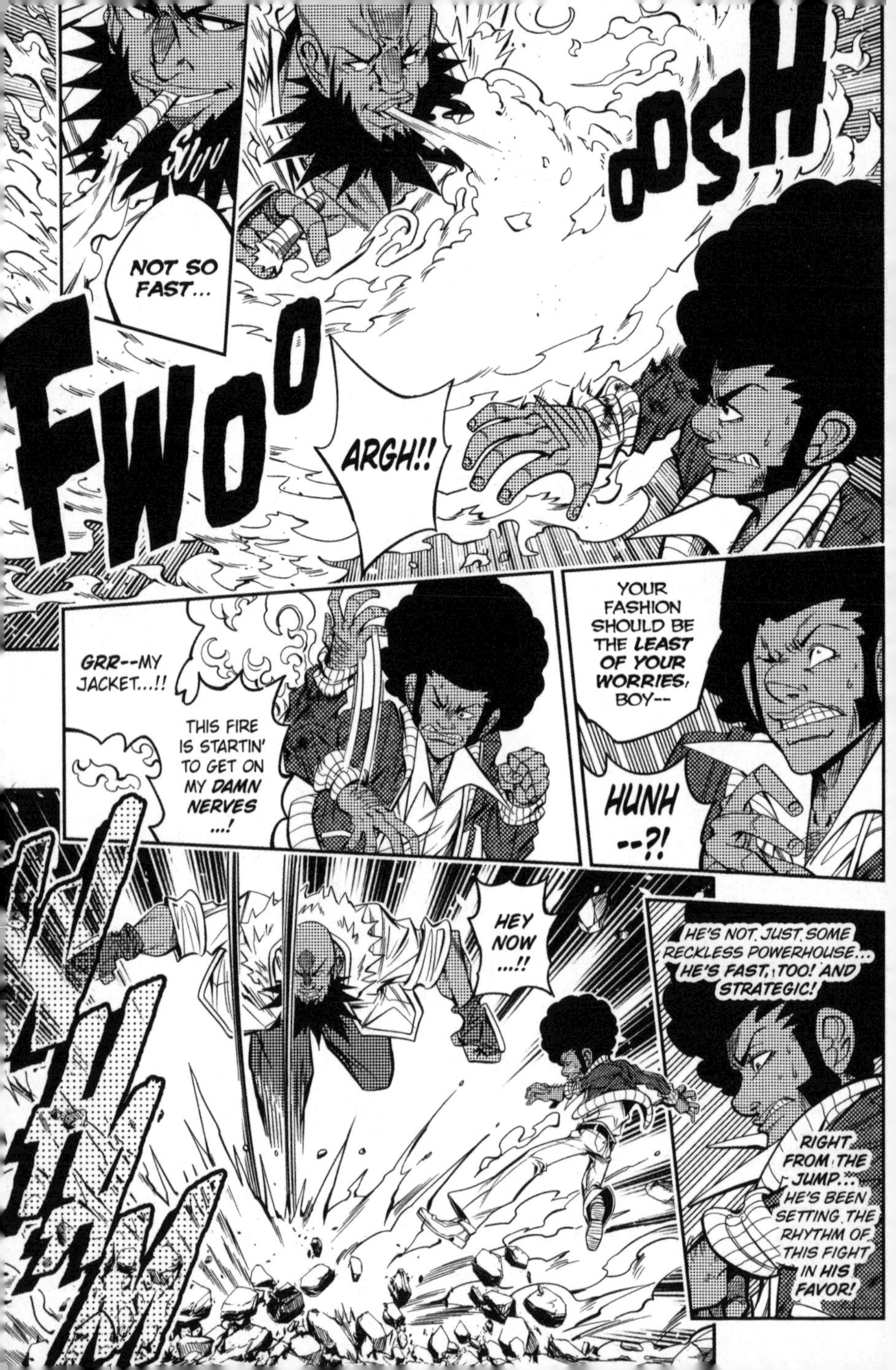
SSSS
NOT SO FAST...
OOSH!
FWOOO
ARGH!!
GRR--MY JACKET...!!
THIS FIRE IS STARTIN' TO GET ON MY DAMN NERVES ...!
YOUR FASHION SHOULD BE THE LEAST OF YOUR WORRIES, BOY--
HUNH --?!
HEY NOW ...!!
HE'S NOT JUST SOME RECKLESS POWERHOUSE... HE'S FAST, TOO! AND STRATEGIC!
RIGHT FROM THE JUMP... HE'S BEEN SETTING THE RHYTHM OF THIS FIGHT IN HIS FAVOR!

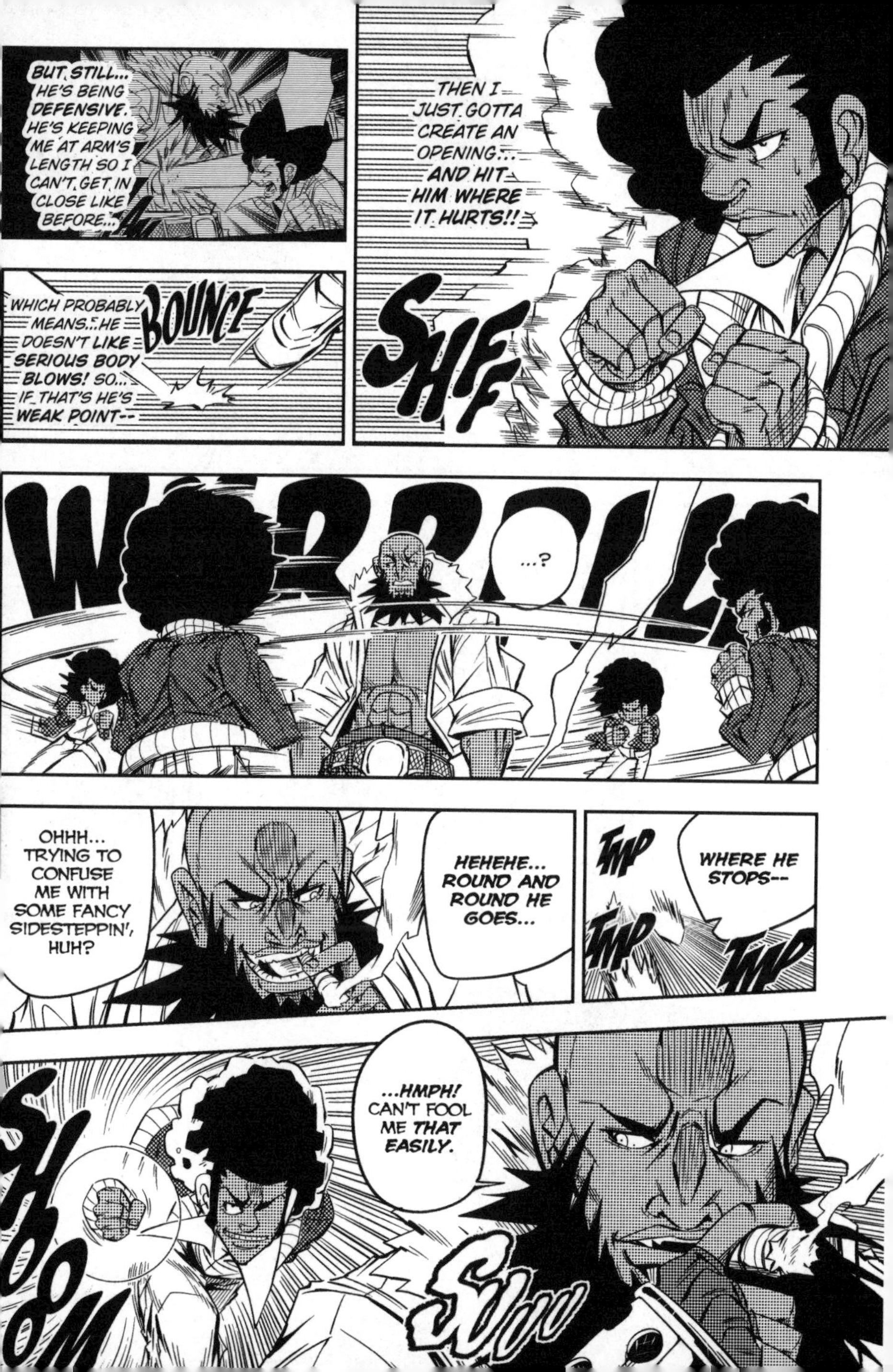
BUT, STILL... HE'S BEING DEFENSIVE. HE'S KEEPING ME AT ARM'S LENGTH SO I CAN'T GET IN CLOSE LIKE BEFORE...
THEN I JUST GOTTA CREATE AN OPENING... AND HIT HIM WHERE IT HURTS!!
WHICH PROBABLY MEANS... HE DOESN'T LIKE SERIOUS BODY BLOWS! SO... IF THAT'S HE'S WEAK POINT--
BOUNCE
SHIFF
...?
OHHH... TRYING TO CONFUSE ME WITH SOME FANCY SIDESTEPPIN', HUH?
HEHEHE... ROUND AND ROUND HE GOES...
TMP
TMP
WHERE HE STOPS--
TMP
SHOOM
...HMPH! CAN'T FOOL ME THAT EASILY.

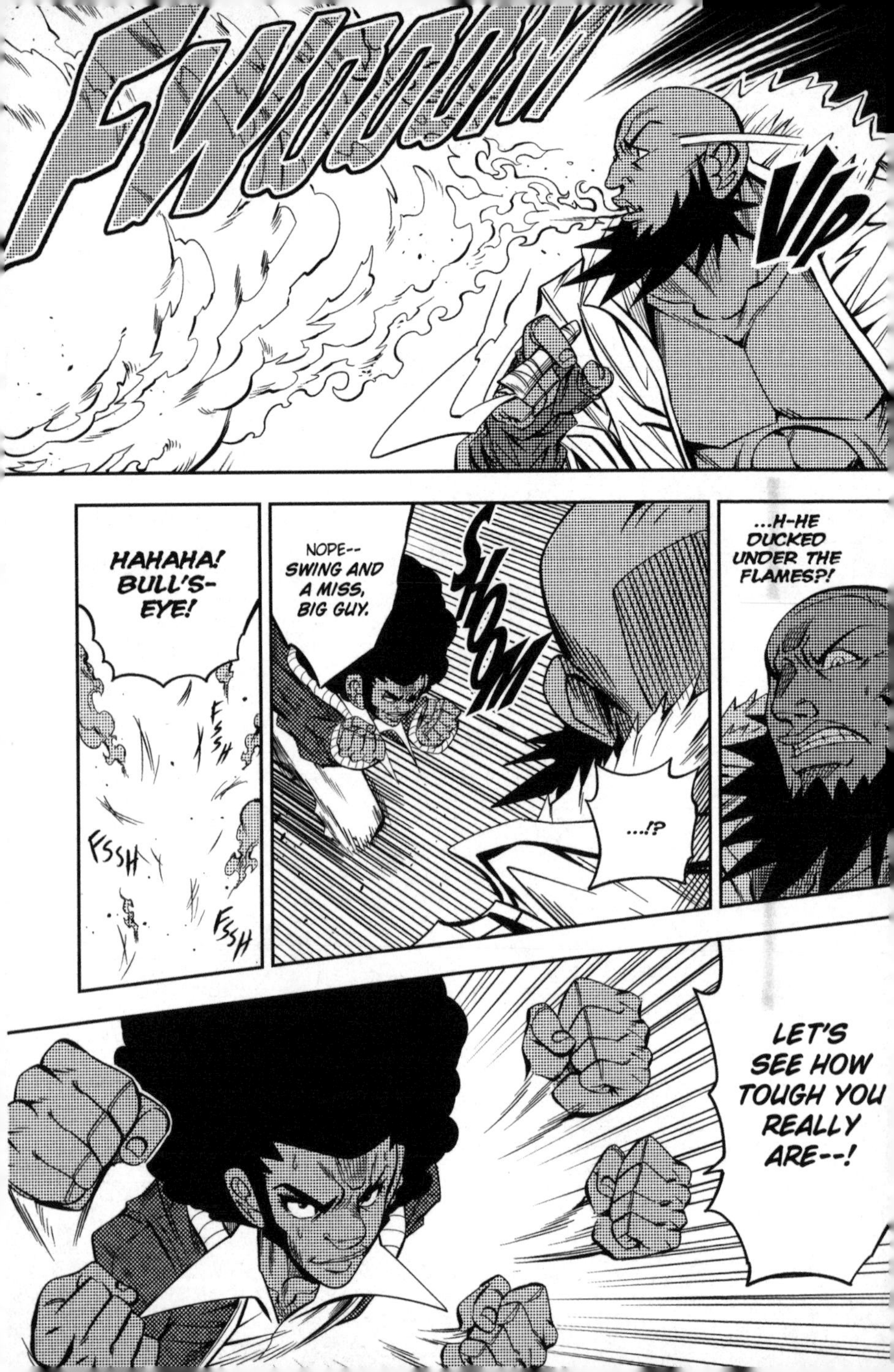
FWOOOM
VIP
HAHAHA! BULL'S-EYE!
FSSH
FSSH
FSSH
NOPE-- SWING AND A MISS, BIG GUY.
SHOOM
...!?
...H-HE DUCKED UNDER THE FLAMES?!
LET'S SEE HOW TOUGH YOU REALLY ARE--!

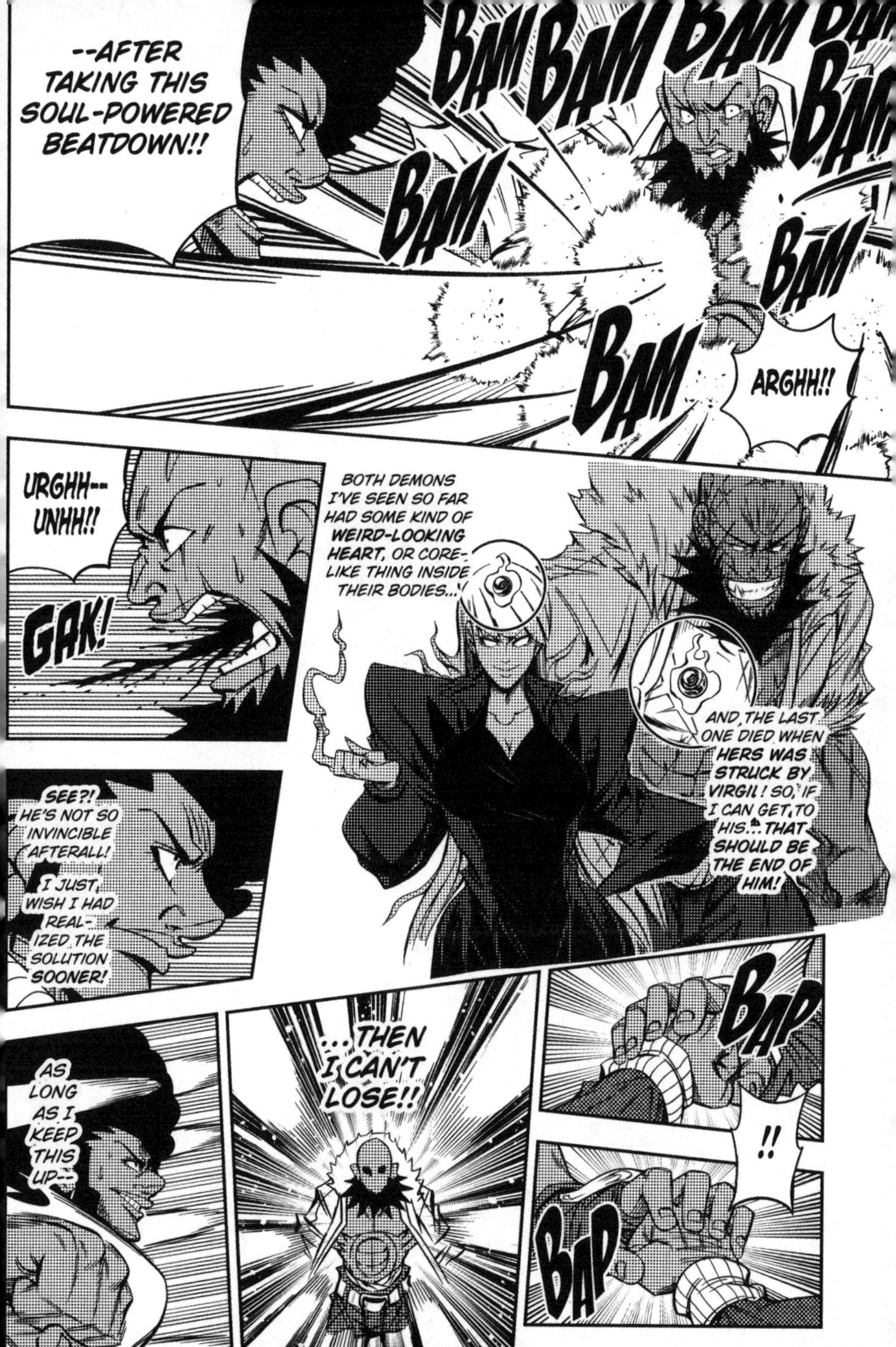
--AFTER TAKING THIS SOUL-POWERED BEATDOWN!!
BAM BAM BAM
BAM
BAM
BAM
BAM
ARGHH!!
URGHH-- UNHH!!
GAK!
BOTH DEMONS I'VE SEEN SO FAR HAD SOME KIND OF WEIRD-LOOKING HEART, OR CORE-LIKE THING INSIDE THEIR BODIES...
AND THE LAST ONE DIED WHEN HERS WAS STRUCK BY VIRGIL! SO, IF I CAN GET TO HIS... THAT SHOULD BE THE END OF HIM!
SEE?! HE'S NOT SO INVINCIBLE AFTERALL!
I JUST WISH I HAD REAL-IZED THE SOLUTION SOONER!
AS LONG AS I KEEP THIS UP--
...THEN I CAN'T LOSE!!
BAP
!!
BAP

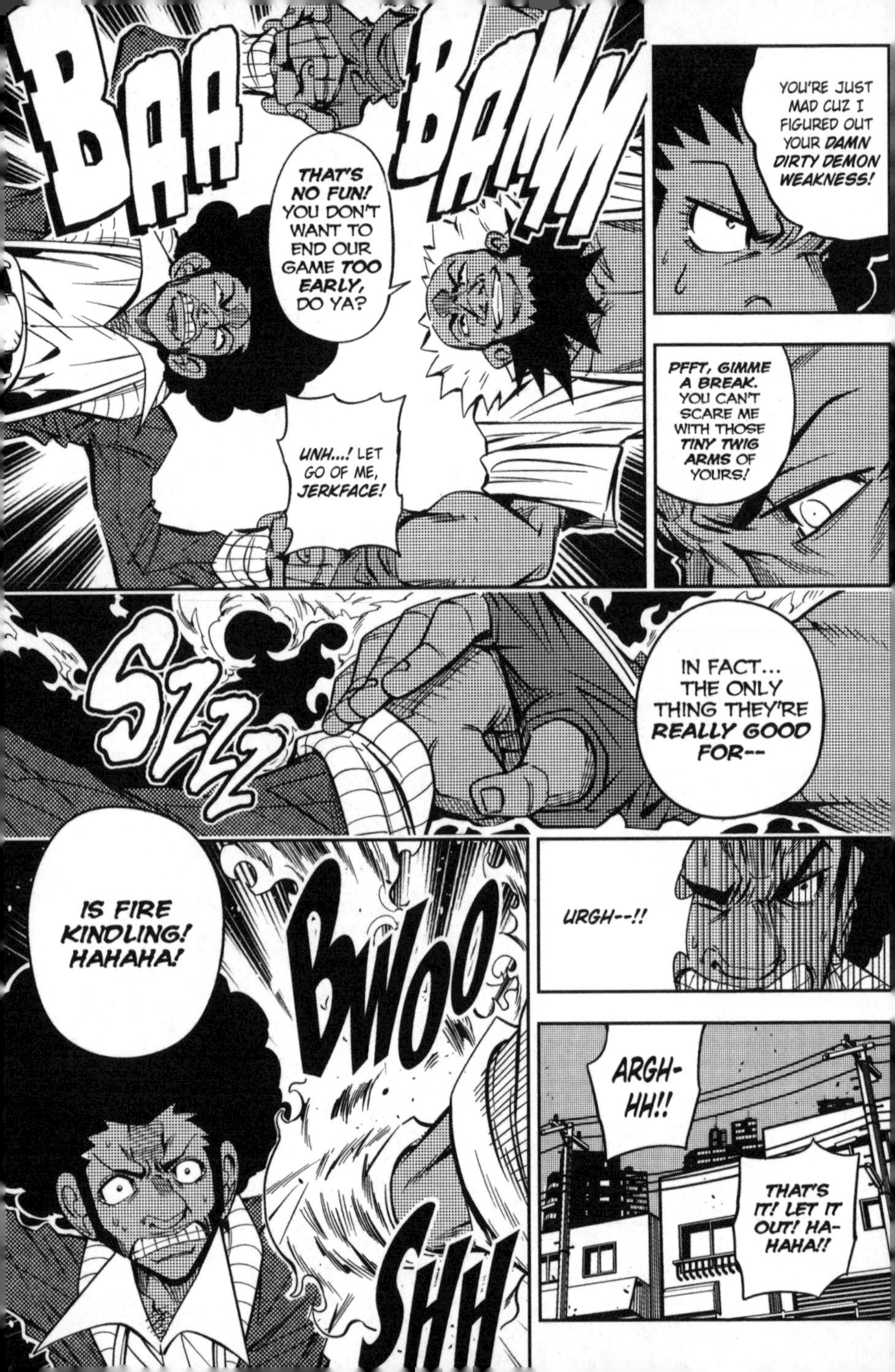
BAA
BAMM
THAT'S NO FUN! YOU DON'T WANT TO END OUR GAME TOO EARLY, DO YA?
UNH...! LET GO OF ME, JERKFACE!
YOU'RE JUST MAD CUZ I FIGURED OUT YOUR DAMN DIRTY DEMON WEAKNESS!
PFFT, GIMME A BREAK. YOU CAN'T SCARE ME WITH THOSE TINY TWIG ARMS OF YOURS!
SZZZ
IN FACT... THE ONLY THING THEY'RE REALLY GOOD FOR--
IS FIRE KINDLING! HAHAHA!
BWOO
SHH
URGH--!!
ARGH-HH!!
THAT'S IT! LET IT OUT! HA-HAHA!!

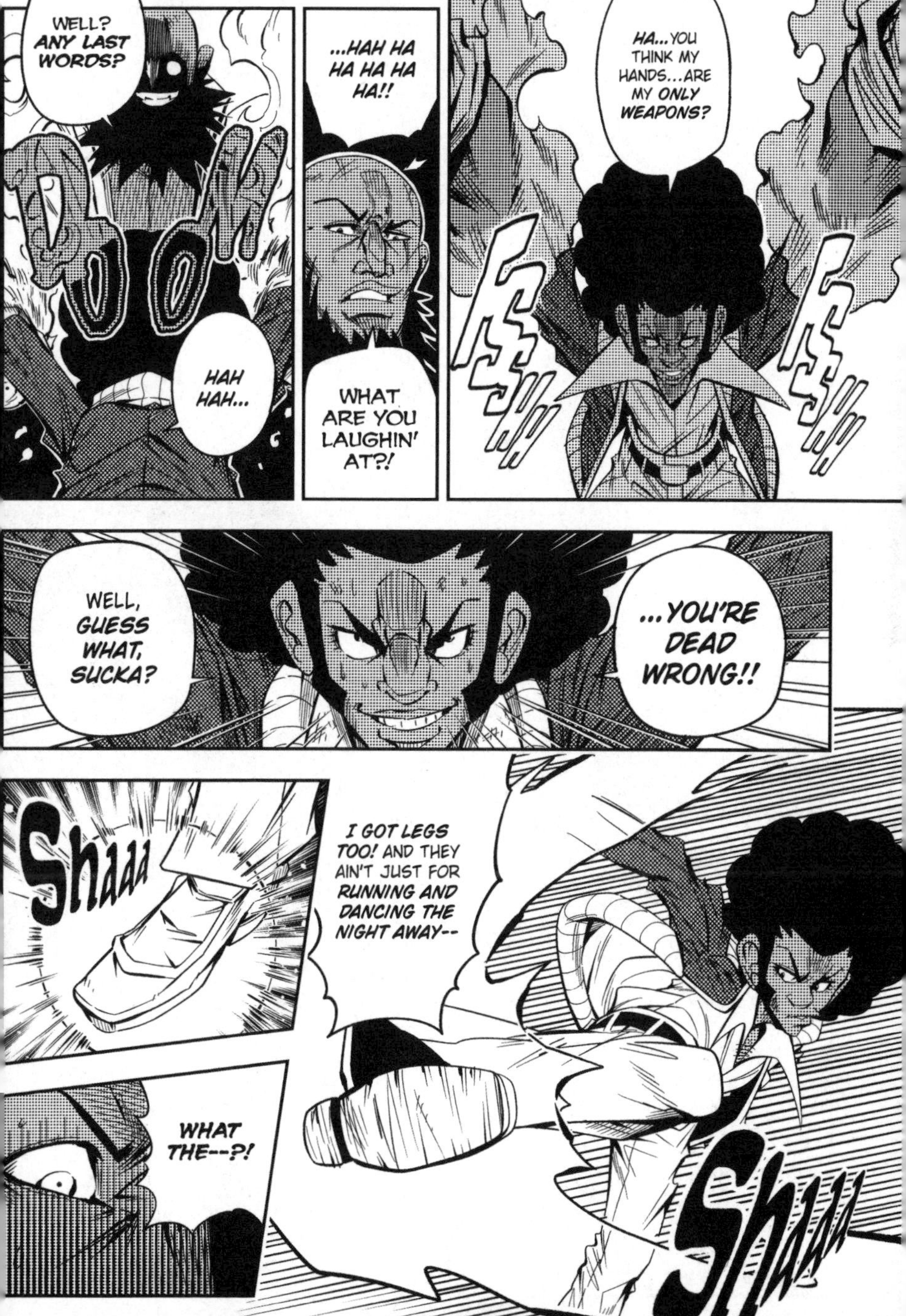
WELL? ANY LAST WORDS?
DOOM
HAH HAH...
...HAH HA HA HA HA HA HA!!
WHAT ARE YOU LAUGHIN' AT?!
HA...YOU THINK MY HANDS...ARE MY ONLY WEAPONS?
WELL, GUESS WHAT, SUCKA?
...YOU'RE DEAD WRONG!!
Shaaa
WHAT THE--?!
I GOT LEGS TOO! AND THEY AIN'T JUST FOR RUNNING AND DANCING THE NIGHT AWAY--
Shaaa

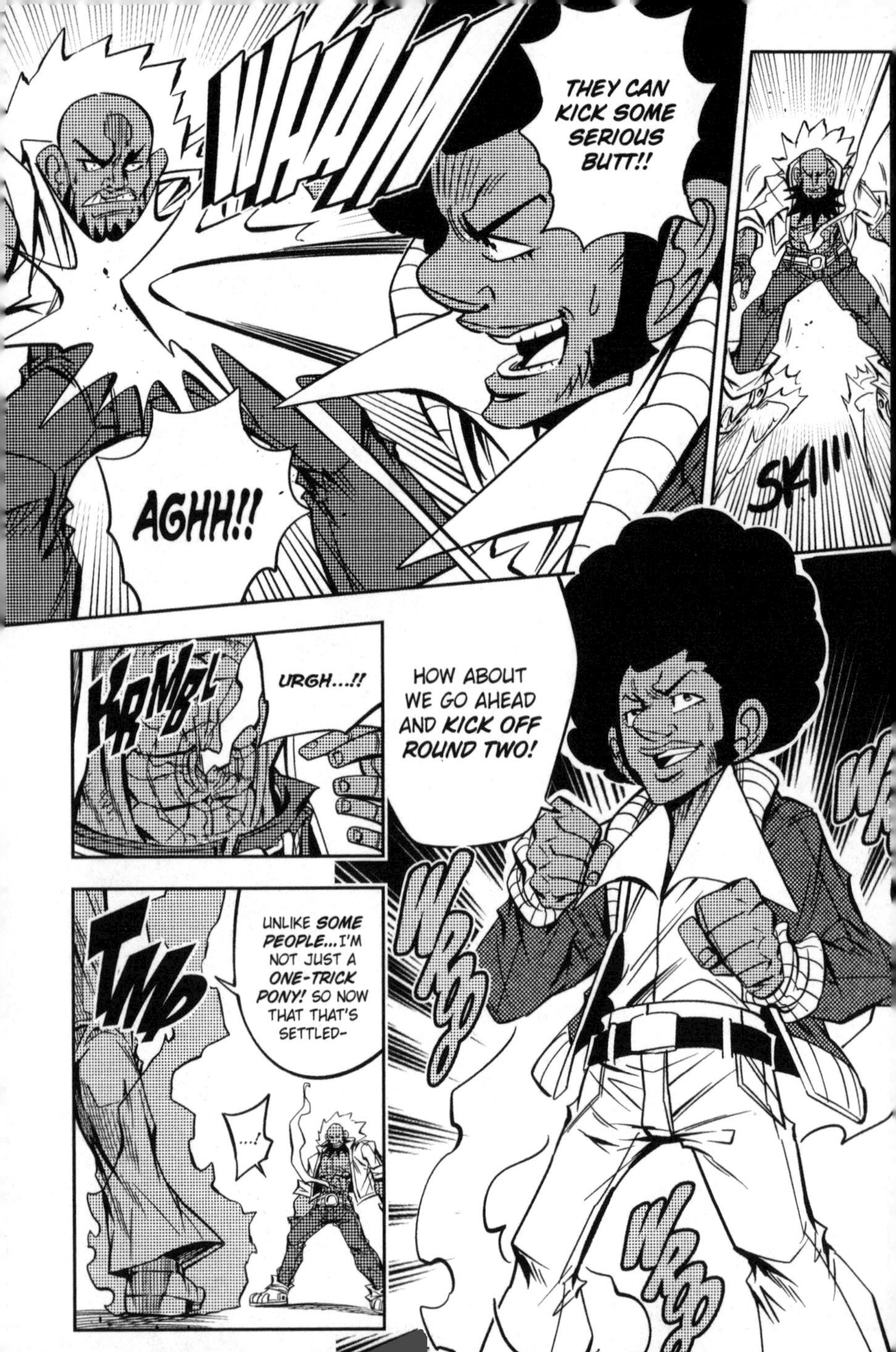
WHAM
AGHH!!
THEY CAN KICK SOME SERIOUS BUTT!!
SKI
HRMBL
URGH...!!
HOW ABOUT WE GO AHEAD AND **KICK OFF ROUND TWO!**
TMP
UNLIKE **SOME PEOPLE...** I'M NOT JUST A **ONE-TRICK PONY!** SO NOW THAT THAT'S SETTLED-
...!

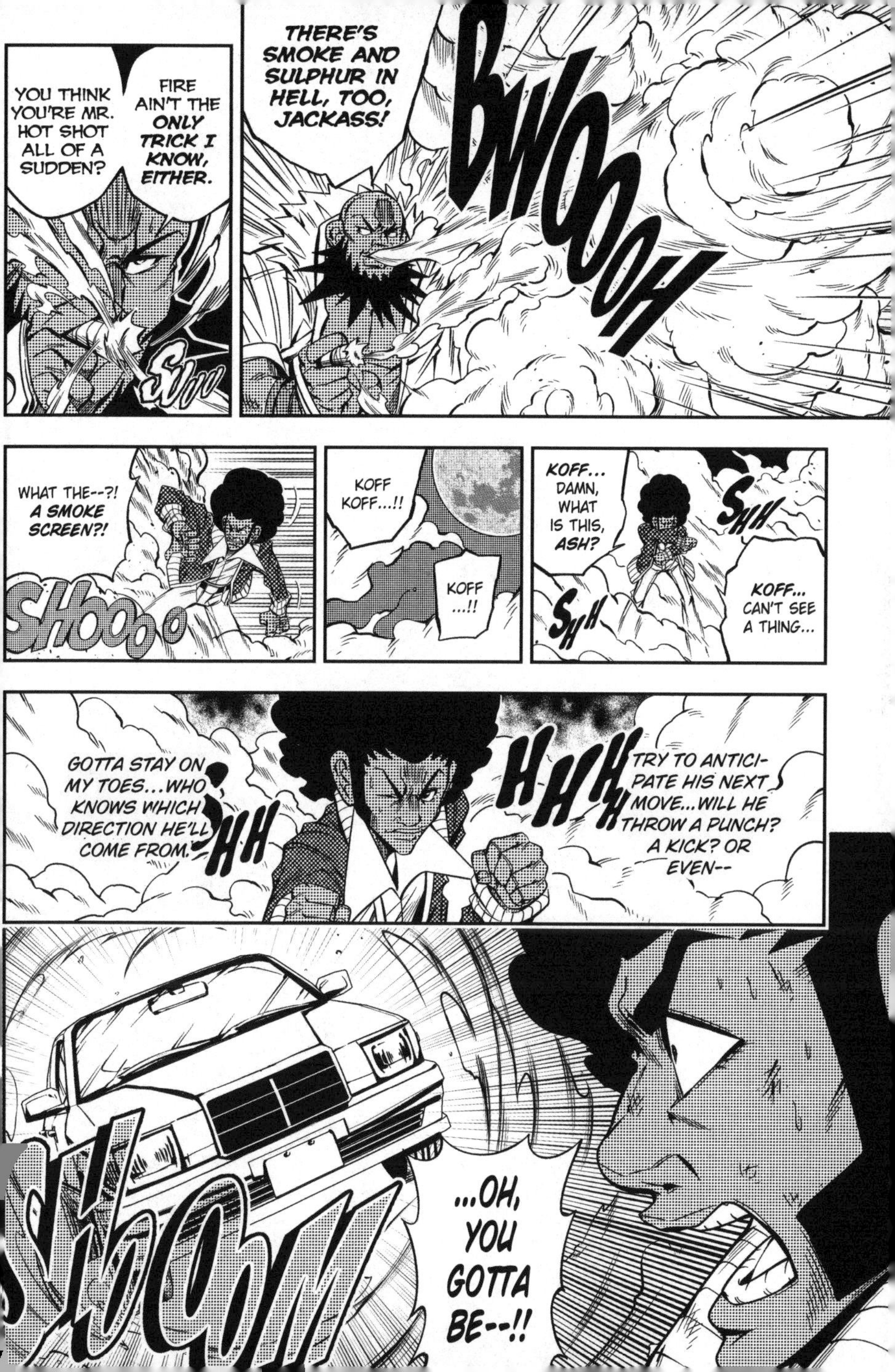
YOU THINK YOU'RE MR. HOT SHOT ALL OF A SUDDEN?
FIRE AIN'T THE ONLY TRICK I KNOW, EITHER.
SHH
THERE'S SMOKE AND SULPHUR IN HELL, TOO, JACKASS!
BWOOOOH
WHAT THE--?! A SMOKE SCREEN?!
SHOOOOO
KOFF KOFF...!!
KOFF ...!!
KOFF... DAMN, WHAT IS THIS, ASH?
SHH
SHH
KOFF... CAN'T SEE A THING...
GOTTA STAY ON MY TOES...WHO KNOWS WHICH DIRECTION HE'LL COME FROM.
HHH
HHHH
TRY TO ANTICIPATE HIS NEXT MOVE...WILL HE THROW A PUNCH? A KICK? OR EVEN--
SHOOM
...OH, YOU GOTTA BE--!!

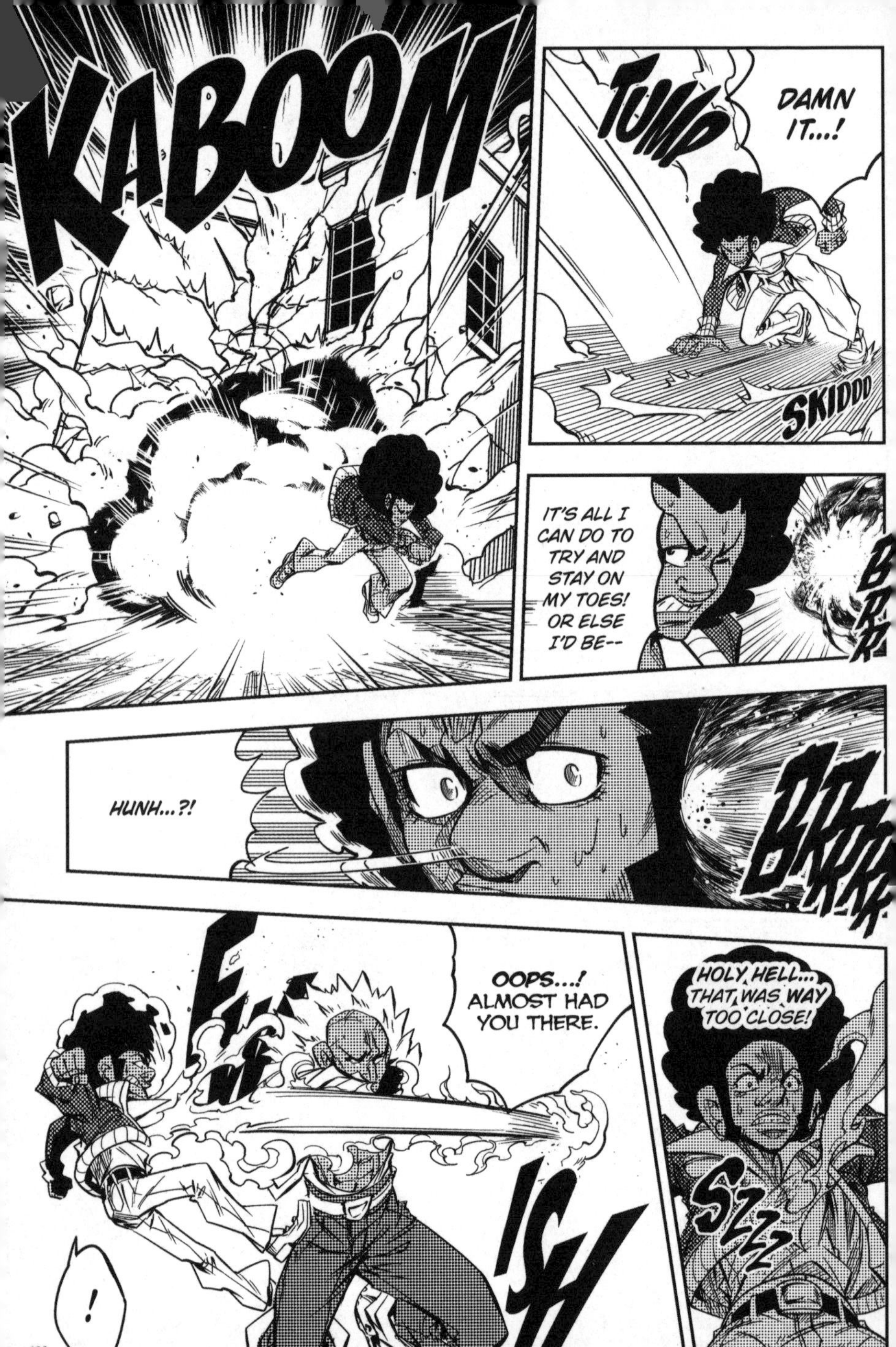
KABOOM
TUMP
DAMN IT...!
SKIDDD
IT'S ALL I CAN DO TO TRY AND STAY ON MY TOES! OR ELSE I'D BE--
BRR
HUNH...?!
BRRRK
FW
OOPS...! ALMOST HAD YOU THERE.
ISH
!
HOLY HELL... THAT WAS WAY TOO CLOSE!
SZZZ

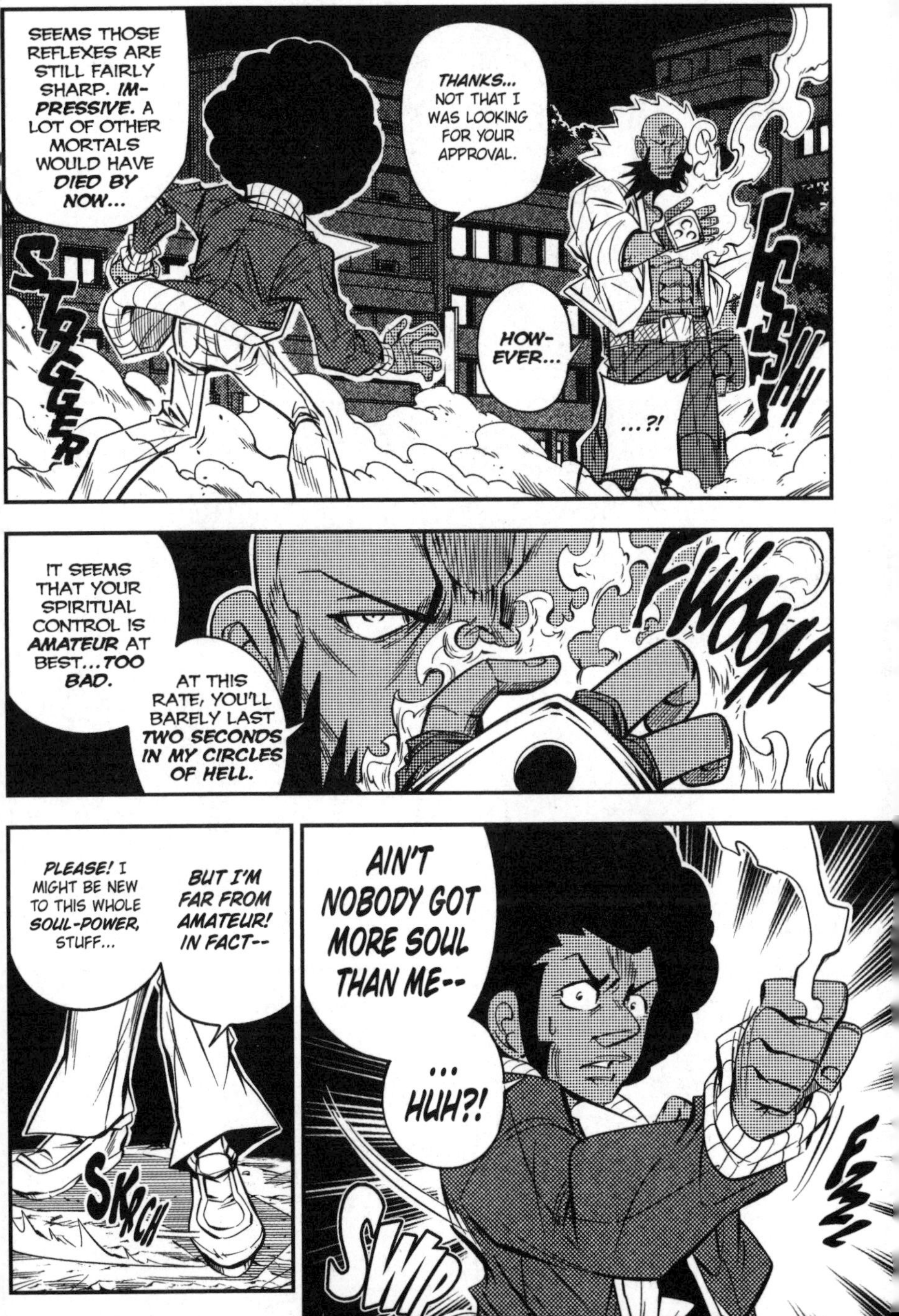

SEEMS THOSE REFLEXES ARE STILL FAIRLY SHARP. *IM-PRESSIVE.* A LOT OF OTHER MORTALS WOULD HAVE *DIED BY NOW...*
STAGGER
THANKS... NOT THAT I WAS LOOKING FOR YOUR APPROVAL.
HOW-EVER...
...?!
IT SEEMS THAT YOUR SPIRITUAL CONTROL IS *AMATEUR* AT BEST...*TOO BAD.*
AT THIS RATE, YOU'LL BARELY LAST *TWO SECONDS IN MY CIRCLES OF HELL.*
FWOOM
PLEASE! I MIGHT BE NEW TO THIS WHOLE *SOUL-POWER,* STUFF...
BUT I'M FAR FROM AMATEUR! IN FACT--
SKRCH
AIN'T NOBODY GOT MORE SOUL THAN ME--
... HUH?!
SWIP

WHAT IS MY SOUL DOING...?!

OR RATHER— WHY ISN'T IT DOING ANYTHING?! IT'S BARELY COMING OUT NOW!

SW OOO

W—WHO TURNED OFF THE TAP?!

HAVING TROUBLE KEEPING THE *FAUCET RUNNING?*

W—WHAT ...?!

WELCOME TO THE MANY *DRAWBACKS* OF BEING MORTAL, SON!

THE FIRST OF WHICH IS THAT *PHYSICAL BODY OF YOURS.*

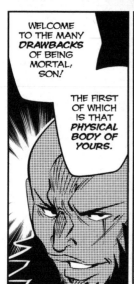

IT'S CALLED *SOUL ARTS*— THE MANIPULATION OF YOUR SOUL MATTER, OR *AETHER.*

FOR SPIRITS AND OTHER SUPERNATURAL BEINGS, CONTROLLING ONE'S OWN AETHER, OR *INVOCATION*, IS AS NATURAL AS BREATHING.

BUT FOR A *MORTAL*— YOU HAVE THE ADDED INCONVENIENCE OF A HUMAN BODY WHICH IS *FRAGILE, TIRES EASILY,* AND REQUIRES MORE STAMINA TO DRAW AETHER OUTWARD...

ONLY MAKING INVOCATION *THAT MUCH HARDER* TO MAINTAIN OVER EXTENDED PERIODS OF TIME.

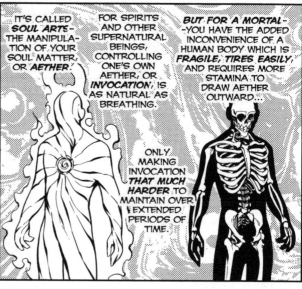

DAMMIT, IS THIS A FIGHT, OR A LECTURE?!

AETHER...? INVO...WHAT-NOW?

IN OTHER WORDS, *SEEMS LIKE YOU'RE RUNNING OUT OF STEAM.*

IF YOU'D LIKE...I CAN GO AHEAD AND END THIS MATCH SO YOU CAN TAKE A NICE *LITTLE NAP* TO RECOVER...

HAHA-HAHA!

URGH...! THE ONLY WAY THIS FIGHT ENDS—

GRGH

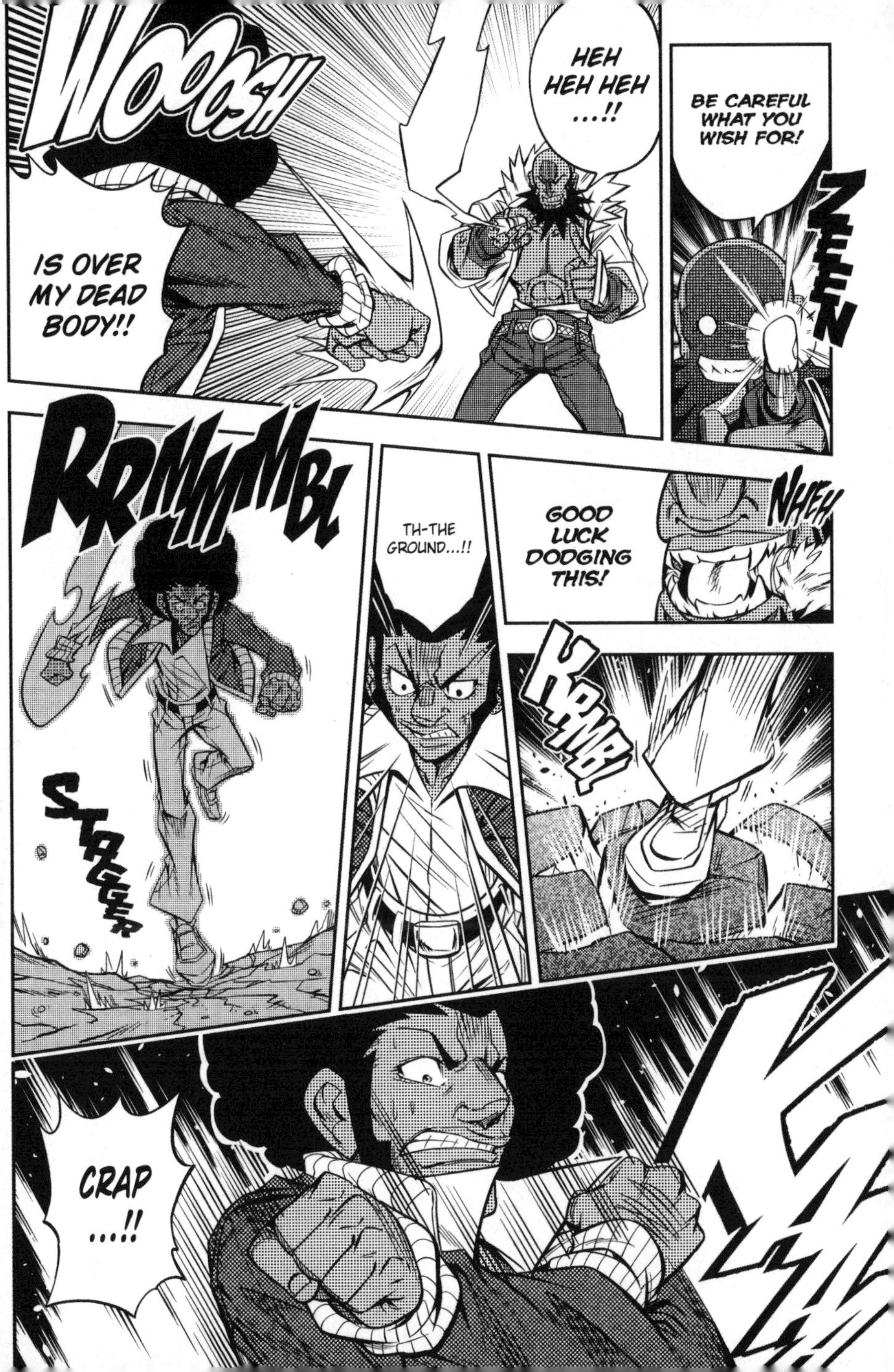
WOOOSH
IS OVER MY DEAD BODY!!
HEH HEH HEH ...!!
BE CAREFUL WHAT YOU WISH FOR!
ZEEN
RRMMMBL
STAGGER
TH-THE GROUND...!!
GOOD LUCK DODGING THIS!
NHEH
KRMBL
CRAP ...!!

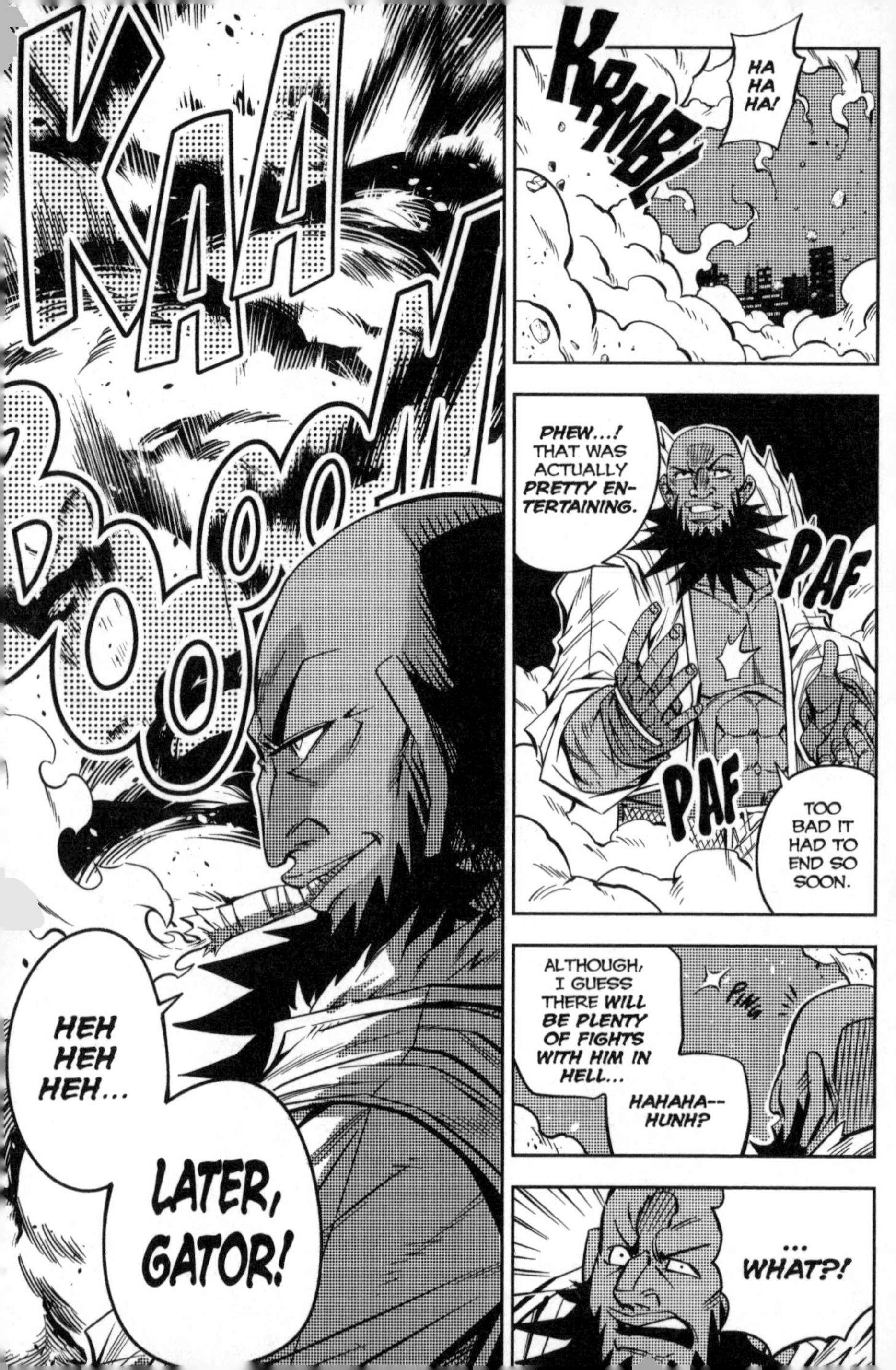
KAA
BOOOOM!
HEH HEH HEH...
LATER, GATOR!
KAMB!
HA HA HA!
PHEW...! THAT WAS ACTUALLY PRETTY EN-TERTAINING.
PAF
PAF
TOO BAD IT HAD TO END SO SOON.
ALTHOUGH, I GUESS THERE WILL BE PLENTY OF FIGHTS WITH HIM IN HELL...
HAHAHA-- HUNH?
... WHAT?!

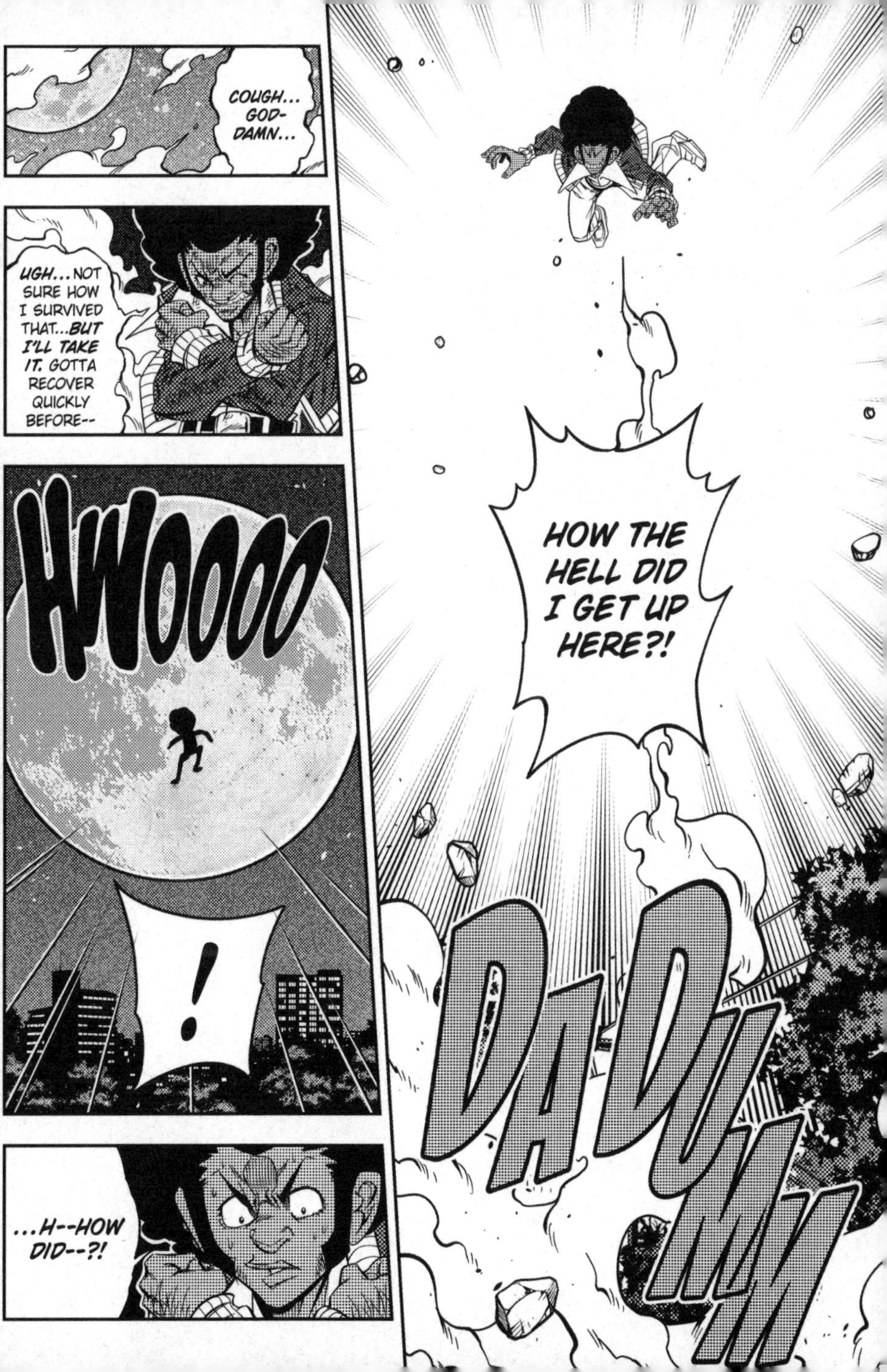
COUGH... GOD-DAMN...
UGH... NOT SURE HOW I SURVIVED THAT...BUT I'LL TAKE IT. GOTTA RECOVER QUICKLY BEFORE--
HWOOOO
!
...H--HOW DID--?!
HOW THE HELL DID I GET UP HERE?!
DADUMM

SOUL BEAT

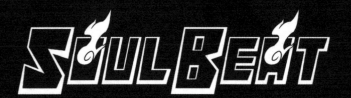

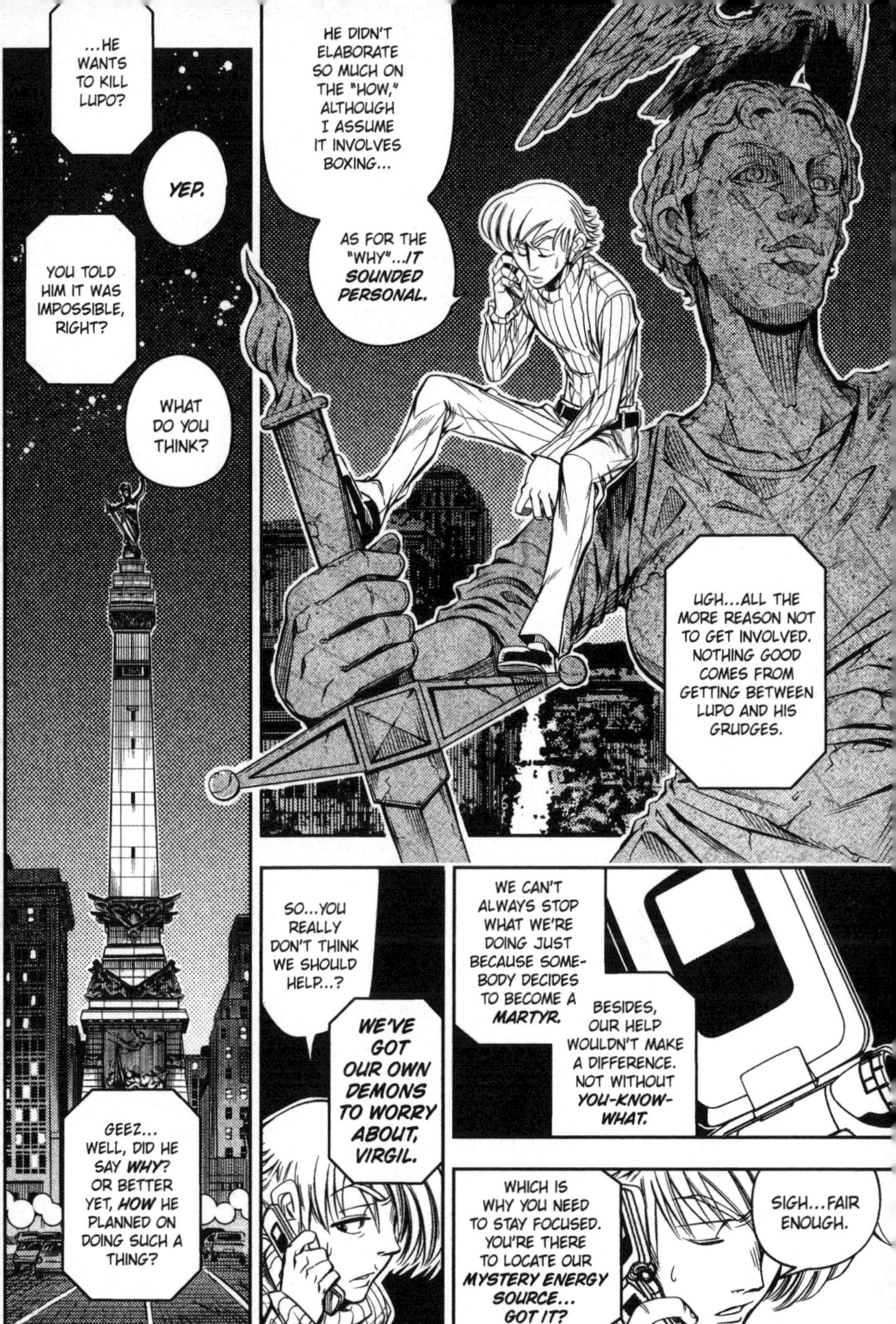
…HE WANTS TO KILL LUPO?
YEP.
YOU TOLD HIM IT WAS IMPOSSIBLE, RIGHT?
WHAT DO YOU THINK?
GEEZ… WELL, DID HE SAY *WHY*? OR BETTER YET, *HOW* HE PLANNED ON DOING SUCH A THING?
HE DIDN'T ELABORATE SO MUCH ON THE "HOW," ALTHOUGH I ASSUME IT INVOLVES BOXING…
AS FOR THE "WHY"…*IT SOUNDED PERSONAL.*
UGH…ALL THE MORE REASON NOT TO GET INVOLVED. NOTHING GOOD COMES FROM GETTING BETWEEN LUPO AND HIS GRUDGES.
SO…YOU REALLY DON'T THINK WE SHOULD HELP…?
WE'VE GOT OUR OWN DEMONS TO WORRY ABOUT, VIRGIL.
WE CAN'T ALWAYS STOP WHAT WE'RE DOING JUST BECAUSE SOMEBODY DECIDES TO BECOME A *MARTYR.*
BESIDES, OUR HELP WOULDN'T MAKE A DIFFERENCE. NOT WITHOUT *YOU-KNOW-WHAT.*
WHICH IS WHY YOU NEED TO STAY FOCUSED. YOU'RE THERE TO LOCATE OUR *MYSTERY ENERGY SOURCE… GOT IT?*
SIGH…FAIR ENOUGH.

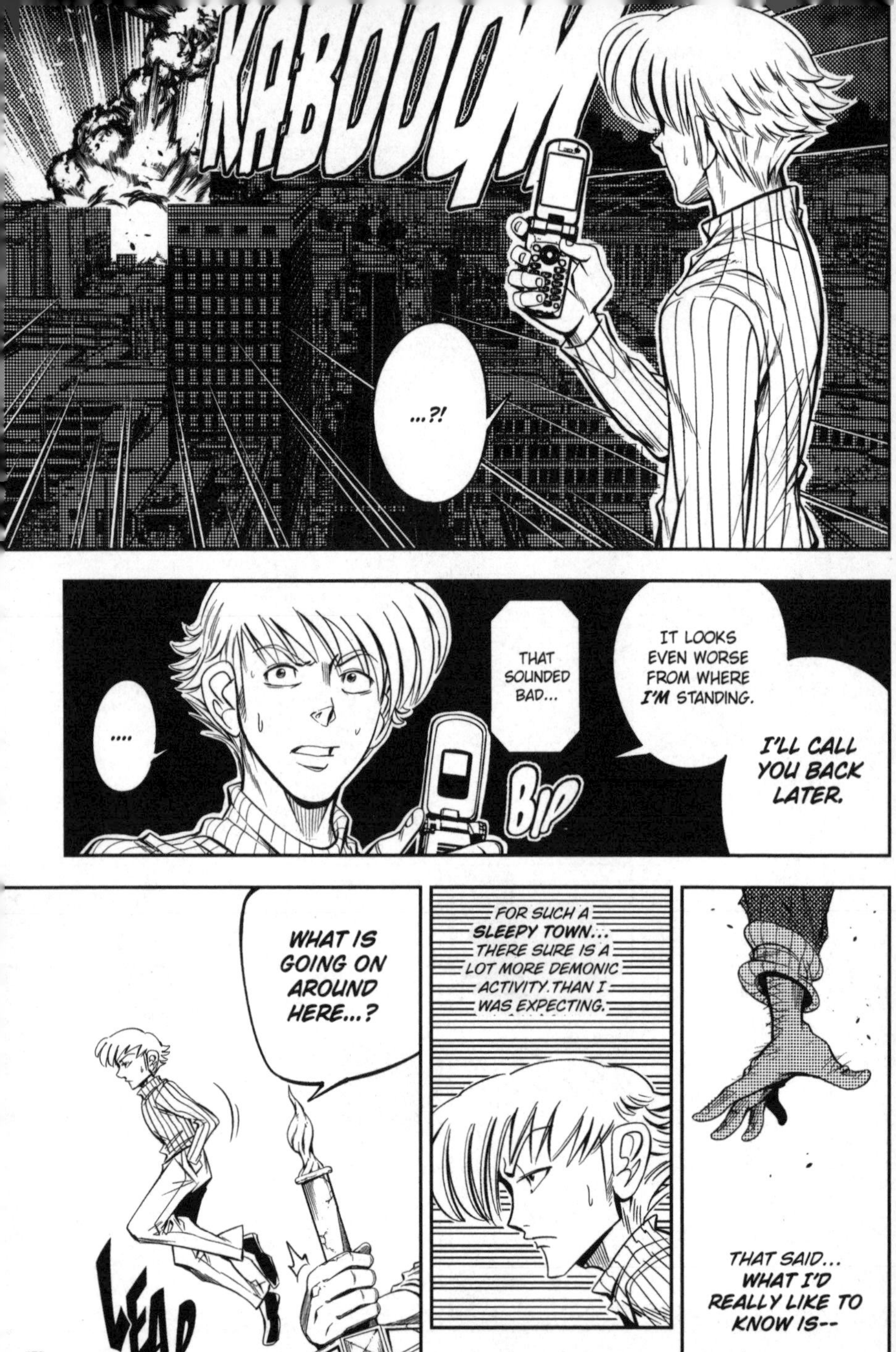
KABOOM
...?!
....
THAT SOUNDED BAD...
IT LOOKS EVEN WORSE FROM WHERE I'M STANDING.
BIP
I'LL CALL YOU BACK LATER.
WHAT IS GOING ON AROUND HERE...?
LEAP
FOR SUCH A SLEEPY TOWN... THERE SURE IS A LOT MORE DEMONIC ACTIVITY THAN I WAS EXPECTING.
THAT SAID... WHAT I'D REALLY LIKE TO KNOW IS--

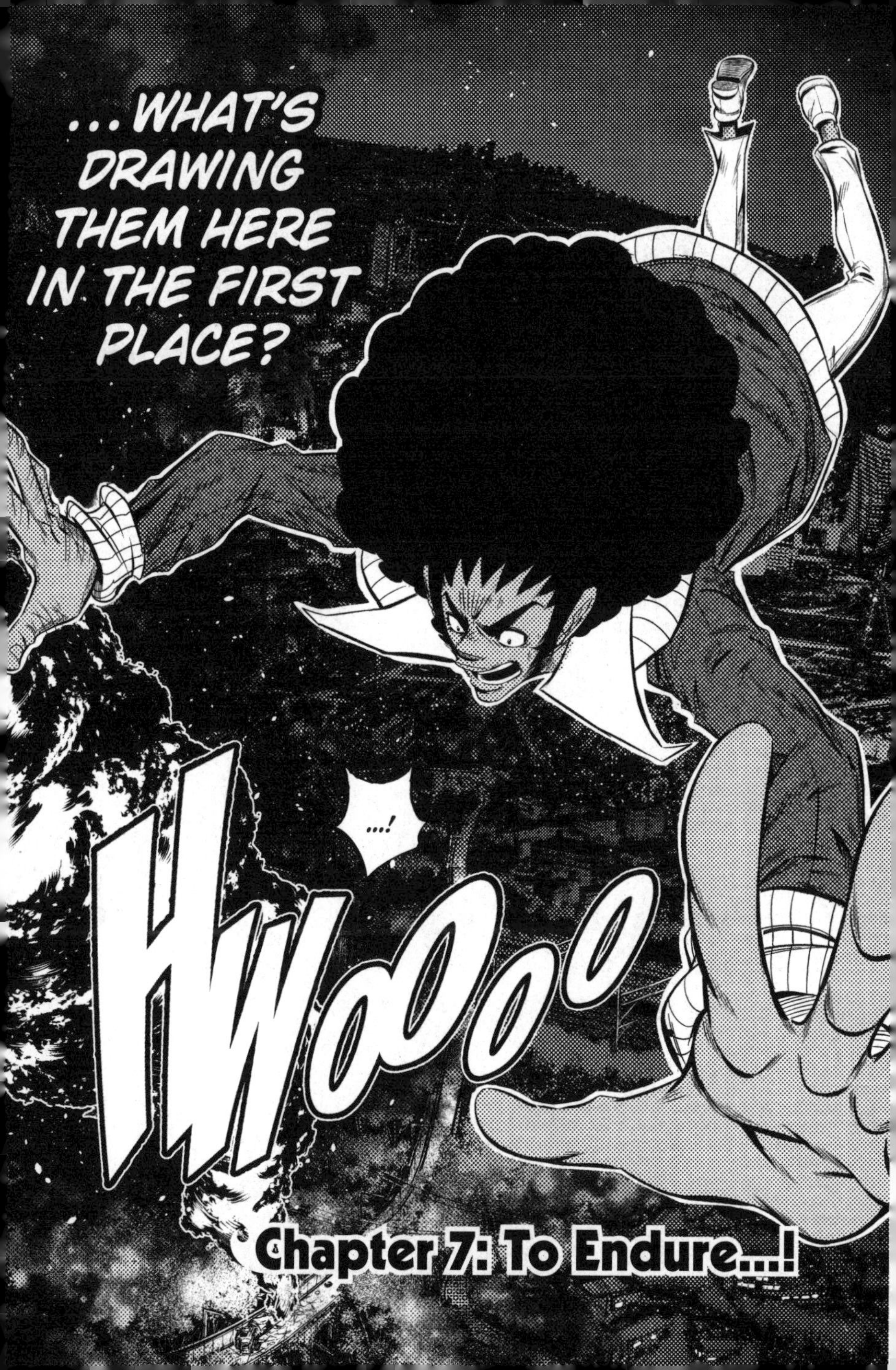
...WHAT'S DRAWING THEM HERE IN THE FIRST PLACE?
...!
HWOOOO
Chapter 7: To Endure...!

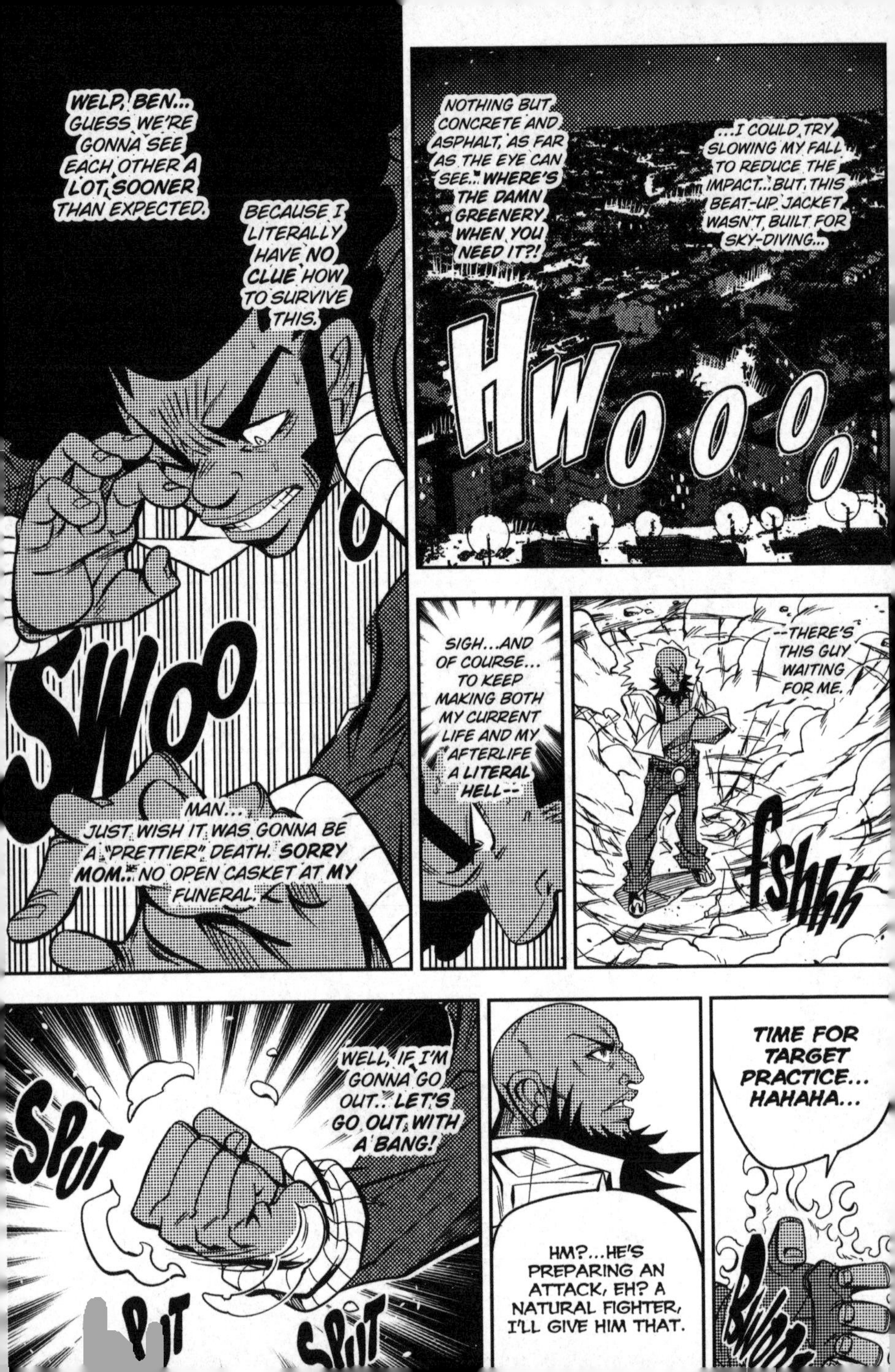
WELP, BEN... GUESS WE'RE GONNA SEE EACH OTHER A LOT SOONER THAN EXPECTED.
BECAUSE I LITERALLY HAVE NO CLUE HOW TO SURVIVE THIS.
SWOO
MAN... JUST WISH IT WAS GONNA BE A "PRETTIER" DEATH. SORRY MOM... NO OPEN CASKET AT MY FUNERAL.
NOTHING BUT CONCRETE AND ASPHALT, AS FAR AS THE EYE CAN SEE... WHERE'S THE DAMN GREENERY WHEN YOU NEED IT?!
...I COULD TRY SLOWING MY FALL TO REDUCE THE IMPACT... BUT THIS BEAT-UP JACKET WASN'T BUILT FOR SKY-DIVING...
HWOOOO
SIGH...AND OF COURSE... TO KEEP MAKING BOTH MY CURRENT LIFE AND MY AFTERLIFE A LITERAL HELL--
--THERE'S THIS GUY WAITING FOR ME.
fshhh
SPLIT
WELL, IF I'M GONNA GO OUT... LET'S GO OUT WITH A BANG!
SPLIT
SPLIT
HM?...HE'S PREPARING AN ATTACK, EH? A NATURAL FIGHTER, I'LL GIVE HIM THAT.
TIME FOR TARGET PRACTICE... HAHAHA...

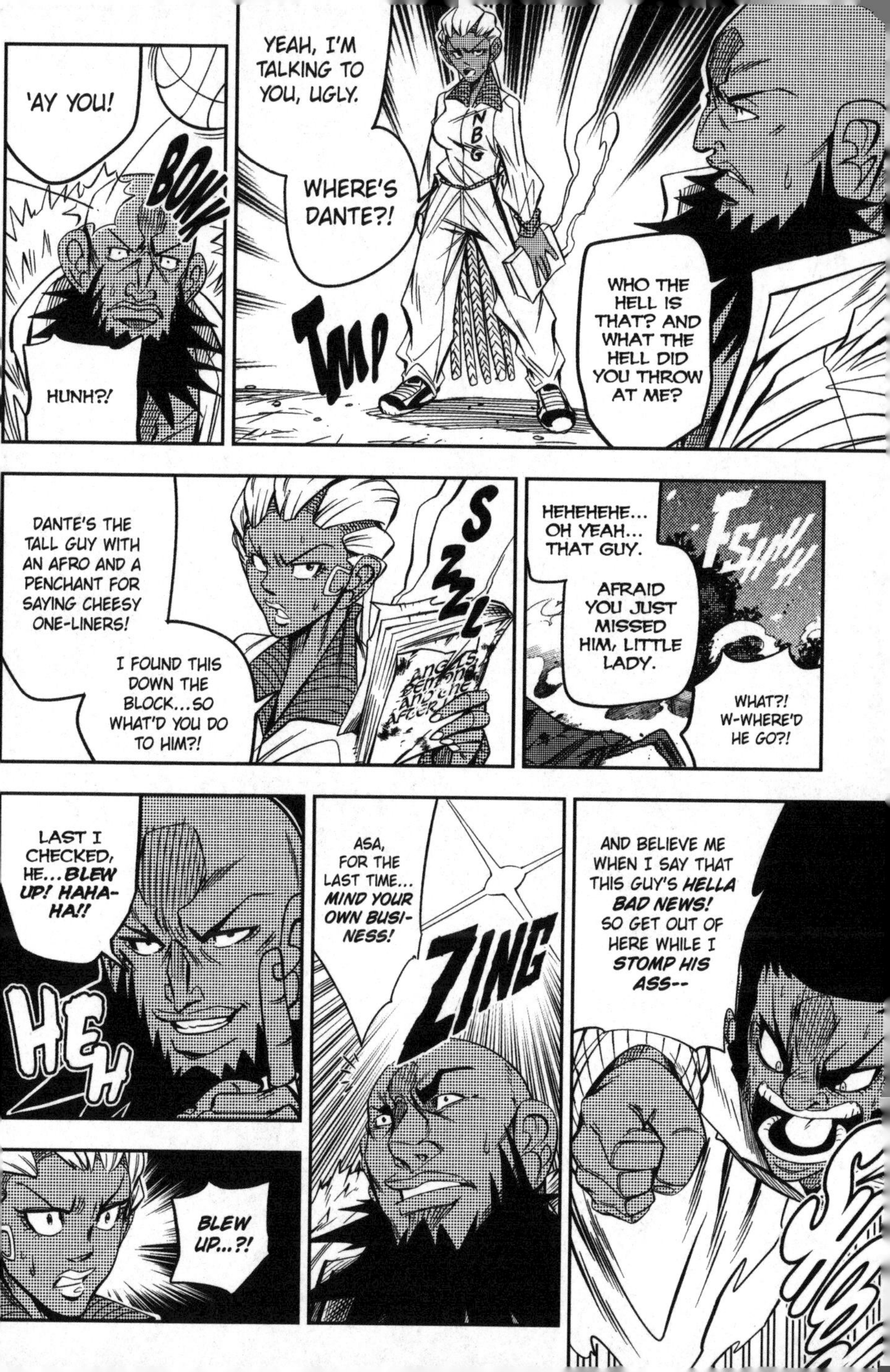

'AY YOU!
BONK
HUNH?!
YEAH, I'M TALKING TO YOU, UGLY.
WHERE'S DANTE?!
TMP
WHO THE HELL IS THAT? AND WHAT THE HELL DID YOU THROW AT ME?
DANTE'S THE TALL GUY WITH AN AFRO AND A PENCHANT FOR SAYING CHEESY ONE-LINERS!
I FOUND THIS DOWN THE BLOCK...SO WHAT'D YOU DO TO HIM?!
SZZL
HEHEHEHE... OH YEAH... THAT GUY.
AFRAID YOU JUST MISSED HIM, LITTLE LADY.
FSHHH
WHAT?! W-WHERE'D HE GO?!
LAST I CHECKED, HE...*BLEW UP! HAHA-HA!!*
HEH
BLEW UP...?!
ASA, FOR THE LAST TIME... *MIND YOUR OWN BUSI-NESS!*
ZING
AND BELIEVE ME WHEN I SAY THAT THIS GUY'S *HELLA BAD NEWS!* SO GET OUT OF HERE WHILE I *STOMP HIS ASS--*

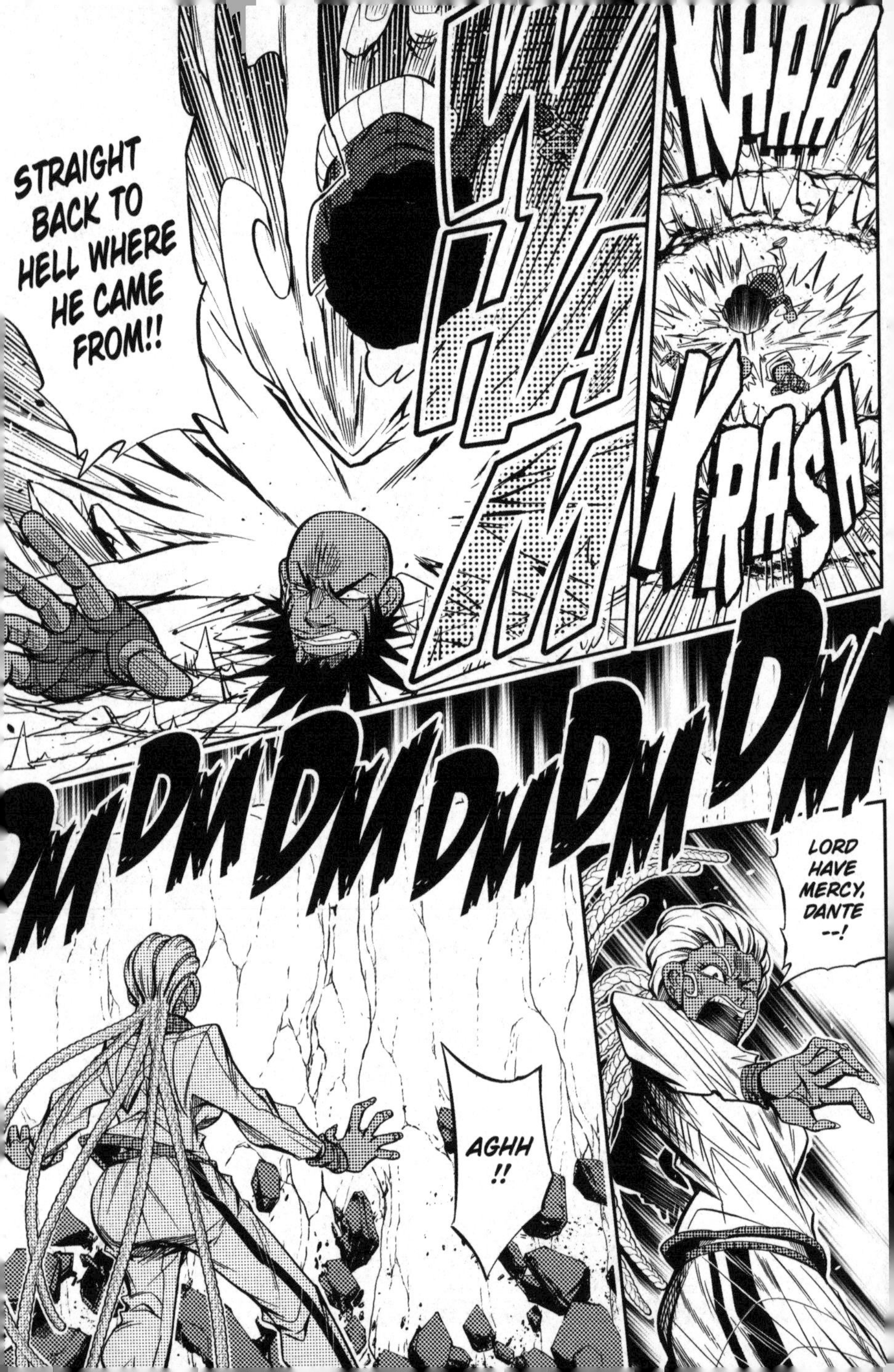
STRAIGHT BACK TO HELL WHERE HE CAME FROM!!
KRASH
DMDMDMDMDMDM
AGHH !!
LORD HAVE MERCY, DANTE --!

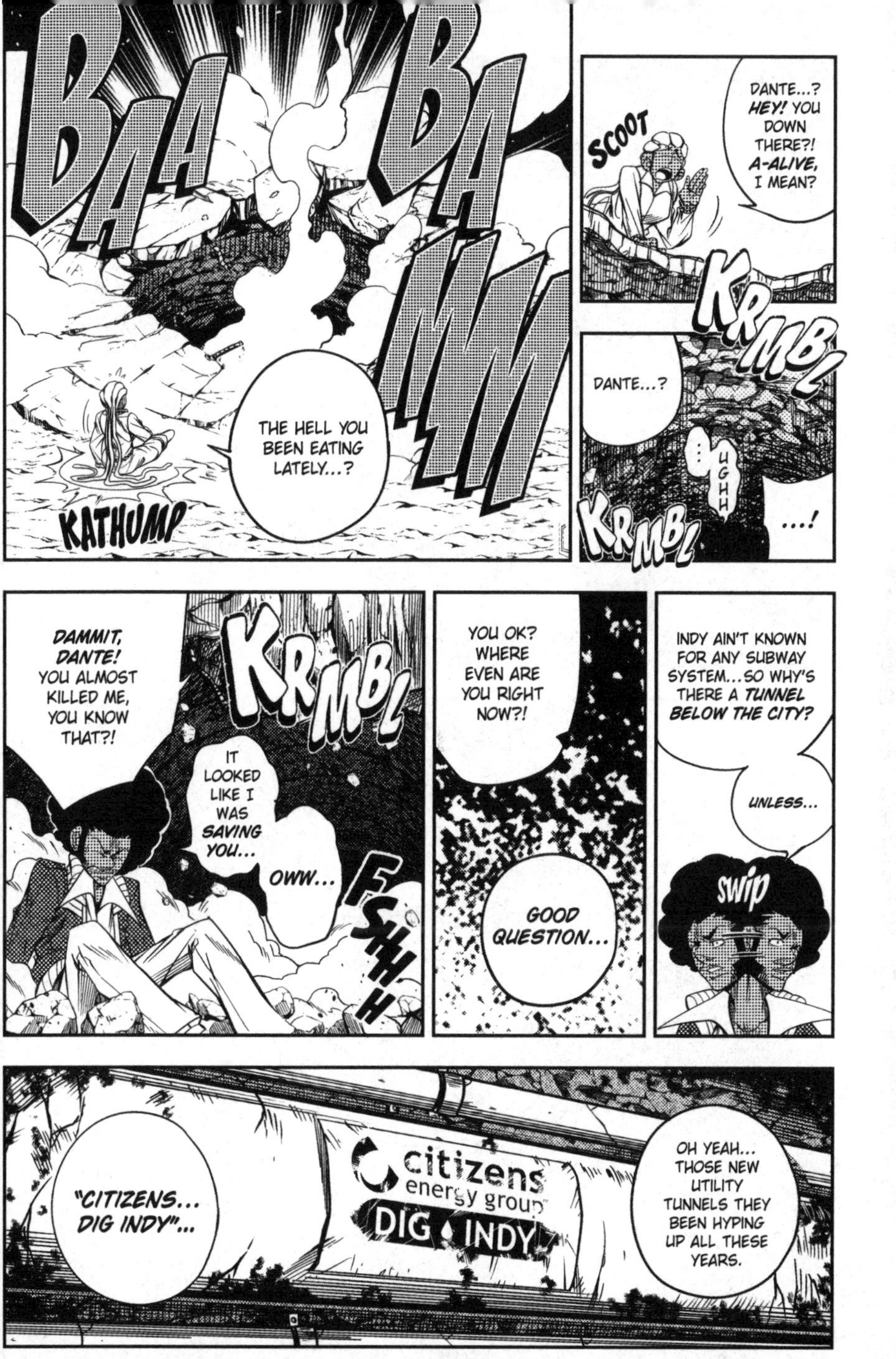
BAA
BADAMMM
THE HELL YOU BEEN EATING LATELY...?
KATHUMP
SCOOT
DANTE...? HEY! YOU DOWN THERE?! A-ALIVE, I MEAN?
KRMBL
DANTE...?
...UGHH
KRMBL
...!
DAMMIT, DANTE! YOU ALMOST KILLED ME, YOU KNOW THAT?!
KRMBL
IT LOOKED LIKE I WAS SAVING YOU...
OWW...
FSHHH
YOU OK? WHERE EVEN ARE YOU RIGHT NOW?!
GOOD QUESTION...
INDY AIN'T KNOWN FOR ANY SUBWAY SYSTEM...SO WHY'S THERE A TUNNEL BELOW THE CITY?
UNLESS...
swip
"CITIZENS... DIG INDY"...
citizens energy group
DIG INDY
OH YEAH... THOSE NEW UTILITY TUNNELS THEY BEEN HYPING UP ALL THESE YEARS.

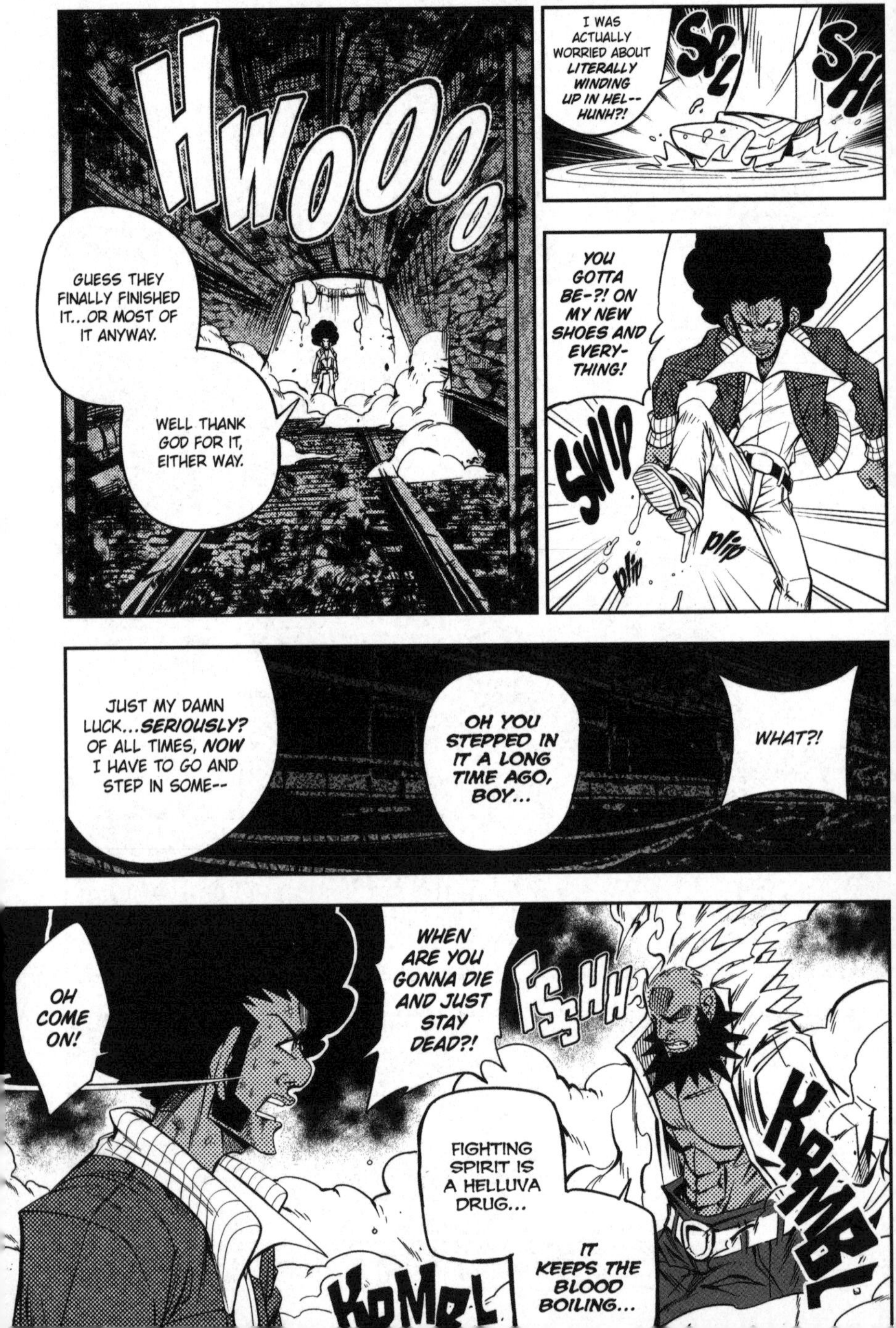
HWOOOO
GUESS THEY FINALLY FINISHED IT...OR MOST OF IT ANYWAY.
WELL THANK GOD FOR IT, EITHER WAY.
I WAS ACTUALLY WORRIED ABOUT LITERALLY WINDING UP IN HEL-- HUNH?!
SPL
SH
YOU GOTTA BE-?! ON MY NEW SHOES AND EVERY-THING!
SWIP
plip
plip
JUST MY DAMN LUCK...SERIOUSLY? OF ALL TIMES, NOW I HAVE TO GO AND STEP IN SOME--
OH YOU STEPPED IN IT A LONG TIME AGO, BOY...
WHAT?!
OH COME ON!
WHEN ARE YOU GONNA DIE AND JUST STAY DEAD?!
FSSHH
FIGHTING SPIRIT IS A HELLUVA DRUG...
IT KEEPS THE BLOOD BOILING...
KOMBL
KOMBL

AND MAKES MY THIRST FOR YOUR SOUL THAT MUCH STRONGER!

WARM-UP'S OVER...NOW WE'RE IN OVERTIME!

FSSHH

GRRRRRR

FSSHH

WHOO-BOY...! FORGET SMACKIN' THE BLACK OFFA YA...

I KNOCKED YOU STRAIGHT INTO A DAMN SEWER MUTANT!

YOU WON'T BE LAUGHING SOON, BOY... LOOK AROUND YOU!

SHIT'S ABOUT TO GET REAL TOASTY!

FWO OOO

HA-HA-HA-HA!!!

...?!

RRRMMRR

THAT AIN'T GOOD...!

...?!

WHOA!

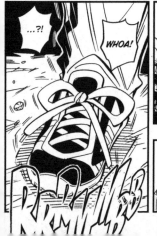

DANTE, WHAT'S GOING ON DOWN THERE?!

RMBL

HUH ...?!

BABABA

!

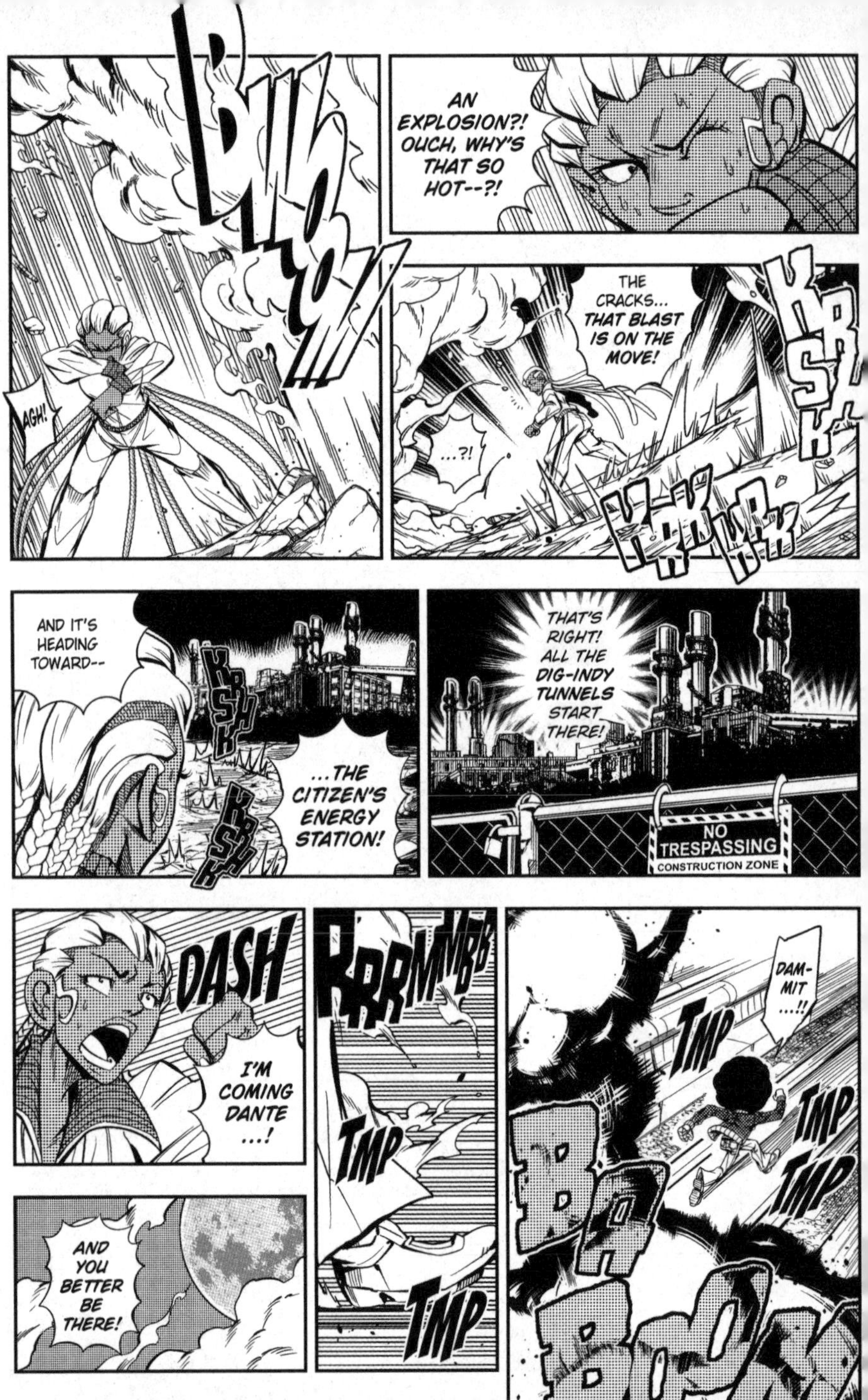
AGH!
AN EXPLOSION?! OUCH, WHY'S THAT SO HOT--?!
THE CRACKS... THAT BLAST IS ON THE MOVE!
...?!
AND IT'S HEADING TOWARD--
...THE CITIZEN'S ENERGY STATION!
THAT'S RIGHT! ALL THE DIG-INDY TUNNELS START THERE!
NO TRESPASSING
CONSTRUCTION ZONE
DASH
I'M COMING DANTE ...!
AND YOU BETTER BE THERE!
TMP
TMP
DAM-MIT ....!!
TMP
TMP
TMP

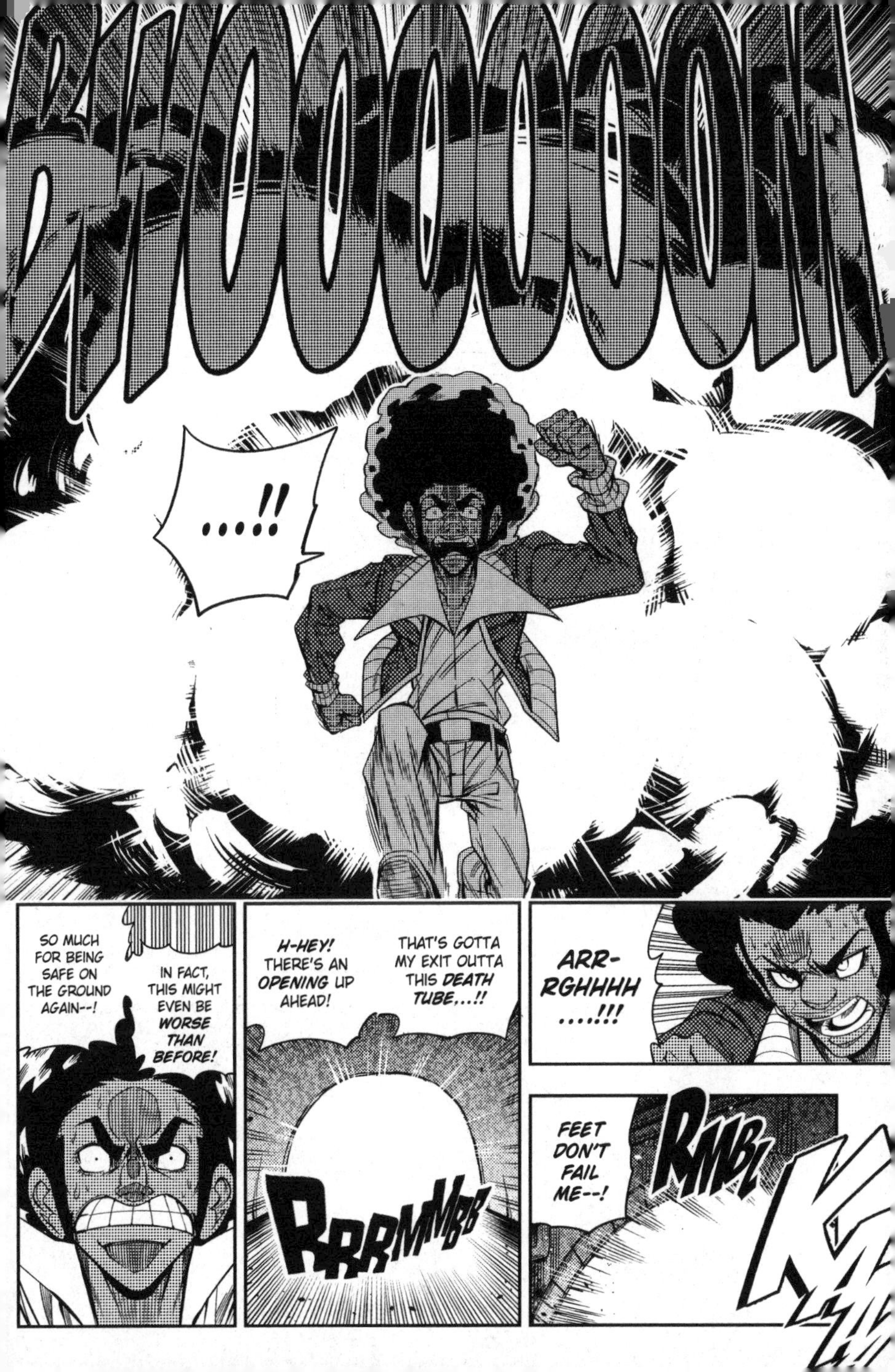

...!!
SO MUCH FOR BEING SAFE ON THE GROUND AGAIN--!
IN FACT, THIS MIGHT EVEN BE WORSE THAN BEFORE!
H-HEY! THERE'S AN OPENING UP AHEAD!
THAT'S GOTTA MY EXIT OUTTA THIS DEATH TUBE...!!
RRRMMMBB
ARR-RGHHHH ....!!!
FEET DON'T FAIL ME--!

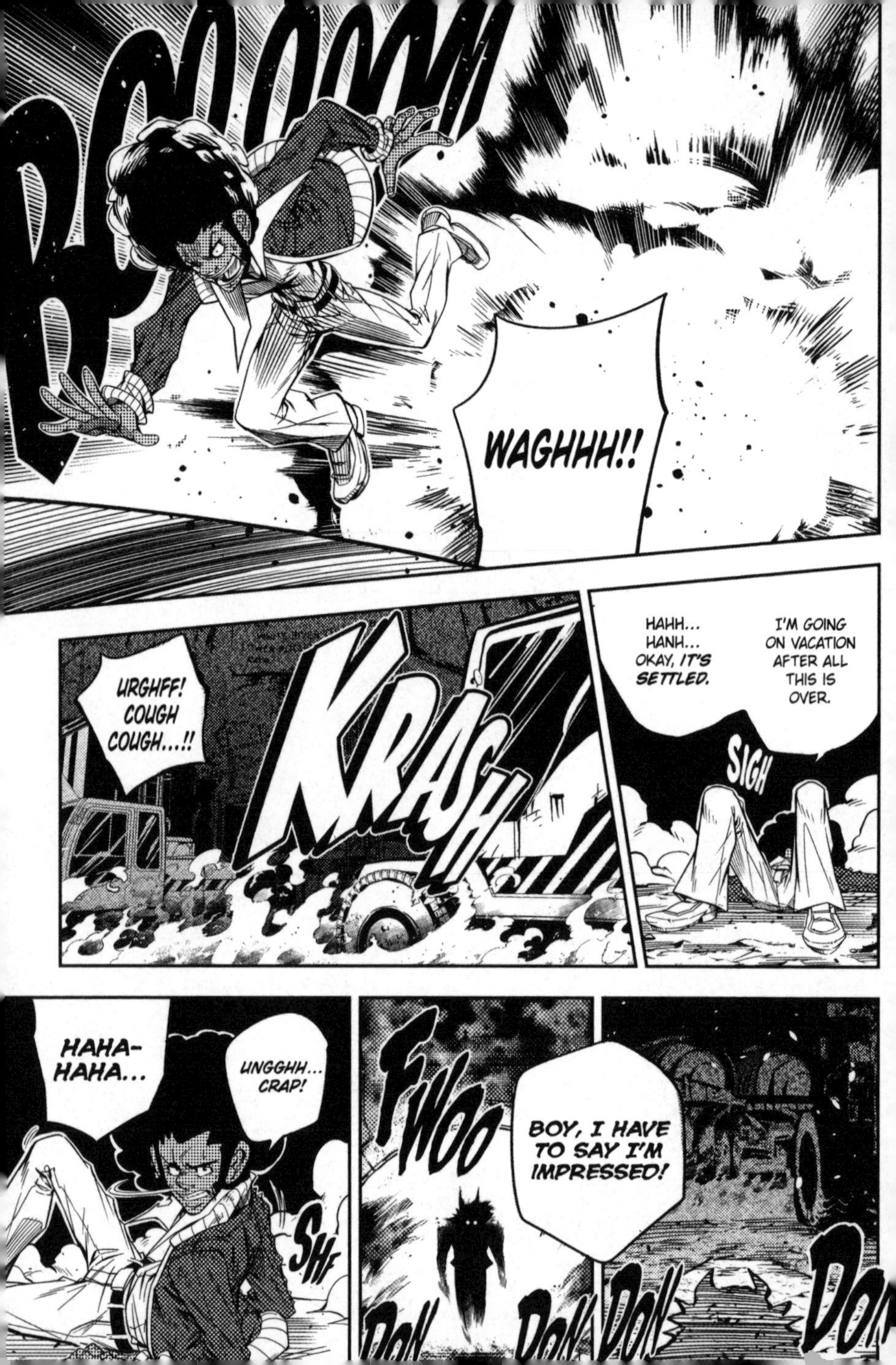
BOOOOOM
WAGHHH!!
URGHFF! COUGH COUGH...!!
KRASH
HAHH... HANH... OKAY, IT'S SETTLED.
I'M GOING ON VACATION AFTER ALL THIS IS OVER.
SIGH
HAHA-HAHA...
UNGGHH... CRAP!
SHF
FWOO
BOY, I HAVE TO SAY I'M IMPRESSED!
DON DON DON DON DON

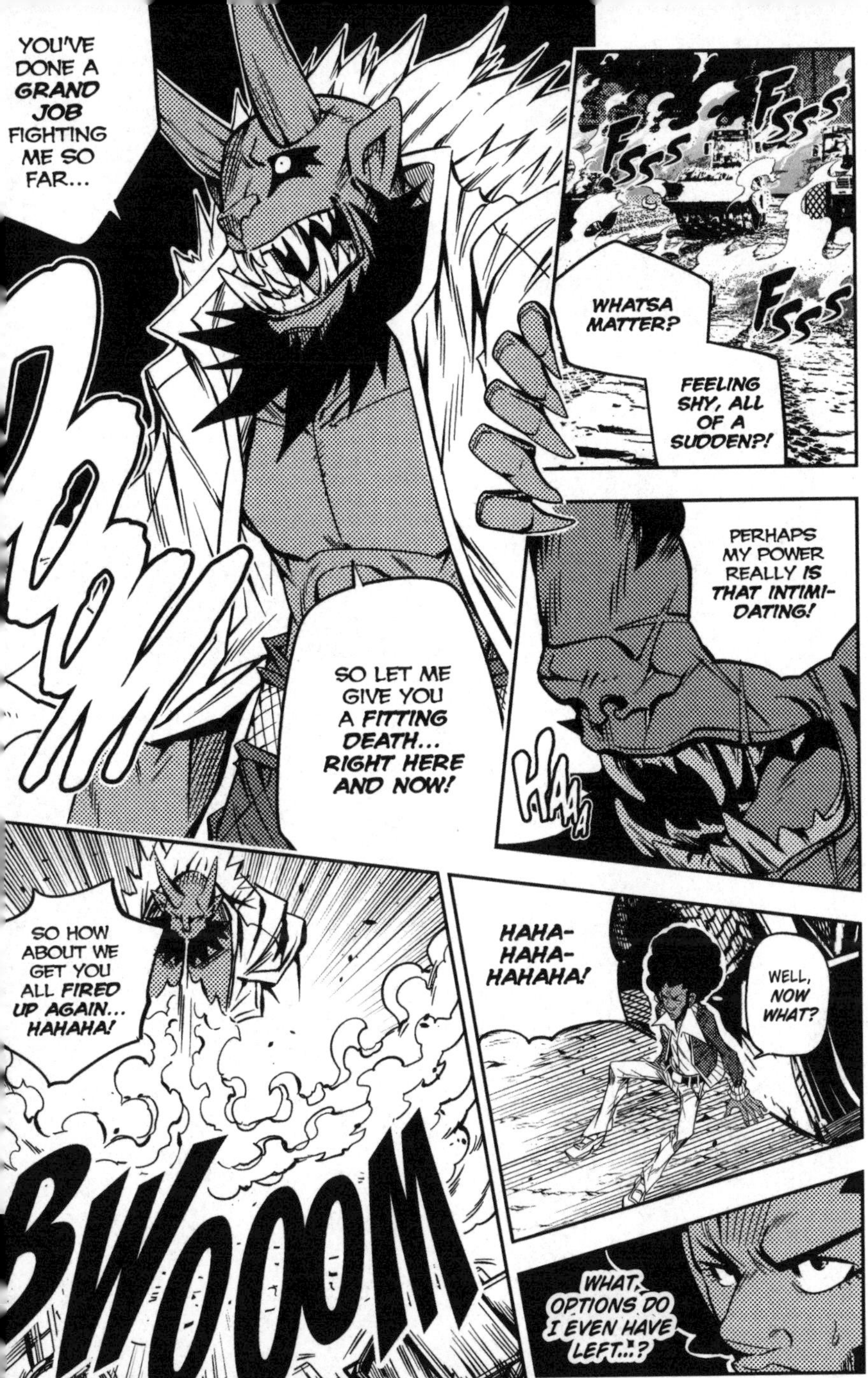
YOU'VE DONE A GRAND JOB FIGHTING ME SO FAR...
SO LET ME GIVE YOU A FITTING DEATH... RIGHT HERE AND NOW!
FSSS
FSSS
FSSS
WHATSA MATTER?
FEELING SHY, ALL OF A SUDDEN?!
PERHAPS MY POWER REALLY IS THAT INTIMI-DATING!
HAAA
SO HOW ABOUT WE GET YOU ALL FIRED UP AGAIN... HAHAHA!
BWOOOM
HAHA-HAHA-HAHAHA!
WELL, NOW WHAT?
WHAT OPTIONS DO I EVEN HAVE LEFT...?

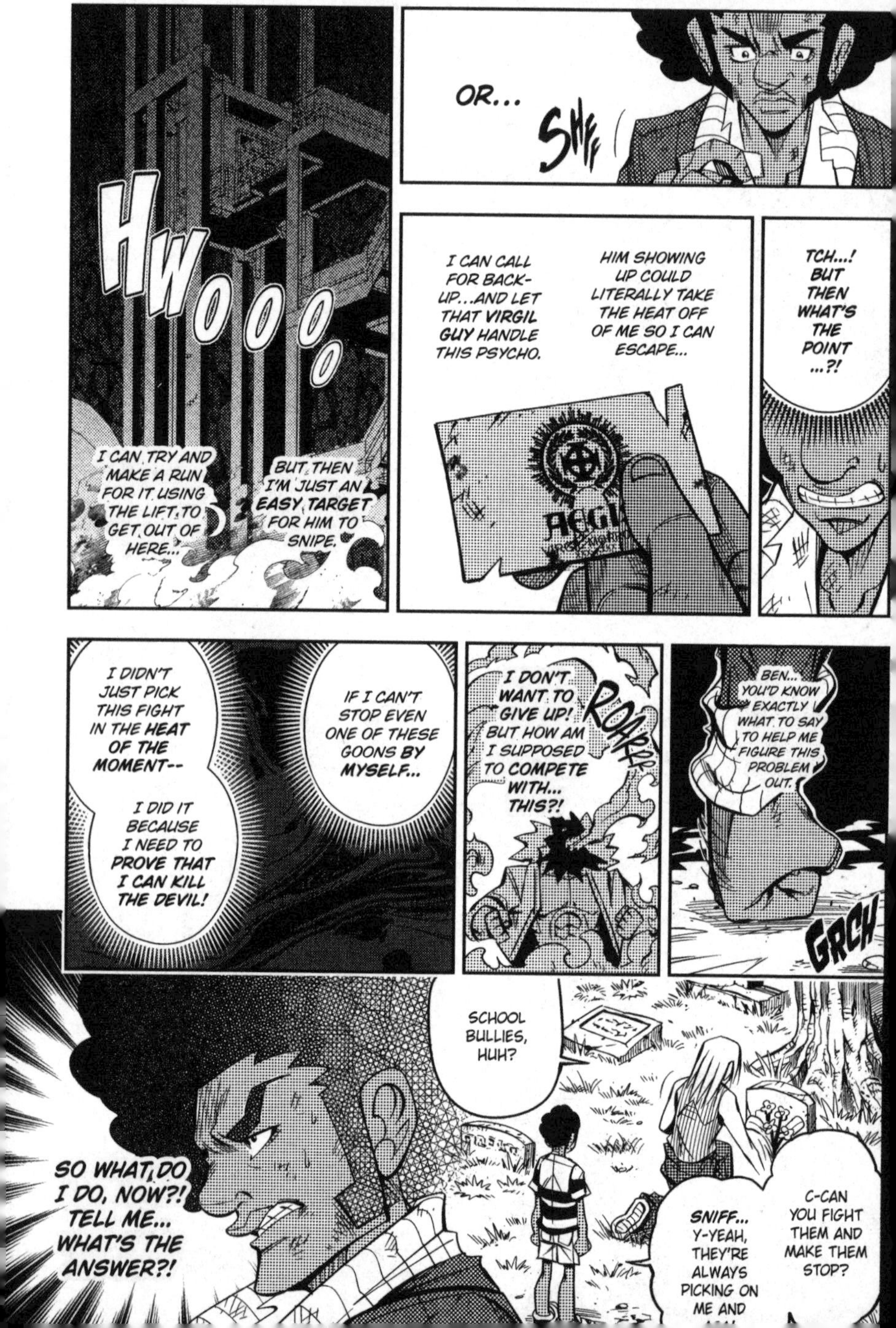
HWOOOO
I CAN TRY AND MAKE A RUN FOR IT USING THE LIFT TO GET OUT OF HERE...
BUT THEN I'M JUST AN EASY TARGET FOR HIM TO SNIPE.
OR...
SHFF
I CAN CALL FOR BACK-UP...AND LET THAT VIRGIL GUY HANDLE THIS PSYCHO.
HIM SHOWING UP COULD LITERALLY TAKE THE HEAT OFF OF ME SO I CAN ESCAPE...
TCH...! BUT THEN WHAT'S THE POINT ...?!
I DIDN'T JUST PICK THIS FIGHT IN THE HEAT OF THE MOMENT--
I DID IT BECAUSE I NEED TO PROVE THAT I CAN KILL THE DEVIL!
IF I CAN'T STOP EVEN ONE OF THESE GOONS BY MYSELF...
I DON'T WANT TO GIVE UP! BUT HOW AM I SUPPOSED TO COMPETE WITH... THIS?!
ROARRR
BEN... YOU'D KNOW EXACTLY WHAT TO SAY TO HELP ME FIGURE THIS PROBLEM OUT.
GRCH
SO WHAT DO I DO, NOW?! TELL ME... WHAT'S THE ANSWER?!
SCHOOL BULLIES, HUH?
SNIFF... Y-YEAH, THEY'RE ALWAYS PICKING ON ME AND
C-CAN YOU FIGHT THEM AND MAKE THEM STOP?

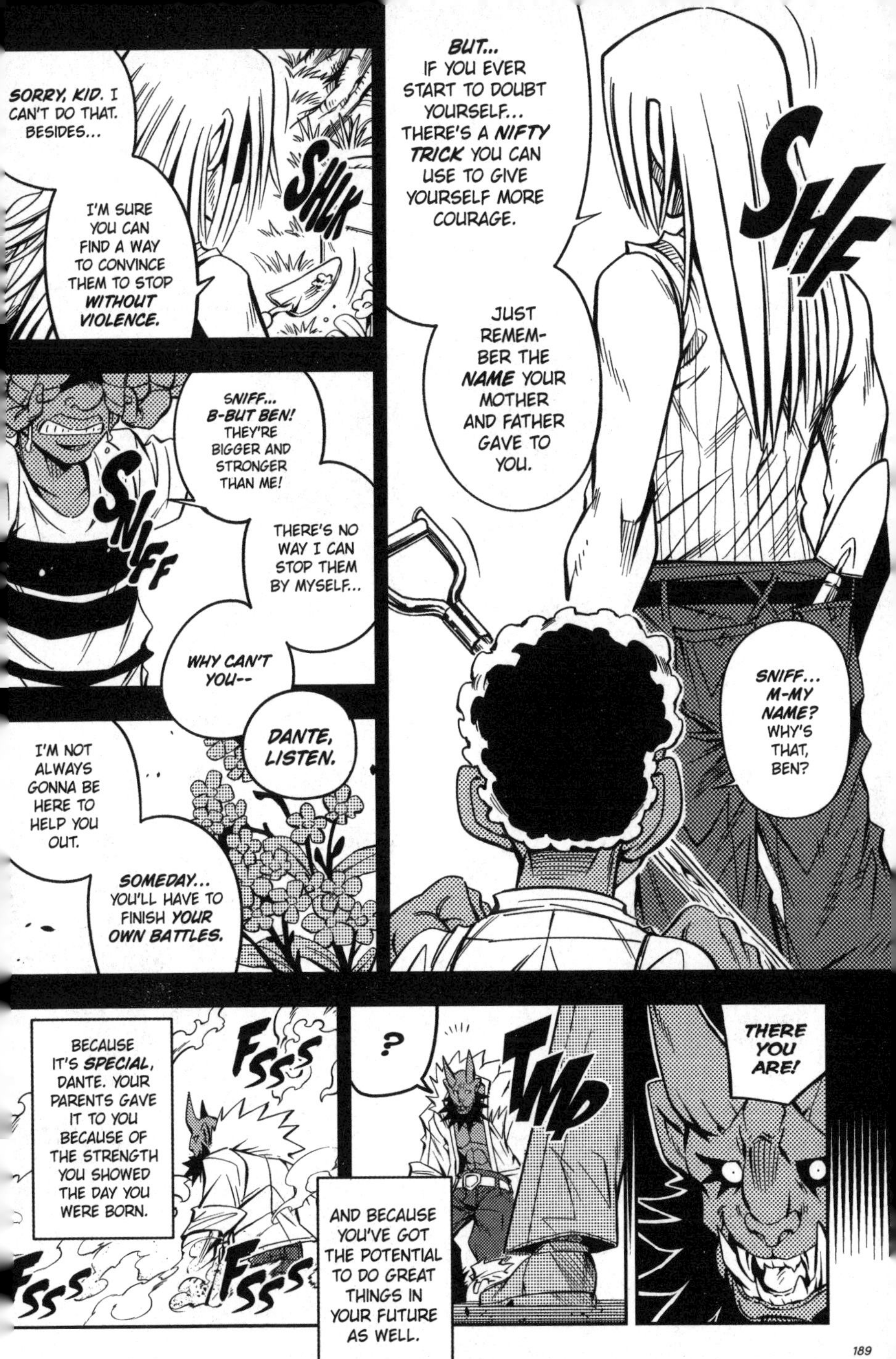
SORRY, KID. I CAN'T DO THAT. BESIDES...
SHLK
I'M SURE YOU CAN FIND A WAY TO CONVINCE THEM TO STOP WITHOUT VIOLENCE.
SNIFF... B-BUT BEN! THEY'RE BIGGER AND STRONGER THAN ME!
SNIFF
THERE'S NO WAY I CAN STOP THEM BY MYSELF...
WHY CAN'T YOU--
DANTE, LISTEN.
I'M NOT ALWAYS GONNA BE HERE TO HELP YOU OUT.
SOMEDAY... YOU'LL HAVE TO FINISH YOUR OWN BATTLES.
BUT... IF YOU EVER START TO DOUBT YOURSELF... THERE'S A NIFTY TRICK YOU CAN USE TO GIVE YOURSELF MORE COURAGE.
SHF
JUST REMEMBER THE NAME YOUR MOTHER AND FATHER GAVE TO YOU.
SNIFF... M-MY NAME? WHY'S THAT, BEN?
BECAUSE IT'S SPECIAL, DANTE. YOUR PARENTS GAVE IT TO YOU BECAUSE OF THE STRENGTH YOU SHOWED THE DAY YOU WERE BORN.
FSSS
FSSS
FSSS
?
TMP
AND BECAUSE YOU'VE GOT THE POTENTIAL TO DO GREAT THINGS IN YOUR FUTURE AS WELL.
THERE YOU ARE!

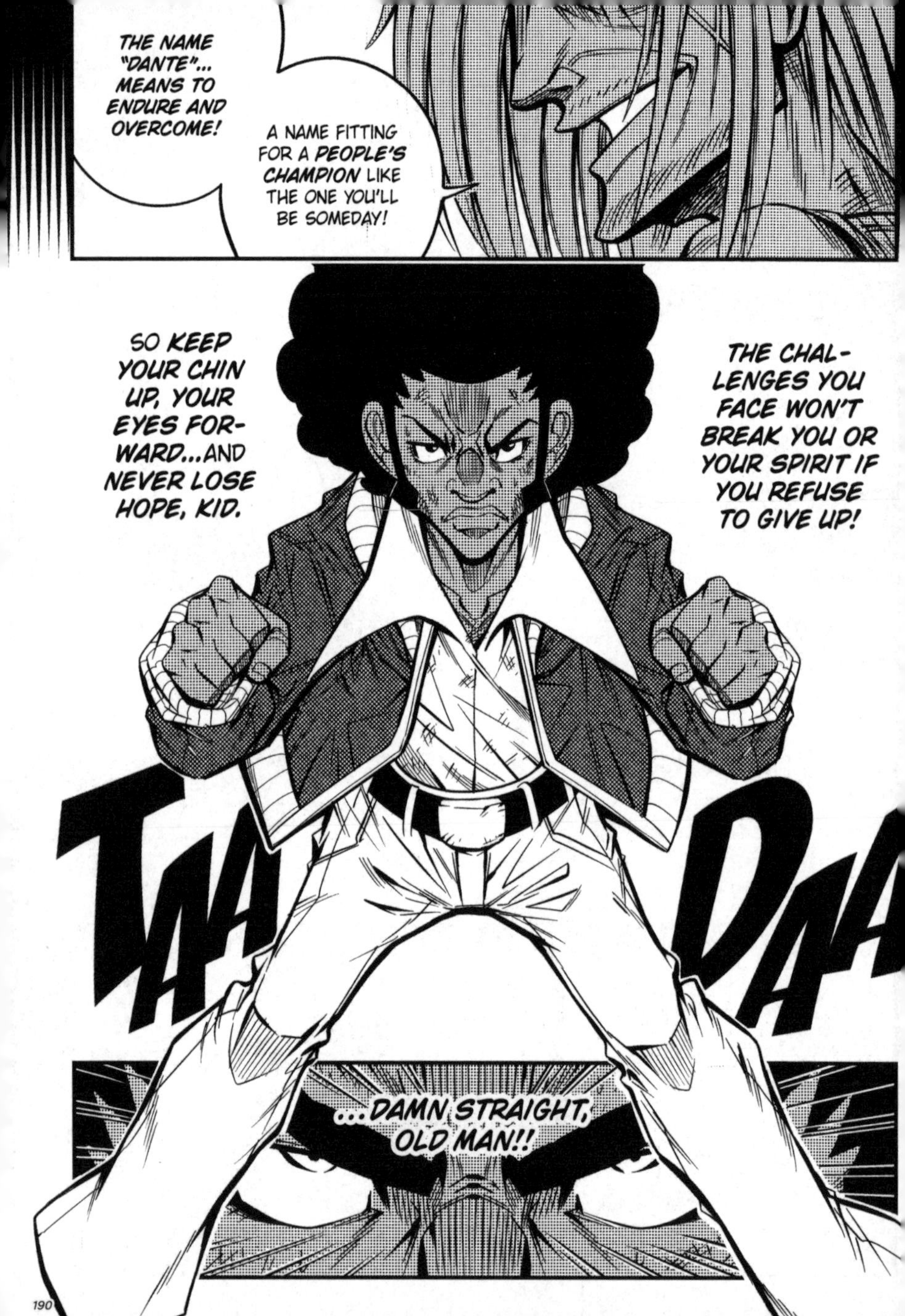

THE NAME "DANTE"... MEANS TO ENDURE AND OVERCOME!
A NAME FITTING FOR A PEOPLE'S CHAMPION LIKE THE ONE YOU'LL BE SOMEDAY!
SO KEEP YOUR CHIN UP, YOUR EYES FOR-WARD...AND NEVER LOSE HOPE, KID.
THE CHAL-LENGES YOU FACE WON'T BREAK YOU OR YOUR SPIRIT IF YOU REFUSE TO GIVE UP!
TAA
DAA
...DAMN STRAIGHT, OLD MAN!!

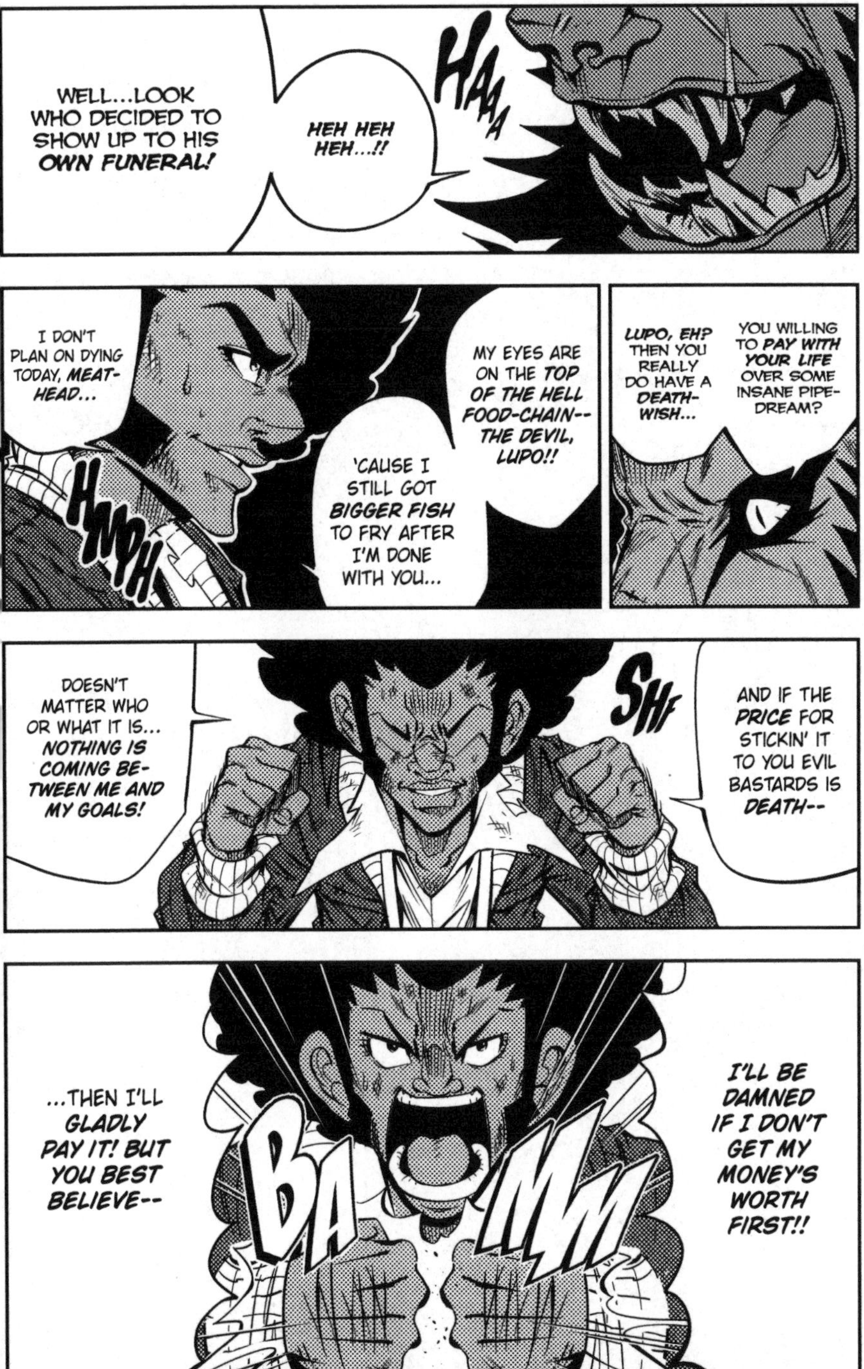
WELL...LOOK WHO DECIDED TO SHOW UP TO HIS OWN FUNERAL!
HEH HEH HEH...!!
HAAAA
I DON'T PLAN ON DYING TODAY, MEAT-HEAD...
HMPH
'CAUSE I STILL GOT BIGGER FISH TO FRY AFTER I'M DONE WITH YOU...
MY EYES ARE ON THE TOP OF THE HELL FOOD-CHAIN--THE DEVIL, LUPO!!
LUPO, EH? THEN YOU REALLY DO HAVE A DEATH-WISH...
YOU WILLING TO PAY WITH YOUR LIFE OVER SOME INSANE PIPE-DREAM?
DOESN'T MATTER WHO OR WHAT IT IS... NOTHING IS COMING BE-TWEEN ME AND MY GOALS!
SHF
AND IF THE PRICE FOR STICKIN' IT TO YOU EVIL BASTARDS IS DEATH--
...THEN I'LL GLADLY PAY IT! BUT YOU BEST BELIEVE--
BAMM
I'LL BE DAMNED IF I DON'T GET MY MONEY'S WORTH FIRST!!

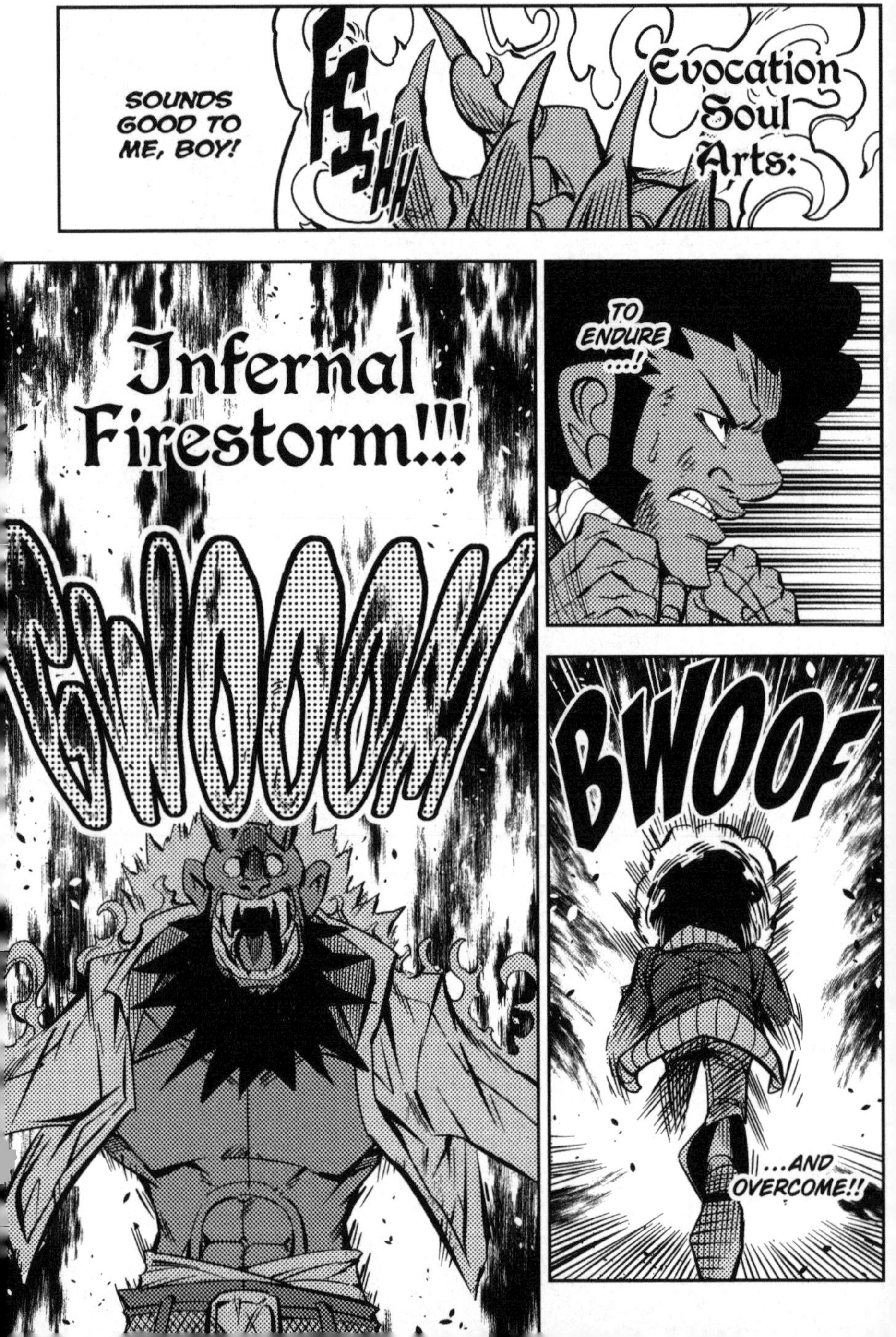
SOUNDS GOOD TO ME, BOY!
Evocation Soul Arts:
Infernal Firestorm!!!
TO ENDURE ...!
BWOOF
...AND OVERCOME!!

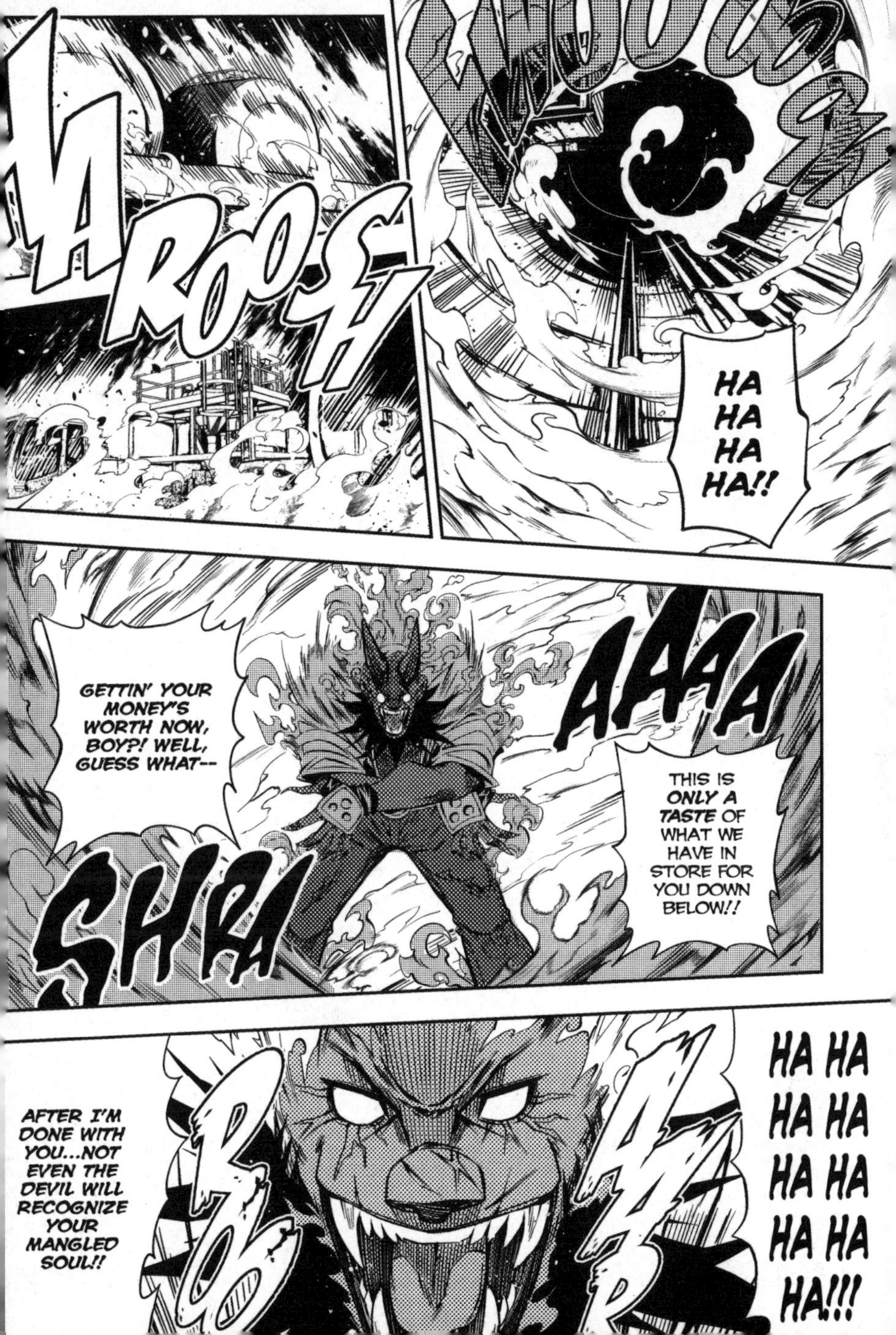
HA
HA
HA
HA!!
GETTIN' YOUR MONEY'S WORTH NOW, BOY?! WELL, GUESS WHAT--
AAAA
SHRA
THIS IS ONLY A TASTE OF WHAT WE HAVE IN STORE FOR YOU DOWN BELOW!!
AFTER I'M DONE WITH YOU...NOT EVEN THE DEVIL WILL RECOGNIZE YOUR MANGLED SOUL!!
HA HA HA HA HA HA HA HA HA!!!

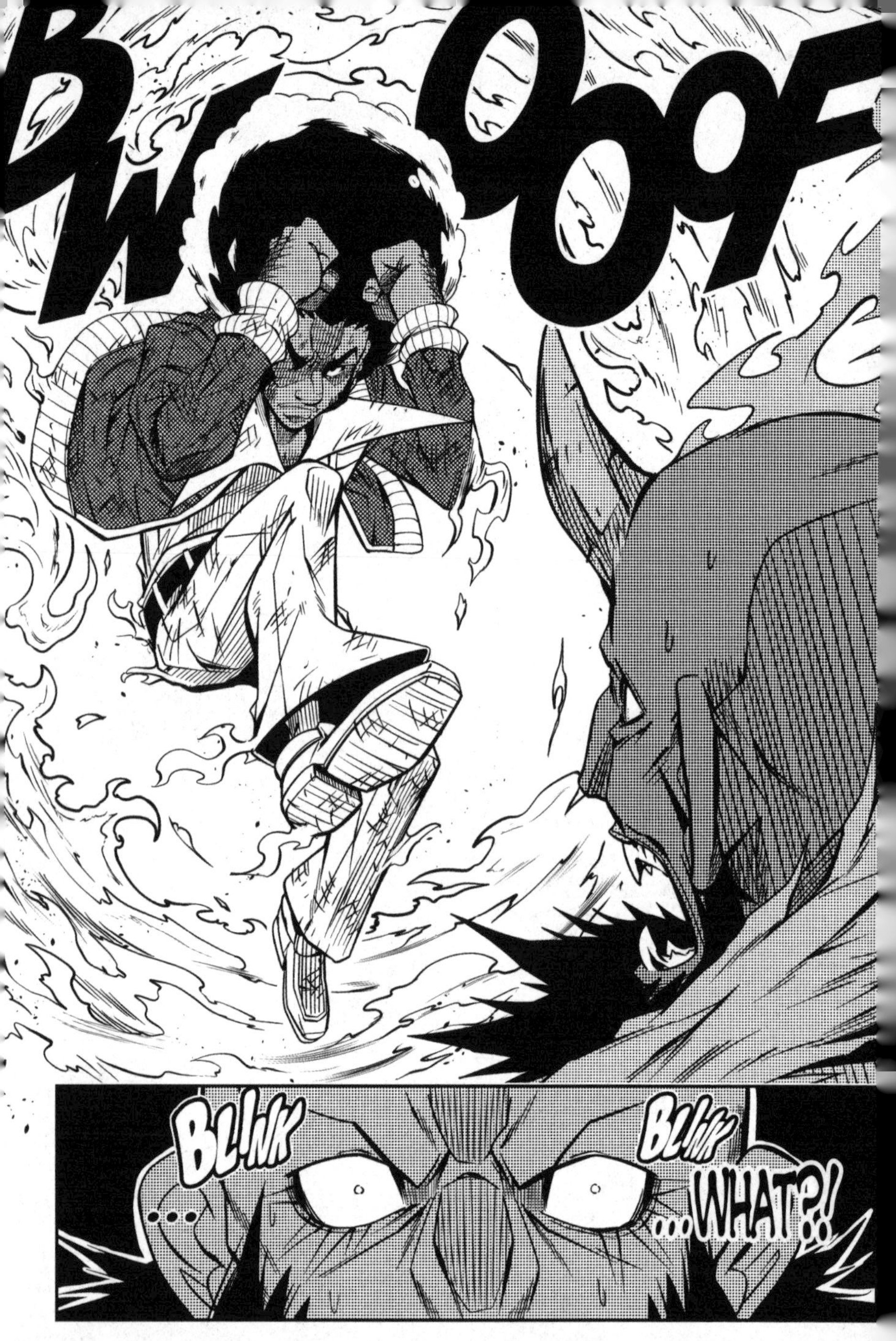
BWOOOF
BLINK
BLINK
...
...WHAT?!

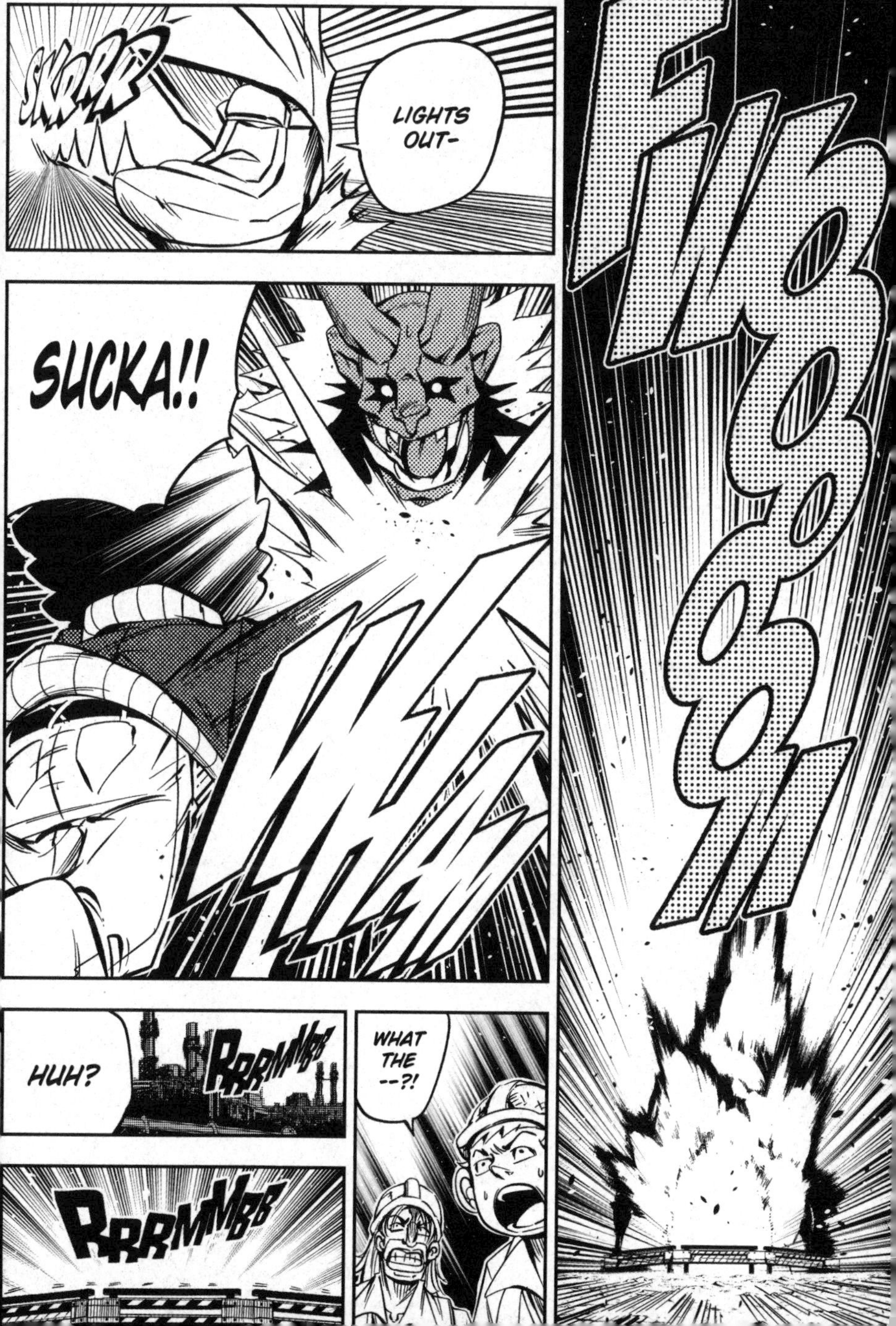
SKRRR
LIGHTS OUT-
SUCKA!!
HUH?
RRRMMBB
WHAT THE --?!
RRRMMBB

SOUL BEAT

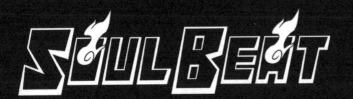

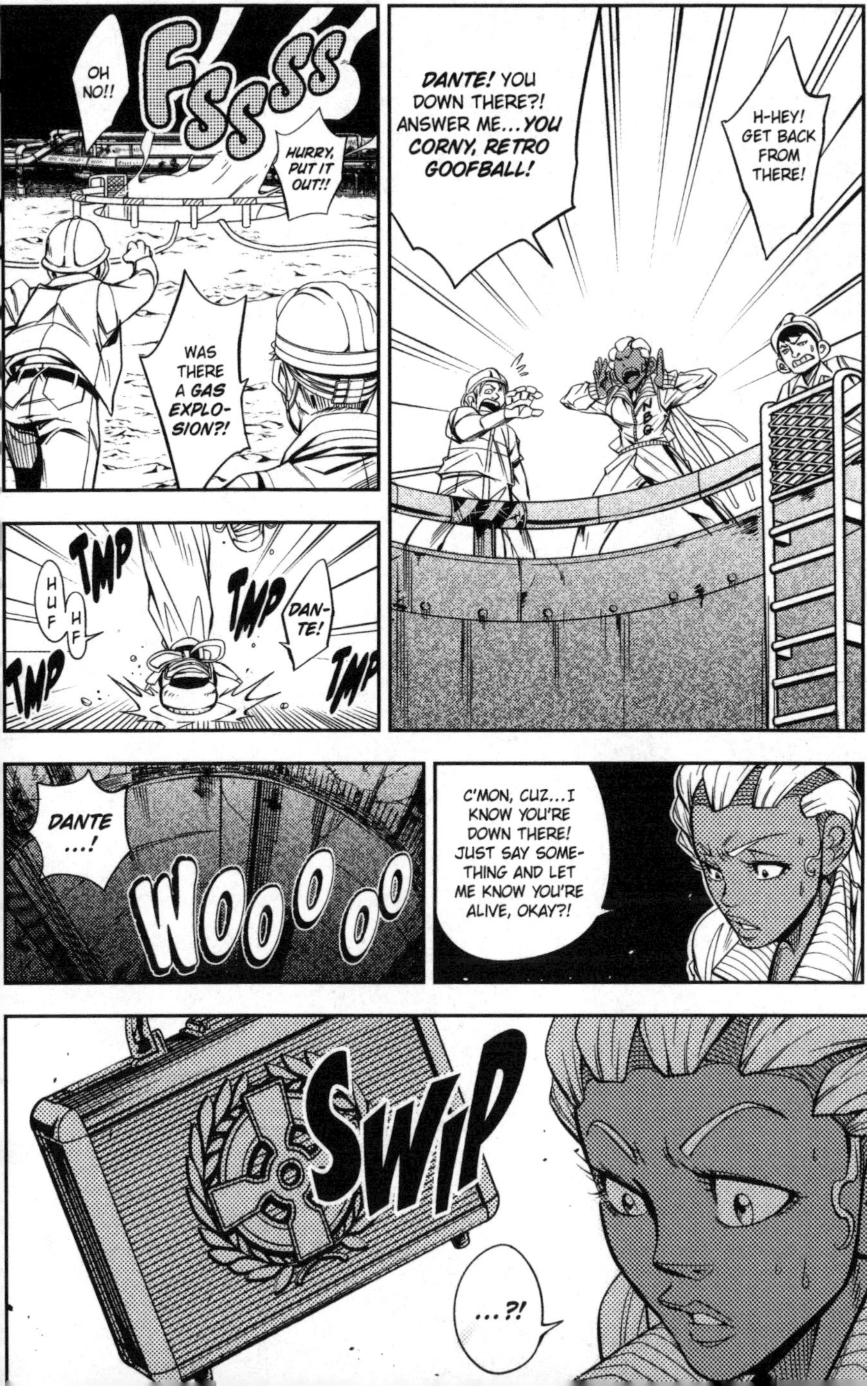
OH NO!!
FSSSSS
HURRY, PUT IT OUT!!
WAS THERE A GAS EXPLOSION?!
DANTE! YOU DOWN THERE?! ANSWER ME...YOU CORNY, RETRO GOOFBALL!
H-HEY! GET BACK FROM THERE!
TMP
HUF HF
TMP
TMP
DAN-TE!
TMP
DANTE ...!
WOOOOO
C'MON, CUZ...I KNOW YOU'RE DOWN THERE! JUST SAY SOME-THING AND LET ME KNOW YOU'RE ALIVE, OKAY?!
SWIP
...?!

Chapter 8: Declaration of War

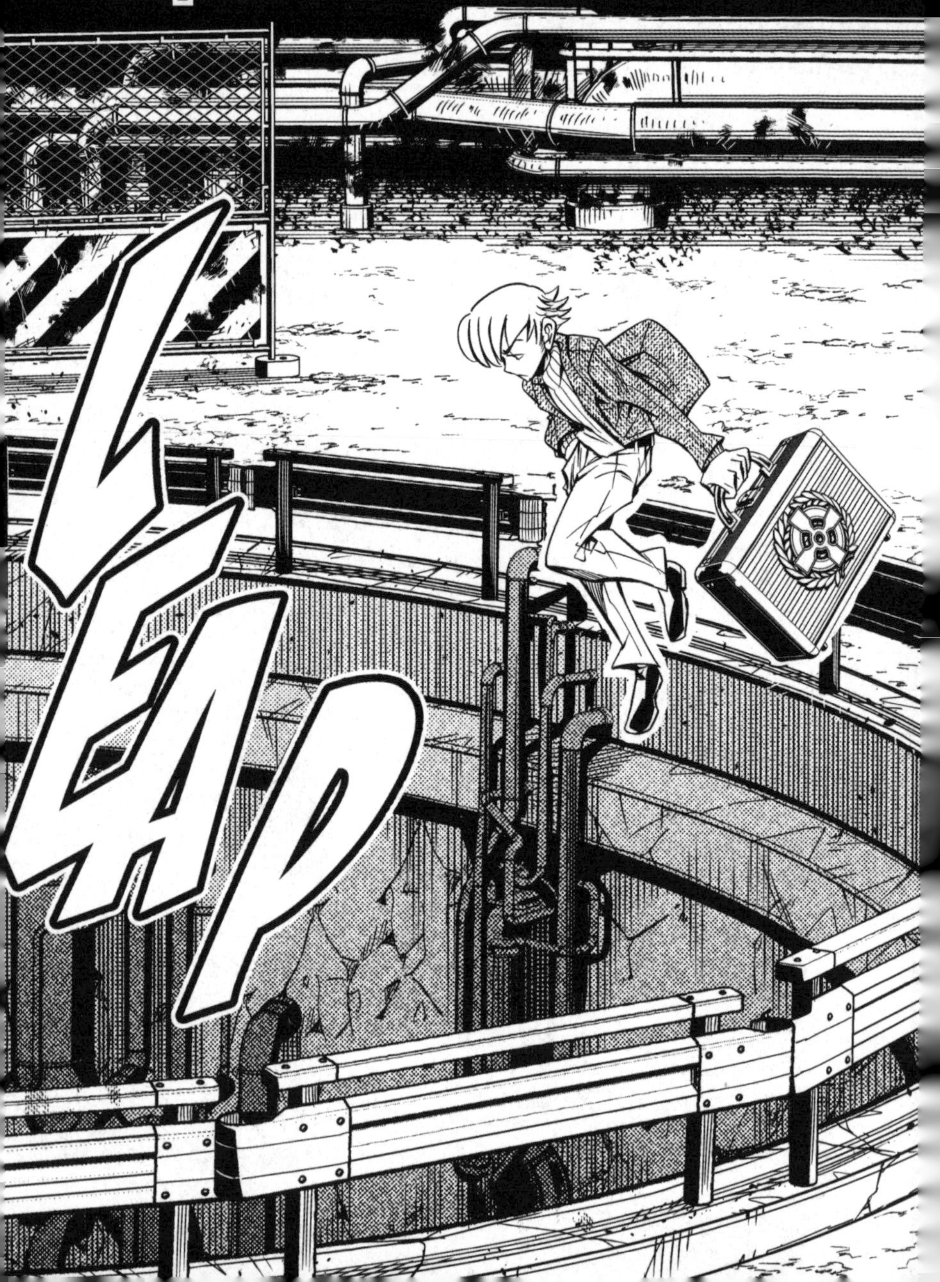
LEAP

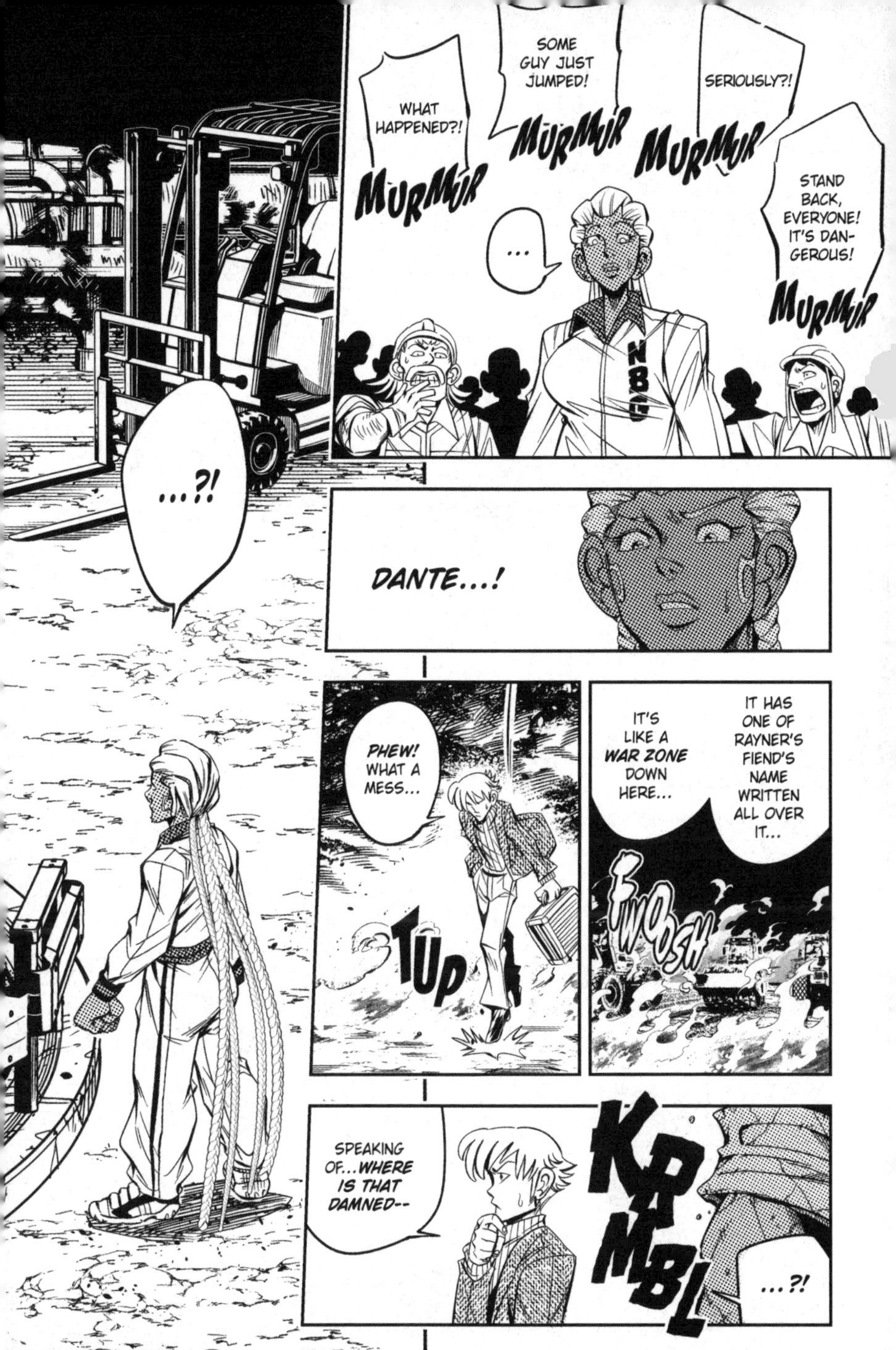
...?!
WHAT HAPPENED?!
MURMUR
SOME GUY JUST JUMPED!
MURMUR
SERIOUSLY?!
MURMUR
...
STAND BACK, EVERYONE! IT'S DAN-GEROUS!
MURMUR
NBC
DANTE...!
PHEW! WHAT A MESS...
TUP
IT'S LIKE A WAR ZONE DOWN HERE...
IT HAS ONE OF RAYNER'S FIEND'S NAME WRITTEN ALL OVER IT...
FWOOSH
SPEAKING OF... WHERE IS THAT DAMNED--
KRAMBL
...?!

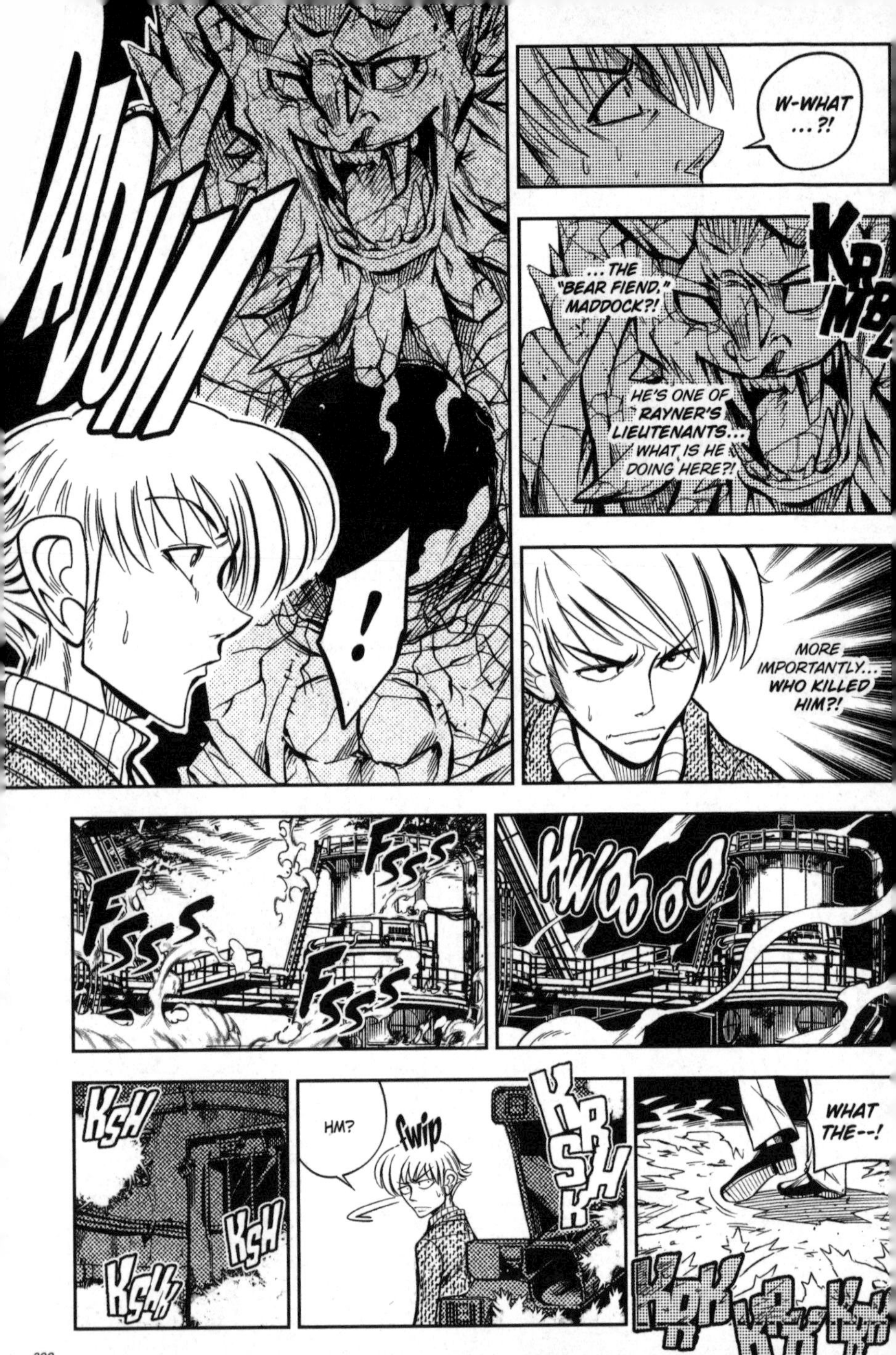
VADUM
!
W-WHAT ...?!
...THE "BEAR FIEND," MADDOCK?!
KRMBL
HE'S ONE OF RAYNER'S LIEUTENANTS... WHAT IS HE DOING HERE?!
MORE IMPORTANTLY... WHO KILLED HIM?!
FSSS
FSSS
FSSS
HWOOOOO
KSH
KSH
KSHK
HM?
fwip
KRSHK
WHAT THE--!
KRK KRK KRK

WHERE IS THIS ICE COMING FROM? IT'S SO UNNATURAL...

B- B- BIP BIP B- BIP

HUH? WHY IS THE *AETHER-OMETER*--

OH... WELL, *THAT* CAN'T BE GOOD...

WARNING
!
X-CLASS DEMON DETECTED

HWOOOO

A PLEASURE TO FINALLY MEET ONE OF *AEGIS' FINEST SHEPHERDS.*

YOUR REPUTATION PRECEDES YOU...*VIRGIL MORROW, I PRESUME?*

Fwip

...!!

FUNNY, THOUGH... WITH THE WAY THINGS ARE GOING HERE ON EARTH...

I FIGURED YOUR ILK HAD ALL BUT GIVEN UP ON SAVING SOULS.

TMP TMP

I SUPPOSE WHAT THEY SAY IS TRUE, THEN...ISN'T IT?

?!

DON DON DON DON

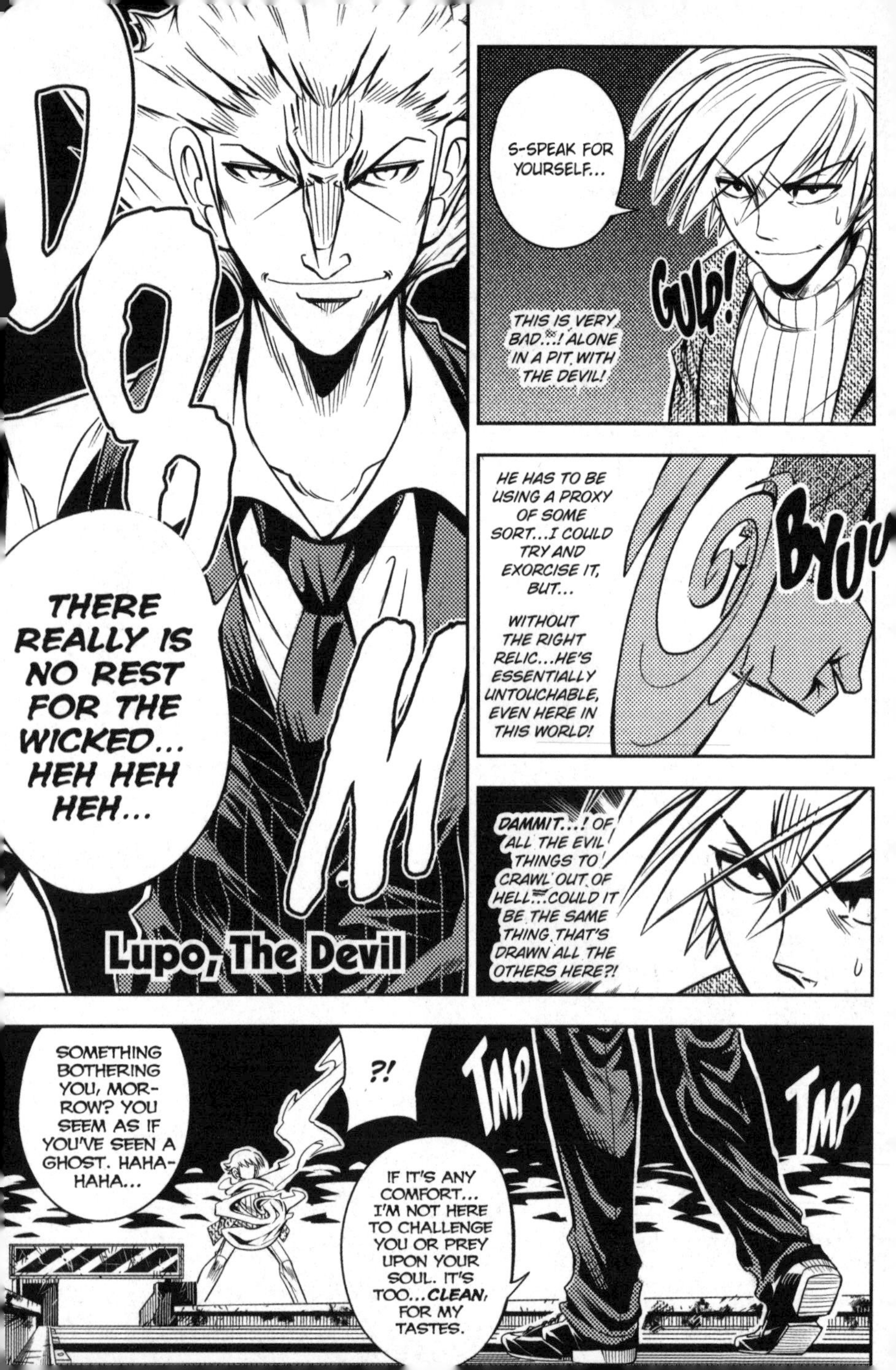
THERE REALLY IS NO REST FOR THE WICKED... HEH HEH HEH...
Lupo, The Devil
S-SPEAK FOR YOURSELF...
GULP!
THIS IS VERY BAD...! ALONE IN A PIT WITH THE DEVIL!
HE HAS TO BE USING A PROXY OF SOME SORT...I COULD TRY AND EXORCISE IT, BUT...
WITHOUT THE RIGHT RELIC...HE'S ESSENTIALLY UNTOUCHABLE, EVEN HERE IN THIS WORLD!
BYUU
DAMMIT...! OF ALL THE EVIL THINGS TO CRAWL OUT OF HELL...COULD IT BE THE SAME THING THAT'S DRAWN ALL THE OTHERS HERE?!
SOMETHING BOTHERING YOU, MOR-ROW? YOU SEEM AS IF YOU'VE SEEN A GHOST. HAHA-HAHA...
?!
TMP
TMP
IF IT'S ANY COMFORT... I'M NOT HERE TO CHALLENGE YOU OR PREY UPON YOUR SOUL. IT'S TOO...CLEAN, FOR MY TASTES.

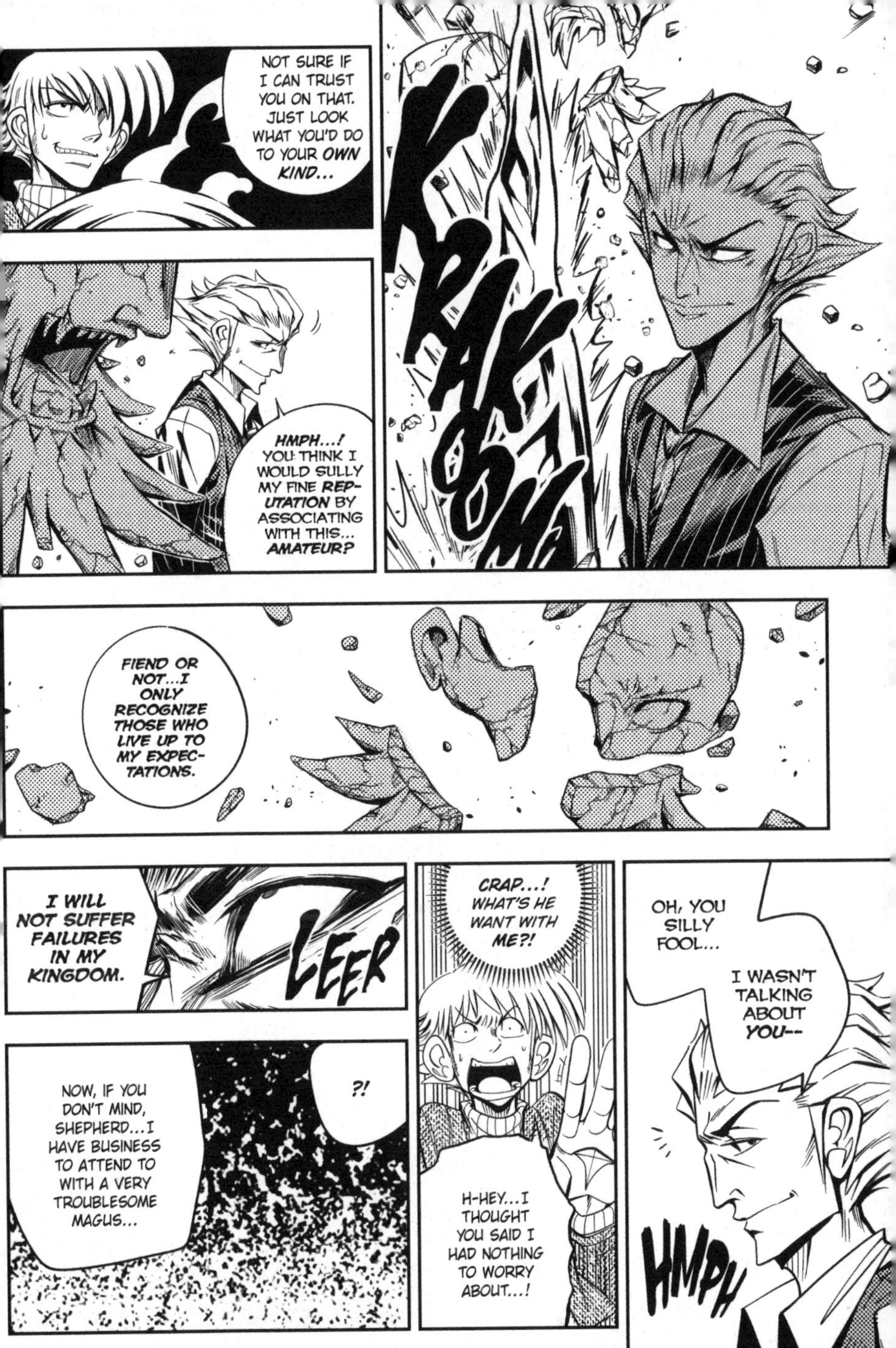

NOT SURE IF I CAN TRUST YOU ON THAT. JUST LOOK WHAT YOU'D DO TO YOUR *OWN KIND*...
HMPH...! YOU THINK I WOULD SULLY MY FINE *REPUTATION* BY ASSOCIATING WITH THIS... *AMATEUR?*
KRAK-BOOM
FIEND OR NOT...I ONLY RECOGNIZE THOSE WHO LIVE UP TO MY EXPECTATIONS.
I WILL NOT SUFFER FAILURES IN MY KINGDOM.
LEER
NOW, IF YOU DON'T MIND, SHEPHERD...I HAVE BUSINESS TO ATTEND TO WITH A VERY TROUBLESOME MAGUS...
?!
CRAP...! WHAT'S HE WANT WITH ME?!
H-HEY...I THOUGHT YOU SAID I HAD NOTHING TO WORRY ABOUT...!
OH, YOU SILLY FOOL...
I WASN'T TALKING ABOUT *YOU*--
HMPH

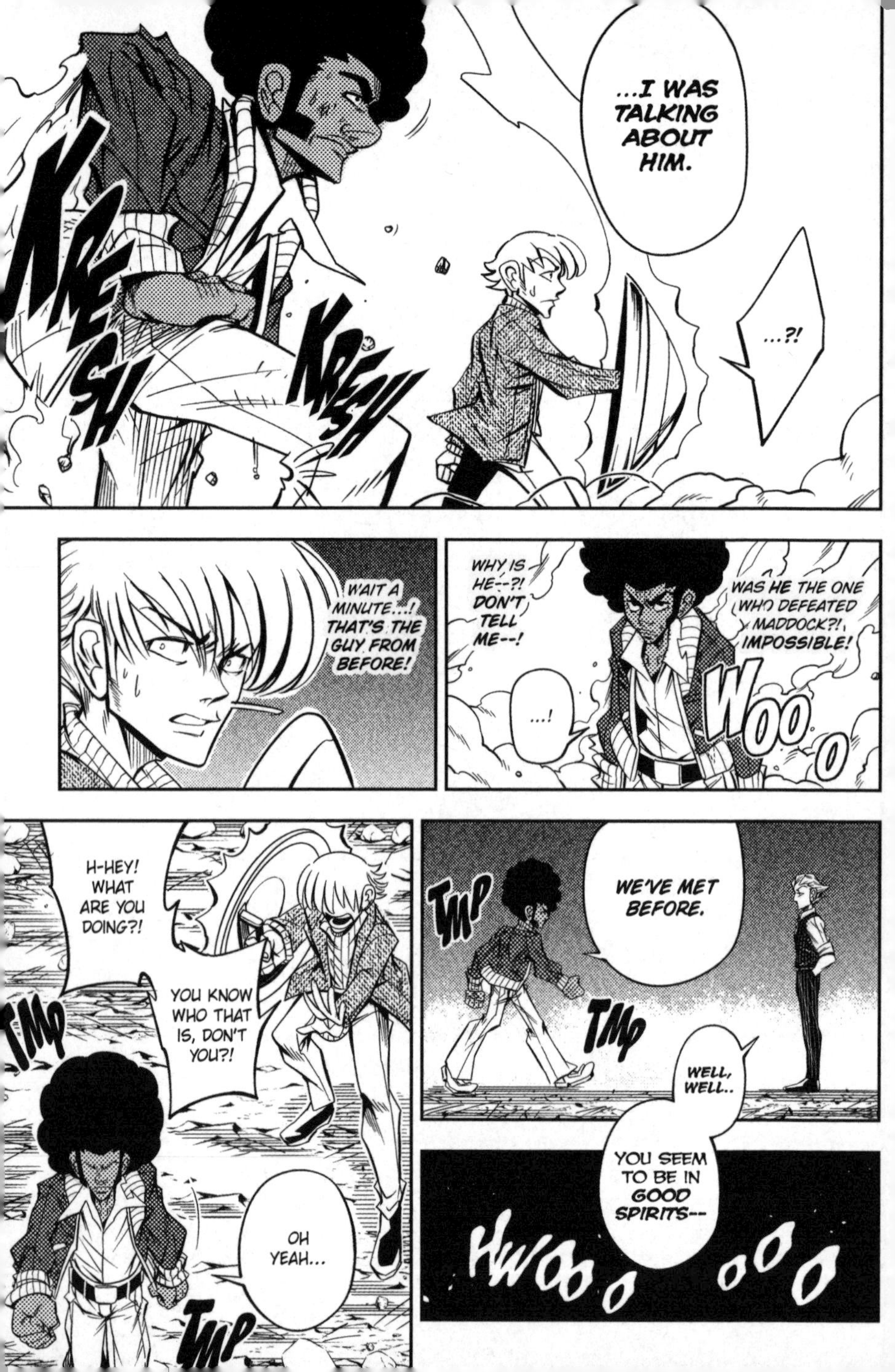
KRESH
KRESH
...I WAS TALKING ABOUT HIM.
...?!
WAIT A MINUTE...! THAT'S THE GUY FROM BEFORE!
WHY IS HE--?! DON'T TELL ME--!
...!
WAS HE THE ONE WHO DEFEATED MADDOCK?! IMPOSSIBLE!
WOOO
H-HEY! WHAT ARE YOU DOING?!
YOU KNOW WHO THAT IS, DON'T YOU?!
TMP
OH YEAH...
TMP
TMP
WE'VE MET BEFORE.
TMP
WELL, WELL..
YOU SEEM TO BE IN GOOD SPIRITS--
HWOOOOOOO

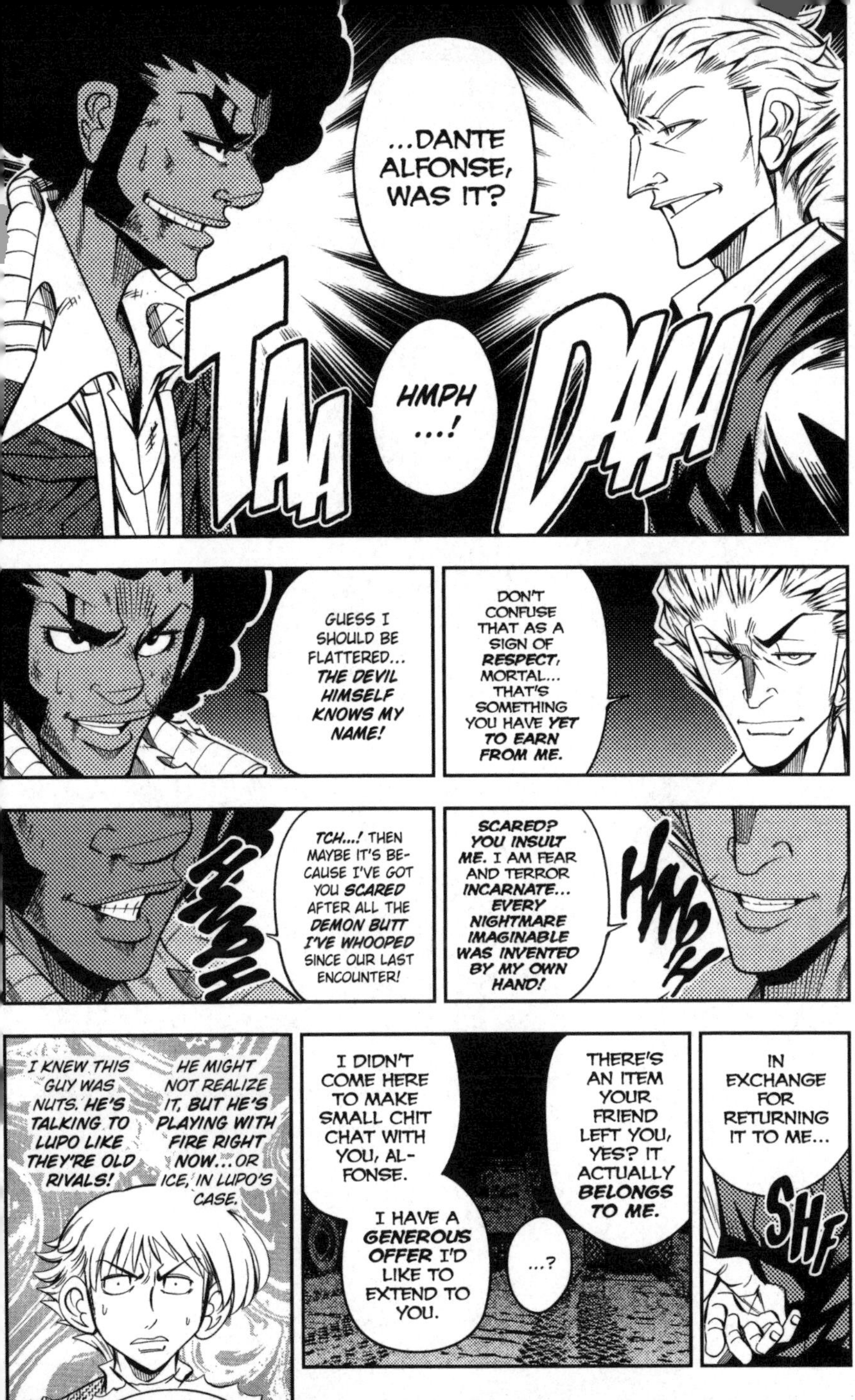
...DANTE ALFONSE, WAS IT?
TAA
HMPH ...!
DAAA
GUESS I SHOULD BE FLATTERED... THE DEVIL HIMSELF KNOWS MY NAME!
DON'T CONFUSE THAT AS A SIGN OF RESPECT, MORTAL... THAT'S SOMETHING YOU HAVE YET TO EARN FROM ME.
HMMPH
TCH...! THEN MAYBE IT'S BE-CAUSE I'VE GOT YOU SCARED AFTER ALL THE DEMON BUTT I'VE WHOOPED SINCE OUR LAST ENCOUNTER!
SCARED? YOU INSULT ME. I AM FEAR AND TERROR INCARNATE... EVERY NIGHTMARE IMAGINABLE WAS INVENTED BY MY OWN HAND!
HMPH
I KNEW THIS GUY WAS NUTS. HE'S TALKING TO LUPO LIKE THEY'RE OLD RIVALS!
HE MIGHT NOT REALIZE IT, BUT HE'S PLAYING WITH FIRE RIGHT NOW... OR ICE, IN LUPO'S CASE.
I DIDN'T COME HERE TO MAKE SMALL CHIT CHAT WITH YOU, AL-FONSE.
I HAVE A GENEROUS OFFER I'D LIKE TO EXTEND TO YOU.
THERE'S AN ITEM YOUR FRIEND LEFT YOU, YES? IT ACTUALLY BELONGS TO ME.
...?
IN EXCHANGE FOR RETURNING IT TO ME...
SHF

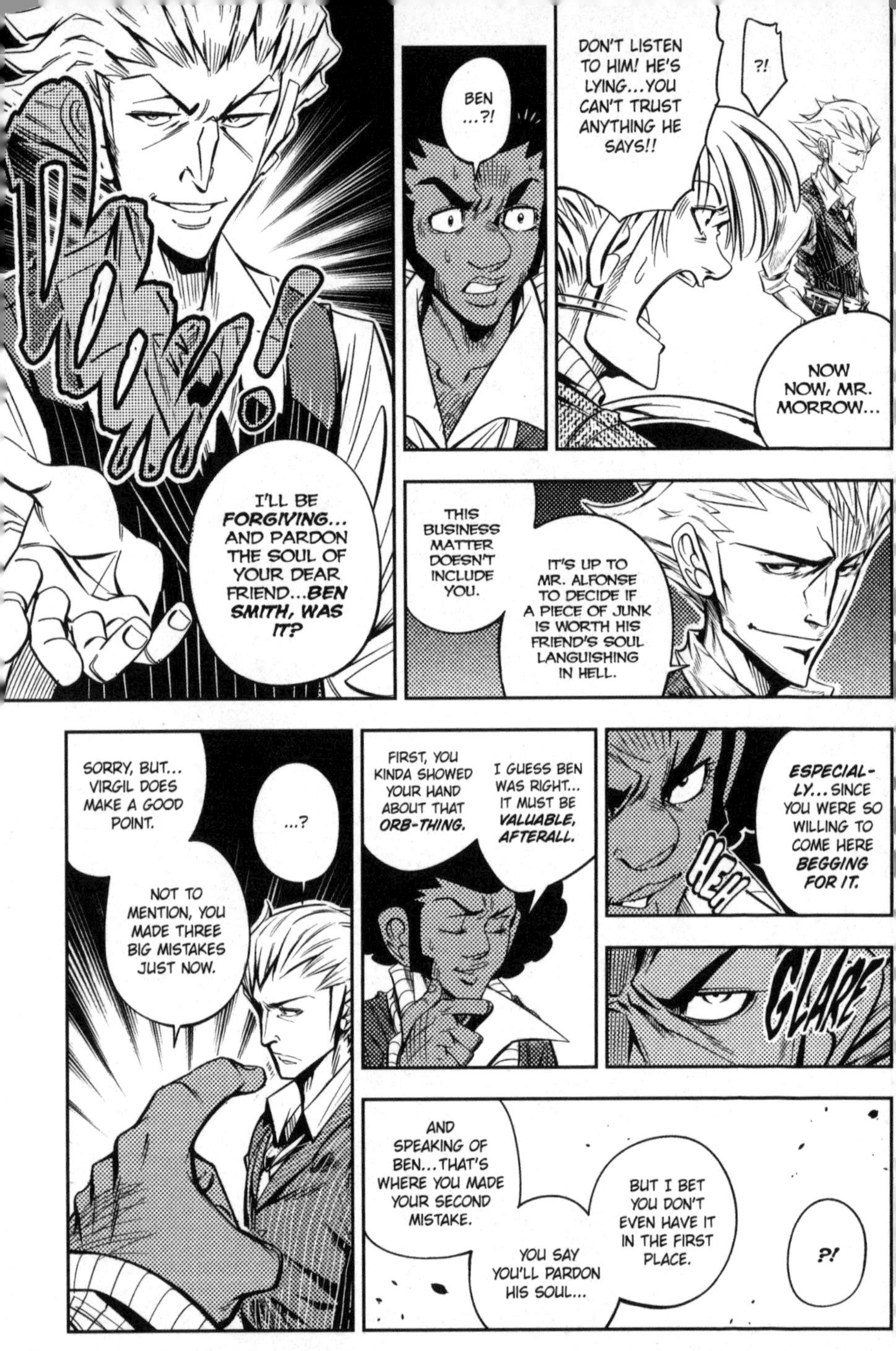
I'LL BE FORGIVING... AND PARDON THE SOUL OF YOUR DEAR FRIEND...BEN SMITH, WAS IT?
BEN ...?!
DON'T LISTEN TO HIM! HE'S LYING...YOU CAN'T TRUST ANYTHING HE SAYS!!
?!
NOW NOW, MR. MORROW...
THIS BUSINESS MATTER DOESN'T INCLUDE YOU.
IT'S UP TO MR. ALFONSE TO DECIDE IF A PIECE OF JUNK IS WORTH HIS FRIEND'S SOUL LANGUISHING IN HELL.
SORRY, BUT... VIRGIL DOES MAKE A GOOD POINT.
...?
NOT TO MENTION, YOU MADE THREE BIG MISTAKES JUST NOW.
FIRST, YOU KINDA SHOWED YOUR HAND ABOUT THAT ORB-THING.
I GUESS BEN WAS RIGHT... IT MUST BE VALUABLE, AFTERALL.
HEH
ESPECIAL-LY... SINCE YOU WERE SO WILLING TO COME HERE BEGGING FOR IT.
GLARE
AND SPEAKING OF BEN...THAT'S WHERE YOU MADE YOUR SECOND MISTAKE.
YOU SAY YOU'LL PARDON HIS SOUL...
BUT I BET YOU DON'T EVEN HAVE IT IN THE FIRST PLACE.
?!

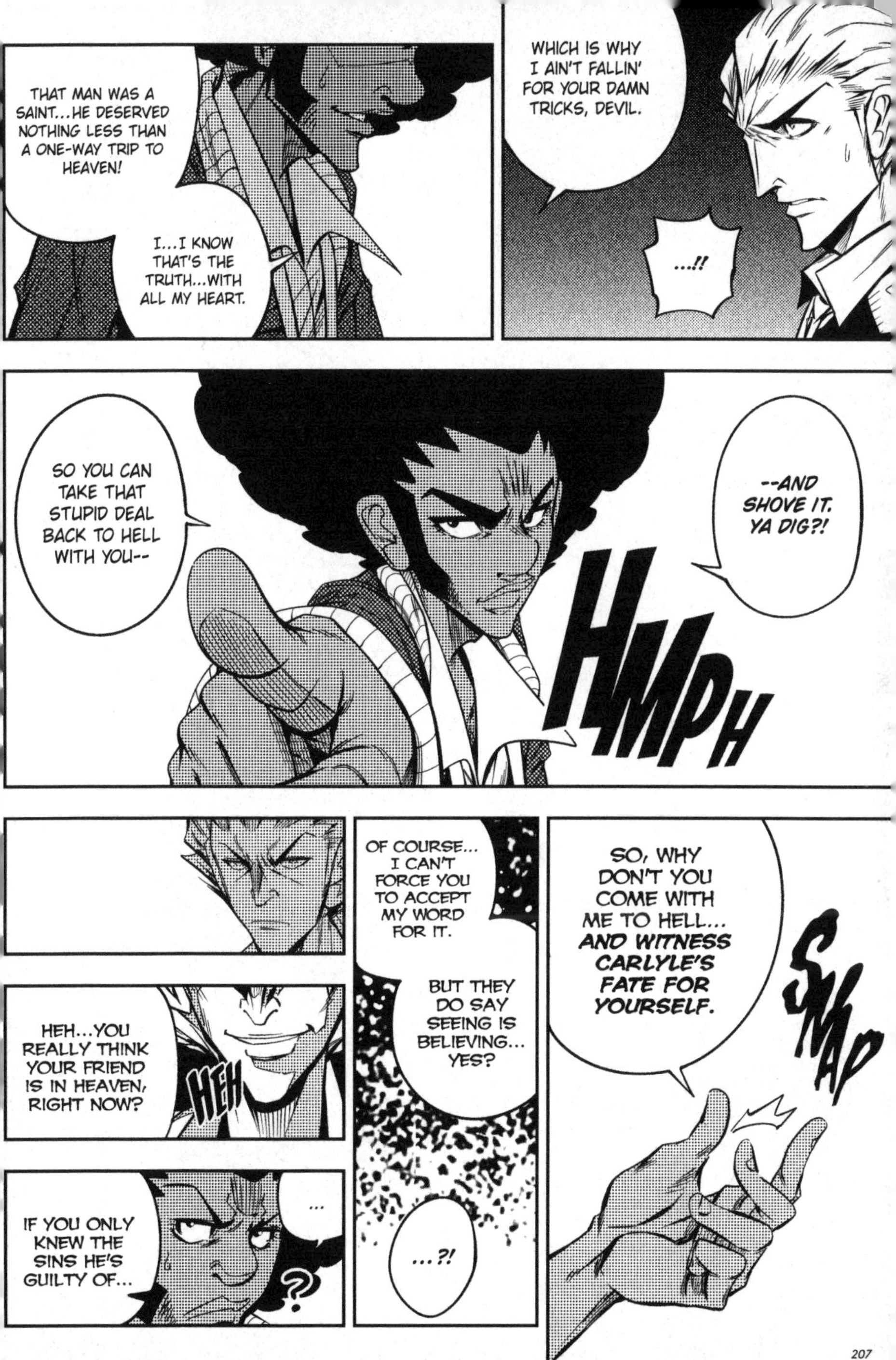

THAT MAN WAS A SAINT...HE DESERVED NOTHING LESS THAN A ONE-WAY TRIP TO HEAVEN!
I...I KNOW THAT'S THE TRUTH...WITH ALL MY HEART.
WHICH IS WHY I AIN'T FALLIN' FOR YOUR DAMN TRICKS, DEVIL.
...!!
SO YOU CAN TAKE THAT STUPID DEAL BACK TO HELL WITH YOU--
--AND SHOVE IT. YA DIG?!
HMPH
HEH...YOU REALLY THINK YOUR FRIEND IS IN HEAVEN, RIGHT NOW?
HEH
...
IF YOU ONLY KNEW THE SINS HE'S GUILTY OF...
?
OF COURSE... I CAN'T FORCE YOU TO ACCEPT MY WORD FOR IT.
BUT THEY DO SAY SEEING IS BELIEVING... YES?
...?!
SO, WHY DON'T YOU COME WITH ME TO HELL... AND WITNESS CARLYLE'S FATE FOR YOURSELF.
SNAP

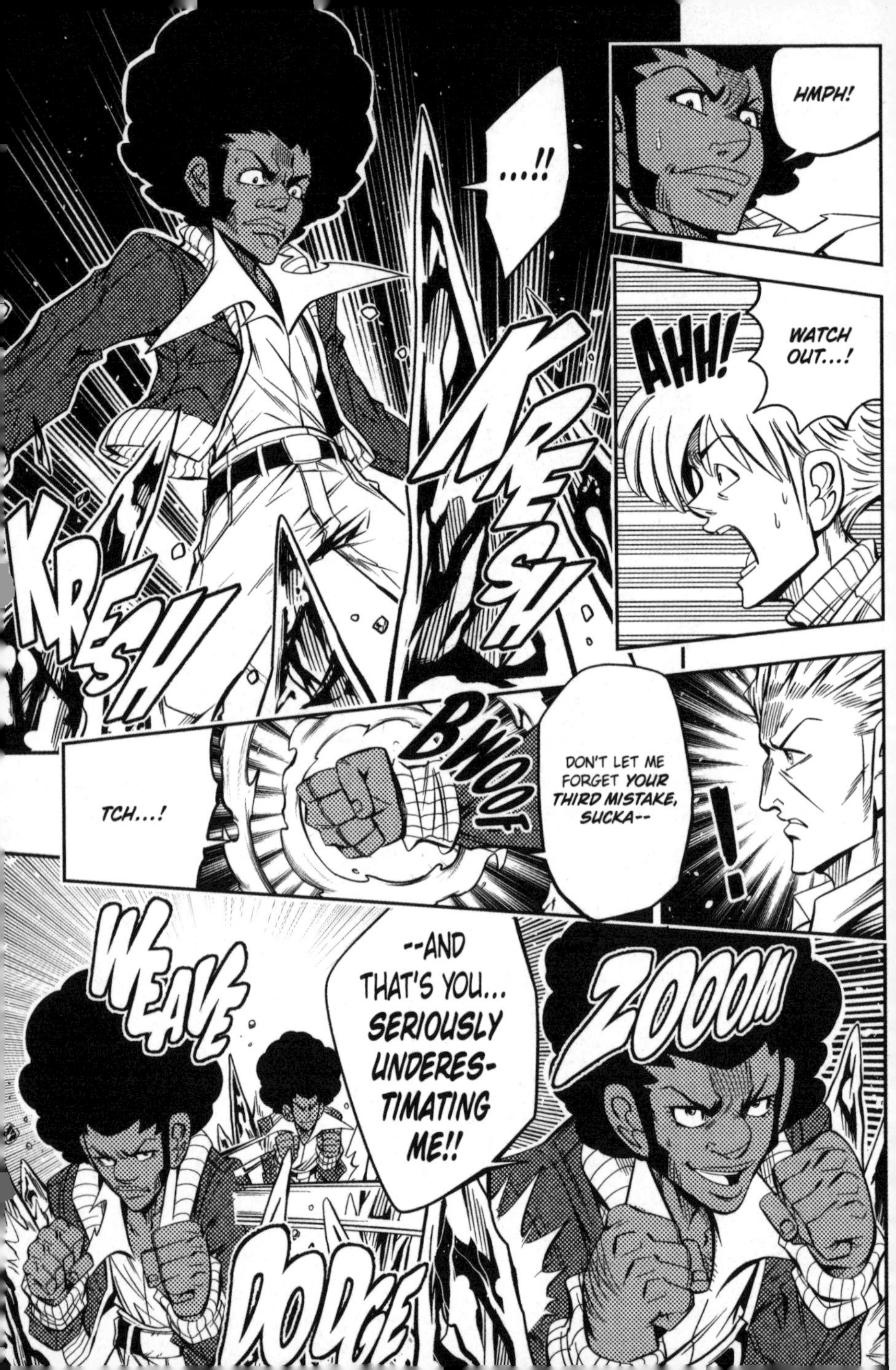
KRESH
...!!
KRESH
HMPH!
AHH!
WATCH OUT...!
TCH...!
BWOOF
DON'T LET ME FORGET YOUR THIRD MISTAKE, SUCKA--
!
WEAVE
--AND THAT'S YOU... SERIOUSLY UNDERES-TIMATING ME!!
ZOOOM
DODGE

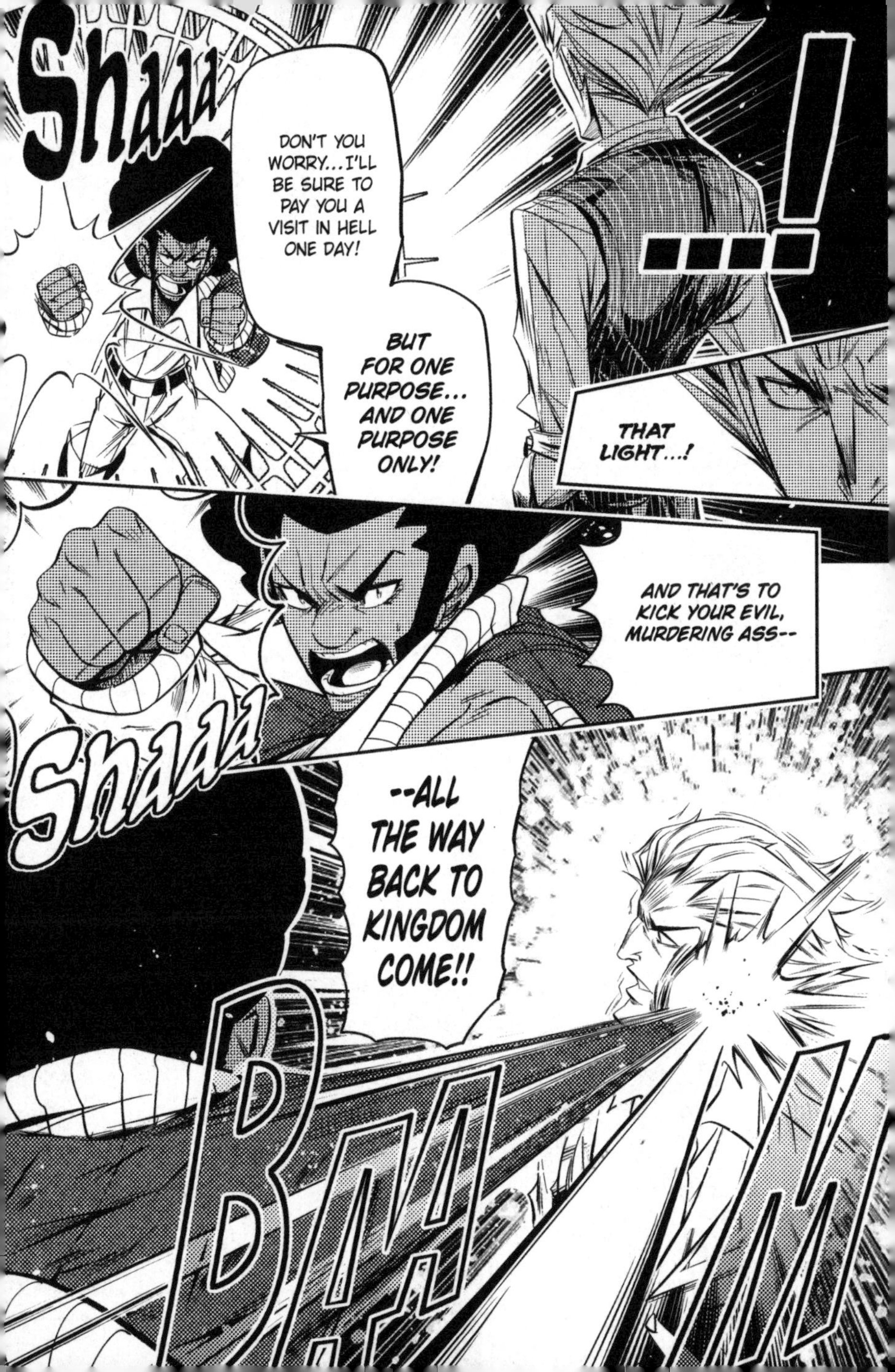
Shaaa
DON'T YOU WORRY...I'LL BE SURE TO PAY YOU A VISIT IN HELL ONE DAY!
BUT FOR ONE PURPOSE... AND ONE PURPOSE ONLY!
...!
THAT LIGHT...!
AND THAT'S TO KICK YOUR EVIL, MURDERING ASS--
Shaaa
--ALL THE WAY BACK TO KINGDOM COME!!

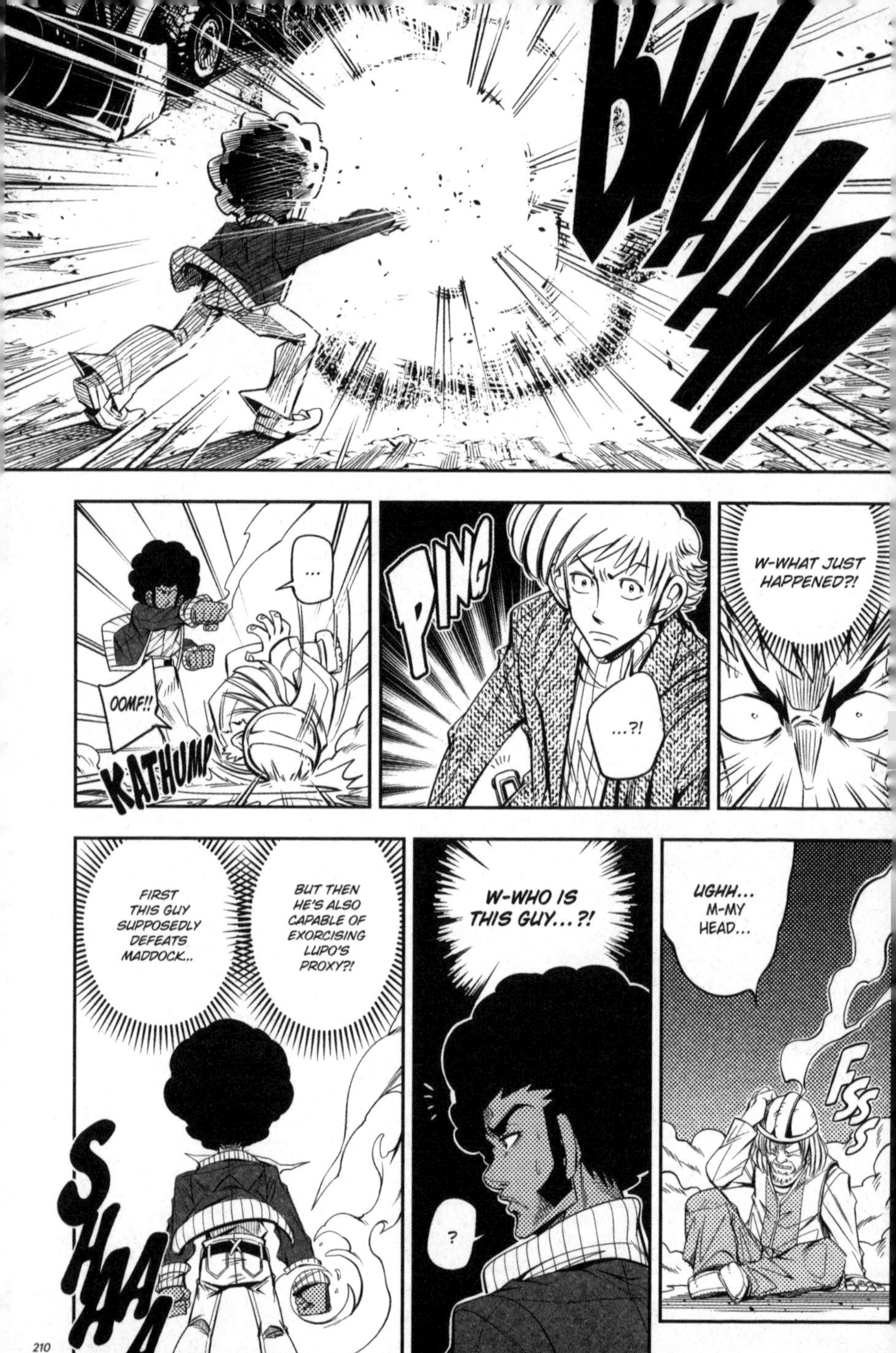
KWAM
...
OOMF!!
KATHUMP
PING
...?!
W-WHAT JUST HAPPENED?!
FIRST THIS GUY SUPPOSEDLY DEFEATS MADDOCK...
BUT THEN HE'S ALSO CAPABLE OF EXORCISING LUPO'S PROXY?!
SHAAA
W-WHO IS THIS GUY...?!
?
UGHH... M-MY HEAD...
FSS

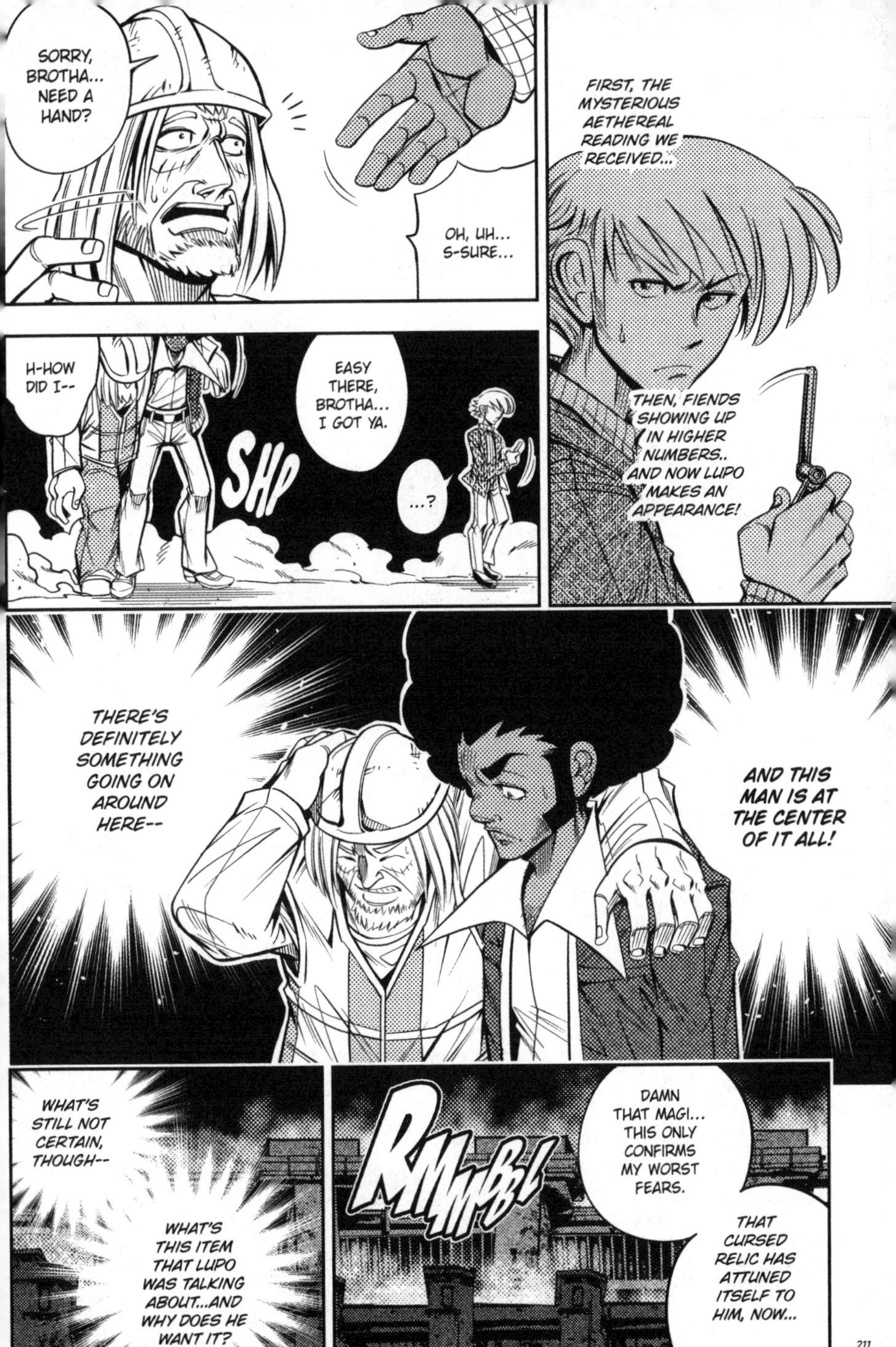
SORRY, BROTHA... NEED A HAND?
OH, UH... S-SURE...
H-HOW DID I--
EASY THERE, BROTHA... I GOT YA.
SHP
...?
FIRST, THE MYSTERIOUS AETHEREAL READING WE RECEIVED...
THEN, FIENDS SHOWING UP IN HIGHER NUMBERS.. AND NOW LUPO MAKES AN APPEARANCE!
THERE'S DEFINITELY SOMETHING GOING ON AROUND HERE--
AND THIS MAN IS AT THE CENTER OF IT ALL!
WHAT'S STILL NOT CERTAIN, THOUGH--
WHAT'S THIS ITEM THAT LUPO WAS TALKING ABOUT...AND WHY DOES HE WANT IT?
RMMBL
DAMN THAT MAGI... THIS ONLY CONFIRMS MY WORST FEARS.
THAT CURSED RELIC HAS ATTUNED ITSELF TO HIM, NOW...

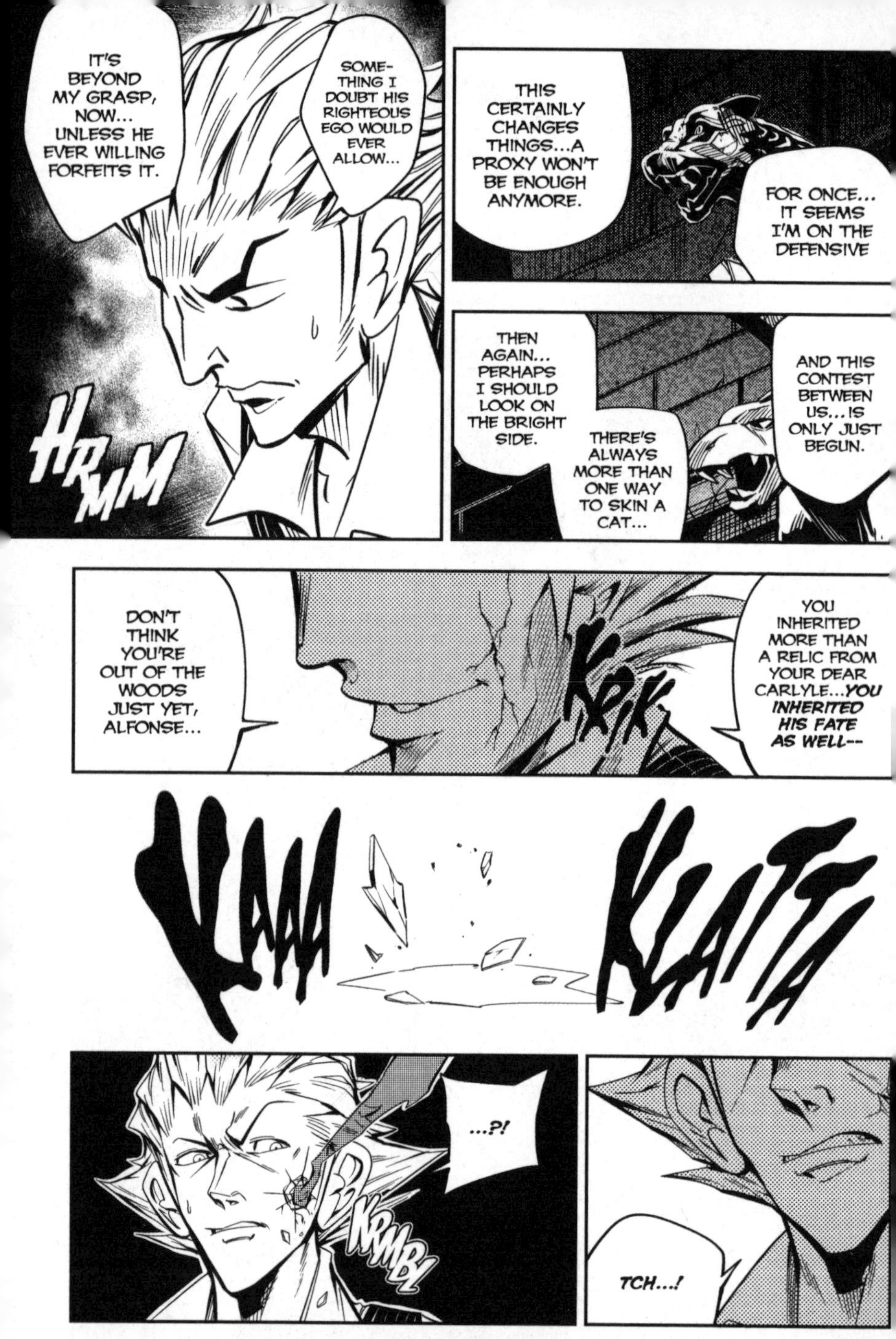
IT'S BEYOND MY GRASP, NOW... UNLESS HE EVER WILLING FORFEITS IT.
SOME-THING I DOUBT HIS RIGHTEOUS EGO WOULD EVER ALLOW...
HRMMM
THIS CERTAINLY CHANGES THINGS...A PROXY WON'T BE ENOUGH ANYMORE.
FOR ONCE... IT SEEMS I'M ON THE DEFENSIVE
THEN AGAIN... PERHAPS I SHOULD LOOK ON THE BRIGHT SIDE.
THERE'S ALWAYS MORE THAN ONE WAY TO SKIN A CAT...
AND THIS CONTEST BETWEEN US...IS ONLY JUST BEGUN.
DON'T THINK YOU'RE OUT OF THE WOODS JUST YET, ALFONSE...
KRIK
YOU INHERITED MORE THAN A RELIC FROM YOUR DEAR CARLYLE...*YOU INHERITED HIS FATE AS WELL--*
KRAA
KLATTA
...?!
KRMBL
TCH...!

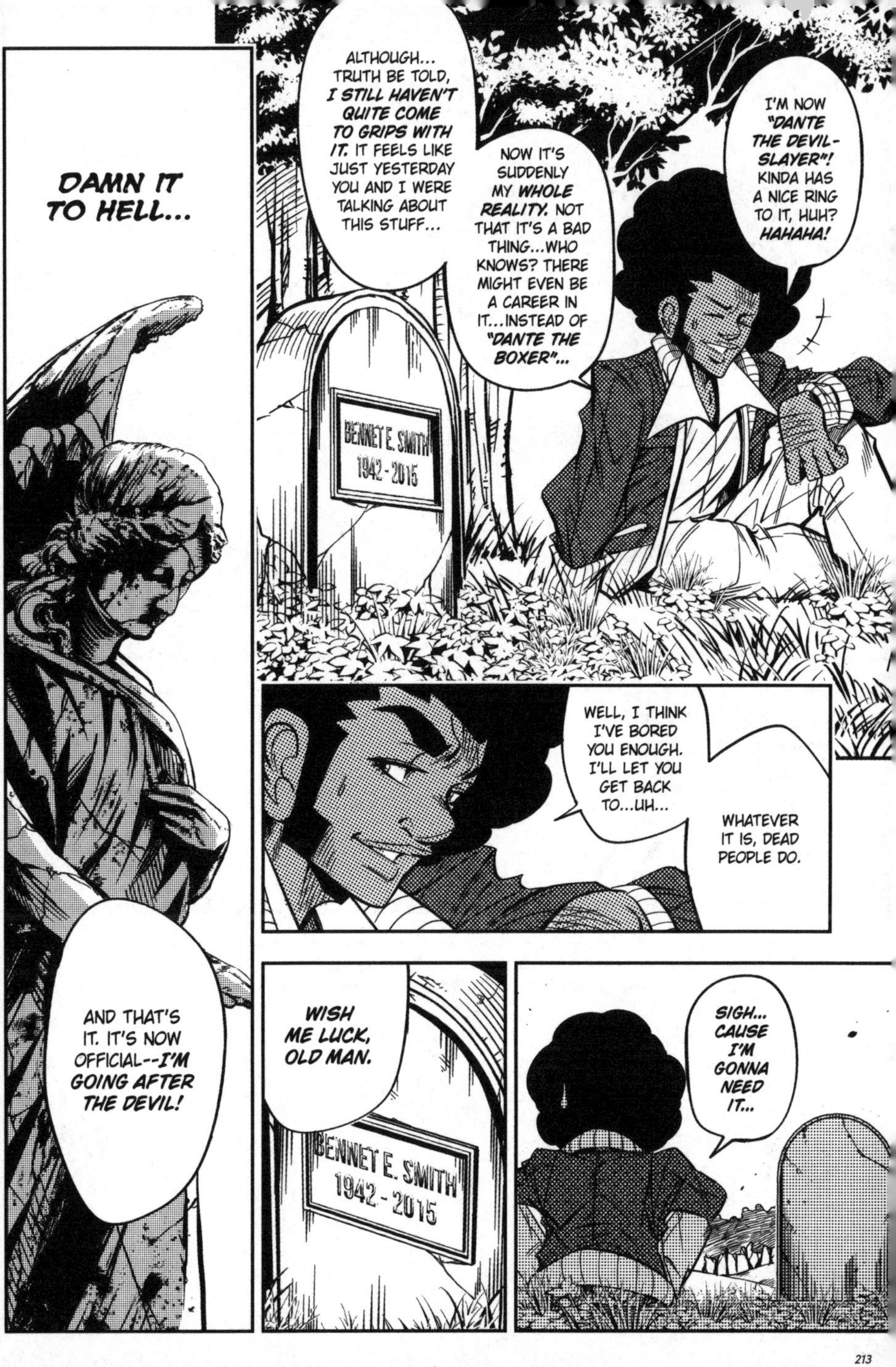
DAMN IT TO HELL...
AND THAT'S IT. IT'S NOW OFFICIAL--I'M GOING AFTER THE DEVIL!
ALTHOUGH... TRUTH BE TOLD, I STILL HAVEN'T QUITE COME TO GRIPS WITH IT. IT FEELS LIKE JUST YESTERDAY YOU AND I WERE TALKING ABOUT THIS STUFF...
NOW IT'S SUDDENLY MY WHOLE REALITY. NOT THAT IT'S A BAD THING...WHO KNOWS? THERE MIGHT EVEN BE A CAREER IN IT...INSTEAD OF "DANTE THE BOXER"...
I'M NOW "DANTE THE DEVIL-SLAYER"! KINDA HAS A NICE RING TO IT, HUH? HAHAHA!
BENNET E. SMITH
1942 - 2015
WELL, I THINK I'VE BORED YOU ENOUGH. I'LL LET YOU GET BACK TO...UH...
WHATEVER IT IS, DEAD PEOPLE DO.
WISH ME LUCK, OLD MAN.
BENNET E. SMITH
1942 - 2015
SIGH... CAUSE I'M GONNA NEED IT...

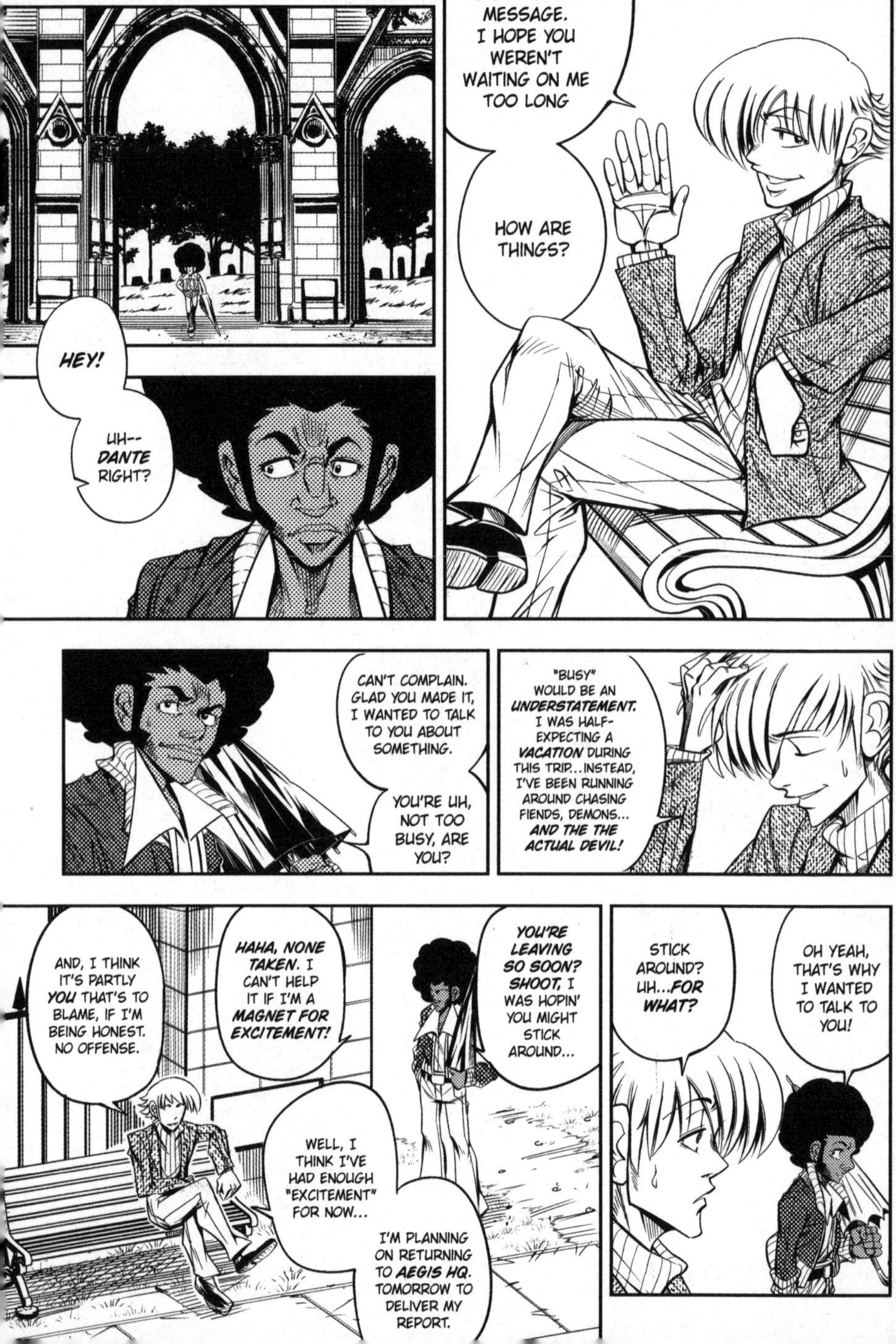
HEY!
UH--
DANTE
RIGHT?
I GOT YOUR MESSAGE. I HOPE YOU WEREN'T WAITING ON ME TOO LONG
HOW ARE THINGS?
CAN'T COMPLAIN. GLAD YOU MADE IT, I WANTED TO TALK TO YOU ABOUT SOMETHING.
YOU'RE UH, NOT TOO BUSY, ARE YOU?
"BUSY" WOULD BE AN UNDERSTATEMENT. I WAS HALF-EXPECTING A VACATION DURING THIS TRIP...INSTEAD, I'VE BEEN RUNNING AROUND CHASING FIENDS, DEMONS... AND THE THE ACTUAL DEVIL!
AND, I THINK IT'S PARTLY YOU THAT'S TO BLAME, IF I'M BEING HONEST. NO OFFENSE.
HAHA, NONE TAKEN. I CAN'T HELP IT IF I'M A MAGNET FOR EXCITEMENT!
WELL, I THINK I'VE HAD ENOUGH "EXCITEMENT" FOR NOW...
I'M PLANNING ON RETURNING TO AEGIS HQ. TOMORROW TO DELIVER MY REPORT.
YOU'RE LEAVING SO SOON? SHOOT, I WAS HOPIN' YOU MIGHT STICK AROUND...
STICK AROUND? UH...FOR WHAT?
OH YEAH, THAT'S WHY I WANTED TO TALK TO YOU!

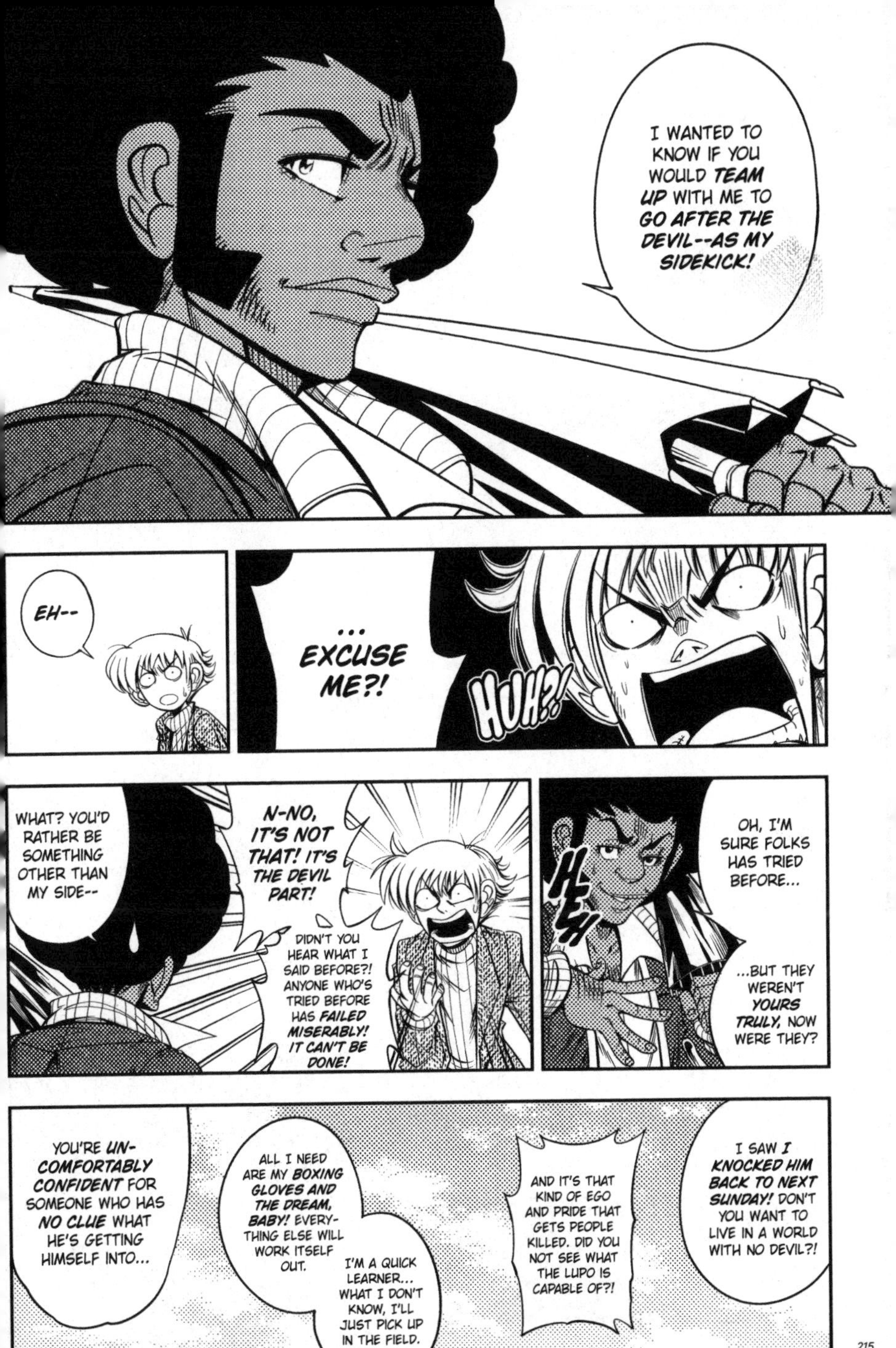
I WANTED TO KNOW IF YOU WOULD TEAM UP WITH ME TO GO AFTER THE DEVIL--AS MY SIDEKICK!
EH--
... EXCUSE ME?!
HUH?!
WHAT? YOU'D RATHER BE SOMETHING OTHER THAN MY SIDE--
N-NO, IT'S NOT THAT! IT'S THE DEVIL PART!
DIDN'T YOU HEAR WHAT I SAID BEFORE?! ANYONE WHO'S TRIED BEFORE HAS FAILED MISERABLY! IT CAN'T BE DONE!
HEH
OH, I'M SURE FOLKS HAS TRIED BEFORE...
...BUT THEY WEREN'T YOURS TRULY, NOW WERE THEY?
YOU'RE UN-COMFORTABLY CONFIDENT FOR SOMEONE WHO HAS NO CLUE WHAT HE'S GETTING HIMSELF INTO...
ALL I NEED ARE MY BOXING GLOVES AND THE DREAM, BABY! EVERY-THING ELSE WILL WORK ITSELF OUT.
I'M A QUICK LEARNER... WHAT I DON'T KNOW, I'LL JUST PICK UP IN THE FIELD.
AND IT'S THAT KIND OF EGO AND PRIDE THAT GETS PEOPLE KILLED. DID YOU NOT SEE WHAT THE LUPO IS CAPABLE OF?!
I SAW I KNOCKED HIM BACK TO NEXT SUNDAY! DON'T YOU WANT TO LIVE IN A WORLD WITH NO DEVIL?!

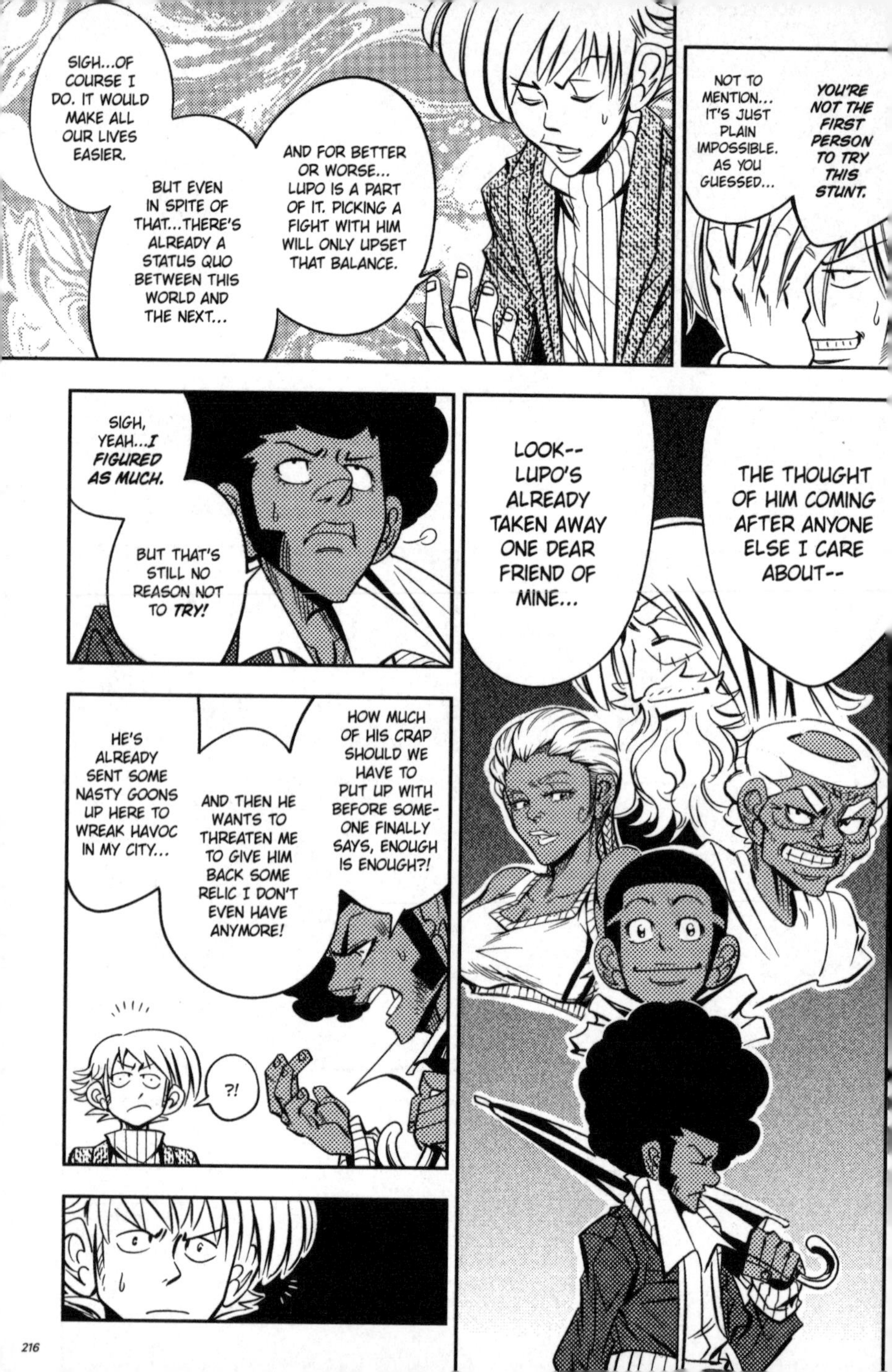
SIGH...OF COURSE I DO. IT WOULD MAKE ALL OUR LIVES EASIER.
BUT EVEN IN SPITE OF THAT...THERE'S ALREADY A STATUS QUO BETWEEN THIS WORLD AND THE NEXT...
AND FOR BETTER OR WORSE... LUPO IS A PART OF IT. PICKING A FIGHT WITH HIM WILL ONLY UPSET THAT BALANCE.
NOT TO MENTION... IT'S JUST PLAIN IMPOSSIBLE. AS YOU GUESSED...
YOU'RE NOT THE FIRST PERSON TO TRY THIS STUNT.
SIGH, YEAH...I FIGURED AS MUCH.
BUT THAT'S STILL NO REASON NOT TO TRY!
HE'S ALREADY SENT SOME NASTY GOONS UP HERE TO WREAK HAVOC IN MY CITY...
AND THEN HE WANTS TO THREATEN ME TO GIVE HIM BACK SOME RELIC I DON'T EVEN HAVE ANYMORE!
HOW MUCH OF HIS CRAP SHOULD WE HAVE TO PUT UP WITH BEFORE SOME-ONE FINALLY SAYS, ENOUGH IS ENOUGH?!
?!
LOOK-- LUPO'S ALREADY TAKEN AWAY ONE DEAR FRIEND OF MINE...
THE THOUGHT OF HIM COMING AFTER ANYONE ELSE I CARE ABOUT--

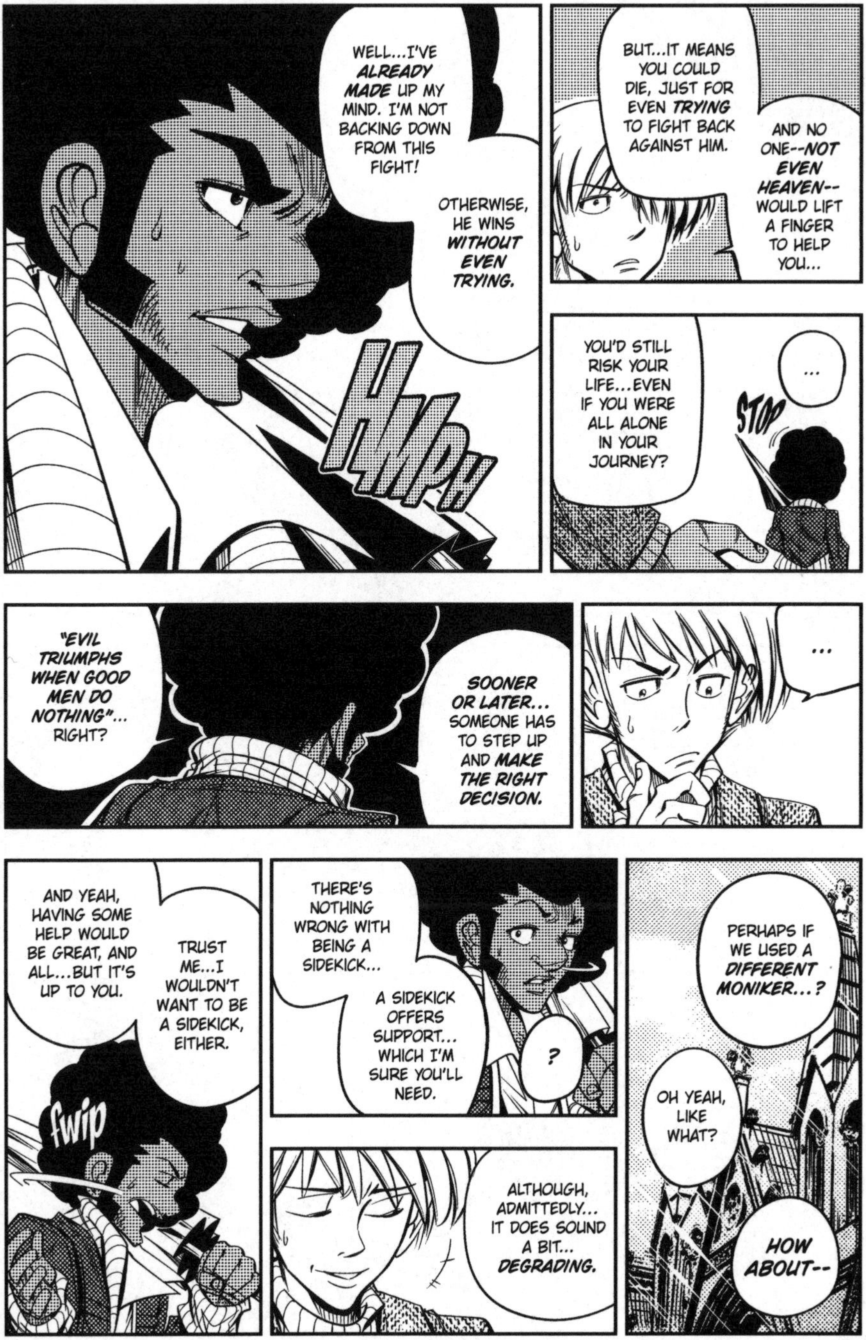
WELL...I'VE ALREADY MADE UP MY MIND. I'M NOT BACKING DOWN FROM THIS FIGHT!
OTHERWISE, HE WINS WITHOUT EVEN TRYING.
HMPH
BUT...IT MEANS YOU COULD DIE, JUST FOR EVEN TRYING TO FIGHT BACK AGAINST HIM.
AND NO ONE--NOT EVEN HEAVEN--WOULD LIFT A FINGER TO HELP YOU...
YOU'D STILL RISK YOUR LIFE...EVEN IF YOU WERE ALL ALONE IN YOUR JOURNEY?
STOP
...
"EVIL TRIUMPHS WHEN GOOD MEN DO NOTHING"... RIGHT?
SOONER OR LATER... SOMEONE HAS TO STEP UP AND MAKE THE RIGHT DECISION.
...
AND YEAH, HAVING SOME HELP WOULD BE GREAT, AND ALL...BUT IT'S UP TO YOU.
TRUST ME...I WOULDN'T WANT TO BE A SIDEKICK, EITHER.
fwip
THERE'S NOTHING WRONG WITH BEING A SIDEKICK...
A SIDEKICK OFFERS SUPPORT... WHICH I'M SURE YOU'LL NEED.
?
ALTHOUGH, ADMITTEDLY... IT DOES SOUND A BIT... DEGRADING.
PERHAPS IF WE USED A DIFFERENT MONIKER...?
OH YEAH, LIKE WHAT?
HOW ABOUT--

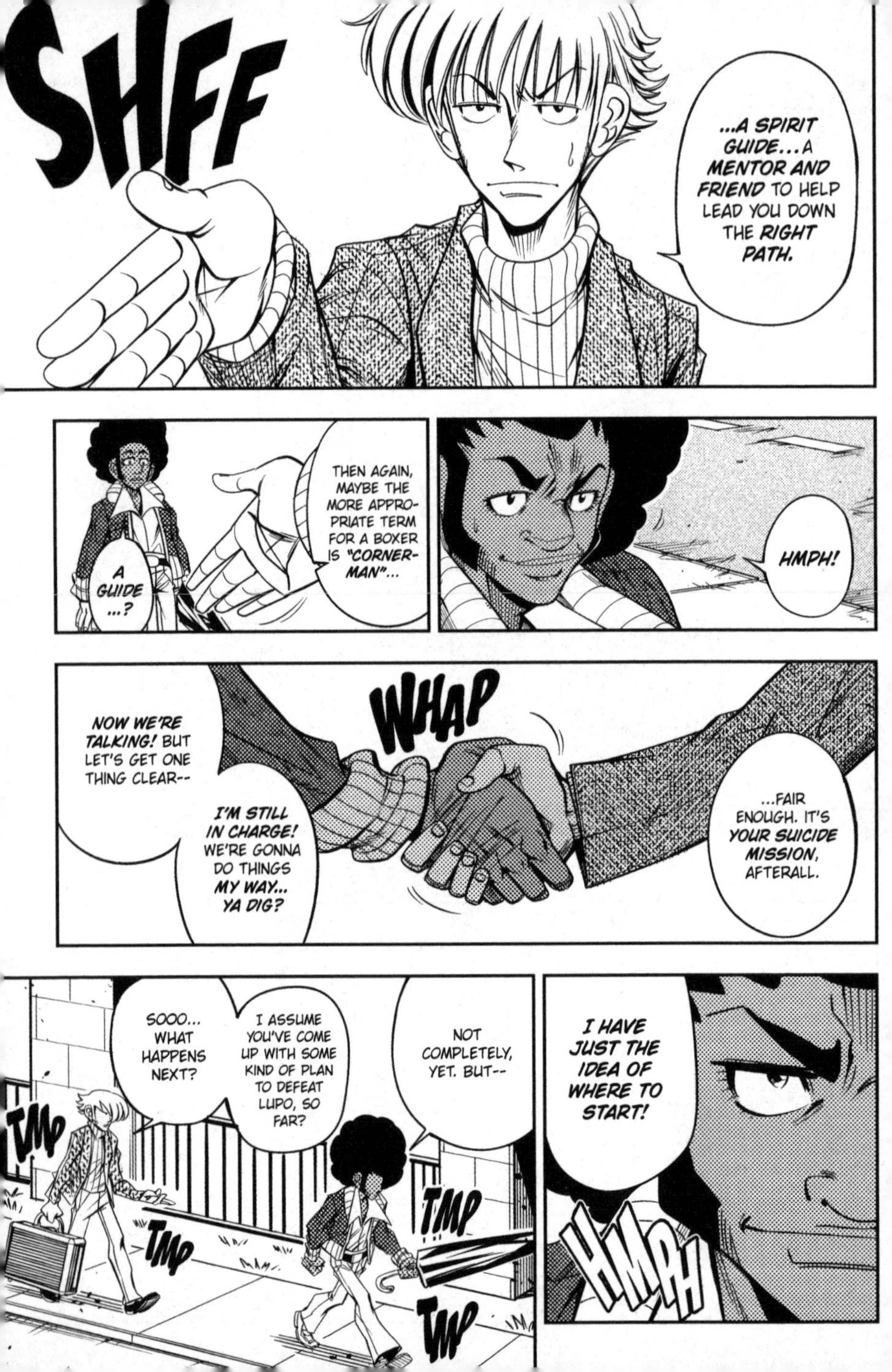
SHFF
...A SPIRIT GUIDE... A MENTOR AND FRIEND TO HELP LEAD YOU DOWN THE RIGHT PATH.
A GUIDE ...?
THEN AGAIN, MAYBE THE MORE APPROPRIATE TERM FOR A BOXER IS "CORNERMAN"...
HMPH!
WHAP
NOW WE'RE TALKING! BUT LET'S GET ONE THING CLEAR--
I'M STILL IN CHARGE! WE'RE GONNA DO THINGS MY WAY... YA DIG?
...FAIR ENOUGH. IT'S YOUR SUICIDE MISSION, AFTERALL.
TMP
SOOO... WHAT HAPPENS NEXT?
I ASSUME YOU'VE COME UP WITH SOME KIND OF PLAN TO DEFEAT LUPO, SO FAR?
NOT COMPLETELY, YET. BUT--
TMP
TMP
TMP
I HAVE JUST THE IDEA OF WHERE TO START!
HMPH

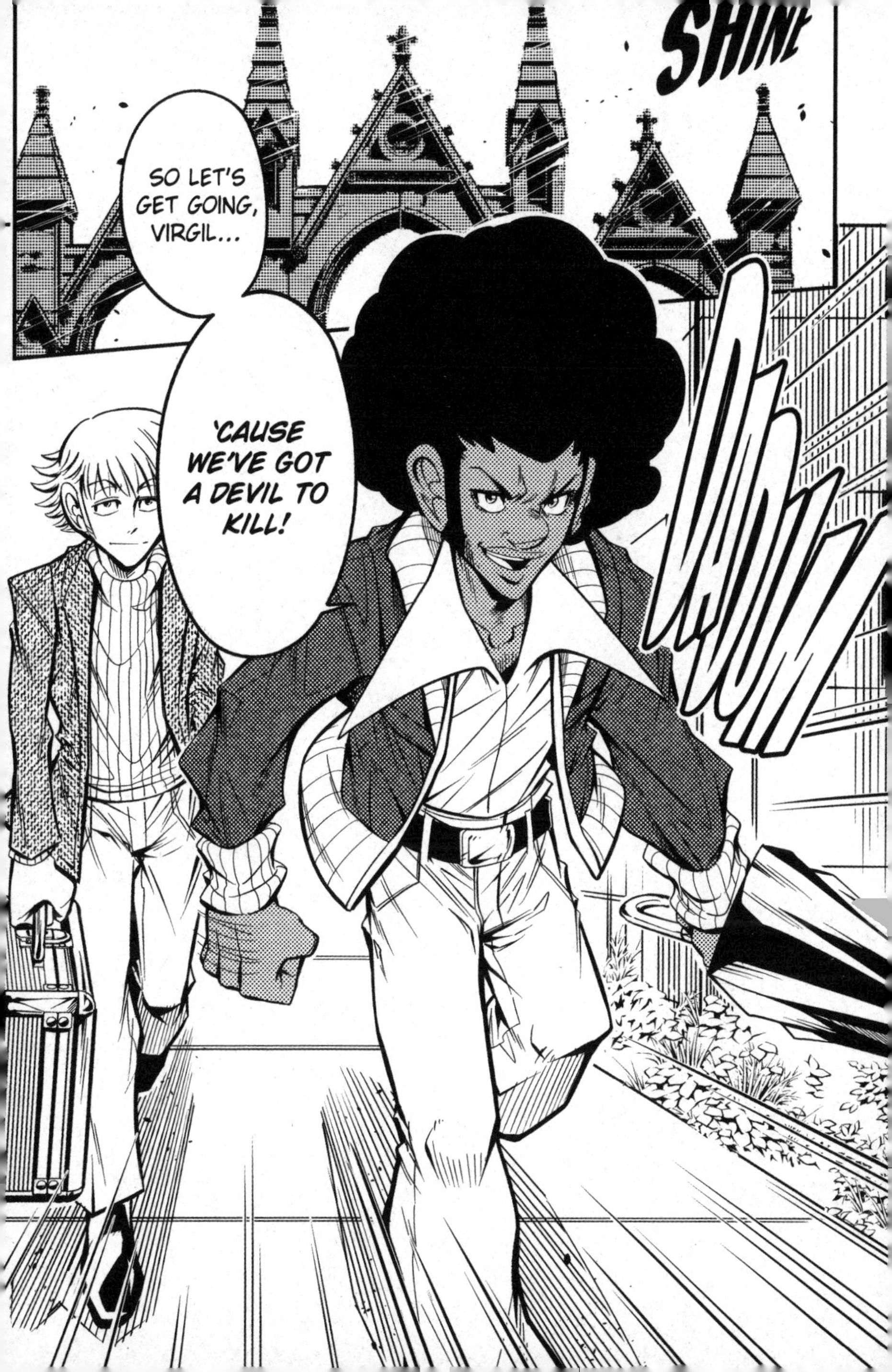
SO LET'S GET GOING, VIRGIL...
'CAUSE WE'VE GOT A DEVIL TO KILL!

SOUL BEAT

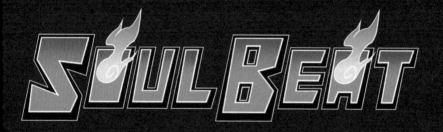

END OF VOLUME 1

Morganne Walker

Morganne Walker joined Saturday AM with the debut of Soul Beat in 2017. In addition to creating manga, she contributes logo designs and professional commentary to many of Saturday AM's signature events, including their annual March Art Madness art contest and #SummerofManga short story competition. An Indiana native (also known as a "Hoosier"), Morganne studied at Ball State University, receiving both a Bachelor's and a Master's degree in Architectural Design. She lives in Indianapolis, Indiana.

ACKNOWLEDGMENTS

MIDWAY THROUGH MY LIFE'S JOURNEY...SOUL BEAT VOLUME 1 HAS FINALLY BECOME A REALITY! IT'S FUNNY TO THINK HOW OVER TEN YEARS AGO, THIS STORY ORIGINALLY STARTED OUT AS SOMETHING OF A THROWAWAY PARODY PROJECT; BUT OVER TIME AND WITH THE HELP OF PEOPLE LIKE FREDERICK JONES AND AUSTIN HARVEY, IT'S REALLY MATURED INTO A STORY I'M PROUD TO CALL MY FIRST MANGA SERIES. IT'S BEEN A HELLUVA ROAD TO GET HERE, SO OF COURSE A BIG THANKS IS ALSO OWED TO MY FRIENDS AND FAMILY FOR THEIR CONSTANT SUPPORT ALL THESE YEARS TO CHASE MY DREAMS; MY ASSISTANTS FOR PUTTING IN THE HOURS TO HELP ME TO (EVENTUALLY) CROSS THE FINISH LINE; MY EDITORIAL TEAM FOR SHOWING ME THE RIGHT PATH, AND GIVING ME THE CHANCE BACK IN 2017 TO TELL THIS STORY; AND A SPECIAL THANKS TO YOU, READER, FOR PICKING IT UP AND INSPIRING ME TO BRING YOU THE BEST EXPERIENCE POSSIBLE. ENJOY!

-Morganne Walker

Quarto.com

© 2023 Morganne Walker

First published in 2023 by Rockport Publishers,
an imprint of The Quarto Group,
100 Cummings Center, Suite 265-D, Beverly, MA 01915, USA.
T (978) 282-9590 F (978) 283-2742

Rockport Publishers titles are also available at discount for retail, wholesale, promotional, and bulk purchase. For details, contact the Special Sales Manager by email at specialsales@quarto.com or by mail at The Quarto Group, Attn: Special Sales Manager, 100 Cummings Center, Suite 265-D, Beverly, MA 01915, USA.

10 9 8 7 6 5 4 3 2 1

ISBN: 978-0-7603-8255-4

Library of Congress Cataloging-in-Publication Data is available.

Story and Art: Morganne Walker
Lettering: Chana Conley
Editors: Frederick L. Jones and Austin Harvey
Book Design: Joshua Thomas & Mitch Proctor

Printed in China

Soul Beat, Volume 1 is rated T for Teen and is recommended for ages 13 and up. It contains mild profanity and some violent action scenes.